I0138172

The Writings of Oliver H. Olney

The Writings of Oliver H. Olney

April 1842 to February 1843 — Nauvoo, Illinois

Edited by Richard G. Moore

Greg Kofford Books

Salt Lake City, 2019

Cover design by Loyd Isao Ericson

Published in the USA.

978-1-58958-762-5 (hardcover)
Also available in ebook.

Greg Kofford Books
P. O. Box 1362
Draper, UT 84020
www.gregkofford.com
facebook.com/gkbooks
twitter.com/gkbooks

Library of Congress Cataloging-in-Publication Data

Names: Olney, Oliver H., 1796-approximately 1847, author. | Moore, Richard G., 1952- editor.

Title: The writings of Oliver Olney : April 1842 to February 1843 : Nauvoo, Illinois / edited by Richard G. Moore.

Description: Salt Lake City : Greg Kofford Books, [2020] | Includes bibliographical references and index. | Summary: "As an early convert to The Church of Jesus Christ of Latter-day Saints, Oliver H. Olney experienced persecution and was forced to flee to Illinois, settling in Nauvoo. In Nauvoo, Olney became disgruntled with Church leadership and began to view Joseph Smith as a fallen prophet. His writings: journal entries, letters, and publications, express his concerns about what he viewed as serious iniquity within the church. His opposition resulted in his excommunication; however, Olney remained in Nauvoo after being expelled from the church and continued recording the things he witnessed. The handwritten papers of Oliver Olney are housed in the Beinecke Rare Book and Manuscript Library at Yale University and are made available in published form for the first time. They offer historical researchers and interested readers of the early Latter-day Saint movement a unique glimpse from the margins of religious society in Nauvoo. Olney's writings add further light to key events in early Mormonism such as the secretive practice of polygamy, theological innovations, as well as growing tensions among disaffected church members and the rising conflict with non-Mormon neighbors"-- Provided by publisher.

Identifiers: LCCN 2020004426 | ISBN 9781589587625 (hardcover)

Subjects: LCSH: Church of Jesus Christ of Latter-day Saints--Controversial literature. | Mormon Church--Controversial literature. | Mormon Church--Illinois--Nauvoo--History--Sources.

Classification: LCC BX8645 .O46 2020 | DDC 289.309/034--dc23

LC record available at https://lccn.loc.gov/2020004426

For Lani, Adam, Travis, and Asia

CONTENTS

Introduction ix
April 1842 1
May 1842 24
June 1842 43
July 1842 77
August 1842 123
September 1842 160
October 1842 176
November 1842 198
December 1842 221
January 1843 229
February 1843 233
Letter from Phebe Wheeler 238
Appendix 1. *The Absurdities Of Mormonism Portrayed* 241
Appendix 2. *Spiritual Wifery Of Nauvoo Exposed* 275
Appendix 3. Olney's List of Proposed Church Leaders 289
Bibliography 295
Index 299

INTRODUCTION[1]

The April 1, 1842, issue of the Nauvoo, Illinois, newspaper *Times and Seasons* carried an article attributed to then-editor Joseph Smith entitled "Try the Spirits." The article discussed the need to detect false spirits in the world so as not to be deceived. It gave examples of the witch of Endor from the Old Testament, Simon the Sorcerer from the New Testament, and contemporaries such as the prophetess Jemima Wilkinson of the United States and Edward Irving of England. Near the end of the article it stated:

> We have also had brethren and sisters that have had written revelations, and have started forward to lead this church. Such was a young boy in Kirtland—Isaac Russell of Mo. and Gladden Bishop, *and Oliver Olney of Nauvoo. . . . Mr. Olney has also been tried by the high council, and disfellowshiped because he would not have his writings tested by the word of God; evidently proving that he loves darkness rather than light because his deeds are evil.*[2]

Who was Oliver Olney, and to what extent was he involved with Mormonism? What did he do that prompted a hearing before the high council, ultimately resulting in Olney losing his standing in the Church?[3] What provoked him to keep a record of what he witnessed at Nauvoo and then publish two exposés of Mormonism? Olney was clearly distressed by Church leaders, yet he remained a resident of Nauvoo for at least nineteen months after becoming disaffected with the Church. His writings, letters, and pub-

---

1. A somewhat different version of this introduction was previously published as Richard G. Moore, "The Writings of Oliver H. Olney: Early Mormon Dissident; Would-be Reformer," 58–78.

2. "Try the Spirits," 748; emphasis added.

3. The *Times and Seasons* article reported that Olney was disfellowshipped. Minutes from his hearing before the high council state, "The charges were sustained and unanimously decided by the Council that the hand of fellowship be withdrawn from him." John S. Dinger, ed., *The Nauvoo City and High Council Minutes*, March 17, 1842. A footnote from *The Nauvoo City and High Council Minutes* states that Olney was "excommunicated in 1842 after claiming to be a prophet." Dinger, *Nauvoo City and High Council Minutes*, March 17, 1842. A brief biographical sketch on the Joseph Smith Papers website also states that Olney was excommunicated. In Olney's writings he asserted that he met twice with the high council. He wrote that after the first meeting "they from me withdrawed [*sic*] the hand of felloship [*sic*] and set me a float." He claimed that at the conclusion of the second meeting he "took from their midst [my] name." Oliver Olney Papers, folder number 2, April 6, 1842 (hereafter OOP). There is no record of a second meeting with Olney in Dinger, *Nauvoo City and High Council Minutes.*

lications dating from April 1842 to his final publication in 1845 afford us an interesting view of what it was like to be a Mormon dissident in Nauvoo.

The writings of Oliver Olney that are currently extant are housed in the Beinecke Rare Book and Manuscript Library at Yale University. The Olney manuscript collection is in one box with twelve folders. Some folders contain loose letters and notes; other folders contain papers that are bound, partially bound, or previously bound but are now loose. Folder number one contains typewritten loose pages with an introduction to the collection and calendar of the Olney documents created by historian Dale L. Morgan. The other folders contain what appear to be dated journal pages, letters, and rewritten entries of certain journal pages that look more like a compilation record than a daily journal. There are also some personal papers and drafts of things Olney intended to publish, including a draft of Olney's 1843 pamphlet, *The Absurdities of Mormonism Portrayed.*[4]

Little is known about the early life of Oliver H. Olney.[5] The most likely place and date of his birth are Eastford, Connecticut, on August 11, 1796.[6] He was the son of Ezekiel Olney and Lydia Brown. Oliver was the eighth of eleven children born to Ezekiel and Lydia. His younger brother Jesse Olney was an educator and author of several textbooks. In 1820 Oliver married Alice Mary Johnson, the daughter of John Johnson and Alice Elsa Jacobs. She was the sister of Lyman and Luke Johnson, two of the original members of the Quorum of the Twelve of the church founded by Joseph Smith Jr., commonly referred to as Mormonism. Oliver and his wife, Alice, became followers of Joseph Smith in the early years of the Restoration.[7] They were likely baptized in 1831 while living in Ohio and moved to Kirtland, Ohio, shortly thereafter.

---

4. Oliver H. Olney, *The Absurdities of Mormonism Portrayed: A Brief Sketch by Oliver H. Olney*.

5. I have been unable to find what the initial "H" stands for in "Oliver H. Olney."

6. A number of genealogical sites have Olney born in 1795, 1796, 1798, and 1800. The sites also list Olney's birthplace as Vermont, New Hampshire, Rhode Island, Ohio, and Connecticut. The most common date given is August 11, 1796, and the place of birth suggested most often is Eastford, Connecticut. In the Olney Papers, there is a letter written to Olney where the author of the letter refers to him and Olney meeting in the land of their nativity: Connecticut. OOP, fd. 8, July 1, 1842.

7. Joseph Smith and his followers viewed their church as a restoration to the earth of the original church created by Jesus Christ. When the Olneys joined the church founded by Joseph Smith, it was called the Church of Christ. It went through several name changes until April 1838, when it became known as The Church of Jesus Christ of Latter Day Saints (LDS D&C 115:4). This section was never included in any of the Community of Christ editions of the Doctrine and Covenants. Throughout his writings, Olney refers to the organization as the Church of Latter Day Saints or the Church of LDS.

Olney was quite involved with the Church during his days in Kirtland. On December 29, 1835, Joseph Smith recorded in his journal that he attended a blessing meeting at Oliver Olney's home with his wife and parents. The journal entry reads, "A large company assembled and Father Smith arose and made some preliminary remarks. . . . [A]bout 15 persons then received a patriarchal blessing under his hand."[8]

The minutes of a Priesthood meeting held in the Kirtland Temple on January 15, 1836, state, "Oliver Olney was nominated and seconded to preside over the teachers in Kirtland ~~and~~ The vote of the assembly was called and passed unanimously."[9] In the September 1836 issue of the *Messenger and Advocate*, Olney is listed as an elder.[10] He was ordained a seventy by Hazen Aldrich on December 20, 1836, at Kirtland, Ohio.[11]

Olney's family left Kirtland and traveled with the Saints to Missouri, where they experienced persecution, mobocracy, and were eventually forced to leave their home and land, fleeing Missouri for the relative peace and safety of Illinois. The Olneys settled in the new Mormon community of Nauvoo, Illinois, where they purchased lot number 135, which was close to the river and only about a half-mile from Joseph Smith's homestead.

Alice Olney passed away at Nauvoo on July 16, 1841, while Oliver was away. Her obituary found in *Times and Seasons* does not list the cause of death. It does mention "Brother Olney is absent from home and probably knows nothing of the afflicting occurrence."[12] The obituary does not reveal where Oliver Olney was at the time of his wife's passing. However, Wilford Woodruff's journal entry for July 15, 1841, reads, "I spent the day at Father Woodruff. Elder Olivor [*sic*] Olney spent the night with us and left us this morning."[13] Oliver Olney was in Connecticut when his wife passed away, likely serving as a Mormon missionary to the eastern states. Wilford Woodruff referred to him as Elder Oliver Olney, and in Olney's September 4,

---

8. Dean C. Jessee, Mark Ashurst-McGee, and Richard L. Jensen, eds., *Journals, Volume 1:1832–1839*, Vol. 1 of the Journals series of *The Joseph Smith Papers*, edited by Dean C. Jessee, Ronald K. Esplin, and Richard Lyman Bushman, 139.

9. Joseph Smith Papers, *Journals, Volume 1*, 155.

10. Thomas Burdick, "Elder's Licenses," 383.

11. "Oliver H. Olney" (bibliographic entry), *The Joseph Smith Papers.*

12. "DIED – In this place July 16th, Alice consort of Oliver Olney," 501.

13. Scott G. Kenney, ed., *Wilford Woodruff's Journal, 1833-1898,* July 15, 1841, 2:112. Wilford Woodruff was visiting his father in Farmington, Connecticut, which is about ten miles southwest of Hartford, Connecticut. Woodruff's August 22 journal entry states that he had just heard about the passing of Alice Olney. He wrote, "Elder Olney is in Connecticut & knows not of the Death of his wife." Kenney, *Wilford Woodruff's Journal,* July 15, 1841, 2:119.

1842, entry he wrote, "One year ago today I returned from a long mission in the Eastern States. I arrived with feelings of no ordinary kind because of the loss and sickness of friends."[14]

Oliver Olney was a faithful follower of Joseph Smith for over ten years. With the Saints in Missouri, he endured trials, persecution, and the loss of home and lands under Missouri Governor Boggs' Extermination Order. But after finding refuge in Nauvoo, Illinois, and suffering the death of his wife, Olney became troubled with what he perceived to be taking place in Nauvoo. He began to view Joseph Smith as a fallen prophet and believed the Church was out of favor with God.

It is unclear when Olney first began to have misgivings about the religion he had joined in 1831, but in his 1842 writings from Nauvoo he looked back at troubling issues in Ohio and in Missouri. While circumstances may have bothered him in Ohio and Missouri, it is also possible they became issues only in hindsight after he settled in Nauvoo and his standing in the Church became tenuous.

Olney must have publicly voiced his concerns about Mormonism and his ideas for correcting what he viewed as serious iniquity in the Church, especially among its leaders. In March 1842, John C. Bennett proffered charges against Olney before the Nauvoo High Council "for improper conduct, for setting himself up as a prophet & revelator in the Church."[15] In Olney's personal record he reported that he was "called before the high council of twelve men and thre[e] to preside" and claimed they demanded his writings.[16]

Olney alleged that his March 1842 hearing before the high council was a result of his keeping a record of the doings of Church leaders, including their sins and misdeeds. The high council was aware of Olney's revelations and did "demand [his] writings." He wrote of his refusal to turn his writings over to the council, stating that he "too well knew their minds to trust them with the record that [he] had kept of the Latter Day Saints as it spoke of their foibles."[17] However, it was his revelations that were the focus of his high council hearing. The newspaper reported that Olney refused to "have his writings tested by the word of God," most likely a reference to revelations he had received. In the hearing there was no mention of any historical record or report of misdoings that he claimed to have been writing. If Olney had been keeping such a record, it is doubtful Church leaders were even aware of it at the time of the high council hearing.

---

14. OOP, fd. 9, September 4, 1842. The loss he refers to was probably his wife, Alice.

15. Dinger, *Nauvoo City and High Council Minutes*, March 17, 1842.

16. OOP, fd. 2, April 6, 1842. A rewrite of this entry by Olney is found in OOP, fd. 3, April 6, 1842.

17. OOP, fd. 2, April 6, 1842.

After his hearing before the high council Olney wrote, "Because of not getting my writings and because of my words, they from me withdrawed [*sic*] the hand of fellowship and set me afloat. I looked at my standing and said I again with the council will meet. I soon met with them with feelings that was good and took the liberty to address them in behalf of my case but they in array moved against me that I took from them my name."[18] In his account of meeting with the high council of Nauvoo, Olney never mentions his revelations or the fact that he was charged with "setting himself up as a prophet & revelator in the Church."

In what is likely the original version[19] of the April 6, 1842, entry Olney wrote, "I have felt it my duty in days past and gone to keep a history of the doings of the Church from the rise until the present time. I have tried to be impartial in what I have wrote, but must say that I have been partial that I have moved in behalf of the saints."[20] He does not say exactly when he began writing this history, except for the claim that he "long [had] been a keeping a record of the Church."[21]

If Olney had been keeping an historical record for a long time, it is no longer extant.[22] It is more likely that his record of the Latter Day Saints and

---

18. OOP, fd. 3, April 6, 1842.

19. Olney's writings include as many as three versions for each date given. It is clear that in these cases he went back and rewrote various entries.

20. OOP, fd. 2, April 6, 1842. A somewhat different version of this entry is found in OOP, fd. 3, April 6, 1842. The only differences in the sentences quoted from the first version to the rewrite are Olney changing "Church" to "LDS" and "saints" to "LDS."

21. OOP, fd. 5, May 8, 1842. This is a rewrite of OOP, fd. 3, May 8, 1842, in which this phrase is not found.

22. There are discrepancies in Olney's claims concerning when he began to keep a record or history of the "doings of the Church." In May 1842 he wrote that he had "long been keeping a record of the Church." Yet, in his *Absurdities of Mormonism Portrayed*, published in 1843, he states, "I commenced about one year ago to write of their doings that occurred daily." In Olney's April 6, 1842, entry he states that the High Council "demanded my writings that they could not attain," and "[b]ecause of not getting my writings and because of my words they from me withdrawed the hand of felloship and set me a float." In *Absurdities of Mormonism Portrayed*, Olney wrote that his writings had been "taken from my custody in my absence, that I have not yet obtained." According to Olney, it was a portion of the new version of the history that was taken from his custody in his absence. He said that the original account he had written was still in his care, "but of their daily doings of late, is what they took from [him], with dates, names, etc., that [he] had designed for publication, of about 130 pages." Olney, *Absurdities of Mormonism*, 3. Although he reported that the original account was still in his possession, none of the purported original account is extant and all of his published writings come from after his separation from the Church. In

the foibles and iniquities of their leaders was begun by Olney *after* his hearing with the high council.[23] As was previously mentioned, based on the article in an April 1842 *Times and Seasons,* it was Olney's efforts to lead the Church, and his unwillingness to have his revelations "tested by the word of God"[24] that resulted in him being excommunicated by the high council. This sounds more like scrutinizing revelations than checking to determine whether some record he had been keeping might prove to be damaging to the Church.

Disaffected with Mormonism and its leaders, Olney eventually published two booklets that were critical of Joseph Smith and Mormonism: *The Absurdities of Mormonism Portrayed*, in 1843, and *Spiritual Wifery at Nauvoo Exposed: A True Account of Transactions in and About Nauvoo*, published in 1845.[25] In preparation for writing the exposés, he kept a personal record of what he viewed as the iniquities of Church leaders "and many doings that is abominable."[26]

In his published writings, Olney never mentions any revelations or spiritual manifestations he had personally received. However, in his personal writings or journal entries, he often wrote of meeting with messengers sent from God. He, at least initially, saw his calling as that of a reformer. He was seeking to "straighten crooked places and make rough places smooth."[27] He felt it his mission to save the Saints from being led astray by corrupt Church officials.

Olney wrote that in 1839 he had been visited by the deceased Latter Day Saint apostle David W. Patten. He reported, "[M]y mind was uneasy because of what I had seen, but I took the same course that I hitherto had until 1840 I was visited again," this time by a group of individuals who met with him daily and "showed [him] of a work that [he] had to do to bring about the order of

---

his unpublished journals, he never mentions any writings being taken from him. He does say in a different version dated April 6, 1842, that he is "writing it anew." Had Olney begun a history of the Saints prior to 1842? Nothing about his writings or his refusing to give up anything he had written are mentioned in the High Council Minutes when he lost his Church membership. Since Olney claimed that he retained his writings and would not hand them over to Church leaders, it would make sense that they would have been found along with what he wrote after his high council hearing. It is more likely that Olney did not keep a record of the foibles and iniquities of Church leaders until after his high council hearing.

23. His claims might have been made to validate his accusations because they would have been written prior to any Church discipline and would not be viewed as a bitter person trying to get even with the church.

24. "Try the Spirits," 748.

25. Oliver H. Olney, *Spiritual Wifery at Nauvoo Exposed: A True Account of Transactions in and About Nauvoo.*

26. OOP, fd. 11, October 31, 1842.

27. OOP, fd. 10, November 16, 1842.

God."[28] He said the people he met with were a council of twelve ancient men of God known as the Ancient of Days. There are entries in Olney's record relating his many visits with this council. In some entries, Olney refers to his otherworldly visitors by name:

> You are to meet in person with the Ancients, with Old Father Adam and receive your anointing even with the oil of gladness that you may have more light that you may be enabled to go ahead in your duty and bring about the purposes of God.[29]

> The gentleman and lady that to me appeared was called Elijah and his companion that had come to turn the hearts of children to their fathers and fathers to children lest gloominess and sorrow should cover the earth.[30]

> I was visited by an ancient that lived in the days of Enoch by the name of Hipsebah that ascended with Enoch's city.[31]

> I was instructed in many good things, often visited by angels in spirit and in person. At last the Savior unto me did come.[32]

The most important visitations took place on June 9, 10, and 11, 1842, following Olney's separation from the Church. He wrote that these dates were "set apart long to be remembered by those that inhabit the earth."[33] It was from this point that Olney was to begin to establish the Kingdom of God on the earth. In the days that followed, he chronicled being anointed with oil and having the Ancient of Days lay their hands upon his head to bless him to accomplish his work. "I received my anointing, it being a spirit of light and intelligence that on me should rest," Olney wrote. "It is another comforter that with me should dwell that should enlighten and expand my mind. It is to be with me and direct me in my doings so fast as my mind can expand. They laid their hands on me and blessed me and said to me to go about my Master's work."[34]

Olney noted that he had been called upon to warn the people of Nauvoo to "speedily repent of your doings . . . straighten crooked and rough paths, and that without delay." He was also instructed to write to and be in contact with "the leaders of the Church again as [his] work [was] not finished with

---

28. OOP, fd. 6, July 12, 1842. There are two versions of this entry, both dated July 12, 1842, and both found in manuscript folder number 6.

29. OOP, fd. 6, June 19, 1842.

30. OOP, fd. 8, August 9, 1842.

31. OOP, fd. 7, July 16, 1842.

32. OOP, fd. 6, July 12, 1842.

33. OOP, fd. 7, July 16, 1842.

34. OOP, fd. 6, June 19, 1842. There is another entry dated June 19, 1842, also found in manuscript folder number 6, which is completely different from the one cited.

them."[35] He was informed that if the Saints refused to repent "that on them is a curse that they cannot get off."[36]

Olney recorded, "[A] council met and ordained me to the authority of the high priesthood after the order of the Son of God to administer in temporal concerns."[37] He also wrote of receiving a special priesthood:

> The messengers of heaven, they now have assembled all as one to ordain Oliver H. Olney to the priesthood that is conferred on them by the Father and Son with the same gifts and blessing to see and to know of the doings of man as the messengers of heaven that a spirit of discernment may have power to foresee iniquity and check it in the bud as this priesthood was decreed but seldom been in force until the present time. It is only for those that have power to move as the angels of heaven in array.[38]

On another occasion, Olney claimed he was "called upon by the Council of the Ancient of Days to consecrate to the Lord the temple, Nauvoo House, also the house in which they [the Ancient of Days] sit."[39] The following day, Olney noted that he again received basically the same instructions. He wrote that he was "called by the Council of the Ancient of Days to consecrate to the Lord the Nauvoo House foundation that it might be preserved for a people that should make their way here from the North—the ten tribes of Israel."[40] He proceeded to the site where the Nauvoo House was being constructed and stood upon the foundation stones of that building "and consecrated it to the Lord that it might be preserved until the time should come for it to be reared up again."[41] Olney then "consecrated the brick house belonging to Brother Nurse," located one street north of where the temple was being built, "that it might stand a witness that the Ancient of Days condescended to meet in its loft and hold a council in honor of the will of God."[42] Olney's writings never mention him consecrating or dedicating the Nauvoo Temple, which was under construction at that time.

---

35. OOP, fd. 6, July 16, 1842.

36. OOP, fd. 6, October 22, 1842.

37. OOP, fd. 6, August 4, 1842, and another version in OOP, fd. 8, August 4, 1842.

38. OOP, fd. 11, December 6, 1842.

39. OOP, fd. 6, June 10, 1842. There are two entries for June 10, 1842, both found in manuscript folder number 6. The words "2nd writing" are found at the top of one entry. The larger of the two, marked "2nd sitting," is where this quotation is found.

40. OOP, fd. 6, June 11, 1842.

41. OOP, fd. 6, June 11, 1842.

42. OOP, fd. 6, June 11, 1842. Evidently, it was in the loft of the home owned by Brother Nurse where Olney was living at the time and where the purported visits with the Ancient of Days took place.

On his forty-sixth birthday, Olney penned, "[A] temporal kingdom is soon to be set up by order and directions of the Ancient of Days," and noted that he had been instructed to do some business to prepare the way for this to be accomplished. He was informed that "it is up the river not far off that a building was established by the Jaredites and new vamped over by the Nephites that reared a city here."[43] In the months that followed, the area designated as a "new stake of Zion" changed locations. Eventually, he was instructed to dedicate a new site "to establish Zion anew in the north part of Illinois near a place called Squaw Grove, as there was once a noted city that was highly extolled for piety called by the Nephites 'Coleon,' but in English is known as a place of rest."[44] Squaw Grove, Illinois, is located about two hundred miles northeast of Nauvoo and about sixty miles west of Chicago.

On several occasions, it was revealed to Olney that he would be provided with the needed wealth to create the temporal kingdom that was to be established under God's direction. One revelation stated, "You are now called to receive and secure the treasures of the earth to do such things as will establish such things as shown to you to do from time to time." He was informed, "You are called on the morrow to receive the treasures of the earth in gold and silver that was put away by the ancient Nephites on the bank of the river below this at a place where you will be shown. You are called to secure it by digging and receiving it to your care."[45] He never reported to have found anything at that time.

Several months later, Olney received another revelation explaining to him that "money must be plenty among certain ones that is called to establish Zion." Again, he was told that "treasures is many which has been laid away in the bowels of the earth."[46] The money he would obtain was to be used to purchase land around Squaw Grove, Illinois.[47] There is no mention of him ever finding any treasure.

In his role as a reformer, Olney felt it was his calling and responsibility to rescue the Saints from the false teachings of fallen Church leaders. At times he appeared hopeful that repentance could take place among the Church leadership. He thought that if Mormon leaders would call upon him, he could be of great assistance, but felt doubtful he would be given the opportunity:

> I think if I for them could devise a plan I could help them much on their way. My course would be easy, simple and plain. I would first call on the Presidency; then on the Twelve; also the high counselors and some few more that says to

43. OOP, fd. 8, August 11, 1842. There are two entries dated August 11, 1842, found in manuscript folder number 8, which are completely different from each other.

44. OOP, fd. 10, December 6, 1842.

45. OOP, fd. 8, June 30, 1842.

46. OOP, fd. 10, November 15, 1842.

47. I have yet to find any record of Olney purchasing land near Squaw Grove.

lead; and set them to fasting and praying both by night and by day until a union could be established that they against each other would not speak or against the members of the Church. But as they look at me with a jealous eye I shall pass by them until I see a change.[48]

In July 1842, Olney wrote a letter to the authorities of the Church threatening to publish against them unless there was "speedy repentance and acknowledgment to the world of [their] faults."[49] He later noted, "I have no hopes of a reformation,"[50] and "their day of reform is over and not to be recalled."[51] He lamented,

> I look back at the time that it was easy for them to be reformed, but when they passed by me their doom was decreed that an utter destruction would eventually be. I have labored; I sought some few to save by showing them the order of God. I, for my doing, before the council was called that they took from me my standing in the Church that I have long a been [*sic*] looked at as an enemy to the Church of Latter day Saints.[52]

Olney believed he was called by God to "put on them a ten-fold curse" and claimed he was shown "the massacre that would follow such ungodly works."[53] There are entries where he prophesied, "An utter destruction is decreed in the city of Nauvoo,"[54] and "Demons in the shape of men will move in array both sides of the river of the Mississippi until a war of extermination will destroy the Latter Day Saints."[55] He explained that this destruction was necessary to cleanse and purify the Saints who chose to repent—that the "war of extermination must needs be to straighten crooked places and make rough places smooth."[56]

When he decided that reformation ceased to be an option, Olney saw himself as an agent of God, called to establish the Kingdom of God upon the earth. He was given names of people to fill positions in his Quorum of Twelve, high council, and other leadership roles. With his negative feel-

48. OOP, fd. 3, May 1, 1842.
49. OOP, fd. 7, July 1, 1842.
50. OOP, fd. 4, August 19, 1842.
51. OOP, fd. 7, N.d.
52. OOP, fd. 7, written on a page dated July 16, 1842, but written upside down on the bottom of that page. It may have been recorded at a later date and this particular page used because there was space at the bottom. Olney appears to have used this page again, using the remaining space at the bottom. He wrote this later date of September 4, 1842, upside down.
53. OOP, fd. 6, July 12, 1842.
54. OOP, fd. 7, N.d.
55. OOP, fd. 10, November 16, 1842.
56. OOP, fd. 10, November 16, 1842.

ings toward Mormon leadership it is surprising that the names he received by revelation to call as authorities in his organization included such Church stalwarts as Orson Spencer, Orson Pratt, Orson Hyde, Lorenzo Snow, and Wilford Woodruff— Pratt, Hyde, and Woodruff already serving as apostles in The Church of Jesus Christ of Latter-day Saints.[57]

There is another puzzling revelation that Olney recorded calling him to select sixty women, thirty at that time and thirty at some future time.[58] "You are called to take those that are young or single that you see fit to take, but few that have companions; . . . you will have five to sit with you as a presidency of female companions."[59] It is not clear for what purpose these women were being called, especially since Olney claimed to be a staunch opponent of plural marriage. He was a widower at the time he received this revelation and was told, "Eliza R. Snow has been raised up for you."[60] It does appear that at least one of these women was supposed to replace his wife who had passed away. He was promised, "[Y]ou will have another that will have a standing on earth in the Millennium that will raise up your children."[61]

Olney's papers reveal other unique information, including the approximate time when the Millennium would begin: "Sixteen hundred years is barely enough time to prepare for the Millennium and one thousand years of rest,"[62] and that the North Star was the abode of the Ancient of Days and "the high and low will center there at the close of sixteen hundred years from this."[63] It was also revealed to him that the Sabbath day, at present, was set apart "in honor of the day the Savior arose," but would from that time forth be observed "to honor the sitting of the Ancient of Days, as they on earth have took a stand to be governed by the Son of God."[64]

---

57. OOP, fd. 10, November 27, 1842.

58. OOP, fd. 6, June 19, 1842.

59. OOP, fd. 6, June 19, 1842.

60. OOP, fd. 6, June 19, 1842.

61. OOP, fd. 6, June 19, 1842. Olney lists thirty women by name and number in this revelation. The first woman on his list is Phoebe Wheeler, whom Olney married in October 1843. He may have been considering these women to serve in leadership roles in his church.

62. OOP, fd. 6, October 22, 1842.

63. OOP, fd. 6, October 23, 1842. It appears that Olney believed that not only was the North Star the abode of the Ancient of Days, but after sixteen hundred years the Millennium would be ushered in by the Second Coming of Christ and at that time all who were worthy, high and low, would be taken to the North Star and it would become their abode as well.

64. OOP, fd. 6, October 23, 1842. October 23, 1842, was a Sunday. Olney was not changing the day of the Sabbath, but saying that it used to be in honor of the resurrection of Christ; but from this point on it would be in honor of the Ancient

One entry is particularly bewildering. Olney wrote, "I am called on a journey to take into the Eastern country at Boston and there from the tomb raise up J. Adams and take her to her parents and leave her until some future time."[65] This is the only time that J. Adams is mentioned in his writings. He does not indicate whether he traveled to Boston. He provides no information as to the identity of S. Adams, nor does he give any explanation for the purpose of raising this woman from the grave.

It is likely that Olney shared many of his dreams, visions, visitations, and teachings with friends and others in Nauvoo who were willing to listen. Undoubtedly, Church authorities became aware of his purported revelations and it was almost certainly for that reason that he was called to appear before the high council.

After Olney lost his membership in the Church, and after the article "Try the Spirits" appeared in *Times and Seasons*, he remained in Nauvoo. He was aware of the newspaper article announcing his evil deeds and reporting that he had been disfellowshipped. In his journal, Olney wrote, "I as of late have been looking at periodicals printed in different parts. My eye catched [*sic*] on the one of our city edited by the Prophet Joseph Smith called the Times and Seasons said to be a standard to the world. I there found my name that causes me now to express my feeling with pen, ink and paper as no other door opens to my view."[66] It is probable at that point Olney began writing about the Latter Days Saints with the intent of publishing his account as an exposé of all their iniquities. Although he reported that the original account was still in his possession, none of the purported original account is extant and all his published writings come from after his separation from the Church.[67]

---

of Days meeting with Olney and "taking a stand" on the earth or establishing a new era on earth.

65. OOP, fd. 8, July 28, 1842.

66. OOP, fd. 3, April 6, 1842.

67. I theorize that Olney had not been keeping a record until he was called in and excommunicated. At that point he began writing his exposé of Mormonism but attempted to differentiate between his writings and those of John C. Bennett by stating "I have wrote on principle of duty and with the best of feelings and Bennett wrote because he was mad." OOP, fd. 8, August 29, 1842. Olney wanted his readers to believe that he was not writing because he had lost his place in the Church, but that he had been keeping this record for some time. He claimed his record was "an impartial account" because he had long been part of the Church and only desired the best for the Latter Day Saints. I believe his claim to be writing simply to defend himself and bring things to light because he felt an obligation to do the right thing was, in part, an effort to hide his bitterness. I tend to think the notion of a record he had been keeping for some time is a fabrication on Olney's part to give the reader the impression that these writings were unbiased and could be trusted. As stated

Olney claimed that both prior to being called before the high council and after his excommunication he heard or saw things that troubled him and caused him to question the veracity of the Church and the integrity of its leaders. In both his personal and published writings, he gave a number of reasons why he had become disaffected with the Church:

First, polygamy. Olney was well aware of the rumors that were circulating around Nauvoo. City Mayor and Church leader John C. Bennett had sought illicit relations with some of the women in Nauvoo by convincing them that they were married to him spiritually. He assured these women that the doctrine of "spiritual wifery" had the approval of the Prophet Joseph. When Bennett's actions were discovered, he lost his leadership positions, his name was removed from Church records, and he left Nauvoo in disgrace.

Gossip, stories, and suspicions were common in Nauvoo, not only because of the John C. Bennett scandal, but also because of secretive plural marriages that were being performed for and by Church leaders. People were talking. Olney's journal states, "I hear of their works being many such as lasciviousness, fornication and adultery, polygamy or certain ones having a plurality of wives."[68] He also wrote that he had heard of "some of the chosen twelve a trying [*sic*] to be very intimate with females." He continued, "I thought as they had wives of their own that they might let the young girls alone."[69] Olney was skeptical of explanations for plural marriages simply being a trial of an individual's faith. He wrote, "[T]hey say when they cut up their rustys (slang for "going courting") they just did it to try their faith."[70]

Olney also rejected the idea that plural marriage came as a revelation from God. He insisted that it was based on their physical desires or from Satan: "The revelations you have respecting many wives is the desire of the heart or from old Blackfoot himself."[71] He wrote of a vision he had seen of fishermen casting a net into the sea and fish of every kind becoming entangled in the net. He gave the interpretation as Church leaders being the fishermen and the fish as women becoming entangled in the net of polygamy being practiced by Church authorities. "Those of high renown went into the water and gathered a plurality of wives. I see contention soon take place as all pick for the hand-

previously, Olney was not brought before the high council to be questioned about any historical record he was keeping or exposé he had been writing, but for revelations he had claimed to receive.

68. OOP, fd. 7, July 16, 1842.

69. OOP, fd. 10, October 20, 1842.

70. OOP, fd. 3, May 7, 1842.

71. OOP, fd. 5, May 13, 1842.

some and young. . . . [T]he old they let go to take others in, that caused many of them to mourn to think that they was left."[72]

Second: Olney's perceived greed of the Mormon leaders. He often complained that, financially speaking, there was a great difference between the leaders of the Church and the rank and file membership. He wrote: "I look at the poor. I see them oppressed. I look at the widows. I see them rejected. I look at the orphans. I see them neglected. I look at the actual saints that is a doing [sic]' the will of God. I see them neglected and counted of no worth."[73] Another entry from his writing states, "I say where is the equality among the [Saints]; some sitting in rags with barely a morsel to eat while others are arrayed in the best and a living in the best style. How, but out of the tithing of the Latter Day Saints?"[74] In addition to criticizing the practice of tithing the Saints, he also complained about the Church establishing the Law of Consecration, whereby the Saints were asked to be willing to dedicate their efforts, property, and wealth to the Church to establish Zion. He viewed this simply as Church leaders glutting themselves on the labor and money of Church members. Olney even connected the tithing of the people with the evil of plural marriage. "Look at their houses," he remarked, "they lack in size, in rooms and convenience to accommodate their numerous wives and maidens."[75] He reasoned that more wives and bigger families would require the leaders to take more money from Church membership through tithing and consecration. The membership would sacrifice and suffer, but not the leaders.

Third: Olney's perceived elitism of church leaders. He referred to the Mormon leaders as the "privileged few," and spoke of their fame or notoriety in the community. In addition to the privileged few, Olney saw what he called a set of office seekers; scores "of young Joseys (would-be Joseph Smiths) . . . of the same species of the twelve, bishops, counselors and those of high blood, say about one hundred, are privileged and the rest must stand back."[76]

Olney viewed the arrival of Masonry to Nauvoo as an unrighteous organization for the privileged few.[77] His remarks about the elite few meeting together coincides with the creation of the Quorum of the Anointed, which

72. OOP, fd. 3, April 6, 1842.

73. OOP, fd. 3, April 6, 1842.

74. OOP, fd. 3, May 6, 1842.

75. OOP, fd. 3, June 18, 1842.

76. OOP, fd. 4, January 1, 1843.

77. In one of Olney's journal entries he wrote, "I am not a Mason." OOP, fd. 3, April 6, 1842. Based on this entry and other things Olney wrote about Masons, and with no existing record of Olney's involvement with Masonry, it is highly doubtful that Olney ever was a Mason.

was a group of people selected by Joseph Smith to receive special ordinances and instruction. He was also troubled by what he considered to be a female chapter of Masonry. He reported that they went under a different name, connecting the formation of the Relief Society with Masonry for women, with a limited number of women being invited to join. He noted, "This society was formed under the charge of the Lady Elect [Emma Smith] and she ruled by the authorities of the Church."[78] Again, Olney felt these things within the church were elitist, only available to the privileged few.[79]

Fourth: Olney believed that Joseph Smith was a fallen prophet and that Church leaders had lost their authority from God. He believed that Joseph Smith had initially been chosen by God to restore the gospel of Jesus Christ to the earth. In his personal writings, he testified of the truthfulness of the Book of Mormon and stated that in its early years, Mormonism had been blessed with God's authority, the Melchizedek Priesthood. Referring to the fallen Joseph Smith, Olney wrote: "I see the priesthood from him took although he does of it boast, yet it is gone that he cannot longer of it boast. . . . I see many by Joseph directed; he said by the authority of the Father and Son, but I said in my heart he lied."[80]

78. OOP, fd. 3, April 6, 1842.

79. If Olney had been a Mason, it would be reasonable for him to be upset by the establishment of a Mormon female Masonic chapter because there were no female Masons. But since Olney was likely not affiliated with Masonry, the question arises, "Why did he appear to be upset by what he perceived to be female Masons?" In one journal entry, Olney states that the Mormons hoped to "obtain the fullness of the priesthood" through their Masonic involvement. OOP, fd. 2, April 6, 1842. Perhaps Olney was bothered that he had not been invited to be involved with receiving the fullness of the priesthood while select women in the community were being provided that opportunity.

80. OOP, fd. 2, April 8, 1842. It is interesting that in his personal writing and in *The Absurdities of Mormonism Portrayed* (written prior to Joseph Smith's death), Olney demonized the Prophet Joseph. However, in *Spiritual Wifery of Nauvoo Exposed* (written after the death of Joseph Smith), Olney refers to the "death of our beloved prophet and patriarch Joseph and Hyrum Smith" (p. 3). Joseph is no longer the fallen prophet, but the man who was raised up by God to restore truth to the earth. Olney also refers to himself as an Elder of the Church in the Church of Jesus Christ of Latter Day Saints, and states, "[I]t is therefore my Priesthood and calling, to teach the pure principles of truth and righteousness" (p. 3). Earlier, he had written that Nauvoo was a dangerous place to live for people who disagreed with Church leaders, yet he continued to live there for some time after he lost his Church membership. Although he had not been received again into the Church, in his 1845 publication he announced, "I visited Nauvoo with the intention and expectation of making it my winter's residence, and for the purpose of receiving blessings and endowments in

After hearing Joseph preach one morning, Olney wrote:

> He will tell them of the gospel plan. He will tell them of the state of their souls. He will tell them of being endowed with power from on high. He will reason both long and loud to show the key word of God's power. The mind that does desire to arise in the estimation of Joseph Smith, he must let him have his money and he will lead him through the golden gate of heaven. But those that kept their money back he says he will leave them far behind that they with him will have no chance to enter through the Pearly gate.[81]

On another occasion he penned,

> [Mormon missionaries] preach from the Bible and say it is true, . . . but when [converts] get to Nauvoo we there find a change in teaching that the Bible is of not much account; . . . we must do as [Joseph Smith] says or he will put on us a curse.[82]

Olney came to perceive Joseph as a power-hungry individual who would establish himself as king. He believed that the plan to go to the Rocky Mountains was well underway and the reason for the move was strategic to the Mormon plan to take over the country. He referred to the Mormons as a dangerous people, and posed the question, "If they was to the Rocky Mountains as they are there designed to go, what would be the consequence if they there should form a home?"[83] He was convinced that with the influx of new members from the states and from foreign countries, the Mormons would establish a kingdom and become a powerful people, and concluded, "They will unite with the Indians as this has long been the theme by them of the leaders of the Church, that they will lead them over the American soil."[84]

In Olney's eyes, it wasn't just Joseph Smith that had become corrupt. He saw most of the Twelve and other Church leaders as fallen people from whom God had withdrawn His Spirit. He questioned the inspiration of Mormon leaders, citing the Church's bank in Kirtland as an example. He wrote, "I moved in accordance with the leaders of the Church of Latter Day Saints as I supposed they had wisdom as they much of it did boast. But alas their bank failed."[85] He also wondered where the gift of discernment was when John C. Bennett "was put forward as a man of God that his counsel was received by

---

the Temple." However, upon visiting Nauvoo, he reported that he found it to be "a sink of iniquity inhabited by a people whose leaders are whoremongers" (p. 5). Olney may have changed his mind about Joseph Smith, but he now saw Brigham Young and the Twelve as being responsible for leading the Saints astray with their unbounded influence.

81. OOP, fd. 3, May 1, 1842.
82. OOP, fd. 3, May 13, 1842.
83. OOP, fd. 7, July 22, 1842.
84. OOP, fd. 7, July 22, 1842.
85. OOP, fd. 3, April 8, 1842.

the most of the Church."[86] Olney wrote of the creation of a secret combination in Missouri called Danites,[87] and the assassination attempt on the life of former Missouri Governor Boggs, which he attributed to Porter Rockwell under the direction of Joseph Smith.[88] He viewed these things as evidence of the corruption of Church leaders. Creative in his use of words, he remarked that those who led the Mormons were worse than Satan:

> I think they have outstripped the devil that he with them will not be catched where there is so much power of combativeness and not-mind-your-own-busitiveness and such feloniousness and comparativeness and perplexitiveness and lasciviousness, fornicationess, adulterousness and many other subteranesses too numerous to mention.[89]

Joseph Smith, Brigham Young, John Taylor, and Orson Hyde received the brunt of Olney's negative comments about Church leaders. In a letter to Orson Hyde, Olney wrote, "If any man in the Church has been unwise, it is you."[90] He referred to John Taylor as one of the "apostles of the Calf," an allusion to the Twelve serving a golden calf as the one designed by Aaron rather than the Lamb of God. "I see [John Taylor] on the stand a puffing and blowing and hear of his doting for writing for the press. Such preaching, such reasoning, such writing is as much as we can expect from the product of the Calf."[91]

Fifth: Olney believed he had been mistreated by Mormon authorities—being called before the high council, having the news of his being disfellowshipped published, and other mistreatments, real or imagined. In a letter to Joseph Smith, Olney wrote, "I feel that I have been shamefully abused by many; I will say I have heard but a little from you; but, hardly a word from you has set scores a barking that I have suffered from the yelping of a dirty mess of pettish pups; that I do not feel in duty bound to bear; but I have

---

86. OOP, fd. 3, August 13, 1842.

87. OOP, fd. 3, May 13, 1842. Olney believed that Danites still existed in Nauvoo as a secret combination. Although a common belief among antagonists, there is no evidence that the Danite organization existed following the Saints' expulsion from Missouri. Olney saw the establishment of Masonry in Nauvoo as a means to conceal Danite operations. OOP, fd. 4, August 19, 1842. He quoted Brigham Young (speaking to a group of Mormons about those that had left the Latter Day Saints) as saying "he would cut their throats if God would give him power." OOP, fd. 4, August 19, 1842. After hearing this Olney concluded, "I look at his agency and Danite oath and said who is safe in their hands, well knowing that several hundreds are in array to put into execution their degraded traits." OOP, fd. 4, August 19, 1842.

88. OOP, fd. 8, August 10, 1842 and August 14, 1842.

89. OOP, fd. 3, July 7, 1842.

90. OOP, fd. 11, February 5, 1843.

91. OOP, fd. 3, June 18, 1842.

borne it until I will not do it much longer."[92] He also spoke of his need "to be on the watch lest [he] come in their way and get catched [*sic*] in their snare," being "threatened by them of being put aside."[93]

Even though Olney noted several times in his journal that it was dangerous for a person considered an apostate to remain in Nauvoo and that his life had been threatened, he continued to live in Nauvoo, attend Church meetings, and associate and communicate with Church members and leaders for some time after his name was removed from the rolls of the Church. He did mention that if they knew of his doings the people would send him down the river on the back of a catfish.[94]

Early in 1843 Olney was arrested in Nauvoo, but his arrest had nothing to do with his anti-Mormon sentiments or writing. The February 15, 1843, edition of *The Wasp* reported:

> On Tuesday evening last Oliver Olney was brought before the Mayor's court, and charged with burglary and grand larceny. . . . About a month ago a great excitement was created in this city in consequence of Mr. Smith's store having been broken into in the night, and robbed both of money and goods. About one thousand dollars worth of goods were stolen, and fifty dollars in money. The officers made diligent search for the goods; but apparently without effect, until, through a variety of small circumstances, suspicion attached itself to Mr. Olney; a search warrant was issued, and the goods were found in his house; he was immediately taken prisoner, and brought before the Mayor's court, where it was fully and satisfactorily proven that he was a thief. This he did not attempt to deny; but openly confessed the whole circumstance of the theft. A bill of Grand Larceny and Burglary was found against him, and as he did not procure bail, he was committed to the county jail, to await the decision of the Circuit Court.[95]

The Wasp went on to report that since his arrest, Oliver Olney, "a large, powerful, athletic man," had escaped and was at large at that time. The article also mentioned that "since his expulsion from the church he has been engaged in a campaign against Mormonism."[96] It is not clear how the theft and escape charges were resolved or whether Olney spent any time incarcerated for burglary.

Joseph Smith's journal entry for February 10, 1843, states:

> Oliver Olney & Newell Nurse were brought in by Sheriff J[ohn] D. Parker as prisoners for stealing goods f[r]om the store of Moses Smith on the night of the 23rd of January last. Olney confessed before the Mayors court that he had been

---

92. OOP, fd. 11, October 31, 1842.

93. OOP, fd. 10, October 8, 1842.

94. OOP, fd. 3, June 30, 1842. The "doings" Olney was referring to was the record he was keeping and the exposé of Mormonism that he was preparing for publication.

95. "Outrageous Theft," 4.

96. "Outrageous Theft," 4.

> visited many times by the Ancient of days. sat with him on the 9. 10. & 11 days of June last.—& shall sit in council with ancient of Days on Tuesday next—have had a mission from him to the 4 Quarters of the world. & have been established the 12 stakes of Zion—I have visited them all but one in the South. I have suffered much for 2 or 3 years—been without clothes & suffered much I despise a theif [sic] but to clothe myself—I opened the store of Moses Smith on the eve of 23d of January . . . and took out the goods.[97]

Olney indicated that the theft was a result of his extreme poverty. In his writings he often complained about the inequity of wealth within Nauvoo. He wrote of "hard times as money is scarce that causes some to mourn because of living in debt to one another."[98] With the death of his wife and being short on finances, he could not take care of his children. "My companion is dead and my children is scattered one here and one there," he wrote. "Until I get through with this order of things I am not disposed much more time to spend but to publish my writings to the world. I then will settle in some pleasant grove on some rich, fertile prairie with my little family and say I have done all I could."[99] In a letter to his friends, the Chapman family, he reported that his children had not lived with him for one year, but he was "about to commence to keep house in a few days with my girls Mary and Laury Elisa, one fourteen the other ten."[100]

Olney's financial situation did not improve after getting some of his children back. On November 19, 1842, he penned these words: "I once had a plenty and to spare that I could go and come as I pleased. But the time has arriven [*sic*] that my clothing is badly worn and my children is destitute and I am destitute of means to clothe, school or have a sustenance."[101] In spite of professing to despise thieves, he appears to have committed the robbery for the welfare of his family.

In October 1843 Oliver Olney married his second wife, Phebe Wheeler. For a time the couple lived in Nauvoo.[102] In a letter to her aunt and uncle,

97. Andrew H. Hedges, Alex D. Smith, and Richard Lloyd Anderson, eds., *Journals, Volume 2: December 1841–April 1843*, Vol. 2 of the Journals series of *The Joseph Smith Papers*, edited by Dean C. Jessee, Ronald K. Esplin, and Richard Lyman Bushman, 259–60.

98. OOP, fd. 9, August 20, 1842.

99. OOP, fd. 5, July 2, 1842.

100. OOP, fd. 5, letter to Brother and Sister Chapman and family, n.d.

101. OOP, fd.10, November 19, 1842.

102. The couple was married in Nauvoo and several months later a letter from Oliver Olney's second wife to her aunt and uncle was sent from Nauvoo. "Phebe Wheeler," in Susan Easton Black, *Membership of the Church of Jesus Christ of Latter-day Saints 1830–1848*, 45:569.

Phebe explained that she was very much a believer in the Prophet Joseph and the Church. She also declared that she and Oliver were not sure where they would ultimately settle, but it likely would not be Nauvoo.[103]

At present there is no information concerning where Olney, his family, and new wife settled or any more details about his life and writings beyond 1843. It is assumed he died in Illinois sometime in either 1847 or 1848.[104] He had friends in the Church who wrote letters to him inquiring after his well-being and as to the reasons why he left Mormonism and encouraging him to come back. He did not return to Church membership through rebaptism but continued to refer to himself as an elder in the Church of Jesus Christ. He wrote that he returned to Nauvoo "for the purpose of receiving blessings and endowments in the Temple."[105] He did not rejoin Mormonism, nor does it appear that he was ever able to establish his own church. There is no record of his organizing his own version of Mormonism or ever having any followers, a mission he felt at one time he had been called of God to accomplish.

Other possible motives for Oliver Olney's departure from Mormonism should be considered. These potential reasons were not listed by Olney in his writings, either because he did not recognize them or was unwilling to admit to them. An examination of possible grounds for Olney leaving Mormonism follows.

During the Kirtland era, Olney may have believed he was on the fast-track of Mormon leadership. He presided over the teachers in Kirtland and shortly thereafter was ordained an elder and then a seventy in the Melchizedek Priesthood. But after Kirtland, no more positions of authority were offered to Olney. Two of his brothers-in-law, Luke and Lyman Johnson, were selected to be members of the Quorum of the Twelve. Other friends and acquaintances from his earliest days in the Church were called to serve in positions of responsibility and notoriety. Olney may have viewed his being passed over as a sign that he was underutilized and underappreciated. This would have been especially irksome to Olney if he saw others whom he considered less qualified rise in the ranks of leadership.

In conjunction with not being called to greater roles of importance in the Church, Olney may have felt slighted when he was ignored by Joseph Smith as the prophet selected men and women from Nauvoo to participate in the Quorum of the Anointed. Todd Compton wrote, "The Quorum of Anointed

103. OOP, fd. 11, January 28, 1844.

104. Genealogical research on Oliver Olney has yet to come up with an actual date or place of death. A number of genealogical or family history websites theorize that he died sometime in 1847 or 1848. Also, each research site places him in Illinois at the time of his death. A few people have suggested to me that Olney moved back to the Kirtland, Ohio, area and died there. I have pursued that rumor, but as of yet have not found any information that would confirm that possibility.

105. Olney, *Spiritual Wifery*, 5.

(also known as the Holy Order) was the secret, elite group which founding prophet Joseph Smith organized and to which he revealed for the first time the ordinances of washing and anointing, the endowment, and the 'fullness of the priesthood'—the foundation of modern LDS temple ritual."[106] If Olney had been invited to participate with this group he might not have viewed it as elitism.

The practice of plural marriage may have been a similar situation. Olney knew of its existence and he was aware that it was being practiced by a select few. In spite of his negative comments concerning polygamy and his published public outrage at the practice, there is that perplexing journal entry about choosing sixty women. Was Olney indignant at the doctrine of plurality of wives or simply irritated that he had yet again not been invited to participate with the select few? Olney's first wife passed away in 1841. As a widower, was he annoyed that eligible women were being taken by men who already had wives and he remained single?

Something else that may have resulted in Olney becoming disaffected with Mormonism was the death of his first wife. Alice Olney must have been a remarkable woman. When she passed away on July 16, 1841, at age forty-one, her obituary in *Times and Seasons* included a beautiful tribute and a poem written by Eliza R. Snow dedicated to the memory of Mrs. Alice Olney. This published eulogy stated:

> The deceased has left a large family[107] and a numerous circle of friends to mourn her loss, a loss which is easier felt than told. Of her worth in society we would freely speak could we paint it to the mind's eye in its true merits, but language would fail us to tell of her virtues, her patience, her endurance, her godly walk, and motherly care to the orphan, &c. &c. In all her afflictions and persecutions, we are confident that she never was heard to complain. She was truly a saint.[108]

It may have been that Alice Olney was a stabilizing influence in her husband's life. He did go through trials in Kirtland and persecutions in Missouri without losing his faith. Perhaps his confidence in the Church and its leaders was shaken during that time, but his wife's faith kept him "in the fold." In addition, who knows what emotional and psychological problems Oliver might have suffered after the loss of his wife.

Eliza R. Snow was very familiar with Alice Olney; perhaps she was a close friend. She was also well-acquainted with Oliver Olney. In a letter from Oliver Olney to Eliza R. Snow, he wrote, "I remember the covenant that I made with

---

106. Todd Compton, foreword to *Joseph Smith's Quorum of the Anointed 1842–1845*, ix.

107. Oliver and Alice Olney had eleven children, seven of whom lived to adulthood. In addition to the immediate Olney family, Alice's extended kin included the families of her brothers, Luke and Lyman Johnson.

108. "DIED – In this place July 16th, Alice consort of Oliver Olney," 501.

you, although you think I am in the fault, yet I will be a great help to you. The time will soon come that the worth of my labors will be known."[109] It is plausible that Eliza had counseled with Olney after his wife passed away and had cautioned him concerning his negative feelings about the Mormon leadership. Was Eliza R. Snow aware of Olney's misgivings about the authorities of the Church and worried what he might do now that his wife was gone? Was the covenant Olney made with her about remaining faithful to the Church and not doing anything that would harm the Church or put his own salvation in jeopardy?

Another viable reason for Olney's dissension from the Latter-day Saints was the Church authorities questioning or rejecting his personal revelations. It is impossible to say what Olney had experienced. What was the source of these otherworldly manifestations he reported to have received? Were they real or imagined? He certainly believed he was experiencing legitimate visitations and visions from heavenly messengers under the direction of God. His argument could have been, "Others have received revelations from heaven that have been accepted by Church members; why are my revelations rejected?"

At one point, Olney believed that it would be revealed to Joseph Smith that Olney was called of God and that Joseph "would unfold [his] mission that [he] might be known in the Church."[110] Olney lamented the fact the Prophet did not do this. It could be argued that "being known in the Church" is what Olney really wanted—recognition, notoriety, and respect. His revelatory gift was not accepted by Church authorities and, instead of receiving higher positions of leadership in the Church, he lost his membership. Add to that the public humiliation of having his name published in the Church-owned newspaper as a person who "loves darkness rather than light because his deeds are evil."[111]

Because of his bitterness toward Latter-day Saint authorities, Oliver Olney's objectivity can certainly be called into question. This is especially true in Olney's case because many of his personal writings were simply a rough draft of an exposé he planned to publish. However, there are insights from his writings that can be considered valuable. His journal reports of rumors that were circulating around Nauvoo of the practice of plural marriage. Olney's writings substantiate the claim that the Mormons were considering removing to the Rocky Mountains years prior to the assassination of Joseph Smith. Journal entries include statements made by Church leaders during public meetings concerning the Saints' need to repent of their evil doings. He expressed his views as the John C. Bennett incident unfolded. Even taking into consideration Olney's adversarial position with the Church at the time,

109. OOP, fd. 9, October 4, 1842.

110. OOP, fd. 9, September 4, 1842.

111. "Try the Spirits," 747–48.

his writings still afford us an interesting view of Nauvoo from someone living in the city during a time of change and controversy in the Church.

Appendices

Appendix 1 is Oliver H. Olney's 1843 publication *The Absurdities of Mormonism Portrayed.* Much of what Olney wrote in his record of the "doings of the Church" was done in preparation to publish this booklet. There is a rough draft of the introduction of the booklet found in folder number three entitled "The Absurdities of Mormonism Portrayed by O. H. Olney."

Appendix 2 is *Spiritual Wifery of Nauvoo Exposed,* a pamphlet published by Oliver Olney in 1845. This publication appears to have been more closely edited than the first one. It is better written than *Absurdities of Mormonism,* with far fewer errors. It is based on more recent information than he had when he wrote *Absurdities of Mormonism,* therefore very little from Olney's 1842–1843 manuscripts are found in *Spiritual Wifery.*

Editorial Procedures

The primary purpose of this publication of the writings of Oliver H. Olney is to make them available to the public in a faithful, readable format. Spelling, punctuation (or lack thereof), grammar, and diction are presented here almost exactly as they are found in the original manuscripts. The one exception is that Olney began virtually every new line of text with a capitalized word. Unless the words appear to be the beginning of a new thought or sentence, the capitalization has been removed.

In some cases, retaining the original spelling may make reading Olney's writings a little more difficult than if they had all been corrected. However, this provides the reader with access to the material in the manner it was written. Context will help the reader recognize the words in most cases. On occasion, a footnote or word in parentheses will clarify meaning or give the editor's "best guess" as to what Olney was saying. In the entire collection there are a little over a dozen words that could not be deciphered. They will be indicated by the notation <illegible>.

Olney rarely used punctuation. The punctuation he did use will appear as it was in the original manuscripts, whether grammatically correct or not. Olney's spelling was often unique, and, at times, it was difficult to determine what word he was using. His spelling on some words was very consistent:

- se (see)
- ben (been)
- orthoroty (authority)
- antient (ancient)

- futer (future)
- traverling or traverlin (traveling)
- Childern (Children – always capitalized for some reason)
- bretheren (brethren)
- ketched (catched – should be "caught")
- citty (city)
- orto (ought to)
- righeous (righteous)
- vew (view)
- senry (scenery)

In other cases, Olney was inconsistent when spelling particular words, sometimes within the same paragraph or even the same sentence:

- lite / light
- straight / straight / strait / strate
- trayning / training
- rote / wrote
- night / knight
- record / recod
- contact / contack (In his use of the word "contact," Olney appears to have meant "in opposition." To come in contact with someone was to disagree with them.)

Because there is no way to determine which documents were written first and which are rewrites with the same date, the writings have been arranged in chronological order, based on the date listed and the folder in which they were found. If there are three documents with the same date, they will be found one after the other, from lower-numbered folders to higher-numbered folders.

There were some loose pages that were not in order found in some folders. I have attempted to put them in order by context. Also, there were some situations where Olney would write on the front side of each page in a booklet, but the backside of each of the pages was from other dates. There were also some writings upside down that did not fit with what was written above on the same page. And there were symbols connecting one part of a document to another of the same document, but on a different page. In most cases it was not difficult to determine what writings went together once the pattern was discovered. Again, context helped determine the correct order of pages.

Olney's handwriting was often difficult to decipher. The entire manuscript was read through carefully over half a dozen times. Each time, more words were recognized and errors corrected. This does not guarantee that there are no errors in the final transcription, but the reader can be assured that serious efforts were made to be as error-free as possible.

Acknowledgments

I express my appreciation to Yale University's Beinecke Rare Book & Manuscript Library, which houses the Oliver Olney papers, for their willingness to provide access to Olney's writings. I am grateful to the John Whitmer Historical Association for allowing me to present a paper on Oliver Olney's writings at their annual conference and then publishing that paper in the *John Whitmer Historical Association Journal.* My thanks to Greg Kofford for inviting me to submit the manuscript to be published and to Brian Whitney, a skilled and very helpful editor. I'm very appreciative for the much-needed help and support I received from Dr. Alonzo Gaskill. I also want to thank my research assistants for their valuable contribution to this project: Dallin Wilcox, Conner Tracy, and especially Daniel Cruz.

APRIL 1842

[Folder number 2] Citty of Nauvo April 6 1842 ILL

I of late have ben alooking at Periodicals printed in different parts My eye ketched on the one of our Citty edited by the Prophet Joseph Smith called the Times and Seasons said to be a standard to the world I there found my name[1] that causes me now to express my feeling with pen ink and paper as no other door opens to my vew I have long ben a member of the Church of the latter day saints I have been conversent with them almost from the rise of the Church Their ways and their doings has ben familiar to me as I first learnt their their faith and have ever since with them ben fre I have look at their doings I have looked at their works I have ben much engaged for them altho at times I have seen much that, I knew was not wright But in hopes for the better I have passed by the worse as I felt it my duty to be in accordance with the Church I have often laboured their foibles to remove that a stigma should not come on the leaders of the Church I with them have traveld I with them have moved I with them as is often exsprest born the burden in the heat of the day They have always have had my feelings and my property to share that I had when I first did with them dwell We have always ben conversent about time and things tho I have often mourned because of what I have seen My mind has been prejudised in be half of the saints as I with them had a standing In the name of the Lord I felt to do in honour of his name as his name to me was

1. An April 1842 edition of *Times and Seasons* carried an article entitled "Try the Spirits" attributed to the editor, who at that time was Joseph Smith Jr. Though it is an editorial, it is not certain that Joseph Smith actually wrote the piece. Nonetheless, Joseph was the editor, so whether he wrote it or not, it is probable that he was familiar with the article and it was published with his approval. "Try the Spirits" was written because recent occurrences that "have transpired amongst us render it an imperative duty to say something in relation to the spirits by which men are activated." The author cites incidents of false spirits deceiving people from Old Testament times and throughout history. He concludes the article with this paragraph: "We have also had brethren and sisters that have had written revelations, and have started forward to lead this church. Such was a young boy in Kirtland—Isaac Russell of Mo. And Gladden Bishop, and Oliver Olney of Nauvoo. . . . Mr. Olney has been tried by the high council, and disfellowshipped because he would not have his writings tested by the word of God; evidently proving that he loves darkness rather than light because his deeds are evil." "Try the Spirits," 747–48. Olney was living in Nauvoo when this issue of the paper came out, and he was markedly upset and angry about this public humiliation. He gives this as his reason for taking up the pen and exposing the foibles of LDS Church leaders.

cheering In looking about on fields and forests his power and wisdom I did se in the formation of the sun moon and stars and the revolution of the Earth I look at the Law by which they was governed I looked at the different seasons of both heat and cold also the reign and snow that fild the pours of the earth Again I look at my bretheren that said to keep Gods Law I se them move in contact to each other I se that was not wright I look at the Law I se it easy and plain to be comprehended by Saint or Sinner that they need not it mistake I looked at man on the Earth to act for him self as his mind and will should direct But to come to my own case as I now feel oprest by a certain few that say to lead the Church I with them have been conversent until a short time We have had feeling that was not of the best kind as I have felt it my duty in days past and gone to keep a history of the doings the Church from the rise untill the presant time I have tried to be impartial in what I have wrote but I must say that I have ben partial to the saints But as I write it a new I will then draw the line a cross the crooked stick without feeling or affection I will tell the tale wright and preserve my writings for ages to come that we may have a history of the work of the Lord performed in the nineteenth Century of time I now have feelings my mind to relate of things that have come under my observation that I think is not wright I was caled before the Council of twelve men with thre[e] to preside without being labourd with or eaven notified But by the by I herd of the trial and when it was to be I then met with them and answerd to my name They soon demanded my writings that they could not attain I to well knew their feelings I to well knew their minds to trust them with the recod that I had kept of the Church as it spoke of their foibles It spoke of their works and the ungodly doings that I have seen amongst the saints Because of not getting my writings and because of my words they from me withdrawed the hand of felloship and set me a float

I looked at my standing and said I will again with the Council meet I soon met with them with feeling that was good and took the liberty to address them in be half of my case but directly arose against me that I took from their midst my name[2] That did not at all hurt my feelings because of what I had

---

2. Olney states that at the second meeting with the High Council of Nauvoo, he "took from their midst my name." Olney claimed he took his own name from the records of the Church. A *Times and Seasons* article reported that Olney was disfellowshipped from the Church. "Try the Spirits," 748. The High Council minutes reported: "A charge was prefered against Elder Oliver Olney by Elder J[ohn] C. Bennett for improper conduct—for setting himself up as a prophet & revelator in the Church. 2nd. Two were appointed to speak on each side. . . . He pled not guilty. The charges were sustained and unanimously decided by the Council that the hand of fellowship be withdrawn from him. His license was then demanded, which

learned as I have had exsperiance amongst those that say to be followers of God and the Lamb I have looked at their works I have [looked] at their ways that is disgusting to a man of the world much more to a man of God I look at the poor I se them oprest I look at the widows I se them rejected I look at the orfan I se him neglected I look at the actual saints that is adoing the will of God I see them neglected and counted of no worth I look at the man that is upright and just that would deal honourbly with his neighbors and well pay his debts I look at the minds that speaks for them selves that would make councilers not to be turned by a nod I se all such stand neglected that would honour the cause of God if they was put in their plase by the orthorotys of the Church But I se a certin few say for to lead that appears to be some informed in the things of the world They know how to manage to accommodate them selves by fleesing their bretheren as fast as they come in They have lands in abundance all over the place at differant prises that of it they can dispose If Uncle Sam should speak and land holders about I am thinking that many habitations would come up missing and many of their one hundred to fifteen hundred dollar lots of which is well known to be an extorianate [extortionate?] prise a prise that is calculated to take the scanty means from those that have ben gathered from the different quarters of the Earth A sound has gone out for all to come in or they will be counted weak in the faith It has not only passed over the American soil it has gone to England and Scotland and Ireland on the Islands of the sea that many have getherd in the name of the Lord with feelings to do their duty and prepare for the Coming of Christ When they arive the 1st thing is to know how much they posses and what they want to do as a company is ready and awaiting as soon as they arise to assist them wait on them in the name of the Lord they soon get an understanding of their minds and their means that they handle them just as they pleas By it many are a suffering all in the name of the Lord as their means are gone by paying an extorshionate prise or lending their substance as wisdom did direct At this time there is many sitting in rags for the want of apparel to go out and get work eaven those that had property and would have ben well of[f] if they had a ben left to have taken their own course In the Citty of Nauvoo this noted place extoled for its righeousness to the Nations of the Earth is an order of things ariseing that must be checked in the land and as no other person has this subject approached I feel in duty bound my mind to relate as I have often

---

he consented to give up." John S. Dinger, ed., *The Nauvoo City and High Council Minutes*, March 17, 1842. A footnote from *The Nauvoo City and High Council Minutes* asserts that Olney was excommunicated (fn. 347). A brief biography of Oliver Olney prepared for the *Joseph Smith Papers* declares that Olney was excommunicated. In any event, Oliver H. Olney lost his standing in the LDS Church in 1842. See "Olney, Oliver H.," *The Joseph Smith Papers*.

ben cherished and nourished by the powers above that rules in the Heavens and on the Earth As much is adoing in the name of the Lord I shall speak in behalf of his Law to man as his Law is easy simple and plain to those that have reason and wisdom If not they are under no condemnation and are freed from sin But those that have wisdom for to opress the poor and take the advantage of and opress the Saints that have labourd and sought their work well to perform as the Law is given by him that has power it must be regarded by man on the Earth that have from choise taken on them a probationary state This Law is said to be upright and just and not to be turned by the folly of man It speaks of principals Noble and good It speaks of Faith words and works being connected as one It speaks of wisdom and knowledge and a oneness of Spirit for the perfecting of the saints that they may arise in a union of feeling a union of mind That speaks of a Savior that died on the Cross His teachings was for man to be upright with his fellow man that the poor and the rich in harmony might move as God has different gifts on them bestowed Then why not a sympethy of feelings between the rich and the poor that have made a covenant by being baptised for remission of sins I think this covenant is broken by some in this as the poor is oprest and entirely neglected by the rich The poor is a morning because of hard times The rich is arayed in apparel of the best kind They have horses and chariots to move in good style They speak of the trials of looking to the saints as they take from them their tithing that is every tenth that they say is the word of the Lord that I all together doubt as I am satisfied that he will not with them chide or convers except to entangle their minds I have looked at their doings I have looked at their works I look at two Jack Asses a roveing about the streets I have thought in my hart if they had the presance of mind that they would put one each side of the river and threw them look for Gods word as many is alooking some light to obtain They must act in wisdom and make use of their best means We have of late herd an institution amongst us set up by a man from a distance said to be Masonry in its best state[3] As I am not a Mason I know not of it

3. Freemasonry (often simplified as Masonry) is a fraternal organization dating back to stone mason guilds of the fourteenth century. In the years that followed, Masons "embellished their legends, which claimed that the institution of Freemasonry could be traced to Adam, Enoch, and Noah and that Masonic rituals were descended from those practiced in Solomon's Temple." See Michael W. Homer, *Joseph's Temples: The Dynamic Relationship Between Freemasonry and Mormonism*, 5. There were a number of men who were Masons prior to their involvement in Mormonism, including Hyrum Smith, Heber C. Kimball, Newel K. Whitney, and John C. Bennett. When the Saints were headquartered in Nauvoo, a petition was made to a Masonic lodge in Quincy, Illinois, to establish a lodge in Nauvoo. In March 1842 Mason Grand Master Abraham Jonas came to Nauvoo to meet with Masons and others interested in

charms but they say threw it to obtain the fullness of the P-hood that I say they have lost because of their unlawful works Again this wise mason that came from the East ~~in the name of the Lord~~ to establish a lodge in the name of the Lord as he caled the Antient Prophets that long since lived as being masons that has much encourged the saints They think soon to arise to perfection as some few secrets they have obtained that doth much encourage them on the way to meet the Coming of the son of Man as he is soon a coming with the saints in the air They now for his second advent are wishing to be prepared that they may ever be with the Father and son This master Mason instructed them in many good things He said there was certain degrees for the Fair sex of the land They soon met in union a lodge to form but changed the name[4] that they mite be distinguished from the Lodge of the men I of tale[5] in brite and sunshiney day was on the high ground near the temple that I had a fair vew of the Citty of Nauvoo and its contents. I se in the lower part of the Citty a jentle man and Lady well arayed on horses of the best They pransed and they moved as beasts of much life one black and one pale red aprancing up the street As they to me drew neer their visage I knew to be President Joseph Smith and his Elect Lady of fame I then soon had a vision or I se a nett cast into the Sea by fishermen far distant from Shore that surrounded fishes of every kind As they had experience in useing a neet [net] they comenced to haul in That much excited the fish but they soon se themselves entangled with cords not a few that they soon became quiet as they see no way to get out as the nett was continually a moveing It soon arived neer

---

Masonry and installed the Nauvoo Lodge. Joseph Smith and Sidney Rigdon became Masons and the Nauvoo Lodge quickly grew in numbers. For a detailed explanation of Mormon Freemasonry, see Homer, 138–78.

4. At the same time that Freemasons were establishing a lodge in Nauvoo, Joseph Smith organized a benevolent society for women called the Female Relief Society of Nauvoo. Olney states that there were certain degrees of Masonry for "the fair sex of the land" and that a lodge was created for them. Women were not allowed to be Freemasons, but Olney's confusion is understandable. The Relief Society was organized on March 17, 1842, just two days after Joseph Smith officially became a Freemason. Also, the Relief Society met in Joseph's red brick store, in the same "lodge room" where the Freemasons met. When Joseph addressed the Relief Society, he used Masonic terminology. According to Michael W. Homer, Joseph Smith taught Relief Society members the Masonic skill of keeping a secret. "He hoped that the Relief Society would help prepare Mormon women for the temple endowment, which the Mormon prophet revealed several weeks later, and he wanted to protect the secrecy of the ever-growing practice (plural marriage) that he was beginning to disclose to his closest associates." Homer, 179–80. See the entire chapter on "The Female Relief Society," in Homer, 179–98.

5. Olney clearly wrote "tale" but certainly meant "late."

Shore that the fisherman put into the water and gethered such as would answer for their uses The rest they let go for some futer haul As the sun was a shining and the air was clear I directly se the interpetation as it came to my mind clear. I se in the Citty of Nauvoo a society formed amongst the Ladys that said to be temperate and benevolent to the poor This society was formed under the Charge of the Lady Elect[6] And she ruled by the influance of the heads of the Church I se the Chords tightened from time to time that exited feelings of no ordinary kind but because of the secrets that they had sworn to keep they had to keep their minds to themselves as this was the first degree The second and third degrees[7] soon came roleing on as the nett gethered to shore by the wisdom of those that over it had power I then se the second degree. It was that those of high renown went in to the water and agetherd a plurality of wives[8] I then se contention soon take place as all pick for the

---

6. Emma Smith was the first president of the Relief Society. Olney would have been familiar with a July 1830 recorded revelation of Joseph Smith directed to his wife, Emma Smith, in which she is designated as an "elect lady." Doctrine and Covenants 25:3.

7. There are three basic degrees of Freemasonry: Entered Apprentice, Fellow Craft, and Master Mason. Scottish Rite Masonry has thirty-three degrees, but this was not the Freemasonry that was practiced in Nauvoo. Joseph Smith did go from Entered Apprentice to Master Mason in three days. However, he only reached the third degree and did not go through thirty-two or thirty-three degrees as some writers have suggested. It is not clear what Olney is referring to when he writes of the three degrees the Mormon women could attain. Perhaps he was equating what he believed to be the female version of Masonry—the Relief Society. Another remote possibility has to do with the Quorum of the Anointed—a select group of men and women Joseph Smith chose to initiate into Mormon temple rites. This particular entry written by Olney is dated April 6, 1841. However, it is possible that he wrote or rewrote this entry at a later date. If that is the case, then he might be equating the first degree of female Masonry to becoming a member of the Relief Society, the second degree to receiving the temple ritual or endowment, and the third degree to becoming a plural wife of one of the Church leaders. It should be noted that this is conjecture on my part.

8. There is evidence that Joseph Smith married his first plural wife as early as 1835 or early 1836. It seems he was not involved in polygamy again until the Saints settled in Nauvoo, Illinois. Joseph slowly and secretly introduced polygamy or plural marriage to a select group of individuals beginning in late 1840. Oliver Olney was not part of the "inner circle" that Joseph Smith instructed about plural marriage. Doubtless, rumors were spread around Nauvoo about the practice of polygamy. Certainly, some of these rumors were true, but some were based on the "spiritual wife" scandal caused by John C. Bennett. Many historians assume that John C. Bennett was one of the polygamy insiders who invented a different version of plural marriage to support his own immoral actions. Brian C. Hales postulates that Bennett did not learn about polygamy from Joseph Smith. Bennett was an adulterer prior to moving to Nauvoo, and his actions in Nauvoo were a continuation of his immorality. He would likely

handsome and young but they soon cast lots for them and desided to make another haul The old they let go to take others in that caused many of them to mourn to think that they was left As my convenience to write is not verry good And much to do that takes my time I think the third and fourth degrees I shall not expostulate on untill an other time I am not disposed to move against or be hard on those that I have in all cases stood up to defend but I look back amongst my friends in the East that I have ben conversent with from time to time about the Church of the Latter day Saints I to them bore my testimony that as is written by the Prophet Isah 11 Chap that the Lord had set his hand to do a work on the Earth or to prune his vineyard for the last time. And open the way for the getherin of the Jews and the second advent of the Savior to reign on the Earth one thousand years to prepare the saints to enter in to a more glorious rest in the presance of God and the Lamb I again bore my testimony that the scriptures of the old and new testa- was true also the Book of Mormon being a recod of the Ancient Inhabitants that once inhabited this Continent of which the Natives of the forest is a remnant that a roveing two and fro without tru light to guide them and must then stand until God in wisdom sees fit to speak to them and untill that time they are under no condemnation as they have no legal orthorised servent amongst them to tel them what to do I bore my testimony of the above and now do the same. I at the same time said if I found that the people was not what they profest to be I would expose them on the house tops I must say it is with feeling of no ordinary kind that I now set down to wield my pen against my onece beloved Bretheren that I have ben conversent with about eleven years they have at all times had my best feeling I have coverd up their falts time and again eaven by streatching the truth to throw a mantle over them on their unwise doings I feel in duty bound to take my pen to defend the inosent that cannot speak for themselves as there is an order of things peculiar to it self in the Citty of Nauvoo. As they have a Corporation they make their own laws to suit their minds If a man is inclined or does lisp[9] a word derogatory to the character of any of the priveleged few is liable to imprisonment and a fine as the case may be Within a few days a man was put under bonds for speaking lightly of the veracity of one of the Twelve of thre hundred dollars for an assurance that in futer he might hold his peace Instead of the Law of God being

have heard the rumors about polygamy that circulated through Nauvoo, and those rumors may have aided Bennett in convincing some women that his sexual advances were appropriate. See Brian C. Hales, *Joseph Smith's Polygamy*, 1:1–29; 547–74.

9. "To utter timidly or secretly; as, to lisp heresy." *A Standard Dictionary of the English Language* 1, s.v. "Lisp." This has nothing to do with a speech impediment. Olney was referring to the private whispering or gossip of Mormons that were critical of Church leaders.

the theme it is the Law of the Citty And scarsely a man dars to express his feelings to come in contact with those that lead ask a man a question and in his answer will denote more fear of comeing in contact with the prophet than God but there is Good reason for that a combined set will move on him that he will have to submit to their terms on the spot But God is not so perticular he is not so afraid of their getting the advantage of him as they are He lets them run a little season and then puts on the screws after shoing them their folly But they like the Childern of Israel do often forget what God has don for them in days past and gone He once met them and on them did bestow the Melchesadeck Priesthood that by it they often was blest The sick in some cases was heald because of Faith works and doings They saints have often ben blest that they have gained much inteligance in things that is of God From time to time the saints have ben blest and received much encourgement by the way of gifts but because of misdoings they have ben often oprest that they have ben driven from place to place that a rod is fixed for them when they get out of the way that they may round up their shoulders and bear it untill they get strait But if I should speak my feelings or eaven think I shall say that many will brake a strateing as I look at them to be crooked set Again I se some that is getting verry faat I supose on the saints tihing as they do not work Saints in all ages as a people have had much to endure but if they would well do their duty and their work well perform no weapon that is formed against them would do them any harm but as the covenant to do and to keep the Law of God this is required of them to well perform. That from them God may fruit obtain. I of late have often ben to meeting to hear the Elders preach Such preaching such reasoning such teaching, There none but a saint could endure They are like gide bords at the corners of the streets They say to go the different of compass but do not go themselves They stand and look to the right and left and speak of things that is past but dare not things to come lest Joseph should with them find falt as he has got his name well up as the saying is he can lay abed till noon B[ut] me thinks there is yet a God above that has power over man that I am not to be turned neither by a wink or a nod as I se many is that say to be the Commissioned servents of God I barly write to express my mind as I se hard feelings towards [me] for they cannot tel what but after I have wrote a few more items I will close my writing for the presant They may think to write to put me down but I have set [yet?] got a bugget[10] that I have not tuched If I have to bring it forth it will make a shakeing among them

10. A bag; a little sack, with its contents. Hence, a stock or store. *Noah Webster's First Edition of an American Dictionary of the English Language—Facsimile 1828 Edition*, s.v. "Budget." Olney was saying that he had much more information about the Mormons that he had not yet shared.

dry bones as they have commenced on me I think they will have their match as they [k]no[w] not my priveleges that I had before I with them do meet I went to Mill and to meeting[11] before I was twenty one Aagain I was raised Connectticut that land of Habits Good in a Noted Town caled Union that in there was a hill caled hejhog that raised high into the air I often got up on it and look all around and vewed many plantation and se nothing that I was aferd of ex[cept] that the snakes should bite my legs as they was often in the sun Again I had priveleges tho of them I cannot bost as I had always rather be a wrestling than to be a studdying my book But I had a master Foster I had a master Horten also Leonard and Strong that took much pains with that I am still their warm friends But I had a master Richerson that of me did lick[12] But his sticks would get worn up before my eyes with tears would wett but now comes the P-hood If you have it put on me a curse that I cannot move against you as now you know I am adoing it or will as soon as this can go to the press Yes I will move against you and crowd you in to the mire and untill you acknowledge beat[13] then I will take hold and help you out

[Folder number 3] (Page 1st) Citty of Nauvoo April 6th ILL

I of late have ben alooking at the Periodiodicals printed In different parts My eye ketched on the one of our Citty Edited by the Prophet Joseph Smith caled the times and Seasons said to be a Standard to the world I there found my name that causes me now to express my feelings with pen ink and paper as no other door opens to my vew I have long ben a member of the Church of the Latter day Saints I have ben conversant with them almost from the rise of the Church Their ways and their doings has ben familiar to me as I first lernt their faith and have ever since with them ben fre I have looked at their doings I have looked at their works I have ben much engaged for them altho at times I have seen much that I knew was not right But in hopes of the better I have passed by the worse as I felt it my duty to be in accordance with the Church of Latter-day Saints I often have labourd their foibles to remove that a stigma should come on the Leaders of the Church of L.D.S. I with them have traveld I with them have moved I with them as is often exsprest borne the burden In

11. "To mill and to meeting" is a phrase likely meaning something like "I'm no novice. I am familiar with and see very clearly the way things are. I have been around." Examples of the use of this phrase can be found. "I have been in a good many places; I have been to mill, to meeting and to the races in North Carolina." Jake Hodges, "What Our Guests Have to Say on the Great Public Question," 3.

12. To strike repeatedly for punishment; to flog; to chastise with blows. *Webster's Dictionary* (1828), s.v. "Lick."

13. Olney likely meant "until you acknowledge that you are beaten" or "until you admit defeat."

the heat of the day They always have had my feelings and my property to share that I had when I met with them We have always ben conversent about times matters and things altho I have often mourned because of what I have seen Yet my mind has ben prejudised in be half of the L.D.S. As I with them had a standing In the name of the Lord I felt to do in honour of his name as his name to me is chearing In looking about on the fields and forests his power and wisdom I did se in the formation of the Sun Moon and Stars and the Revolution of the Earth I look at the Law by which they are governed I looked at the seasons of both heat and cold also the reign and Snow that fills the pores of the Earth Again I look at my Bretheren that say to keep Gods Law I se them move in contact with each other I se that was not wright I looked at the Law to be easy and plain to be comprehended By Saint or Sinner that they need not it mistake I look at man on the Earth as an agent to act for himself as his mind and will him directs But to come to my own case as I now feel oprest by a certain few that say to lead the Church of L.D.S. I with them have ben conversent untill within a short time We have had feelings that was not of the best kind as I have felt it my duty in days past and gone to keep a history of the doings of the L.D.S. from the rise untill the presant time I have tried to be impartial in what I have wrote but must say that I have ben partial that I have moved in behalf of the L.D.S. But in writing it a new I will then draw the line across the Crooked Stick without feeling or affection I will tell the tale wright and preserve my writings for ages to come that we may look back and se what took place in the ninteenth Century I now have feelings my mind to relate of things that have come under my observation that I think is not wright I was caled before the High Council of twelve men and thre to preside without being Labourd with or eaven notified But by the by I herd of my case and when it was to be I there met with them and answerd to my name They soon demanded my writings that they could not obtain I too well knew their feelings I too well knew their minds to trust them with the record that I had kept of the L.D.S. as it spoke of their foibles It spoke of their works and the ungodly doings that I have seen a mongst the L.D.S. Because of not getting my writings and because of my words they from me withdrawed the hand of fellowship and set me a float I looked at my standing and said I again with the Council will meet I soon mett with them with feeling that was good and took the liberty to address them in behalf of my case but they in aray moved against me that I took from them my name That did not at all hurt my feelings because of what I had Learned as I have had experiance amongst those that say to be followers of God and the Lamb I have looked at their works and vewed them in their ways that is disgusting to a man of the world much more to a man of God I look at the poor I se them oprest I look at the widows I se them rejected I look at the orfan I se him neglected I look at the actual saints that is adoing the will of God I se them neglected And counted of no worth I look at the man That is upright and just that would deal honourbly with his neighbour and well pay his debts I look at the minds that speaks for themselves that would make Councilers that is not to be turned by a nod I se all such stand neglected that would honour The cause of God if they was put in their place by the Orthorotys of the L.D.S. But I se a certin few say for to lead that appears to be some informed in the things of the world They know how to manage to accommodate them selves by fleesing their Bretheren as fast as they come in They have lands in abundance all over the place of different prises that of it they can dispose But if Uncle sam should speak and the land holders around I am thinking that many habitations would come up missing And many of their one hundred to fifteen hundred dollar lots of which is well known to be an extorshitant price a prise that is calculated to take the scanty means from those that have ben getherd from the differant quarters of the Earth A sound has gone out for all to come in or they will be counted weak in faith It has not only passed over the american soil it has gone to England Scotland Ireland and the Islands of the sea that many have getherd in the name of the Lord with feelings to do their duty and prepare for the coming of the son of man When they arive the 1st thing is to know how much they possess and what they want to do as a company is a ready and a waiting as soon as they arive to assist them wait on them in the name of the Lord They soon get an understanding of their minds and their means that they handle them Just as they pleas By it many are a suffering all in the name of the Lord as their means is gone by paying an exorbitant price or lending their substance to those that say Thus saith the Lord At this time there is many sitting in rags for the want of apparel to go out and work eaven those that had property and would a ben well of[f] if they had a ben left to have taken their own course In the City of Nauvoo, This noted place extoled for its righeousness to the Nations of the Earth I se an order of things araising that must be checked in the bud and as no other persen has this subject approached I feel in duty bound my mind to relate as I have often ben cherished and nourished by the powers above that rules in the Heavens and on the Earth As much is adoing in the name of the Lord I shall speak in behalf of his Law to man as his law is easy simple and plain to those that have reasen and wisdom If not they are under no condemnation and are freed from sin But those that have wisdom for and opress the poor and take the advantage of them and opress them that have labourd and sought their work well to perform. As his Law is given by him that has power it must be regarded by man on the Earth that have from choise taken on them a probationary state This Law is said to be upright and just not to be turned by the folly of man It speaks of Principals Noble and Good It speaks of Faith words and works of being connected in one It speaks of wisdom and knowledge and a oneness of Spirit for the perfecting of the Saints that they may arise in a Union of feeling a union of mind That speaks of a Saviour that died on the Cross His teachings was for man to be upright with his fellow man that the poor and the rich in harmony might move as God has on them differant gifts bestowed Then why not a sympethy of feelings between the rich and the poor that have made a covenant by being baptised for remission of sins I think this covenant is broken by some in this as the poor is oprest and entirely neglected by the rich The poor is a mourning because of hard times The rich are arayed in apparel that is of the best kind They have horses and Chariots to move in good style They speak of their hardships of looking to their saints as they take from them Their tithing that is every tenth that they say is the word of the Lord that I altogether doubt As I am satisfied that he does not with them coincide I have looked at their doing I have looked at their works I have looked at two Jack Asses a roveing about the streets that is said to belong to the Church I have thought in my heart that if they had the presance of mind that they would put one each side of the river of Missippi and threw them look for Gods word as many is alooking much lite to obtain They must act in wisdom and make use of their best means We have of late had an institution set up by a man from a distance said to be Masonry In its best state As I am not a mason I know not of its Charms but they say threw it to obtain the fulness of the Priesthood that I say they have lost because of their unlawful works Again this wise mason that came from the East to establish a lodge in the name of the Lord as he caled the Antient Prophits that long since lived as being masons that has much encouraged L.D.S. They think soon to arise to perfection as some few secrets they have obtained that doth much encourage them on the way to meet the comming of the Son of man as he is soon a comming with the saints in the air They now for his second advent are a wishing to be prepared that they may ever be with the Father and Son This master Mason Instructed them in many good things He said there was certin degrees for the fair sex of the land They soon met in union a loge to form But changed the name that they mite be distinguished from the lodge of the men I of late in brite and sunshiney day was on the high ground near the temple that I had a fair vew of the Citty of Nauvoo and its contents I se in the lower part of the Citty a jentle man and lady well arayed on horses of the best They pransed as beasts of much life one black and one pale red They moved up the streets As they to me drew neer their visage I knew to be President Joseph Smith and his Elect Lady of fame I then soon had a vision or I se a nett cast into the sea far distant from Shore by fisherman of power that surrounded Fish of every kind As they had experiance in useing a nett they commenced to haul in that much exited the fish but they soon se themselves entangled with Chords not a few that they became quiet or submissive as they see no way to get out as the nett was continually a moveing It soon arived near Shore that the fisherman put into the water and getherd such as would answer for their use The rest they let go for some futer haul As the sun was a shineing and the air clear I directly se the Interpetation. As it came to my mind I se in the Citty of Nauvoo a sosiety formed by the Ladys that said to be benevolent to the poor This society was formed under the Charge of the Lady Elect And she ruled by the Orthorotys of the Ch— I se the chords tightend from time to time that exited feelings of no ordinary kind but because of the secrets that they had sworn to keep they had to keep their minds to themselves as this was the first degree of Masonry The second and third degrees soon came roleing on As the nett getherd to shore by the wisdom of those that over it had power I then se the second degree It was those of high renown went in to the water and getherd a Plurality of wifes I then se a contention soon take place as all picked for the handsome and young but they soon cast lots for them and desided to make another haul The old they let go to take others in that caused many to mourn to think that they was left As my convenience to wright is not verry good and much to do that takes my time I think the third and fourth degrees I shall not expostulate on until some futer time It is not my mind to be hard on those that I have in all cases stood up in defens of their characters in all cases I have moved for their good and am still determined to do the same I now consider it a favor to them to unridle their doing that will needs produce a reformation in some If it is possible to save a part it is better than to have the whole lump spoil But the smoke that daily arises dampens the prospect but in looking back on past events I am supprised that God would bear to be mouthed as he has ben by the Church of Latter day Saints. They say to move in his name and keep the command of God They say to be a blest people of God and move in accordance to his will But what do they do to honour his name but move in dark paths both early and late They move in darkness at noon day they baffle the mind of the honest by sayings that is not of God They speak of the power of which they are propeld that is the spirit of lustful desires They lust for grandeur and applause also that is forbidden in the word of God They think to move by proxy as it is with them a common word to take the advantage of those that comes in contact with them. But I look at some thats looking on that is not to be duped by smooth words I look at the Editoral department and of it I cannot for bear to speak When I see the use that is made of it such a use made of letters as they by them are placed disgrases our language much more the subject on which they wright They write of their doings at home and abroad and put the best side out in all cases In looking at their doings and daily moves I se them determind to carry their own points I se they are determined the cepter to sway wright or wrong that will cause many to mourn that move under their wach care As many is a looking and say all is well that our leaders are a blest people that in them we are willing to confide as this by many is the sayings at and abroad No shadow of turning will by them be received They speak of their Prophit word as being the word of God that it must be fulfild to the letter He has aids around him to back up his word thats utterd in the name of Lord that many of it is a feard lest something mite be said that would dampen their influance as they are established to do as fast as the way opens But the order is established that the head must lead

[Folder number 2] Citty of Nauvoo April 8 1842

I have ben to conferance and meeting and a writing as gratifyed my mind and as I was out of the Church I exspected to be let alone and soon go to some retired station and mind my own concerns to be sure I have for two days ben a writing but mostly to fre my mind not that I cared about such an ungodly mess of stuff agoing to the world as I have wrote But I think I will look it over and fix it for the press as they still sing my name from the East to the west They bear on me both in public and private whire ever they have a chance that I plainly se I must defend myself I have lately had a vision or vew in a sun shiny day of a company that said to have great wisdom in the Order of God I look at their doing I looked at their works I some times felt doubtfull whether it was of God but I said in my heart I will stand still and see Perhaps good may come out of it I looked at it over and over again I said in my heart it is veryy smooth It is verry brite It is verry fair I think of it I soon will share But behold unto my supprise the interpetation came the interpetation came as clear as the sun that shined I se it begin I se it end I se it caused much trouble threw out the land In every mouth in every mind more or less was said or thought to know whether God needed an armed force on the Earth to propel his work to prepare for his second advent on the Earth I look amongst the saints of God that first clad in a military garb I se a man apearently come to teach and tell them of good things He in structed them in things that was verry good He told them of the order of God He told them if they would wish to become wise and great to make friends with the Mammon of unrigheousness that in as much as time should come that they should be streighened by a mob that the world would receive them into their arms I thus did se companys formed all said to be in the name of the Lord that in aray they often did meet all equipt by the Orthor[ity] of the state I se them long in order move in pomp and splendor they did stand that said to be the light of the land I se them dote from time to time of Gods power in their behalf I se them stand I se them gase in hopes to se some messenger of power come to teach them how to manover but to their supprise they have yet to stand barely in the streanth of man I se the Prophet Joseph arayed at the head because of his power of with God I se him stand I se him move I se him gain in the eyes of the world at the same time loose his power with God On one hand he raised on the other he fell tho often blest because of man as many stood a looking to know Gods will I se him strive to be verry great in goods and chatels around did much exalt his mind I se him have a taste to know Gods will and well contend for good things but because of popularity and pride God left him a season to him self that he mourned he wept both knight and day that caused much excitement amongst the saints. In his behalf I se the P-hood from him took altho he does of it bost yet it is gone that he cannot longer of it boast He has had a teacher that was not of God that has brought darkness to him instead of light I se the P-hood took from the Church that not a man either big or small had power to baptise for a remission of sins much more for the Dead that long have lain. As unto them was said such a company for preaching would have made me a stared if I had not a ben aversed they received their charge to scour the Country in all parts as several hundreds came forward this great work for to do The priests of Babilon must begun to look out as rag shag and bob tail will soon beguin their under pinning to slip out If they are greesy dirty and raged they from the Apostles of the Calf[14] have received their charge so of course their work will be performed They will speak of the getherin as they rove around It will be well for the sisters to have their eyes on the first and second degrees of Masonry as the sosiety is now being organised they may possibly come in amongst the first Again there has many ben baptised at the Conferance some in the River others at the font that I am satisfied did them no hurt as I was to the River I se many by by Joseph directed he said by the Othoroty of the Father and son but I said in my hart he lied but we read that the sin of ignorance is to be winked at so it is not laid to his charge Altho I could a told him long since of his standing before God that had no more power with him than any other man I then went up to the font the above named apostles in part was there to work in connection with others that had no light The sick and the lame into the font did go They did not wait for the Angel to trouble it before they went in If they a wated they would have had to a wated in vain As

14. This is a derogatory term based on Jesus being the Lamb of God and his apostles being commonly called the apostles of the Lamb. Viewing LDS Church leadership as having left the path designed by God and no longer following Him, Olney mixes metaphors and describes Church leaders as "Apostles of the Calf." Olney is clearly referencing the golden calf that Aaron made—a false god that the Children of Israel sinfully worshiped. (Ex. 32). Olney was referring to Church leadership as apostles of a false god.

I think the[y] have more wisdom than to get among such a dirty set I looked at them as they went in I thout a scrub broom and soap would have ben of much use So I pass by the Conferance as of not much account as there did not appear to be much Business to be don altho they spoke of ling and tatling and some of the twelve a having to be verry intimate with females But if it was so I thought as they had wives that they might a wated untill the woman takes the second degre of Masonry I now come to a close as I did once before in hopes that I shall no more from them hear but if I do I have other bugets that is ready to burst that will make an explosion that I do not want to hear as I am satisfied when this is as public as your proceeding against me I now with you will reason of things that have past You well know that you have always tried me to opress and this to get a union and honour God law If we have lost our Credit from it we cannot run We may as well repent of the past and set out anew God will to do I had rather be licked if noboddy knew it than to expose myself with you but we mus[t] round up our sholder and in a reformation go ahead that we may no more disgrase the American soil or our Children that is is agroing up to manhood and this to get a union and honour God law If we have lost our Credit from it we cannot run We may as well repent of the past and set out anew God will to do I had rather be licked if noboddy knew it than to expose myself with you but we mus[t] round up our sholder and in a reformation go ahead that we may no more disgrase the American soil or our Children that is agroing up to manhood

[Folder number 3] Citty of Nauvoo April 8th

I have ben to Conferance and to meeting and a writing As Gratified my mind and as I was out of the Church I exspected to be let alone and soon go to some retired station and mind my own concerns I of late have ben a writing but bearly to fre my mind but as my name is mouthed by them both in private And on the stand exspress my feelings and to tutch on a subject that is familiar to me as I have seen much of it since I have ben with The L.D.S. It is a spirit of bosting of wisdom or to move by proxy they say in takeing the advantage of their fellow man We hear them speak of the Gentiles as a low and a degraded set hardly fit for the Kingdom of God but my mind gets a running on doings that I have seen at Kirtland Missouri and of their decit I will recite them to Kirtland to the scores of Farms barly one and two payments made then the farms went back Why was the prise rais[ed] from ten to one hundred dollars per acre it may easily be said by proxy In the mormons out buing one another how was it with the bank gether and to it did subscribe some from one to one hundred thousand Scores came to gether In the name of the Lord and liberally subscribed to help the bank The amount subscribed

I will not say but it was heaps upon heaps They caled for their enstalments but them that si[g]ned the most I think in most cases paid the least But gold and silver was flush in their hands that much encouraged many of the business men about They soon isued their Currency abroad that mad[e] a fine show of pictures but as many had feelings to sound them that had moved in the name of the Lord they daily caled on them to redeem bills but by proxy They ment no one should doubt their ability to redeem their bills They had boxes in abundance that they filed with sand well neer the top and then put on the clean coin that made a fair prospect This paper was flush to those that wanted to Borrow or buy that caused much to be a doing in differant parts as many as was sent to distribit it to the fore quarters of the Earth Thus by proxy it moved and went untill the bills silver gold and dirt all got mixed up to gether and the Prophesi failed that caused many to mourn all in the name of the Lord I was in the mire as others in the mud as I moved in accordance with the Leaders of the Church of L.D.S. as I supposed they had wisdom as they much of it did bost But alas their Bank failed for the want specie to back it up

[**Folder number 3**] Saturday the ninth

They received their charge the country to scour Several hundred came forward this great work to do The Priests of Babilon must beguin to look out as rag shag and bobtail[15] will soon beguin, Their underpinning to root out If they are dirty greesy and ragged they from the apostles of the Calf gethering as they rove around It will be well for the Sisters to have their Eye on the First and second degrees of Masonry as the Sosiety is now in being organised They may posibly come in amongst the first So I pass by the Conferance as of not much account as their did not appear to be much business to be don altho they spoke of Lying and tatling and some of the twelve a trying to be verry intimate with females mite as well a wated untill the women takes the second degree of masonry I now come to a close As I did once before in hopes that I shal hear from them no more but if I do I to them will speak of things that they suppose is in the dark that will make an explosion on you that I do not want to hear as I am satisfied when this is as public as your doings with me I now with you will reason of things that have transpired You well know that you have in all cases tried me to oppress You think that you now have don it that pleases you much but we have nothing to brag of as we are all of a mess

15. An idiom meaning an assortment of people, typically of the lowest mien. From an 1883 publication comes this example: "The devout itinerant . . . gazed upon the motley crowd that surrounded him for a few moments in silence, then rose to his feet, and said, 'Well, here you are, rag, shag, and bobtail!'" Harvey Rice, *Pioneers of the Western Reserve*, 108.

Our ungodly doing is known in part You well know what has ben published in the differant Periodicals[16] tri to get a union in honour of Gods Law If we have lost our Credit from it we cannot run We may as well repent of the past and set out a new to serve God I had rather be licked in the dark than to expose my self with you but we must round up our shoulders and in a reformation go ahead that we may no more disgrase the American Soil Also our children that is a groing to manhood

[Folder number 3] Citty of Nauvoo April 10th 1842

I still continue my writings of things that daily transpires as we have ben engaged in a conferance a few days past as I have ben in the habit of keeping a record of things that transpires in the Church The conferance commenced April 6th but few came to gether the first day as they had to meet out of doors for the want of a house as it was verry wett They mett with good feelings and with each other shook hands They commenced teaching and reasoning of matters and things The second day they came together but little was don As it was wett cold and uncomfortable because of heavy rains The third day they came together they spoke of the temple[17] and the necesity of its being don that the Elders mite be endowed with power from on High to go forth and bind up the Law and seal up the testimony of the gentile race The Nauvoo house[18] came up that of it remarks was made The necesity of its being finished

16. Many newspapers in the Midwest and nationally carried articles about Mormonism—typically negative in tone. A small sampling of the newspapers reporting on Mormonism include *The Alton* [Illinois] *Telegraph*, *The Quincy* [Illinois] *Whig*, *The Sangamo* [Illinois] *Journal*, *The Peoria* [Illinois] *Register and North-Western Gazateer*, *The Warsaw* [Illinois] *Signal*, *Iowa News*, *The Iowa City Standard*, *Fort Madison* [Iowa] *Courier*, *Hawk Eye* [Iowa], *St. Louis* [Missouri] *Pennant*, *Missouri Reporter*, *American Bulletin* [St. Louis, Missouri], *The Sun* [New York], *The New York Evangelist*, *The Ohio Observer*, *The Arkansas Gazette*, and *The Boston Recorder*. For a large collection of articles about early Mormonism in newspapers all around the United States, see *Uncle Dale's Readings in Early Mormon History*.

17. The Nauvoo temple was the second temple built by the Latter-day Saints, the Kirtland, Ohio, temple being the first. Three other temple sites were dedicated prior to Nauvoo: Independence, Missouri; Far West, Missouri; and Adam-ondi-Ahman, Missouri. These three Missouri temples were not built because the Mormons were driven out of the state. In January 1841 instructions were given for building the Nauvoo temple. Cornerstones were laid on April 6, 1841, and construction began. Persecution and financial setbacks interfered with the construction of the Nauvoo temple. Joseph Smith was killed in 1844, prior to the temple's completion. However, work on the temple continued until its dedication in April 1846.

18. A published revelation of Joseph Smith dated January 19, 1841, now known as section 124 in the Doctrine and Covenants, included a charge to build a temple

for the high and the noble of the Earth They caled for volenteers I make use of their words Rag Shag and bobtail And the ofscourings[19] of all Gods Creation You now are caled to come forth and receive Ordinations from under our hands as many is a setting in darkness that have not herd the gospel sound You are caled as fishers and hunters to look up the good And leave the bad that all things may move in order as God has decreed Thus by scores and hundreds, They came forward to honour Gods cause Rag Shag and bobtail as unto them was said Such a Company for preaching would have made me a staired if I had not been a versed in their doings They soon received their ordination mostly from those That said to be apostles of the Lamb

[Folder number 2] Citty of Nauvoo April 12 1842

As I am yet looking about the citty to se what is a going on I often meet with those that say to have much wisdom in the things of God as they daily are a preaching and teaching in the name of the Lord I often look at them and think of the storys that I have of them herd I said in my heart I will say its not so as I want my teachers to appear fair I want to se them stand without being sensurd if they are wrong as I did not se the inquity of it I did not know that I was glad in my heart that I could not against them testify but as visions verry plain altho I do not know as they will be received as I have them when I am wide a wake and generally on a high hill I of late had a vision that that spoke of a set that was noted for their good qualities esspesily by them selves I se them bost

in Nauvoo and also a hotel. Of the hotel the revelation declared, "And it shall be for a house for boarding, a house that strangers may come from afar to lodge therein; therefore let it be a good house, worthy of all acceptation, that the weary traveler may find health and safety while he shall contemplate the word of the Lord; . . . And let the name of that house be called Nauvoo House; and let it be a delightful habitation for man, and a resting–place for the weary traveler" (D&C 124:23, 60). The Nauvoo House should not be confused with the Mansion House where, for a time, Joseph Smith's family lived and took in boarders. There is a difference of opinion concerning the revelation recorded in section 124 relating to the Mansion House. One view is that, in addition to the temple and the Nauvoo House, section 124 also includes a directive to build the Mansion House (see vs. 115). Lachlan Mackay, historic sites coordinator for Community of Christ, believes that verse 115 is referring to the Nauvoo House, which was supposed to have a suite of rooms for Joseph and Emma Smith. Because the Nauvoo House was to serve as a home for Joseph Smith's family, the Mansion House likely had not been contemplated when the January 1841 revelation was received. (Personal correspondence from Lachlan Mackay to the Editor, April 8, 2015.)

19. That which is scoured off; hence, refuse; rejected matter; that which is vile or despised. *Webster's Dictionary* s.v. "Offscouring."

of their goodness of their welth influance over all the land I se them stand in contention with many around and eaven defied the powers of man I se many look at them with feelings to do them no harm but because of their folly and because of their works a contention a rose on the fourth of July clens and puryfy the saints From that time they was no more humble that sin a mongst them did not so much abound The Law of God was regarded by many around A union of feeling a Union of mind was the theme of those of the Latter day Saints I se the Sin of Leciveousness and fornication and Audultory was from that time put down I then se an order of things that was Noble and good The kingdom spoken of by Daniel was then set up it moved in order by legal orthorised servents on the Earth upheld by the power of God I se many a looking that said to be wise to get assistance from those that they had oprest I se many stubborn because of mismoves that had to suffer the penalty of God Law I se many that God took to him self because of the evil to come that caused a Lamentation marvelous to relate amongst those that said to be the Latter day Saints but their name did not save them because they lacked in good works As my vision is ended whether for the better or worse I am not perticular as I can only speak for my self but I have feelings for the well fare of man I am willing to spend and be spent in the Service of God altho I am alone At the same time friends all around At the same time dare not speak lest they are censured with a delusive spirit some thing that is not of God But spirits are many that invade the land but I am not sensurd for opressing the poor or takeing the widows mite or the Orphans Crumb or liying or tattleing or backbiting Laciveousness fornication Audultery or takeing the advantage of my fellow man as is alleged on some of my Clan Yet I take from them forever my name bretheren that is scatterd abroad to stand still and se the salvation of God I[f] you come here you will add sorrow to gloom that will not be of any use to you to further you on as here in an order perculiar to itself If I am permitted I will make a comparison seilor had been a roveing oer the briney great deep that he got wearyed and worn out that he could not climed a rope he from water on to land did go and hired to be a farmer to plow He in to the field with a thre beast team and commenced to plow for to sow The plow it hitched and the old mare kicked The oxen began for to baul All was confusion discord and disunion The old mare and the oxen all tangled in to gether The plow on its side turned The sailor he gased at its site but lest he with them should get entangled he run to his master and said all is not write The master he inquired into the matter The sailer in reply said the Labbourd ox is on the scabbord side the scabbord ox is on the Labberd side[20] The old mare has fell foul in the rigging The plow is

20. Larboard: the left side of a ship when the spectator's face is towards the bow. Starboard: the opposite of *larboard* or *port*; the distinguishing term for the right side

on her beams end they are all a going A_s fore more mast to the Deavil So it is with order of the latter day saints Let you that have feelings to be up and a doing stand still in untill the old mare and oxen do all get streightend and the plow on its Nose aready to perform it labours as said time is approaching and the Labours a waiting their seed to thrust in The time will soon be that the team will be a plowing the old mare and oxen together will draw The plow will perform its duty haveing hands of skill to manage the team I of late have ben a looking and vewing the situation of the Church of latter day Saints espesily the Elders that say to be the lites of the world I again to at the Church that says to be like a Citty on a hill I look at their doings that speaks hard things I say in my heart whire is their reasen whire is the economy or wisdom of God displayed As property is lavished frolickin and Dansind and a traverling too and fro on the <page torn> and all to no purpose Look at Kirtland se money there exspended for scores of Farms and barly the 1st payment made eaven at a fourfold price day saints Look at their goods in abundance that brought a slur on the saints because of their debts due to the world Look at the men caled on to do business for them It was these that could be turned by a wink or a nod or by those that had wisdom to gathe[r] their treasures and put them to their own use Look at the many names that have ben trusted with treasures of the Latter day Saints eaven those that have ben as teachers to stand in defens of the Law of God have taken the advantage of the honest in hart Again look at the Elders from Prophit to teacher all that have had a chance to get a quainted and se them arise in contention oth[er] They are often in Law and contending and oppresing each other that brings sorrow and Lamentation amongst the Latter day saints Again I se many that would do their duty if they was well

---

of a ship when looking forward. Rigging: a general name given to all the ropes or chains employed to support the masts and arrange the sails according to the direction of the wind. Mast: a long cylindrical piece of timber elevated perpendicularly upon the keel of a ship, to which are attached the yards, the rigging, and the sails. Foul: generally used in opposition to *clear*, and implies entangled, embarrassed, or contrary to. Nose: often used to denote the stem [the foremost piece uniting the bows of a ship] of a ship. Beam-ends: a ship is said to be on her beam-ends when she has heeled over so much on one side that her beams approach a vertical position; hence a person lying down is metaphorically said to be on his beam-ends. Admiral W. H. Smyth, *The Sailor's Word-Book: An Alphabetical Digest of Nautical Terms*, s.v. "Larboard," "Starboard," "Rigging," "Mast," "Foul," "Nose," "Beam-ends." Olney uses this humorous anecdote about a sailor on a farm not knowing what he is doing and likens it to the leaders of Mormonism being similarly ignorant. Wording similar to that used by Olney for larboard and starboard is found in *The Adventures of Tom Sawyer*. A boy named Ben Rogers is coming down the street imagining himself to be a riverboat captain, giving orders to his crew: "Set her back on stabboard! . . . Let her go back on the labboard!" Mark Twain, *The Adventures of Tom Sawyer*, 15.

instructed in things that is good that is a wandering in darkness from morning untill knight I say the Law of God is broken and underfoot troden by those that say to be the Latter day saints I mite continue my writing in speaking of their foibles from time to time but suffise it to say I have written of the foibles of the Church and in doing it I am not disposed to wholy screen my self as our teaching is and has ben to move in accordance with the orthorotys of the Church but as I have been out of their hands for a little season a preaching and teaching and endeavouring to persuade man to keep the Law of God but as I have of late returned from an estern mission vewed a senry of things that to me is disgusting to speak of that is prevalent amongst the latter day saints They are often seen in contention one with another The rich is much respected the poor their is those that say to have wisdom that cannot bear to se any person as wise as them selves I now with good feeling speak to them and tel them of things that mite do them good if they give heed to them If not well and good that they have not so much wisdom but what they can learn more Now if a union could be established in honour of the Law of God I with you will endeaver to regain our characters that we may be counted as worthy inhabitants of the Earth But if you persist in your doings I shall move my squil[21] [quill?] against you until I break you all up Yours with out fear or affection

Oliver Olney

[Folder number 3] Citty of Nauvoo April 12th

As I am yet looking about the Citty I see much a float that I will minet[22] and say it is correct If it is doubted I have no more to say to such but those that can think and speak will with me coincide As much has ben said and don to take the attention of those that are arayed in riches in high life as this sample before them is set they for to imitate it have often the poor stript of their property in an unlawful way a way that is disgusting to those that can speak and think for themselves They borrow with a promise to refund and act on a principal to the Contra[23] they deal much in land that takes the orthorities of

21. According to Webster's 1828 dictionary, a squill is a lobster or prawn; a crustaceous animal; an insect resembling a fish; and a plant with a large bulbous root not unlike an onion. Olney likely meant "quill." The large strong feather of a goose or other large fowl; used much for writing pens. Hence, the instrument of writing. *Webster's Dictionary*, 1828 ed., s.v. "Quill." Olney was threatening to write more damaging information about the Latter-day Saints.

22. To set down a short sketch or note of any agreement or other subject in writing. *Webster's Dictionary*, 1828 ed., s.v. "Minute."

23. A Latin preposition signifying *against, in opposition,* entering into the composition of some English words. *Webster's Dictionary*, 1828 ed., s.v. "Contra."

many They sell and they by to serat times But of it I am one daily informed theyr titles are good for nothing or the most of them I look at their doing as they pass and ask the wise a question How will it be with them Five years hence if they go ahead as they are now on the looked at his team as he goes a plowing with or three heart team as he was sloly a plowing all untill the plow hit a stone that all came up standing at once The old hores he kicked and the oxen commenced to baul that much excited the Sailor as he had just come on land He ran to his master and said all is not well His master enquired Why it was thus The Sailor replied The Labbord ox is on the scabbord side The scab. ox is on the Lab. side The old horse has fell fowl in the rigging The plow is on her beams end and they are all a going A—ss foremost to the Deavil The above is a sample of the L.D.S.

MAY 1842

[Folder number 3] May 1st 1842 Citty of Nauvoo

This morning to meeting I went and desided that the mind that would wish to be great must be attentive to meeting and hear Joseph Preach He will tell them of the gospel plan He will tel them of the state of their soles He will tell them of being endowed with power from on high He will reason both long and loud to show the key word of Gods power The mind that does desire to arise in the Estimation of Joseph Smith he must let him have his money and he will lead him threw the Golden gate of Heaven But those that kept their money back he says he will leave them far behind that they with him will have no chance to enter Threw the Pearly Gate into a Heavenly rest a rest of which the Prophits spoke if they it understood If they it understood Between them and Joseph is a contrast The Prophit spoke of being endowed with power from on high They spoke of power that was of God They spoke of works By it performed to heal the sick by the prayer of faith to cast out Deavils raise the Dead and well declare the Council of God This in connection with all the gifts compose the endowment[1] of those sent to preach But says Joseph Smith if you with me desire to share in blessings that is good On me depend and I will take you all a long If I for you do say to do you in return must do for me in Money Goods and Chatels or I will leave you far behind as the keys of the Kingdom of God like the Apostle Peter I possess Thus I can save you or dam you as I pleas Such Preaching and teaching as I of late have herd denotes the degraded situation that the Church of L.D.S. is in I now ajourn for afternoon At two oclock to meeting I went and attentively set and attentively set to hear them preach They spoke of many things that I said was good They caled for a reformation both long and loud They desided on next Thursday to meet to beguin to mend and repent of all their ungodly deeds I se they well understand of what they have ben about They spoke of their sins Cases of Audultry fornication and others too numerous to mention If they

---

1. In 1836 Joseph Smith introduced a temple ordinance in the Kirtland Temple referred to as an endowment with power. "Between the completion of the Kirtland Temple in March 1836 and his death at Nauvoo in June eight years later, the Prophet expanded the meaning of the endowment." By May 1842, Joseph began to introduce to selected Church members this expanded version of the endowment. The first endowments in Nauvoo were performed in the upper room of Joseph Smith's red brick store, prior to the completion of the Nauvoo Temple. Before the Mormons left Nauvoo, many endowments were performed in the Nauvoo Temple. Glen M. Leonard, *Nauvoo: A Place of Peace, A People of Promise*, 255–61.

hole harted in a reformation go ahead I think with them will be a change I think If I for them could devise a plan I could help them much on their way My course would be easy simple and plain I would first cal on the Presidancy then on the twelve also the High counsilers and some few more that say to lead and set them to fasting and praying both by knight and by day untill a union could be established that they against Each other would not speak or against the members of the Church But as they look at me with a jealous Eye I shall pass by them untill I se a change I think as they have commenced they have got the Cart before the horse as they have caled on the members soon to meet and reform I have ben conversant with them both far and near I find not much falt with them except they suffer themselves to be brought into bondage by the Leaders of the Church I think their chance for a reformation is but small As the Leaders of the Church as they said by Presidant Vanburen is a getting verry fatt When my pen gets a running in connection with my mind it is hard to stop as its inclined to run If I have to take a second round I shall no more daub with soft soap but tell the tale as it actually is the daily moves That I have seen would establish a king In the City of Nauvoo or we may say in one sense he has took a stand that a lisp against him a man is in danger of his life as a secret combination now is formed[2] to stand by each other at the expens of their lives This is one chord that is on them drawn that

2. The term "secret combination" is found in Restoration scriptures (eighteen times in the Book of Mormon, once in the Doctrine and Covenants, and once in the Pearl of Great Price). A secret combination is a group of conspirators, seeking for power and wealth through acts of evil. "Secret combinations may be brotherhoods, groups, societies, or governments. They operate in secrecy to perform evil acts for the purpose of gaining power over the minds and actions of people." Daniel H. Ludlow, ed., *Encyclopedia of Mormonism* 3, s.v. "Secret Combinations." During the violence against the Mormons in northern Missouri in 1838, a group of Mormon men created a defensive paramilitary band calling themselves "Danites." The Danites were led by Sampson Avard, "who instituted initiation rites and secret oaths of loyalty and encouraged subversive activities." They attacked and looted non-Mormon settlements and forced Mormon dissidents to flee Far West, Missouri, through intimidation. Although the existence of Danites was short-lived and there is no actual evidence of any such group later, the stereotype of lawless, Mormon avenging angels persisted for decades. See Ludlow, *Encyclopedia of Mormonism* 2, s.v. "Danites"; and Garr, Cannon, and Cowan, eds., *Encyclopedia of Latter-day Saint History*, 275. Olney believed that the secret combination known as the Danites had formed again in Nauvoo, putting the lives of those critical of the Church in danger. In a later writing, Olney states, "A secret combination that was formed in Missouri is a dread to those that would act for themselves. It was a combination formed by the male members caled Danites, said to be in honor of the law of God. They took an oath to defend each other to the expense of their lives, whether wright or wrong. It is now newly vamped over by men

hundreds is kept down for fear They dare not lisp their minds for fear of what may follow God that knows my heart knows that I wish them well and always have but from principal of honour and good will to man I feel as no other one has this Subject approached to take my stand in behalf of the Laws of the United States not by a mob Law as that is low and mean It will dishonour a people that will to it give heed But let the people that have power look well to their duty and releive the oprest When first an oak beguins to grow if it is streight and thrifty and would honour a grove nourish it and cherish it on its way But if it is crooked coarse and rough and would dishonour a forest to check it when it first beguins to grow it is easily don But if it is left untill its roots gets pronged and boddy strong it is hard to roust From its bed Thus I look at the L.D.S. and hear them bost of their power with God. Show them their weakness now in time before it is to late to save many minds that would be an honour to our state They say our Military forse is strong They say a Choir of Angels to our Cohort would come if invaded by an armed forse Thus they reason From day to day that darkens the minds that mite be wise if they would give vent to their minds Whire is the God that rules in Heaven and on Earth Is he a God of order and of light and truth If he is who are those That disgrase his name like those that say to do in his behalf but do not according to his word Whire is the drunkard and the man of sin that makes no pretentions to do his will Is he dishonoured by those No not as he is by those that profess to do ~~but do not~~ and reject his council and take to themselves ways and means and dote in his power In their behalf Does God need a set of office seekers and a Nauvoo Legion to propel his power on Earth What is their characters amongst them selves even amongst The first of the Legion but of the basest kind If testimony is to be received After speaking of what I have in my remarks There is not a statement that I have made but what is well known to be the truth But not the whole truth An abundance of testimony could be provided If people could speak without fear of being delt with afterwards The question now arises does God move in Unholy temples Will he move threw men of ill fame to display his power in honour of his name If so the principal Officers of the Nauvoo Legion may look for the Angels to help them And if not they stand in the strength of men

[Folder number 5] Dear Brother and Sister Chapman and Childern

I with no ordinary sit down to write you a few lines That you may know of my welfare I at this time enjoy good health an my Childern are all well I do not keep house nor have I since I broke up one year ago I got my Childern

of pleasure that are well off by tithing the Latter day Saints." See Oliver Olney Papers, folder number 3, May 13, 1842; fd. 5, May 13, 1842 (hereafter OOP).

out to good places that I have got along with them well But now I am about to commence to keep house in a few days with my girls Mary and Lany Eliza one fourteen the other ten I think to get along with them untill some other door opens I have not herd in perticular from you since I was at your house last fall a year ago but have often thought of my Brother and Sister also their Childern that seems neer to me but when I look at the distance between us I find thought will go quick but not the boddy I am often with you but not but by thought in meditation I well reccollect how I roved around over the hills and threw the vally both early and late But I am engaged now other ways I have something more serious I have had that to do that causes me often to mourn and Lament bearly to do my duty It is that I have volenteerd to do on a principle of honouour And good will to man I have for years ben with the Ch of LDS I have known of their doings that some times was not wright but in hopes of reform I moved ahead said not but that all was well But for som ten months past I have seen much afloat that I with them could not coincide I from them took my name and on a principal of wright have felt it my duty to unridle their works I commenced by writing of their doing of which I have plainly wrote that will speak loud of the Iniquity of L.D.S. They have become a fallen people because of their bad works In the form of a a pamphlit my writings will soon go forth that I am sorry to publish to the world But as I have commenced I feel in duty bound to well do my duty in the fear of God as no other person has ben engaged to come out with good feelings and speak of facts of their doings My mind is the same as it was when I with you Conversed of Gods Law to man but man is changeable That does not alter the truth If the way opens I shall give you a call I think some time next season I mite write much to you about matters and things but I hardly know whire to beguin as I se much again I[n] different parts that takes my attention that I look upon as of not much account Money is scarse Crops is good Many is sick Some dies that causes many to mourn because of the loss of Friends Much is said but little don because of hard times at home and abroad In a word I will say all with me is well I am in hopes that these few lines will find you the same I have added "H" to my name Please to give my respect to all of the connections Elias and Abbalena Chapman[3]

O. H. Olney

3. This letter was addressed to Elias and Abbalena Olney Chapman. Abbalena was an older sister of Oliver Olney. She was born at Union, Connecticut, on April 14, 1790. Abbalena married Elias Chapman, and the couple had six children.

[Folder number 5] May 1st Nauvoo

This morning to Meeting I fixed up and went And decided that the mind That would arise and become wise and great must be attentive to Meeting and hear the Prophit Joseph Preach He will tel them of the gospel plan He will tel them of the state of their souls He will tel them of being endowed with power from on High He will reason both long and loud to show the key word of Gods power The mind that does desire to arise in the Estimation of Joseph Smith he must let him have their money and he will lead them threw the Golden gate of Heaven But those that have kept their money back he says he will leave them far behind that they with him will have no chance to enter threw the Pearly Gate into a Heavenly rest a rest of which the Prophits spoke if they it understood Between them and Joseph is a contrast The Prophits spoke of being endowed with power from on High They spoke of power that was of God They spoke of works by it performed to heal the sick by the prayer of faith to cast out Deavils raise the Dead and well declare the Council of God This in connection with all the gifts composed the endowment of those sent to preach But said Joseph Smith if you with me desire to share in blessings that is good On me depend and I will take you all along If I for you do say to do you in return must do for me in money and Goods and Chattels or I will leave you far behind as the Keys of the Kingdom like Peter I possess Then I can save you or Dam you as I pleas Such Preaching and teaching as I of late have herd denotes the degraded situation that the Church is in I must now draw to a close and to meeting go This afternoon According to apointmen[t] at two O clock To meeting I went and Attentively set to hear them Preach They spoke of many things that I said in my heart was good They caled for a reformation both long and loud They decided on next thursday to meet to beguin to mend and repent of all their ungodly deeds I se they well know of what they have ben about They spoke of their sins being cases of Audultry and Fornication and others to numerous to mention If they whole harted in a Reformation go ahead I think with them I will have a home But they must first do as well as say I think if I for them could devise a plan I could help them much on their way My course would be easy simple and plain I would first cal on the Presidancy then on the twelve Then on the High Councilers and some few others that says to lead and set them to fasting and praying both by knight and by day Untill a union could be established amongst them that they against Each other would not speak or against the members of the Church or a buse them in the least Then I would cal a general Conference at a time apointed To come together and to Confess to Each other their falts and continue to gether from day to day and fast and pray untill we got the whole lump leavend But as they look at me with a jealous eye I shall pass by them Untill I se a change I think as they have Commenced they have got the Cart before the horse They have caled on the members soon to meet And Commence a Reformation in the Church of latter day saints I have ben Conversant with them both far and near I find not much falt with them except they suffer themselves to be brought in to bondage by the leaders of the Church I think their Chance for a Reformation is verry small As the leaders of the Church as they said by President Vanburen they are agettin verry Faat How fleety are the ways of man when in orthoroty he does arise Thus we se the minds of those that mite a ben valient men of God They have had a chance to well improved on their talents If they had a ben wise But now we se their presant state rejected by God And discountinanced by man because of their unwise doings The mistakes they have took that I am ashamed to rehearse has put on them a stain that time will not rub of[f] But on a principal of Mathimatics take nothing from nothing nothing remains so it is with those that have not power of mind to come out and take a stand in the name of the Lord and then keep their pledge They are of no worth As they are of no act[4] but to be oprest by the rabble of the day When my pen gets a running in connection with my mind it is hard to stop It is inclined to run If I have to take a second round I shall no more daub with soft soap but tel the tale as it actually is The dayly moves that I have seen would establish a king in the City of Nauvoo or we may say in one sence he has took a stand that a lisp against him a man is in danger of his life As a secret Combination now is formed to stand by each other to the exspens of their lives This is one chord that is on them drawed that hundreds are kept down for fear They dare not lisp their minds for fear of what may follow God that knows my heart knows that I wish them well and Always have But from principal of honour and good will to man I feel as no other one has this subject approached to take my stand in behalf of the Laws of the United States Not by a mob Law as that is low an mean It will dishonour a people that will to it give head [heed] But let the people that have power look well to their duty and releive the Oprest When first an Oak beguins to gro if it is strait and thrifty and would honour a grove nourish it and cherish it on its way But if it is crooked coarse and rough and would dishonour a forest to check it when it first beguins to grow is easily don But if it is left untill its rotts [roots] gets pronged and its boddy strong its hard to roust from its bed Thus I look at the Latter days saints and hear them bosts of the power with God Show them their weakness now in time before it is to late to save many minds that would be an honour to our state They say our Military forse is strong They say a Choir of Angels to our Cohort would come if invaded by an armed forse Thus they reason from day to day that darkens the minds that mite be wise if they would give vent to their minds Whire is the God that rules in Heaven and on Earth Is he a God of order and

4. Likely a truncated version of "account."

of light and truth If he is who are those that desgrase his name like those that say to do in his behalf but do not according to his word Whire is the drunkard and the man of sin that makes no pretentions to do his will to be dishonoured by those No. Not as he is by those that profess to do and reject his Council And take to themselves ways and means and dote in his power in their behalf Does God need a set of office seekers and a Nauvoo Legion to propel his power on Earth What is their Characters amongst themselves eaven amongst the first of the Legion but of the basest kind If reports is true Even amongst them selves they say is to be proved if tested After speaking of what I have in my remarks there is not a statement that I have made but what is well known to be the truth but not the whole truth And abundance of testimony could be produced if people could speak without fear of being dealt with after wards The question now arises Will God dwell in Unholy temples Will he move threw man of ill fame to display his power in honour his name If so the principal officers of the Nauvo Legion may look for the Angels to help them And if not they stand in the strength of man I now draw to a close by subscribing my name

O. H. Olney

[Folder number 3] Citty of Nauvoo May 6th 1842

I of late have ben a traverlin and vewing the Citty of Nauvoo I se much a doing That looks to me strange amongst those that say to be saints of God I se them armed and equipt with weapons of war that is said to answer the Laws of the State But in looking at Their movements and the weapons they bear also the time they spend in trayning denotes something more than mierly to answer the Law As much is a doing in the nam[e] of the Lord there weapons looks to me savage to be used by men of God Also their daily trainings when I se so many a suffering for the necessarys of life Several days is now spending in trayning Besides time to come in from ten to sixty miles of[f] At the best much time is spent in training. They say to answer the Law of the state but I find it is the Law of the Citty of Nauvoo not the Law of the state of Ill I look at the poor and destitute of the place I look at the officers and draw a contrast I say whire is the Equality among the L.D.S. some sitting in rags with bearly a morsel to eat while others are arayed in the best and a living in the best stile. How but out of the tithing of the L.D.S.

[Folder number 5] Citty of Nauvoo May 6th 1842

I of late have ben a traverling and vewing the Citty of Nauvoo I se much adoing that looks to me strange amongst those that say to be Saints of God I see them armed and equipt with weapons of war that is said to answer the Laws of the State But in looking at their movements and the weapons they bear also the time they spend in trayning denotes something more than merly to answer the Law As much is adoing in the name of the Lord there weapons looks to me savage to be used by men of God Also their daily traynings looks to me strange when I se so many a suffering for the necessarys of life Sever-al days is now spending in trayning besides time to come in From ten to sixty miles of[f] At the best much time is spent In trayning They say to answer the Law of the state but I find it is the Law of the Citty of Nauvoo not the law of the state of Illinois I look at the poor and destitute of the place I look at the officers And draw a contrast. I say whire is the Equality among the Latter day Saints some sitting in rags with bearly a morsel to Eat while others are arayed in the best and a living in the best stile How but out of the tithing of the Latter day saints

[Folder number 3] Citty of Nauvoo May 7th

This day has ben a senry of things as I have seen much a doing all in the name of the Lord We have had a great muster of the Legion of Nauvoo They together In the morning did meet and parade that made a noble appearance for those that had gethered to se They was armed and equipt with swords Rifles and guns Tomahawks spears cutlasses and Cannon as they mostly was equipt to answer their Law Some said their was seven thousand That made a fine Show A show that would be an honour to any of our western States if that was the object of the Legion of Nauvoo but those that are conversant with them well knows the fact, That they are a making ready to stand in their own defens in case of an attact They speak of Missouri from whence we was drove that they shall yet receive their dues for driving us out Again they Prophesi in the name of the Lord that they will be six hundred thousand strong In ten years Thus a spirit of encouragement is held out By those that lead that they will gain in numbers and become a terror to the Nations of the Earth They have now sent to England and to all parts for the saints to come in and that without delay Thats no mistry to solve as they want tithing and strength The day past away in good order that not much against could be said if they had not ben a doing in the name of the Lord as this is the theme with them I with them do much disagree as I think God is able to bring about his own purposes without an armed forse The impliments of war has caused many to bleed to establish doctrin in the name of the Lord But when we get better informed in principals that is good we find that God by the still small voice or the sword of the spirit produces lite a light that shines in dark places and makes crooked strait and rough places smooth Let those that have wisdom set reason to work and Ask this question Do we or do we not need an armed forse to establish the order of God in the Land in this the nineteenth Century of time on a land of freedom For which our Fathers fought a land that is noted to be a land of freedom amongst the Nations Both far and near Let us reason for a moment How was it with the antient Saints How was their faith established Was it but by faith and good works We will now look at the Latter D. Saints and their faith and works and make a contrast We look at their doing at home and abroad There is no union amongst their Elders If a few get together they all or a part want to lead that makes divisions and scisims amongst the Latter day Saints They then go to the Prophit to get the word of the Lord He recites them to the high Council They there have a hearing according to testimony and receive their destiny and go home ashamed to think of the things That against them was proved They make their confession that all with them may be well that they may be esteemed by the orthorotys of the Church of L.D.S. But with the heads of the Church it is not so They say when they cut up their rustys[5] they just did it to try their faith This is the whip roe[6] they take when they get ketched in a dirty scrape and they slip – out – as – easy all – in – the – name – of the Lord

---

5. This is clearly an idiom or colloquialism. There are a number of possible meanings: to show off; behave foolishly; to explode with anger. Robert Hendrickson, *The Facts on File Dictionary of American Regionalisms*, s.v. "Cut a rusty." Another use of the phrase "cut a rusty" has to do with wooing a woman, courting, or soliciting in marriage. In the context used by Olney, the meaning is likely slang similar to "go courtin." *Western Slang, Lingo, and Phrases—A Writer's Guide to the Old West*, s.v. "Cut a rusty." Olney probably used the phrase in connection with married Mormon men wooing women other than their wives for the purpose of plural marriage. According to Olney, a Mormon leader caught trying to unsuccessfully seduce a woman or take another man's wife could simply use the excuse that he wasn't serious in his attempts. Rather, it was a test to try the faith of the individual. There are instances like this in Mormon history. Probably the best-known case is Heber C. and Vilate Kimball. Kimball's grandson and biographer recounts the circumstance of Heber being introduced to plural marriage by Joseph asking for his wife, Vilate: "Three days [Heber] fasted and wept and prayed. Then, with a broken and a bleeding heart, but with soul self-mastered for the sacrifice, he led his darling wife to the Prophet's house and presented her to Joseph. . . . Joseph wept at the proof of his devotion, and embracing Heber, told him that was all that the Lord required." Joseph then performed a ceremony making Heber and Vilate husband and wife for eternity. Orson F. Whitney, *Life of Heber C. Kimball*, 323–24. Todd Compton expressed his belief that there were cases in which "Joseph was not simply asking for wives as a test of loyalty; sometimes the test included giving up the wife." See Todd M. Compton, *In Sacred Loneliness: The Plural Wives of Joseph Smith*, 18–19.

6. "In agriculture, the row easiest to hoe; hence, the inside track; any advantage: as, to have the whip-row of a person (to have an advantage over him)." William Wight Whitney, ed., *The Century Dictionary: An Encyclopedic Lexicon of the English Language* 8, s.v. "Whiprow." Olney is accusing LDS Church leaders of immorality or attempted immorality. He alleges that if they are caught in their attempts to seduce women, they claim that it was a planned ruse to test their faith. Thus, they use the "trial of faith" excuse to their advantage. That is their "whip-row."

[Folder number 5] Nauvoo Saturday 7th 1842

This day has ben a senry of things as I have seen much adoings All in the name of the Lord We have had a great Muster of the Legion Company They to gether in the morning did meet and parade that made a Noble appearance To be seen to those that had gethered to se They was armed and Equipt with swords rifles and guns tomahawks spears and cutlasshes and Cannon As they mostly was equipt to answer their Law Some said their was seven thousand That made a fine show a show that would be an honour to any of the western States if that was the object of the Legion of Nauvoo But those that are conversant with them well knows the facts That they are makeing ready to stand in their own defens I[n] case of an attact They speak of missouri from whence we was drove that they shall receive their dues For driving us out Again they prophesy in the name of the Lord that they will be six hundred hundred thousand strong in ten years Thus a spirit of encourgement is held out that they will gain in numbers And soon become a teror to the Nations of the Earth They have now sent to England And to all parts for the saints to come in with out delay That is no mistry to solve As They want tithing and strength The day passed away in good order that not much against them could be said if they had not ben adoing in the name of the Lord as this is the theme with them I with them do much disagree As I think God is Able to bring about his purposes Without armed forse The implements of war has caused many to bleed to establish doctrin that was said to be of God But when we get better informed in principals that is good we find that God by the still small voice or the sword of the Spirit produces light A light that shines in dark places and makes crooked straight and rough plases smooth Let those that have wisdom set reason to work and ask this question Do we or do we not need an armed forse To establish the order of God on the Earth in this the nineteenths Century of time on a land of freedom for which our Fathers fought a land that is noted to be a land of fredom amongst the Nations both far and near Let us reason for a moment How was it with the antients saints How was their Faith established Was it but by Faith and good works We will now look at the Latter day saints and their Faith and works And make a contrast We look at their doings in differant parts There is no union amongst their Elders If a few get to gether they all or apart want to lead that makes divisions and schisms amongst the Latter day Saints They then go to the Prophit to get the word of the Lord He recites them to the High Council They there have a hearing according to testimony and receive their destiny and go home ashamed to think of the things that against them was proved They make their Confessions That all with them may be well that they may be essteemed by the heads of the Church But with the heads of the Church It is not so They say when they cut up their rustys they first did it to try the saints They say if you want to stumble stumble over it as I did thus and so to try your Faith This is the whiproe they take when they get ketched in a dirty scrape And – they – slip – out – as – easy All done in the name of the Lord

[Folder number 3] Nauvoo May Sunday 8th

This morning to meeting I did go to hear and se what was a going on One of the presidancy took the stand and commenced Preaching and teaching As I am willing and a waiting to give each one their due I must say I was edified at what I se and herd Altho he was feeble Because of ill health yet he spoke with freedom in honour of God as no embarisments on him did rest He spoke freely his mind to us that I said to my self he is not turned by a nod I se he had a spirit planted within to move without being turned by every wind Altho he is said to be under the weather by some of hig[h] renown and those that turn on a pivot but when I first herd him speak I se his independance and understood his case He spoke some two hours and took his seit and was followed by one of the twelve I found no falt with him he spoke freely his mind Then arose another John Taylor by name that seemed desirous to be great He spoke loud and heavy but in matter he much lacked as the spirit of Inteligance did not on him rest But in puffing and bloing he to us did show that he must to go ahead whether or no They administerd the sacriment in honour of the Saviour that died on the Cross That some little excited my feelings as I thought by it he was not honoured because of their daily walk altho I said in my mind it is nothing to me as I would not a partook with them if they had a given me a chance They then caled on the High councilers all in order to meet at H Smiths office They soon assembled twelve men and thre to preside with Prst H. Smith over them The agreeved and the agressor soon took their stand and brought forward their testimony to make the Crooked strate and the rough places smooth Testimony after testimony did come to settle a difficulty Amongst the Elders of the Church of L.D.S. that had before the Council come I se the witnesses well understood which sid[e] they belonged as they was much engaged in behalf of their side that they did well for it contend Thus they submited the case to the Council Some few on it spoke and said those that preside knows better than we do We submit it to your better judgement Thus the Councilers got along easy with the case The thre that presided said Br Hirum we will submit the case to you Brother Hirum arose with feelings that was good and commenced to expostulate to the edification of all around He spoke of their folly of haveing a fuss about mearly nothing not so much as there was between an old man and his wife respecting a rat or a mouse that run a cross the floor The old man said it was a rat The old woman said it was a mouse That caused a contention that they broke up keeping house They of-ten together did meet but no oftener did they come together than the rat and the mouse had to be mouthed by them that by them it was disgraced At last the old man desided that a home he would have The old lady said I have no objection to live with you my Dear but I [k]now it was a mouse Thus he argued the case both long and loud and I took my hat and went out

[Folder number 5] Nauvoo Sunday May 8th 1842

This morning to meeting I did go to hear and se what was agoing on One of the presidancy took the stand and commenced Preaching and teaching As I am willing and a waiting to give each one their dues I must say I was edified at what I se and herd Altho He was feeble and low because of ill Health yet he spoke with fredom in honour of God as no embarishments on him did rest He spoke freely his mind to us that I said in my heart that he can neither be turned by a wink or a nod I se he had a Noble spirit imprinted within that would govern his person and make him a wise and upright man Altho he is said to be under the weather for a number of months past By those of hig[h] renown And those that turns on a pivot but when he first commenced to speak I se his independance And[und]erstood his case He spoke some two hours and took his seit and was followed by one if the twelve I found no falt in perticular with him except he seemed to be verry large Then arose another one of his mates that seemed to desire To be a man of importance He spoke loud and heavey but in matter he much lacked as the spirit of intelligance did not on him rest But in puffing and blowing He to us did show that he ment to go a head whether or no They administerd the sacriment In honour of the saviour that Died on the Cross That some little exsited my feelings as I thought by it he was not honourd because of their daily walk Altho I said in my mind it is nothing to me as I would not a pertook with them if they had a given me a chance They then caled on the High Councilers all in order to meet At Hyram Smith office They soon assembled twelve men and thre to preside with President Hiram Smith over them The agreeved and the aggressor soon took their stand and brought forward their testimony to make the Crooked strate and the rough places smoothe Testimony after testimony forward did come to settle a difficulty amongst the Elders of the Latter day Saints that had before the Council Come I se the witnesses well understood which side they belonged as they was much engaged in behalf of their side that they did well for it contend Thus they submited their Case to the Council Some few on it spoke and said Those that preside knows better what to do with the case than we do We submit it to you[r] better judgment Thus the Councilers got along easy with the case The thre that presided said Broth Hiram we will submit the case to you Broth Hiram arose With feeling that was good and commenced to expostulate to the Edification of all around He spoke of their folly of having a fuss about mearly nothin Not so much as there was between an old man and his wife respecting a rat or a mouse that run across the floor That man said it was a rat The old woman a mo[u]se that caused a contention that they broke up keeping house They often to gether did meet but no oftener did they come to gether than the rat and the mouse had to suffer the approach of being mouthed by thes toothless Crechurss [creatures] At last the old man desided a home he would have The old lady said I have no objections to it but my dear it was a mouse Thus he argued the Case both long and loud and I took my hat and cleard out As I long have ben a keeping a recod of the Church of the latter day saints I shall now draw to a close by saying to them that I think their doing is to simple to read much more to wright At the same time I will say to them that when I was a boy my papa set me to work at plowing planting and Hoing that I got a notion of skiping hills that I could with my father keep up That is a tipe of my writings So move if you ~~dare~~ think best against me Then I will go back and hoe the left hills But let you conduct your selves as you may of your doings in futer I will not write as you can no longer stand to disgrase the name of the Lord You have no power with him Your light has gone out for the want of oil in your Lamps Now to prove it as you are so flush with your curses we know that many you have surprised Just make up a bundle and put on me that I cannot write against you or in behalf of the Law of God Put me down and I will acknowledge [beat?] or that I am wrong in what I have wrote If not I say there is a veto on you that you cannot get of[f] I have refferance to the leaders of the Church or more perticular those that are getting as they said by Presidant Vanburen verry Fatt I hardly know how to subscribe myself as I am not your Enemy or much of a friend

[Folder number 3] Citty of Nauvoo May 13th

With feelings that is good I sit down to write of things that comes under my observation As it is a time of reformation amongst the Latter day Saints, I met with them in meeting and herd them freely speak their minds Thre that said to preside took the stand and opened meeting in the name of the Lord The members followed and spoke freely their minds with much candor and good feelings to honour the cause of God They spoke of a determination to do as well as say that it should be well with them in a futer day I se they was willing in a Reformation to go ahead that nothing could be said against them exscept they was easily turned by those who say to lead I think If I had a standing with them that I could devise a plan that would open a door for a reformation I would topsy turvy turn them and set the good old mothers to work that have raised large familys and had some experience I would cal on the Fathers that have heads silvered ore [o'er] to assist the mothers in the work If this plan could be devised and the bees set to work I would cause a reformation that would be marvelous to relate But as things stand I hard can se as I can be much help to them as I am looked upon to be out of the way But suffise it to say I look at them as frogs of a pond That puffs and sweaIls or like a weathercock in the wind as the wind is often a changing So it is with their Political doings that keeps many in commotion that belongs to the Church of the L.D.S— They go for their friends without respect to party that denotes a mind that is contracted I[t] would not establish principals for which our Fathers fought but would establish a principal of a monarchal goverment in a land of liberty of which we much bost But this order of teaching is not congenial to the majority of the L.D.S— There is many that has a spirit of independance that would freely speak their feelings if it was not for certin chords that on them is drawn A secret Combination was form[ed] in Missouri is a dred to those that would act for themselves It was a combination formed by the male members caled Danites said to be in honour of God They took an oath to defend each other to the exspense of their lives whether wright or wrong It is now newly vamped over by men of pleasure that are well of[f] by tithing the L.D. Saints. All things are a moveing in good order Horses Chariots and harnnesses is gaining that makes a fine show For men of pleasure I now in ernest ask a question While hundreds are a suffering for food and rayment does this tend or not to establish the work of the Lord in this the ninteenth Century of time Again what has Politicks to do to establish the work of the Lord Again does God need a secret Combination such as Danites His work to roll forth Pleas to give me your reasons why you thus are a doing all in the name of the Lord Is his name honoured by your doings As you are a passing and repassing I look at a few that bosts of Gods power that by it they lead in to bondage and opress all that comes under their watch care by saying thus and thus saith the Lord Such teaching such reasoning unless I am mistaken is an abomination In the site of God Has he power to remove mountains and dry up fountains and speak by Earthquakes and thunder and lightnings and puts the Earth in commotion once in twenty four hours in honour of the sun Look at your doings Look at your works Look at your shortsightedness a puffing and blowing a seeking to be of much importance in the Eyes of the world Look at your preaching at home and abroad and se the course of the Elders that are a traverling and preaching the word They preach from the bible and say it is true and hold out good principals but when they get to Nauvoo we there find a change in teaching that the Bible is of not much account as modern Revelations will direct all wright They by them say to be governed in their daily concerns As the Bible has ben translated by uninspired men of God they say not be governed by it but the Prophit Joseph Smith as he is a Prophit that God has raised up we must do as he says or he will put on us a curse Thus they are governed by the few that say to be chosen men of God They well know how to perform their works If they cannot depend on the Law of God they form laws of the Citty to suit their case and say we like Peter the keys posess that we can save you or dam you as we pleas I now draw my writings to a close by advising you to go ahead in a reformation and let the old mothers and Fathers take the lead Again I would say to you respecting a plurality of wives they will be a trouble to you as they will harrass you both knight and day They will depend on you for a living that will come out of the tithing of the L.D.S. Be satisfied with one as is the custom around with you in the end it will be as well I now draw to a close By saying to you the revelations you have received respecting manny wives it is the desire of the hart or from old Smootfoot himself Other things I pas by at present

[Folder number 5] City of Nauvoo May 13th 1842

With feeling that is good I sit down to write of what has come under my observation this day as it is a time of Reformation amongst the latter day Saints I met with them in meeting and herd them freely express their minds Thre that said to preside took the stand and opend meeting in the name of the Lord The members followed and spoke freely their minds with much candor and good feeling to honour the cause of God They spoke of a determination to do as well as say that it should be well with them in a futer day I se they was willing to reform If they was rong but I desided they was honest so far as they knew that nothing could be said against them. But I must say they honourd Gods cause The presidancy looked with out much being said and dismised the meeting and all went home I think if I had a standing with them that I could devise a plan that would cause a Reformation In the Church of the Latter day Saints I would topsisy turvy turn them and set the good old Mothers to work that have raised large familys and have had some experiance I would cal on the Fathers That has heads silver and come to assist the mothers in this work If this plan could be devised and the bees set to work it would cause a fermentation Marvelous to relate But as things stand I hardly se as I can help them as I am looked upon with a jealous eye But suffise it to say I look at them as Frogs of a pond that puffs and swells or like a weather Cock on a pivot in the wind as the wind is often a changing so it is with the Political doings that keeps many in commotion that belongs to the Church of the Latter day Saints They go for their Friends with ou[t] respect to party that denotes a mind that is contracted It would not establish principals for which our Fathers fought but would establish a principal of a monarchal goverment in our land of liberty of which we so much bost but this order of teaching is not congenial to the feelings of the majority of the Latter day saints They have a spirit of Independance that they would freely speak their feelings if it was not for certin chords that on them is drawn. A secret combination that was formed in Missouri is a dread to those that would act for themselves It was a combination formed by the male members caled Danites, said to be in honour of the law of God They took an oath to defend each other to the expens of their lives whether wright or wrong It is now newly vamped over by men of pleasure That are well of[f] by tithing the Latter day saints All things are a moveing in good order Horses Chariots and Harnises are a gaining that makes a fine show For men of pleasure but I in earnest ask a question While hundreds is a suffuring for the want of food and raiment does this tend or not tend to establish the work of the Lord in this the nineteenth Century of time Again what has politicks to do to establish the work of the Lord Again does God need a secret Combination or a set of Danites To bring about his purposes Pleas to give us your reasons why you are thus a doings In the name of the Lord Is his name honourd by you in your daily doings as you are passing and repassing here and there I look at a few that bosts of Gods power that by it they lead in to bondage and opres all that comes under their care by saying thus saith the Lord Such reasoning and teachings unles I am mistaken is an abomination in the sight of God Has he power to remove mountains and dry up fountains and speak by Earthquakes and thunder and lightning and puts the Earth in commotion that it performs its revolutions once in twenty four hours in honour of the sun Look at your doings Look at your works Look at your short sightedness a puffing and blowing Aseeking to be of much importance in the eyes of the world Look at your Preaching at home and abroad and se the course of the Elders that are traverling and preaching the word They preach from the bible and say it is true and hold out good principles to their hearers but when we get to Nauvoo we there find a change in teachings that the bible is of not much account as our modern Revolations will direct us wright We by them will be directed in our daily concerns as the bible has not ben translated by inspired men of God we are not to be governed by it but by the Prophits Joseph Smith As he is a Prophit that God has raised up we must do as he says or he will put on us a curse Thus we are governed by the few that say to be the chosen ones of God They well know how to stand and perform their works If they cannot depend on the Law of God they form Laws in the Citty to suit their case and say we like Peter the keys posses that we can save you or dam you as we pleas I now draw my writings to a close by advising you to go a head in a reformation and let the old mothers and Fathers take the lead Again I would say to you respecting a plurality of wives They will be a trouble to you as they will harrass you Both night and day They will depend on you for a living that will have to come out of the tithing of the saints Be satisfied with one As is the custom all around and with you in the end it will be as well I now draw to a close by saying to you the Revolations you have respecting many wives is the desire of the Heart Or from old blackfoot him self and other things I pas by for the presant

[Folder number 3] Citty of Nauvoo May 17th 1842

With feelings of no ordinary kind I sit down to write of things that transpire under my observation in the Citty of Nauvoo I look at things as they pass and to speak my own feelings I cannot but say that I daily mourn I look at the people of this place and knowing the reasons why they are here I look at their doings I look at their works I se some at hard Labour others ~~a~~ riding about I se some in trouble Because of what they se and hear others disgust~~ing~~ and clearing out Others saying of us the advantage is taken that we cannot get our dues Again I se others dote of their honesty in their teachings on the stand in their Sabbath devotions as they meet saying to worship in honour of God They say our bretheren you know us of old that we are determined to bild in the name of the Lord We want your money and your money we will have If you do not give it up for it we will search untill we obtain it that we can our purposes bring about Here is our honesty Of which we bost that we will not deceive you but tell you the truith We as Councilers know what is for your good Give us your property whatever it is We in return will bless you in the name of the Lord but will not reccompens you in temporal Concerns If you want further testimony cal on the Prophit Josep Smith and he will give you the word of the Lord Then you will know we are right Again I look at the Laws of the Citty that are published in the times and seasons and a weakly Periodical Caled the wasp that I think is wrongly named altho wasps are of many sises and colours and forms but take either of the above dimentions there is nothing but buty [beauty] wisdom power and Independance if not much love The wasp in an animal that often does Sting When insulted and soon returns to his bis business because his work is don As his weapon is severe when once it is used It lasts a long time But the little wasp that sits on a srub in the noted Citty of Nauvoo I think has mistook the name as by his moveing I think it was hatched by a bug that I have seen in the dark caled a lightning bug but when we get neer it no lite could be found That I cal a sample of the papers published at the Citty of Nauvoo They as the story is when the Devvel ketched a hog for a sheep said there was a great Cry and but a little wool The little bug that flies from the scrub in the Citty of Nauvoo I am some little aquanted with those that gives it a start Several are engaged in it They all profess to be men of God and set an example to the world

Look at the controversy with Thomas Sharp the Editor of the Warsaw Signal Se their abuse towards him week after week, when he took no notice of them not in the least Except like the wasp he once did them sting, And let them alone But we find the wound is a smarting as they cry and howl aloud If I had the privelege To give them some advise I would say to them to Crop the wasps wings and let it stay neer home as the bug is no honour to them in flying about the world After writing what have written I was about to keep my writing to myself but whether I publish them or let them lay it does not make much differance as they are fast a telling the story themselves I will recite to the 1st volum 5 No of the wasp in connection with the previous numbers and many Items of the Times and Seasons that speaks of the laws of the Citty of Nauvoo and of their unwise doings all in the name of the Lord Trayning Frolicking Rioting Feasting and takeing the benefit of the Insolvent act, Who the first men of the Church of L. D. Saints from ten to sixteen of them I give one item of their Law entire as a sample of their doings Sec 1st that with other items will establish the most of my writings I now take leave of them to be gone some few weeks Then will I look to them and minit what is afloat

[Folder number 5] Citty of Nauvoo May 17th 1842

With feeling of no ordinary kind I sit down to write of things that transpire under my observation in the Citty of Nauvoo I look at things as they pass and to speak my own feeling I cannot but say that I daily mourn I look at the people of this place and knowing the reasons why they are here I look at their doings I look at their works I se some at hard Labour Others riding about I se some in trouble Because of what they se and hear Others disgusted and clearing out Others saying the advantage is taken of them that they cannot get their dues Again I se others dote of their honesty in their teachings on the Stand in their Sabbath devotions as they meet saying to worship in honour of God They say my bretheren you know as of Old that we are determined to build In the name of the Lord We want your money And your money we will have If you do not give it up We for it will search untill we obtain it That we can our purposes bring about Here is our honesty of which we bost That we will not deceive you But tel you the truth We as councilers know what is for your good Give us your property whatever it is We in return will bless you in the name of the Lord but will not recompense you for it In temporal concerns If you want further testimony cal on the Prophet Joseph Smith and he will give you the word of the Lord Then you will know we are wright Again I look at the Laws of the Citty that are published in the Times and seasons and a weekly Periodical Caled the Wasp that, I think is wrongly named Tho wasps are of many sises and Colours and forms But take either of the above dimensions there is nothing but buty and wisdom and power and Independance if not much love The wasp is an animal that often does sting when insulted And as soon returns to his business because his business is don As his weapon is severe when once it has ben used It lasts a long time But the little wasp that sits on a scrub at Nauvoo I think has mistook the name As by his moveing I think he has ben hatched by a bug that I have seen caled in the dark a lightning bug But when we get neer him No light could be found That I cal a sample of the Papers published at the Citty of Nauvoo They as the storys is What the Devil said when he ketch a hog for a sheep said there was a great Cry and a little Wool The little bug that flies out from Nauvoo I am some little aquainted with those that gives it a start Several is engaged in it They all profess to be men of God and set an example to the world Look at the Controversy with Thomas Sharp the Editor of the Warsaw Signal Se their abuse to wards him week after week when he takes no Notice of them not in the least Except like the wasp he once did them sting And let them alone But we find the wound is a smarting as they cry and howl aloud But If I had the privelege to give them some advise I would say to them to crop the wasps wings and let it stay neer home As the bug is no honour to those a flying about the world I have ben ashamed of my writings after writing what I have written I was about to keep my writing to myself but whether I publish them or let them lay it does not make much differance as they are fast telling the story them selves. I will recite to the 1st volum 5 No of The Wasp in connections with the previous Numbers and my own Items in the times and seasons that speaks of the Laws of the Citty of Nauvoo and of their unwise doings. The 5th No of the Wasp must speak for itself As in it we find much adoing all in the Name of the Lord Trayning frolicking [X] rioting feasting and taking the benefit of the Insolvent act Who the first men of the Church from ten to sixteen of them I give one Item of their Law entire as a sample of their doings Section 1st that in connection with other Items will establish the most of my writings I have written mostly my mind to releive and have now and then said I would publish them To the world when I have herd of their slander toward me at different times because I do not coincide with them in their daily doings If they are wright I am wrong Again if they are wright God has turned topsi turvy his word and we will throw away the Bible and the antients teachings of what was then wright I must now take a Journy some hundred miles of[f] and when I return I will se what is afloat

JUNE 1842

[Folder number 3] Citty of Nauvoo June 4th 1842

I again have arived at the Citty of Note with feelings of no ordinary kind as there is yet much a doing in the name of the Lord The Inhabitsants of the Citty Together did meet to establish an order of things that zion may be great They apointed Candidates The county to rule some of the Church others not that a sympethy of feelings mite exist Again I Look at the storys that takes the daily rounds that raises much smoke if there is not much fire As there is a connection Between smoke and fire so I must say of the doings of the Citty and the storys afloat Some noted ones of the Citty is said to have power to seal the assurance of an eternal rest if their doings have ben ever so bad It is don threw the orthoroty of the P-hood that threw the institution of masonry they have received Of masonry I cannot speak But of their works I will venture to say will far excede anything that can be found in the history of our American soil since our fathers fought And gained their Independance By the shedding of blood Report says much is adoing amongst the two sex that is unlawful unwise and degrading in every sense of the word The heathen would blush at it As I of late have herd that daily salutes my ears as I am a passing and repassing threw the Citty of Nauvoo that infants are found of which no account has ben given of them I pass by the perticulars and speak on general terms and say their is to much smoke to say their is no fire I now draw to a close and say The half is not told

[Folder number 5] Citty of Nauvoo June 4th 1842

I have arived at the Citty of Note with feeling of no ordinary kind as there is yet much a doing in the name of the Lord The Inhabitants of the Citty Together did meet to establish an order of things That Zion may be great They apointed candidates The County to rule some of the Church Others not that a sympethy of feeling mite exist Again I look at the storys that takes the daily rounds that raises much smoke If there is not much fire As there is a connection between smoke and fire so I must say of the doings of the Citty and the storys afloat Some noted ones of the Citty Is said to have power to seal the assureance of an eternal rest if their doings have ben ever so bad It is don by the othoroty of the Priesthood that threw the institution of Masonry they have received Of masonry I cannot speak But of their works I venture to say will far excede anythin that is found in the history of our American soil since our father fought and gaind their Independance by the shedding of blood Report says much is adoing amongst the ~~differant~~ two sex that is unlawful unwise and degrading in every sense of the word The heathen would blush at it As I of late have herd That daily salutes my ears as I am a passing and repassing through the Citty of Nauvoo that infants are found Of which no account has ben given of them I pass by perticulars and speak in general terms And say there is too much smoke to say there is no fire I now draw my writings to a close and take them to the press and say the half is not told

[Folder number 3] June sixth Citty of Nauvoo

I will now speak to the travlin Elders as I se them much engaged to convert souls To the faith of the L.D.S. By scores they go out into the viniard of the Lord to preach and baptise for remission of sins I by the way of a caution would say to those that they deserve to be whiped and sent back as they well know what is a doing in the Citty of Nauvoo that it far excedes Any other place for wickedness that is known in our American soil Clens first the fountain head that the streams may be clear Let those that have ben long absent aproclaiming the word Stand still or come to Nauvoo That is the fountain head and se the abominations That is a going on Again I say to the people that have minds to speak in behalf of things that is wright that if they do not stop preaching to give them a jack knife and send them home If they don't take the hint put on them a mark that they may be distinguished in their moves about

[Folder number 5] June 6th 1842 Citty of Nauvoo

I now speak to the traverlin Elders[1] as I se they are much engaged to convert souls to the faith Of the Latter day saints By scores they go out in to the viniard of the Lord to preach and baptise for the remission of sins I by the way of a caution would say to those that have lately gone out That they deserve to be whipt and sent back as they well know what is adoing in the Citty of Nauvoo that it far excedes any other place for wickedness known in our American Soil Clens first the fountain That the streams may be clean Let those that have ben long absent a proclaiming the word Stand still or come to Nauvoo that they say is the fountain head and se the abominations that is agoing on Again I say to the people That have minds to speak in be half of things that is wright that if they do not stop preaching to give them a Jack knife And send them home If they dont take the hint put on them a mark that they may be distinguished In their moves about

1. In the Doctrine and Covenants, the Quorum of the Twelve Apostles are referred to as "traveling high priests" (D&C 102:23), "twelve traveling councilors" (D&C 107:23), "Traveling Presiding High Council" (D&C 102:33), and the "traveling high council" (D&C 107:34). Doctrine and Covenants 124:138–139 states that the quorum of seventies is "is instituted for traveling elders." However, men from various quorums were sent out as missionaries. Olney writes of scores of Latter Day saints going "out into the viniard [vineyard] to preach and baptise [*sic*]." He was likely not referring to men of any specific quorum, but to traveling missionaries in general.

[Folder number 6] Citty of Nauvoo June 9th 1842

Being caled upon to meet in Council with the Antient of Days at this time as they have assembled in Council twelve Antient men of God That was resorected with the Saviour at the meridian of time As I am caled upon to pen their doings It I cheerfully perform as I by them am shone As I with them assemble their visage to me is plain looks and doings not to be explained simply by the scratch of the pen But to have a vew of the Antient of Days is not the same as looking at our fellow man altho in sise and form they much agree But in looks they far dissemble the fallen state of man as they are the spirits of just men made perfect that is caled to fill an important post that they on Earth have took a stand to be conducted by the Savior In their daily moves as he with them has assembled and in Council set To preside that they by him are Instructed in their fervant paths to take to put all things in order as is congenial with the word of God

[Folder number 6] Nauvoo Citty June 9th 1842

What do I discover That speaks to me loud of a fallen people in the Citty of Nauvoo What can I do for them as they are against me that I cannot with them dwell I cannot have a home with them as they do me much opress They treat me as an enemy except now and then a place I get housed up out of site I am weary of them as I am often shone they desire my destruction to get me out of the way But I think my time with them must be verry short as a messenger has come to me To set me to work He cals on me a temporal Kingdom to set up That will gro and florish and put down all others It will be established and by many propeld that has lived in differant ages of the world They to the Earth are returning in the power of God to baffle the wicked and prepare a home for the Saints They cal on their agents And set them to work by the spirit of Elijah From this time forth I now am caled to be ready to do that my work may be accomplishd so far as I am shone to do work

[Folder number 6] June 10th 1842

2nd sitting

This morning I arise in the name of the Lord and with the Antient of days take a (stand?) a work to prepare For the coming of the son of Man In the flesh The Antients have come To the Citty of Nauvoo and have taken a stand Gods will to do They speak of their power To reinstate and to liborate the Captive That sits in the dark That sits in the dark[2] That sits a looking desiring the time to

2. Olney wrote "that sits in the dark" on the last line of a page and then wrote it again on the first line of the next page.

arive for light and inteligance on him to rest But the people of the Citty first must be clensed or this noted stake of Zion of which so much is said light and Inteligance must be the theme of the streams that put out from the fountain head This noted Citty is destined to fall with many of its leaders by the Antient of Days Its fall is determined soon to take place That will cause sorrow and siing[3] [sighing] by many that is wright But alas they have to suffer because of the fountain head But let it be purified That all may be clean that a Kingdom may be reard in honour of God as Old Father Adam in council has set with his Decendants to establish his order on the Earth His order is light and Inteligance by the spirit of God It is honour and riches It is what will boy [buoy] up And strenthen the mind that the gifts of the gospel may make crooked strait The Antients have come In honour of God and took up their abode on Earth They first will purify and make clean at the same time make ready a foundation for a remnant of the saints As a few will be preserved a testimony to bear of a fallen people that disgrased the name of the Lord that have long said to do his will

[Folder number 6] June 10th 1842

2nd setting

This morning I arise in the name of the Lord and with the Antient of Days take a stand a work to prepare for the comming of the Son of Man In the flesh The Antients have come to the Citty of Nauvoo and have taken a stand Gods will to do They speak of power to reinstate and to liborate the captive That sits in the Dark That sits a looking Desiring the time to arive for light and inteligance on him to rest But the people of the Citty first must be clensed or this noted stake of Zion of which much is said that light and inteligance may be the theme of the streams that put out from the fountain head This noted Citty is desined to fall with many of its Leaders by the Antient of Days Its fall is determined soon to be that will cause sorrow and sighing by many that is upright But alas they have to suffer because of the fountain head But let it be purified That all may be clean that a Kingdom may be reard in honour of God As Old Father Adam ~~has on Earth took a stand~~ in Council has set With his decendants to establish his order on the Earth His order is light and inteligance by the spirit of God It is honour and riches It is what will boy [buoy] up And strengthen the mind that the Gifts of the Gospel may make crooked streight The Antients have come In honour of God to bring about an order

3. The act of suffering a deep respiration; taking a long breath. *Noah Webster's First Edition of an American Dictionary of the English Language—Facsimile 1828 Edition*, s.v. "Sigh." Olney is using "sighing" as a sign of the anxiety and grief of the Mormons who, he believes, are following their leaders to destruction.

that the name of the Lord will be acknowledged They first have feelings with the weak to sympethise teach them and instruct them in paths of light They then will display the power of God that will cause Sorrow and sighing in all parts of the Land that the wicked will mourn because of their Lot as scourges will rest on them because of their works But the time will come that the wise and learned Will se their folly in what they have ben adoing As I am caled upon by the Council of the Antient of Days to consecrate to the Lord The temple[4] Nauvoo house Also the house[5] in which they sit That the foundations

---

4. Olney writes that the Ancient of Days have called upon him to personally consecrate to the Lord the temple, Nauvoo House, and the house where he has been living because it was there that the Ancient of Days had appeared to him a number of times. In the LDS Church, buildings are dedicated by an ecclesiastical authority offering a dedicatory prayer. Perhaps this is what Olney meant by consecrating these sites unto the Lord. The official dedications by Church leaders did take place. The cornerstone dedication of the Nauvoo Temple took place on April 6, 1841. During the construction of the Nauvoo temple, specific spaces were dedicated as they were completed. The baptismal font located in the basement of the unfinished Nauvoo Temple was dedicated on November 8, 1841. See Richard Neitzel Holzapfel, "The Nauvoo Temple," 421–36. On Sunday, October 5, 1845, a meeting was held in the temple. Brigham Young "opened the services of the day in a dedicatory prayer, presenting the Temple, thus far completed." See "First Meeting in the Temple," 1017–18. On November 30, 1845, Brigham Young and twenty others gathered in the temple to dedicate the attic story for ordinance work. See Richard O. Cowan, *Temples to Dot the Earth*, 63. "The corner stone of the Nauvoo House was laid by President Joseph Smith on the 2[d] of October 1841." Dean C. Jessee, Mark Ashurst-McGee, and Richard L. Jensen, eds., Volume 2 of the Journal series of *The Joseph Smith Papers,* edited by Dean C. Jessese, Ronald K. Esplin, and Richard Lyman Bushman, 19. After many delays in the building process, there was another ceremony held on August 18, 1845, to mark the commencement of the brickwork for the Nauvoo House. On this occasion Heber C. Kimball "offered up a prayer, dedicating the works and workmen to the Lord and recommending them to his mercy and protection from accidents and sickness." William Clayton, *Journal*, August 18, 1845, Church History Library, The Church of Jesus Christ of Latter-day Saints, Salt Lake City, Utah. Only the foundation and part of the first floor of the Nauvoo House were completed during Joseph Smith's lifetime. Still incomplete when the Saints fled Nauvoo, it is unlikely that the Nauvoo House was officially dedicated. On June 11, 1842, Oliver Olney stood upon the foundation of the Nauvoo House "and consecrated it to the Lord." He also "consecrated the brick house belonging to Brother Nurse . . . that it might stand a witness that the Ancient of days condescended to meet in its loft and hold a council." Although he was also called upon to consecrate the Nauvoo Temple, Olney does not mention consecrating that building. See Oliver Olney Papers, fd. 6, June 11, 1842 (hereafter OOP). Thanks to Alex Smith and Lachlan Mackay for information about the Nauvoo House.

5. The house here refers to the home of Newell Nurse where Olney had been boarding. It was located "one street north of the temple atoal 1/2 mile East on the

shoud stand as a living monument that God had once had a people that he communicated himself to But alas they are fallen Because of their works They have broken their Covenant because of bad works They wander in paths of gloominess both Early and late and know not of Gods work As the work of the Lord is now to commence as is spoken that long since lived They on Earth had a standing in different ages of the world They rote their feelings should be to bring about the purposes of God They on the Earth have taken a stand the Latter day glory to usher in and took up their abode on Earth They first will puryfy and make clean At the same time make ready a foundation for a remnant of the Saints as a few will be preserved a testimony to bare of a fallen people that disgrased the name of the Lord that have long said to do his will

[Folder number 6] Saturday 11th 3rd

I am agained caled in the chamber to take my seit with those of the antients that sets in council on the Earth as it is a time of Counciling by the messengers above Much is now to be accomplished in honour of God The day has ariven for light to shine that dark sayings may be streightend by enlightened minds By minds that are united God will to perform As the day star has risen the vale will be rent by the power of faith By man on the Earth Let a union be established amongst the few that is singled out from the mass Gods work for to do That the stone from the mountain may move ore the land And Create principals that have lain long in the dark There was once a people By faith and good works moved in the power and majesty of God They had power invested in them in order to move That threw them God manifested his power on Earth The time has ariven And the ancients have took their stand To bring about an order that the name of the Lord will be Aknowledged They first have feelings with the weak to sympethise teach them and instruct them In paths of light They then will display the power of God that will cause sorrow and sighing in all parts of the land That the wicked will Mourn because of their lot As scourges will rest on them because of their works But the time will come that the wise and the Learned Will se their folly in what they have ben adoing Being caled on by the Council of the Antient of days to consecrate to the Lord the Nauvoo house foundation that it mite be preserved for a people that should make their way here from the North the ten tribes of Israel Also consecrate to the Lord the house in which you meet in council that it may be seen in futer ages by a people that shall rear up this fallen Citty no more to be thrown down I took my course and stood upon the Nauvoo house and consecrated it to the Lord that it mite be preserved untill the time should come for it to be reard up Aagain

north side of the street." See OOP, fd. 6, June 11, 1842.

I consecrated the brick house belonging to Brother Nurse[6] one street north of the temple atoal ½ mile East on the north side of the street that it mite stand a witness that the Antient of days condescended to meet in its loff and hold a council in honour of the will of God As the work of the Lord is now to commence as is spoken by the Antients That long since died They on the Earth had a standing in differant ages of the world They wrote their feelings of what in the last days should be don to bring about the purposes of God They on the Earth have taken a stand the latter day glory to usher in As is by God decreed that workman of pleasure they may move together to form and create anew. The time is at hand for man to arise in honour of God by displaying his power By raising the dead and changeing the elements from heat to cold or revers Also wet or dry will be subject to their word again as Moses had power over the Egyptians to opress them with plagues from time to time So will be the order of the destruction of the wicked that all may be left without excuse against the comming of the son of man as He soon is a coming with his saints in the air

[Folder number 6] Nauvoo June 11th 1842

The word of the Lord is unto the[e] at this time to attend strictly to your business as you now have much to do in a short time to fetch things round as you have to do You are caled to go to Quincy and get your writings published or to Warsaw as you see fit of the foibles of the Church Get them under way then come back here and take a vew of things as they are agoing in the name of the Lord I last knight had a vew of a beast something in looks as a bear of strong looks and dark colour I vewed him about me at a short distance often looking at me I again se him with two horns as a he goat in looks but kept at a propper distance as I made up my mind to tackle him if he came neer me The interpetation came to me that the beast denoted a Lepard that was spoken of by John while on the Isle of patmos that he had come to take his stand on the Earth to scare terify disharten change in look appear in fearful sites to the saints that he had took his stand with the antients of days to lead into bondage opress disharten terify the weak throw them into confusion I again found myself surrounded by many that appeard to me en-

6. Newell Nurse was a member of the Nauvoo 2nd Ward. Susan Easton Black, comp, *Membership of the Church of Jesus Christ of Latter-day Saints, 1830–1848,* 32:933. Nurse and Olney were arrested together in February 1843. "Oliver Olney & Newell Nurse were brought in by Sheriff J[ohn] D. Parker as prisoners for stealing goods from the store of Moses Smith on the night of the 23rd of January. Last." It was the decision of the court that "Mr Nurse be discharged—& Olney be remanded to prison for trial or bound under $5,000 bonds." Andrew H. Hedges, Alex D. Smith, and Richard Lloyd Anderson, eds. *Journals, Volume 2: December 1841–April 1843.* Vol. 2 of the Journals series of *The Joseph Smith Papers,* edited by Dean C. Jessee, Ronald K. Esplin, and Richard Lyman Bushman, 259–60.

emys they seemed friendly in words but seemed desirous to opress I look at them as enemy and made my calculation to get away from them but they seemed to keep neer me but at last I extricated myself from them that I found myself alone I desired the interpitation That came to me that the men was eavil spirits that had took their stand on the Earth to overpower the doings of the Antients and as I was the only one that they had appeard they would first take me in hand and as the work spread they would continue their doings untill they would establish an order that would be said to be of God that would lead the natural mind into bondage by sings [signs] and mericals that they would do by power given them of the prince of Darkness that as the saints should arise this power would arise but the saints would have pow[er] to deteck them by the gifts of the gospel that on them will rest in asmuch as they do the will of God As God is a looking his power to display he will stand by his servents that propel his work by giving them power to bring his purposes about His power is invested in those that holds the P-hood and well does their work As to them is shone by the messengers that from Heaven comes The day is at hand for the saints to arise and contend for the faith of antient saints By faith words and doing much will be don in honour of the cause of God Let the mind that would arise and establish his name by good works

[Folder number 6] 3rd Setting June 11th

Saturday 11th I am caled in to the Chamber to take my seit with those of the Antients that sits in Council on the Earth as it is a time of Counciling amongst the messengers above Much is now to be accomplished in honour of God The day has ariven for light to shine that dark sayings may be streightend by enlightened minds by minds that are centerd Gods will to do As the Day Star has arisen the vale will be rendt By the power of faith by man on the Earth Let a union be established amongst the few that is singled out from the mass Gods will for to do That the stone from the mountain may move ore the Land and create principals that have lain long in the dark There was once a people By faith and good works moved in power and magesty of God They had power invested in them in order to move That threw them God manifested his power on Earth The time has ariven and the Antients have took a stand His path was easy and plain His sayings was plain familiar and Easy that no one need mistake the way that should say to follow his Example in performance of the Law of God as his Law was given at the meridian of time to prepare for a Melineum rest

[Folder number 3] City of Nauvoo June 12th 1842

I now sit down to write a history or journal of the Church of L D Saints I today went to meeting And herd them Preach They spoke of many good things that they did soon expect to receive such as the establish ment of a Citty that would be a lite unto the world They spoke of Kings aray to assist in building Zion in honour of God with their silver and gold and precious stone orthorotys of the Church of the L. D. Saints I said in my heart whire has reason gone as one of our noted teachers reasoned thus that all was a doing in honour of God I looked at the doings of the L. D. S— that I have now and then rehersed to write it over would be time spent in vain and say in my heart how long is people to be duped by dupes I said he was honest in his remarks but his mind had got so contracted[7] that him with others are bearly tools to be used by Joseph Smith afinding falt with the Complaining of the poor Sacriment in honour of the Son of God but I think it was by him imputed to their ignorance as I think they have lost the path of wright Again I look at their doings that says to be in the name of the Lord and vew the daily movements that I se atakeing place in the Citty They by scores and hundreds are daily a comeing in that speaks to me loud of what is to come I look at those that long have ben here that are of the lesser Class that cannot speak for themselves I look at the doings of the Citty of both high and low and se a saying fulfild that is often true that the big fish eat up the little ones if their boddys is saved Their substance is gone to pay tithing cals in the name of the Lord Again the Laws of the Citty raises a tax that collex in their scanty pitance that causes many to mourn because of Opression That on them does rest Whire is their reason and minds of those that lead this people It looks to me Strange To se such doings in a land of freedom of which we much bost that a company should come together as is now the case

[Folder number 5] Nauvoo Citty June 12th

I now sit down to write my Journal or History of the Church of Latter day saints I today went to meeting and herd them preach They spoke of many good things that they did soon expected to receive such as the establishment of a Citty that would be a light unto the world They spoke of Kings and rulers that they to it would flock To learn wisdom and to get the word of the Lord That, they with their subjects would come in aray to assist in building Zion in honour of God With their silver and gold And precious stone would soon come bowing to the Orthorotys of the Church of the Latter day Saints I said in my heart whire has reason gone as one of Our Noted teachers reasoned thus that all was adoing in the honour of God I looked at the doings of the Latter day Saints that I have now and then rehersed to write it over would be time spent in vain and said in my heart how long Is people to be duped by dupes I said that he was honest in his remarks but his mind had got so contracted that he in connection with others are bearly tools to be used by Joseph Smith I look

7. Drawn together, or into a shorter or narrower compass. Narrow; mean; selfish; as a man of a *contracted* soul. *Webster's Dictionary* (1828), s.v. "Contracted."

at the doings of this people and notised a noted bishop on the stand afinding falt because of the Complainings of the poor He made a Comparison respecting their habitations that they was no better than hog pens or hogs in a pen I will make a Comparison as I have a chance and say they are more take them as they pass like a sow that has returned to her wallowing in the mire They administerd the sacrament in honour of the Son of God but I think it was by him imputed to their Ignorance as I think they have lost the path of wright I again look at their doings that says to be in the name of the Lord and vew the daily movements that I se takeing place in this Citty They by scores and hundred are daily coming in that speaks to me loud of what is to come I look at those that long have ben here that are of the Lesser Class That cannot speak for themselves I look at the doings of the Citty of both high and low and se a saying fulfild That is to often true that the big fish Eat up the little ones if their boddys is saved There substance is gone to pay tithing and Labouring in the name of the Lord Again the Laws of the Citty raises a tax that collex [collects] in their scanty pitance that causes many to mourn because of Opresion That on them does rest Whire is reason whire is the minds of those that lead this people It looks to me strange To se such doings in a land of fredom Of which we much bost that a Company should come to gether as is now the case

[Folder number 6] Nauvoo June 12th 1842

I now sit down my journal to keep along of the doings of the Church of the Latter day Saints I to day have ben in meeting and herd them teach They spoke of many good things that they exspected to receive such as the establishment of a Citty that would be a light unto the world They spoke of Kings and rulers that they to it would flock to learn wisdom And get the word of the Lord that they with their subjects would come in aray to assist in building Zion in honour of God With their silver and gold and precious stones would soon come bowing To the Othorotys of the Church of the Latter day Saints I said in my heart whire is reason gone as one of our noted teachers reasoned thus That all was adoing in honour of God I looked at the doing that I need not again reherse and said in my heart how long is people to be duped by dupes I said in my heart he is honest in his remarks but is so contracted in his mind that he in connection with others are bearly tools to be used By a Prophet Smith Look at the doings of this people as was by one of their Bishops said in comparison that they resembled a Hogs nest but I will make a Comparison a little differant from that that they are more like a Sow returned to her wallowing in the mire They adminesterd the sacrament in honour of the son of God But I think it would be by him imputed to their Ignorance as I think they have lost the path of wright I now am caled my story to change and to look at things that is to come as the stone beguinning to move

In honour of God Much is to be don the path to clear as it brakes in pieces and puts down obsticles that comes in the way The First obsticle is a fallen people of the Latter day Saints that are much in the way of those that have a wish to do wright They are first to be delt with as they sit and put in order first Then comes the wicked that is scatterd abroad in the land They will have to submit to a man

[Folder number 3] June 15th Nauvoo

As my mind has led me of late so I have ben a looking at things as they pass I have ben over hills and threw vallys both rough and smooth as the way opened as I was in a low vally in mud up to my knees I looked for a way out to get clear of tods and snakes I looked all around me and se it was dark but the more I labourd The worse I was of that it seemed impossible to extricate my self But at last I made a struggle that cleared me from the place that I arose on a hill and shook of the mud I looked back in to the mire from whence I did arise and what did I se that did me supprise The old and young all mixed up together some big and some little all in confusion I se some a scolding because of their lot of getting ketched in such a Company Others a looking and saying is this of God Others stood a looking on to se what was to come I se an other company apadling around to get better foot hold and go a head as their faces was downward they said another platform we will lay that we can go and come as we pleas As dark shades rested on all that was in the mud they made an appearance strange to relate I looked at them with supprise after seeing who they was in the mud I se many that I well knew to be the leaders of the L D Sa[i]nts I looked on a plain some little way of I took a vew of them to be members There was men women and Childern all a looking at their leaders in the mud Many commented at the sight but concluded That they would not get ketched in such a scrape But I soon se a move made or snare set The members to ketch I see it in a vision as I was moving around the temple Lot that made me gase I hardly spoke but now I will wright it as I se it so plain I know it is true with out iffs or anns [ifs or ands] I se this noted Company apadling in the mud They there desired to raise up a Righeous Branch of fruits of their own I looked at a sosiety By the females formed that had took a degre of Masonry and the second about to receive At an instant sudenly a rush was made but because of the mud, a blunder ensued that caused some room for meditation and the females cleared out They thus became dis hartened and sunk deep in to the mire and wallowed and tumbled untill I got out of sight I had a vew of others degree of Masonry that would soon a ben the theme but I se the institution broke up and the females not serious injured by it as I se a snare set far in the dark that was desined by a perticular set The females should run afoul that they it could Spring Again I have had inteligance or a vision of what they have don since they have ben in the mud that they have abused Their own Companions by being fre with femáles of ill fame and others they have taken the advantage of by saying thus and thus saith the Lord that many is a mourning because of what they have don in the dark as they supposed But it has come to light and it is wright that they should suffer for such ungodly works But let the villings [villains] suffer that have them abused Leaders or no leaders Prophit or no Prophit If my vision is not received I will then write it in prose and speak in plainness And prove facts Names I will mention That stands high in the estimation of some that are as deep in the mud As themselves But I will speak again of the people of the Citty of Nauvo and its surburbs If they had good institutions amongst them they would have honoured The cause of God But look at the teaching altho by the most of them It is swallowed because of those that say Thus saith the Lord In passing over a vally on another high Hill I again had a vew or vision clear and plain North of the temple lot I se the poor on every side Their houses was open And fare hard I looked at all parts of the Citty and se some few rich but mostly poor I se many daily a comming in from different parts some with much but mostly poor They all stood a looking And said it looks dark I se a law about to be made that would not only take the tenth as tithing[8] but a consecration Law[9] is soon to be put in

8. Although referred to earlier, the law of tithing was revealed in greater detail to Joseph Smith in July 1838 at Far West, Missouri. Prior to this time, tithing had meant to the Saints not just one-tenth, but all free-will offerings, or 'contributions' to the Church. The law of tithing came to mean the annual payment of one-tenth of a person's income, interest, or increase. See Daniel H. Ludlow, ed., *Encyclopedia of Mormonism*, 4 vols., s.v. "Tithing."

9. Olney is bothered that the Mormon leadership is trying again (there had been failed efforts prior to this time) to establish the law of consecration in addition to asking Church members to pay tithing. It is true that in 1842 Joseph Smith "sought to perfect a program of sacrifice and consecration among those whom he believed to be faithful and loyal. He proposed to accomplish this by placing a few (and later many) of the Saints under explicit covenants of obedience while at the same time teaching them exalting keys of knowledge and power." See Arnold K. Garr, Richard O. Cowan, and Donald Q. Cannon, eds., *Encyclopedia of Latter-day Saint History*, 241–43. The Law of Consecration is a principle whereby Mormons voluntarily dedicate their material wealth, their time, and their talents to the establishment and building up of God's Kingdom. It is a necessary aspect of establishing Zion described in latter-day scripture: "And the Lord called his people Zion, because they were of one heart and one mind, and dwelt in righteousness; and there was no poor among them" (Moses 7:18). The Book of Mormon also describes a Zion-type of society where "every man did deal justly one with another. And they had all things common among them; therefore there were not rich and poor, bond and free, but they were all made free, and partakers of the heavenly gift" (4 Ne. 1:2–3). Joseph Smith introduced the Law of Consecration to the early Saints based upon revelations he received. Initially, the revelations appear to have been more focused on economic

forse The rich and the poor All as one will be cald and be put under oath To tell what they have They then must fetch forward whatever they have and lay it to the Apostles feet They then will manage with it as they pleas and it is All in the name of the Lord I then se a confusion Immediately take place as but few would come forward that had much of temporal Concerns They said to draw the line between wright and wrong and cut of from the Church all that would not to them conform After passing over an other vally I again looked about to se what was a going on I se some noted ones that Lead in the mire stopt and seemed asstonished to think that they did not come forward after haveing the word of the Lord They looked for many thousands to so[o]n be at their feet but bearly a few thousand to them was put down They looked astonished to se so little notice taken of Gods word They then began to query amongst them selves They often asked questions To know each others minds that many became dishartened to se the daily moves Some sad is it not possible that we are mistaken in the course we have took All has ben well with us We much have ben blest in our doings for many months past The word of the Lord has ben to us to go a head or was we mistaken was it bearly the impulse of the mind O yes you have got the wright of it The Lord has forsaken you And the Deavil is ashamed of you Altho he has now and then given you a wink I se he was uneasy lest you should get ahead of him especily in Politicks

---

matters to assist the poor and to finance various Church undertakings. "And behold, thou wilt remember the poor, and consecrate of thy properties for their support that which thou hast to impart unto them, with a covenant and a deed which cannot be broken. And inasmuch as ye impart of your substance unto the poor, ye will do it unto me; and they shall be laid before the bishop of my church. . . . [A]fter they are laid before the bishop of my church, and after that he has received these testimonies concerning the consecration of the properties of my church, that they cannot be taken from the church, agreeable to my commandments, every man shall be made accountable unto me, a steward over his own property, or that which he has received by consecration, as much as is sufficient for himself and family. And again, if there shall be properties in the hands of the church, or any individuals of it, more than is necessary for their support after this first consecration, which is a residue to be consecrated unto the bishop, it shall be kept to administer to those who have not, from time to time, that every man who has need may be amply supplied and receive according to his wants. Therefore, the residue shall be kept in my storehouse, to administer to the poor and the needy" (D&C 42:30–34). There were several failed attempts by the Church to live the law of consecration. Although a Church-directed, formalized living of the Law of Consecration does not presently exist, the principle has not been rescinded. Latter-day Saints today voluntarily live the law to the best of their ability by dedicating their time, talents, and a percentage of their income to the Church, viewing the fulness of the Law of Consecration as a promise for the future. See Ludlow, *Encyclopedia of Mormonism*, s.v. "Consecration."

[Folder number 5] June 15the Nauvoo

As my mind has led me of late so I have ben looking at things as they pass I have ben over hills and threw vallies both rough and smoth As the way opened As I was in a low vally in mud up to my knees I looked for a way out to get clear of tods and snakes I looked all around me And se it was dark but the more I Labord the wors I was off that it seemed to be impossible to extricate my self But at last I made a struggle that boosted me up That shook of the mud and set my feet on a high hill I looked back in to the mire From whence I did arise And what did I se that did me supprise I se old and young All mixt up together some big and some little All in confusion I se some a scolding because of their lot of getting ketched in such a company but Others a looking and saying is this of God Others stood a looking on To se what was to come I se an other Company a padling around to get better foothold And go ahead As their faces was downward They said an other platform we will lay that we can go and come as we pleas As dark shades rested on all those that was in the mud they made an appearance strange to relate I look at them with much supprise after seeing who they was all in the mud I se many that I well knew to be Leaders of the Latter day saints I looked on a plain some little way of off I look a vew of them and se them to be members of the Church There was men women and Childern all a looking at the leaders in the mire Many commented at the site but concluded that they would not get ketched in such a scrape But I soon se a move made Or snare set the members to ketch I se it in a vision as I was moveing around the temple lot that made me gase That I hardly spoke But now I will write it As I see it so plain I know it is true without iffs or anns I se this noted Company a padling in the mud They there desided to raise up a righeous branch Of fruits of their own I looked at a sosiety by the females formed That had took one degree of masonry and the second about to receive At an instant sudenly a rush was made but because of the mud a blunder was ensued that caused some room for meditation and the females cleard out They thus became dishartened and sunk deep in to the mire And wallowed and tumbled untill I got out of sight I had a vew of other degrees of masonry that would soon a ben the theme but I se the institution broke up and the females not dishonerd by it at all As I se a snare set by a perticular set in a path far in the Dark that was desined the females should run a foul of it That they could it spring Again I have had visions of what they have don since they have ben in the mud that they have abused their own Companions by being fre with other women of Ill fame and others they have taken the advantage of by saying thus and thus saith the Lord that many is a mourning because of what they have don in the dark as they supposed But now it has come to the light and it is right that they should suffer for such ungodly works But let the villings [villains] suffer that have them abused Leaders or no Leaders Prophit or no Prophit theye will have to try another round of a probationary State[10] I will stake my salvation to that amount I have testimony if my vision is not received I will next write in prose and speak and prove facts Names I will mention that stands verry high in the estimation of some that is as deep in the mud as themselves but I will speak again of the People cald the Latter day Saints If they had good instruction at Nauvoo and other places whire they have getherd they would have honoured the cause of God But look at the teaching altho by the most it is swallowed because of those that say thus and thus saith the Lord In passing over a vally on another high hill I again had a vision Clear and plain North of the temple lot I se the poor on every side Their houses was open and fare hard I looked at all parts of the Citty and some few rich but mostly poor I se many daily comeing in from different parts some with much Others poor They all stood looking And said it looks dark I se a Law about to be made that would not only take the tenth as tithing but a consecration Law is soon to be put in forse The rich and the poor all as one will be cald and put under oath to tel what they have They then must fetch forward whatever they have and throw it down to the Apostles feet They then will manage with it as they pleas and it is all in the name of the Lord I then se

---

10. Although it is not official Church doctrine, Olney appears to have believed that, at least in some cases, individuals would be required or allowed to have "another round" for the purpose of either serving God in some capacity or preparing themselves to dwell with God. It is uncertain whether he meant life in the post-mortal spirit world, life in a lower kingdom, or life in another mortality. However, it would seem that he was referring to another mortal experience. He writes that those who have abused others "will have to try another round of a probationary state." In OOP, fd. 9, September 22, 1842, Olney writes that the Holy Ghost "in a person grown to manhood in an early day condescended to take another round." In OOP, fd. 6, October 13, 1842, Olney discusses Latter-day Saint leaders who began with righteous motives but who have become corrupt. He writes, "[T]hey stand on the ground as they did before they was born so all those that have not well done their work must remember the penalty of the Law of God But because of their doings in days past and gone they now are permitted to take another round that they may yet enter in to the presence of the Farther and Son that they may yet have a chance a work for to gain a Celestial rest." It is not clear where Olney's belief about "another round" originated. In contrast, but related, Joseph Smith recalled an experience he had with a man named Mathias. Mathias told Joseph "that he possessed the spirit of his fathers, that he was a literal descendant of Matthias, the Apostle, who was chosen in the place of Judas that fell; that his spirit was resurrected in him; and that this was the way or scheme of eternal life-this transmigration of soul or spirit from father to son." Joseph told him "that his doctrine was of the devil." Dean C. Jessee, Mark Ashurst-McGee, and Richard L. Jensen, eds., *Journals, Volume 1:1832–1839*, Vol. 1 of the Journals series of *The Joseph Smith Papers*, edited by Dean C. Jessee, Ronald K. Esplin, and Richard Lyman Bushman, 95.

a confusion immediately take place as but few would come forward that had much of temporal concer[n]s They said to draw the line between wright and wrong and cut of from the Church all that would not to them Conform After passing over an other vally I again looked about to se what was a going in the name of the Lord I se a company in deep trouble because of what was a going on I se some few noted ones That lead in the mire Stop and say is it possible we are mistaken in the course we have took all has ben well with us we much have ben blest in our doings for many months past the word of the Lord has ben to us to go a head or was we mistaken was it bearly the impulse of the mind Yes You are wright You have hit the nale on the head The Lord has forsaken you and the Deavil is ashamed of you Altho he has now and then given you a wink But I se he was uneasy lest you should get a head of him esspecially in Politicks I have long ben a looking and writing of things that daily transpired but I find a serious difficulty attend me as I think something of my time But I think I have gained some little ground by looking a head That I can leave them a few days and then I to them will return with some pamphlets That they may learn what the Church is about

[Folder number 6] City of Nauvoo June 16th

A theme of the gospel Has often ben a theme of strife and Division In this and foren lands but with it a testimony That speaks for itself It is a spirit of inquiry To do what is wright and establish principals In honour of God It speaks of a union That is not known but amongst the saints of God The plan of salvation was first devised at the beguinning of time by the Father and Son It was an ordinance Preparitory to light that was to be received threw the P hood The gift of the wholy Ghost By the laying on of hands after believing in the Father and Son and repenting of their sins and be baptised for the remission thereof They then have the promise the gifts to obtain by saying and doing as the scriptures directs that doth boy up and Expand the mind untill man becomes familiar with The messengers above He thus has before him a theme of things that tends to enlighten Threw the gift of the Holy Ghost I of late have ben a looking at one here and their and say why do those That have the same privelege disagree in doctrinal points Why not se alike as the teachings of the Antients is simple and plain No one need mistake the path of right that desires to do what is wright In order to become an heir of the Kingdom of God First belief and submission to his word then comes a blessing on the honest in hart that they can testimony bear of the goodness of God by conformation of the Spirit That they receive Again we will reason of our duty to God Why have we a standing on his footstool Is it not from our own choise That we are here to well do our duty To arise far higher than the place we left Now comes the point if we well do our duty and Labours perform we have don wise in passing threw this probationary state If not it would aben better to a not ben born

[Folder number 3] Citty of Nauvoo Saturday June 18th 1842

I to meeting and trayning did go to se and to learn, All that is agoing on Meeting and trayning All turned into one They then did expostulate about many things They took up a case of a noted man that they caled a rascal that had a long and high standing in the Church of L D Saints that he had been a noted rascal a long time that he had abused and seduced females time and again They proved his character to be of the blackest die That looked to me strange why they should put him forward as one of the first of the Church After hearing his character defamed I said why was he not looked to sooner or why was he put forward and kept in Orthoroty when they knew of his bad works I looked at their doings and works I se it to be in accordance with their former works I look back to Kirtland To missouri and se the same order As with J C Bennet[11] that men is put forward In all cases that is to be swayed by those that rule I look at many that is said was dishonest and took the advantage of the

11. John Cook Bennett was born at Fairhaven, Massachusetts, on August 3, 1804. Well educated, Bennett studied medicine and became a licensed doctor. Married and living in Ohio, Bennett became a follower of Alexander Campbell. He met Sidney Rigdon prior to Rigdon's conversion to Mormonism. In the years that followed, Bennett became interested in the military and sought to adopt a military image. He moved to Illinois and was appointed to a high position in the Illinois militia. During this time, he also earned a reputation of being a huckster. Joseph Smith and John C. Bennett may have become acquainted during the 1830s in Ohio. There was correspondence between the two in 1840, and Bennett was invited to come to Nauvoo and join with the Saints. In Nauvoo, Bennett was baptized and experienced a meteoric rise to power, becoming a major general in the Nauvoo Legion, university chancellor, mayor of Nauvoo, and counselor to Joseph Smith. In 1841 it was discovered that Bennett, who had claimed to be a bachelor, had a wife and children in Ohio. When confronted, he admitted the truth, affirmed his repentance, and remained in his positions of leadership. Secretly, Bennett was having illicit affairs with women in Nauvoo, claiming that there was no sin in it because they were "spiritually" married to him, a doctrine he convinced the women had been approved by the Prophet Joseph. Although this was done without Joseph Smith's approval, Bennett may have been aided in this charade by the fact that Joseph Smith had secretly begun the practice of plural marriage at this time in Nauvoo. As the truth about Bennett began to emerge, the relationship between Joseph Smith and John C. Bennett deteriorated. Joseph initiated disciplinary proceedings against Bennett in May 1842. By June, Bennett had resigned from all leadership positions and had removed his name from Church membership. He left Nauvoo and became a bitter enemy of Joseph Smith, lecturing on the evils of Mormonism in various cities, publishing scandalous newspaper articles, and ultimately writing *History of the Saints or an Exposé of Joe Smith and Mormonism.* After the

Ch— Why did they do it, It was because power was put in their hands by those that dote of haveing wisdom to desern the hart of man in their outgoings and incomeings that nothing can escape their desernment I look at the thousands that have ben took unlawfully from the Church by those that is boosted up by those of Orthoroty Look at J C Bennet how has it ben with him he was extold to the highest untill with in a few days eaven above the virtue of any man now what has this day ben said but that he is the meanest lowest In a word language is mad[e] use of to slander him beyond my act of writing When I say that I say the same of those that have put him forward as a tool to bring about their purposes I look on J C Bennet as on them all of a mess They have moved together hart and hand in all their windings. If Bennett had not a moved quite so fast all would a ben well now, As I look at things with them I look at the teachings on the stand What is it but give me your money and we will be your friends and conduct you in to Heaven Whire is your reason of which you bost Is it flead is it gone No more to return I have looked at a noted man on the stand by the name of John Taylor one of the twelve apostles of the Calf I often se him on the stand a puffing and bloing and hear of his doting Of writing for the press Such preaching reasoning and writing is as much as we can exspect from a product of a Calf But not a gold one As by Aaron was made to eumer [humor] the Children of Israel in the woods No a calf of that discription would exalt them that they could hardly be tuched with a ten foot pole But it was hatched by a beast of which John The Revelator spoke that was to come forth in the Last days in the shape of a he goat If I am permited To comment on scripture I will reason some little from that as I se as I se much a doing by the watchman in the mud or they would say on the tower teaching and instructing the Latter Day Saints How do they teach them contra from scripture and lead them in to bondage By being combined together they lead in to bondage as they pleas How do they do it But put a man forward untill he runs in to Iniquity that he cant hold up his head They then come out against him all in a mass In it they are united to throw out their slang untill they have pored out their epothets as is strang[e] to hear from from a lot of calves But when they all get a bawling and the JackAsses a naying and the members a laughing a fellow had better be in a wasps nest than to speak for him self As that would set them to whineing in all in the name of the Lord Curse after curse would sail around him That he would be worse of than a Cat in a strange Garret[12] I commenced to cout [quote] scripture but I got of the subject I will come mence a new and make use of some

death of Joseph Smith, Bennett became involved with several schisms of Mormonism. He died in Iowa in 1867. See Garr, Cannon, and Cowan, *Encyclopedia*, 88–89.

12. A watchtower. That part of a house which is on the upper floor, immediately under the roof (attic). *Webster's Dictionary* (1827), s.v. "Garret."

reasen altho it it may not be counted of use amongst the bawling calves But I am not a writing in perticular but to the members of the Church of L D Saints I ask you to use some reason Is God a God of order Does he move in unholy temples Look at the wild Beasts of Nachure that dont come under the care of man Have they not an independance of action Is there not an Equality of the differant grades Look at the Deer in the forest the fish in the ocean the brutes in the Mountains also the fowls That fills the immensity of space Each school fitted to its part Now look at your selves and then vew your teachers Look at the inequality between them and members Then ask a question If nachure has not took a joy you must desid in the affirmative and say all is not well Why are they a takeing from you the Last Pirtance [Pittance] It is because of their greediness to agrandise themselves and you know they a talking about raising up a Righeous Branch look at their houses They lack in sise in rooms and conveniencies, To accomodate their numerous wifes and maidens As they say old David and Solomon had that they say was the antient order of God They say you have ben a praying for the Antient order and your prayers have ben herd in the Ears of the Lord of Sabeath And because of your faith the antient order is a coming like a tornado on us And you must put hand to and help build and assist by putting all your means in our hands that we may not lack in substance to do on our part As God is anxiously a looking and a waiting to role forth his work on the Earth to prepare for his comming and Kingdom on ~~the Earth~~ You well know that the royal Blood must arise, As we can make nothing with this presant jentile uncircumcised race I suppose you have not all herd them come out with their strong reasoning of thus and thus saith the Lord but they think it good to keep a profound secret O yes they by the eye of faith look at a people That soon will be in it there is a union as I se it on a high hill in a brite and sunshiny day it being a connection between the first to the forth degrees of masonry I se many a looking to se who they would ketch but the calves made a blunder I se after wards and the females cleard out and their Sosiety Broke up It caused a confusion The calves looked sad as their plans were broke up many felt bad but it set some a laughing because of looks and troubled many because of their lot They went into the mire up to their Ears without getting any foot hold They there stood a gapping all in the mud and became a public example and I cleard out of their sight and glad was I as I long have herd them bost of their honour wisdom and Influance in this and foren lands I looked at their influance amongst those that have come from afar and hear them tell how they have ben used while on their way that the advantage has ben taken of them In differant ways under a cloak of religion or thus saith the Lord

[Folder number 5] Citty of Nauvoo Saturday June 18th 1842

I fixed up and to tray-ning and meeting did go to se and to learn all that was a going on Meeting and training all limited in one They then did expostulate About many things They took up a case Of a noted man that they caled a rascal that had a long and high standing in the Church that he had ben a noted Rascal a long time that he had abused and sedused females time and again They proved his character to be of the blackest die That looked to me strange why they should put him forward as one of the first of the Church After hearing his character defamed, I said why was he not looked to sunner or why was he put forward By the Leaders of the Church We have herd much of him from time to time and of his unwise doings, That he did Lead in to darkness the Church of Latter day Saints I spoke of it by the way of a vision lest I should caled to prove the fact that he was leading in to darkness the church and caused confusion discord and disunion amongst the Church of Latter day Saints I said to myself why is it so That such men is put forward and entrusted With treasures Also to be highly thought of in the Church I look back to Kirtland It would be easy for one to cal names that was counted dishonest By the Leaders of the Church yet many they have put in to office that have taken their thousands from the Church and left without giving of it any account I look back at many That is said That is said they have much abused the Church and say its my opinion if they had not a ben put forward By the Leaders of the Church that many of them would a ben at this time worthy members in the Church But it was with them as others they was willing to go ahead that a little urgin put on their high heel shoes so by the by many have fallen because of being boosted up By noted men They say if they want to go ahead we will give them rope to hang themselves Why not check them in the bud as well as to let them go ahead untill they have disgrased A whole Community which would a ben at the best When two of the presidancy Found he had a wife in the East And J. C. Bennet caled him self a single man and was a keeping Company With young girls in the Church of latter day saints What have you gaind by bo[o]sting him up in office after you knew of his ungodly doings as you have born testimony against him Why did you not expose him that he mite no more abuse the inosent But no you say you wanted to save him What have you gained by it I can let you [know] what you have gained he says if reports is true that he has ben intimate with you[r] own wives no doubt but it is the facts not only so many has to bear the reproach of being with him on your account of continuing to extol him to the hiest and keeping him along untill he had took his name from the Church and is a moving in flying colours As you say he did as you said went and come at your command no doubt but he has ben a tool for you but in the end he has outwitted you all and brought a disgrase on your Familys that time wont wash of You speak of your wisdom This day on the stand what do you do that is so brite What do you bring about but display your folly and weakness Look at your teachings on the stand What is it but give me your money and we will be your friends and conduct you in to heaven Whire is your reason, of which you se much lost Is it flead is it gone No more to return I have looked at a Noted man on the stand by the name of John Taylor one of the twelve Apostles of the Calf I often se him on the stand a puffing and bloing and hear of his doting of writing for the press Such preaching such reasoning such writing is as much as we can exspect from the product of a Calf But not a gold one as by Aaron was made to eumer the Childern in the woods No a calf of that discription would exalt them that they could not be tuched with a ten foot pole But it was hatched by a beest of which the ~~Prophit~~ John the Revelator spoke was to come forth in the Last days in the shape of a he goat If I am permitted to comment on scripture I think I will reason some little from that as I se much adoing by the watchman in the mud or they would say on the tower teaching and instructing The Latter day Saints How do they teach them Contry [contra or contrary] From scripture and lead them in to bondage by being combined together that they lead in to bondage the members as they pleas How do they do it They first put a man forward untill he runs in to iniquity That he cant hold up his head They then come out against him All in a mass In it they will be united To throw out their slang untill they have pored out Their epothets as Is strange to hear from a flock of calves But when they all get a bawling and the Cows a bellowing And Jack A—s a naying and the members of the Church a laughing a fellow had better be in a hornets nest than to speak for him self As that would set them to whinein all in the name of the Lord curse after curse would fly around him that he would se himself worse of than a cat in a strange Garret I commenced to cout [quote] scripture but got off of the subject I will now commence a new and make use of some reason Altho it may not have on the bawling calves but to them I am not a writing as I look at them not worth of my notice Or the notice of any decent person Neither am I a writing in perticuler but to the members of the Church of Latter day Saints I ask you to use some reason Is God a god of order Does he move in unholy temples Look at the wild beasts of Nachure that dont come under the care of man Have they not an independance of action Is there not an Equality Of the differant grades Look at the deer in the forest The fish in the Ocean The brutes in the mountains Also the Fowls that fills the immensity of space Each school fitted to their part Now look at your selves and your teachers Look at the inequality Between them and members Then ask a question If nature has not took a <illegible> you must decide the affirmative and say all is not well Why are they takeing from you the last Pisense [Pitense] It is because of the greediness to agrandise them selves And you know they are a talking about raising up a Righeous Branch look at their houses they lack in size in rooms and conveniences to accommodate their numerous wives and maidens as Old David and Solomon had that they say was the antient order of God They say you have have ben apraying for the antient order and your prayers have Assended the Lord of Sabeoth and because of your faith the antient order is now comeing like a tornado on us and you must put hand too and help build and assist by putting all your means in to our hands that we may not lack in means to do on our part as God is anxiously alooking and awating to role forth his work on the Earth to prepare for his coming and Kingdom on the Earth You well know that the royal blood must arise as you know that we can make nothing of them that are of this gentile race I suppose you have not all herd them come out with their strong reasonings of thus saith the Lord but they think it is too good to keep a profound secret O yes they look at a people That soon will be in it there is a union as I se it on a high hill in a brite and sunshiney day it being a connection of the first to forth degrees of masonry Amongst the females I se many alooking To se who they would ketch but the calves made a blunder I se after wards and the females cleard out and then society broke up It caused a confusion the calves looked sad as their plans was broke up Many felt bad But it set some a laughing Because of looks that troubled many because of their lot They went in to the mire up to their Ears without getting any foot hold They there stood gaping all in the mud They became a public Example and I cleard out of their sight and glad was I to do it As I long have herd them bost of their honour wisdom and influance in this and foren lands I looked at their influance amongst those that have come from afar and hear them tel how they have ben used while on their way That the advantage was taken of them In differant ways under a cloak of religion or thus saith the Lord I again look at this Priveleged few that say to be a light to the world from Prophet to teacher and say that another such a set cannot be found on our American Soil But I think their days is numberd as I had another vision of them apassing threw a low and miry swale They there got a contending about a lobster and snale They thay continued their contention some few weeks That caused an excitement all over the land That all as one arose and said we will no more have such works on this our American Soil I se they was as good as their word I then took my course over the Prairies some si[x]ty miles of threw fresh bresses [breezes] that much comforted my mind After visiting and Conversing about matters and things I with the best of feelings started back I soon arived at the Citty of Nauvoo and found my vision fulfild as on tuesday 21st of June they met and came forward with the Law of God that all must come forward and lay to their feet their mites They had thus saith the Lord for it as I am well informed by eye witnesses that caused sorrow and Lamentation amongst many of the Rich of the place as they first was caled on there effects to give up Som soon came forward and others kept back

[Folder number 6] June 19th 1842

The word of the Lord is unto the[e] at this time to prepare your self for a differant order of things than what you have had experienced in You are caled to understand an order of things that lies in the dark to the world and will untill it is reveld threw those that is caled to teach by the gift of the Holy Ghost that brings to light things both presant past and futer and that by the wisdom of God which is a comfater sent from God that is no less than an ministering spirit that takes up his abode with man that has fully submitted himself to the will of God By faith and works Amaseing what comes to my vew but a messenger from the Mansions of Glory that speaks in language not penned that God is a preparing A work for to perform All Nations will understand it as much is to Zion that will s[p]eak of antient writers as as their record now is to be fulfild as many have written of the Latter day Glory It now beguins to unsolve mistrys that have long lain in the dark Let the wise now have feelings Gods will to be adoing As he by the Antients on the Earth has took a stand his will to perform and has cald on a mortal of foibles and vanitys to be an agent to his Agents on the Earth I am some times much wearyd in what I am adoing to learn and understand his order of teaching It takes all my time his will for to do but as I much depend on him I am still determined to persevere untill what I have to do is accomplished and the Kingdom of God is Established as is spoken of by the Antients Prophhits no more to be baffled by the folly of man As the little stone is amoveing it will soon beguin to Cripple and brake in pieces all kingdoms As there is none on Earth that is of God It must soon be established In power and glory that will baffle the wicked th[at] on Earth have a standing in this the nineteenth Century of time. It will speak to the Righeous or those that are honest that have Laberd and sought Gods will to do A field will open to them That will far excede the wisdom of man. As much is adoing in the name of the Lord That is not of him decreed let those that have feeling His will for to do remember the Condesention of the Saviour at the meridean of time As much then was don to prepare an order of things that in the last days was to be performed by man on the Earth as agents for those that doth Desend from the Father and Son As administering spirits to bring about Gods purposes That the time may come that the Son of man may With all the Saints come and take up their abode on the Earth The word of the Lord is unto you at this time to prepare your self for more light and inteligance You are to meet in person with the Antients with Old Father Adam and receive your anointing eaven with the Oil of Gladness that you may have more light that you may be enabled to go ahead in your duty and bring about the purposes of God you are caled to take your course on to the Prairie that you will not be baffled in mind by Friends or Enemys you then will be caled to return and write what took place I accordingly took my Course on the open Prairies whire the Air was clear And the breses fresh and no opposite spirit To baffle my mind I there was visited by messengers from Heaven that long since had a standing on the Earth They to me exprest good feelings and administerd to me in the name of the Lord I with them had a union That was to me encourageing I received my anointing It being a spirit of light and Inteligance That on me should rest It is an other Comforter That with me should dwell that should enlighten And expand the mind It is to be with me and direct me in my doings so fast as my mind can expand They laid their hand on me and blest me and said to me to go about my Masters work that all things may be a moveing in honor of God I cheerfuly Labour In honour of my maker that my work may be adoing As to me has ben don

[Folder number 6] June 19th 1842

Thou art caled at this time to understand your duty to realise at all times what you have to do to bring about the purposes of God You are caled to understand an order of things that is of much importance for you to understand you are caled to select sixty females of such as you shall choose thirty at this time and thirty at some futer time You are caled to take those that are young or single that you se fit to take, but few that have Companions none unless you have a testimony that such is your duty after haveing this testim[on]y write their names You will have five to sit with you as a presidency of female Companions you have had two that are on planets of rest Eliza R Snow has ben raised up for you As you do not get her you will have an adopted one to live long with Again you will have another that will have a standing on Earth in the melinium that will raise up your Childern that have died or that you will have that dies in their youth[13]

13. This is a curious entry. Olney makes it clear in other parts of his writings that he felt polygamy was an abomination. He includes polygamy with the sins of fornication and adultery. But here he is called to select sixty women, thirty at this time and thirty more later. What was the purpose of this list of women? Perhaps he was considering the names of women to serve in leadership positions after the Church went through his hoped-for reformation. He does write that five of the women are to "sit with him as a presidency of female companions." However, this explanation makes little sense when considering that one of the women on his list (Alvira Atwood) was already deceased. Also, he does not write "female leadership," but rather "female companions." The more likely possibility is that these were names of women with whom he was hoping to have a relationship in this life or the life to come. He will later marry number one on his list, Phebe Wheeler . He mentions that "Eliza Snow has been raised up" for him. He writes that he will have one that will live long with him and another to raise his children during the Millennium. His comment that he "has had two that are on planets of rest" is confusing. Certainly, he could be referring to his late wife, Alice Johnson Olney, but it is not clear who the other would be. It is possible that Olney was not so much anti-plural marriage as he was irritated that he had no wife at this time and yet there were married men who were taking second

<1> Phebe M Wheler[14] / <2> Mary Bennet[15] / <3> Axy White[16] / <4> dau[17]

---

and third wives. It may be that Olney felt slighted that he was not invited to be part of the inner circle of men in the Church who had been instructed in the doctrine of plural marriage and had been authorized to secretly participate in the practice. It is difficult to identify positively all of the women in the list. I have attempted to identify the names on the list, but based on limited information in many cases these are only possible identifications. In some cases, Olney only gives the last name of the individual. In other cases, there are many possibilities because several women have the same name. I have taken into consideration Olney's statement, "You are caled to take those that are young or single that you se fit to take, but few that have Companions none unless you have a testimony that such is your duty." The possible individuals listed are based on age and proximity to Nauvoo, Illinois, in 1842.

14. Phebe Wheeler was married to Oliver H. Olney at Nauvoo, Illinois, on October 19, 1843. Wheeler was a member of The Church of Jesus Christ of Latter-day Saints and belonged to the Nauvoo 4th Ward. D. Michael Quinn relates the Olney-Wheeler marriage being performed by Hyrum Smith in D. Michael Quinn, *The Mormon Hierarchy: Origins of Power*, 348n39. However, both Susan Easton Black and Lyndon W. Cook state that the marriage was performed by Joseph Hadlock in Black, *Membership*, 45:569; and Lyndon W. Cook, comp., *Nauvoo Deaths and Marriages*, 107.

15. Several women with the name of Mary Bennett lived in the vicinity of Nauvoo in 1842. The following are possible candidates for Olney's list: (1) Mary Bennett born December 9, 1786. She received her endowment in the Nauvoo Temple on February 6, 1846. Based on the criteria that the women he chose should be young and single, she is probably not the Mary Bennett that Olney was referring to. She was ten years older than Olney. However, it is possible that Olney may have selected some older women. See Black, *Membership*, 4:735. (2) Mary Bennett born May 3, 1788, at Alleghany, Pennsylvania. She received her patriarchal blessing from Hyrum Smith in Nauvoo on September 10, 1843. Again, she was older than Olney and may not be the one he was considering. See Black, *Membership*, 4:736. (3) Mary Twimberrow Bennett born August 26, 1819, at Alfrick, Worcestershire, England. She immigrated to the United States and married Williiam Kay on February 10, 1845, in Nauvoo, Illinois. See Black, *Membership*, 4:471–72.

16. According to Susan Easton Black, Axy White was born at Worcester, Massachusetts, on March 15, 1789. She received her endowment in the Nauvoo Temple on December 23, 1845 and was sealed to Erastus Snow in the Nauvoo Temple on January 30, 1846. See Black, *Membership*, 45:667. However, according to Erastus Snow's entry on familysearch.org, he was married to Minerva White (who might have gone by the nickname "Axy.") Minverva White was born at Northbridge, Worcester, Massachusetts, on March 22, 1822. She was married to Erastus Snow on April 2, 1844, in Nauvoo, Illinois. Minerva White Snow made the pioneer trek to Utah, had nine children, and died on April 1, 1896, in Manti, Utah. Minerva White is likely the Axy Snow on Olney's list.

17. Likely meaning "daughter."

Susan White[18] / <5> [ ] Aldridge <6> dau [ ] Aldridge[19] / <7> Carolin Crony[20] <8> [ ] Craine <9> [ ] Craine <10> [ ] Craine[21] <11> Betsy Chase[22] <12> Mary Chase[23] / <13> Polly Chase[24] <14> Sally Hatch[25] <15> Genelle Russel[26] <16>

---

18. Several possibilities for Susan White. Susan Rebecca White, born June 18, 1812. See Black, *Membership*, 45:745. Susan Twing White, married at Nauvoo, Illinois on June 9, 1844, to William Wade. See Black, *Membership*, 45:476.

19. There are two Aldridge women on Olney's list with no first names. In OOP, fd. 10, October 18, 1842, there is a rewritten version of Olney's list of thirty women. On the updated version, Olney lists Leita Aldridge. I could not find any information on this name. Possibilities for the other Aldridge on the first list are Amy Aldridge, who was born June 30, 1804, and received her endowment in the Nauvoo Temple on January 23, 1846. See Black, *Membership*, 1:308. Sophia Aldridge is listed as a member of the Nauvoo 3rd Ward. See Black, *Membership*, 1:329.

20. Could find no information on Carolin Crony, even using various possible spellings.

21. Numbers nine, ten, and eleven are listed as "Craine" with no first name given. It is likely that Olney was aware of these women but did not know them well enough to be familiar with their first names. In the rewritten list (OOP, fd. 10, October 18, 1842), Olney includes only two women with the name of Crane: Abigail Crane and Leita Crane. I could find no information on either Abigail or Leita Crane. Other possibilities for the third Crane woman on the first list include Electa Crane (born 1813), Elizabeth Crane (born 1826), and Sarah Watson Crane (born 1795). It is certain that Electa and Sarah did live in Nauvoo. It is not known whether Elizabeth lived in Nauvoo. It is also unknown if these three had any familial relationship. See Black, *Membership*, 12:304–7.

22. Betsey Ann Chase, born September 23, 1818, at Lysle, New York. She received her endowment (January 18, 1846) and was sealed to her husband (January 27, 1846). Betsey Ann Chase was married to Horace Sunderland Eldridge on July 20, 1836, at Buffalo, New York. See Black, *Membership*, 9:354–55. This may have been a case where Olney chose a married woman to put on his list.

23. Mary Chase, or Maria Chase, or Mariah Chase. Born March 29, 1825, at Lewiston, Illinois. She was endowed in the Nauvoo Temple on January 30, 1846, and is listed as a member of the Nauvoo 4th Ward.

24. There is a Polly B. Chase in Susan Easton Black, comp., *Early Members of the Reorganized Church of Jesus Christ of Latter Day Saints* 2:150. Polly B. Chase was born December 1831, making her only eleven years old when Olney wrote his list, which makes her a questionable candidate. Also, it is not known whether she ever lived in the Nauvoo area or was ever a member of The Church of Jesus Christ of Latter-day Saints.

25. Sally Hatch is found in both OOP, fd. 6, June 19, 1842, and OOP, fd. 10, October 18, 1842. There was a Sally Hatch who was married to George Snyder on April 17, 1842, at Hancock County, Illinois. Nauvoo is located in Hancock County. If this is the Sally Hatch mentioned by Oliver Olney, her marriage took place prior to the writing of the lists, making her another possible married woman on the list.

26. Genelle or Genette Russel are on both of Olney's lists. If her name was Genette, he neglected to cross the two t's on the first list. No information could be found on any variation of the name Genette Russell.

Juliette Atwood[27] <17> Elisabeth Sikes[28] <18> Emily Thompson[29] / <19> [ ] Crandall[30] / <20> Alvira Atwood (dead)[31] <21> Rebecca Atwood[32] <22> Leonora

[Publisher's note: The blank space here is intentional to accommodate multiple footnotes. No text is missing.]

27. There is a Juliette Atwood on both of Olney's lists. Her name may have been Jenette Atwood. She was born May 16, 1818, at Mansfield, Connecticut. She married George Wyrick (Wirick, Warwick) on December 8, 1842, at Nauvoo, Illinois. See Black, *Membership*, 2:762.

28. Elizabeth Sikes was born November 16, 1822, in Monroe County, New York. She married Wilson Law at Nauvoo on December 25, 1842. Joseph Smith performed the marriage. See Black, *Membership*, 39:357.

29. Emily Thompson was born August 13, 1819, at Mansfield, Connecticut. She married Hiram Spencer on January 1, 1843, at Nauvoo, Illinois. See Black, *Membership*, 43:258–59.

30. Crandall, no first name written by Olney. There is a Crandall on Olney's rewritten list in OOP, fd. 10, October 18, 1842. No first name is given on the second list. The following are possible Crandalls Olney was referring to: (1) Emeline Crandall (Crandell), born June 27, 1824. Married Richard Bird on March 7, 1845. Their first child was born at Nauvoo. See Black, *Membership*, 12:271–73. (2) Mary Crandall, born on July 28 (July 30), 1820, at Middletown, Vermont or Danby, Vermont. There is no record of her living in Nauvoo. See Black, *Membership*, 12:281.

31. Alvira Atwood is on Olney's list, but he writes a notation that she is dead. It is unclear why he would have a deceased person on his list, unless he is planning on a relationship in a post-mortal existence. There is an Alvira Atwood in the *Membership of the Church of Jesus Christ of Latter-day Saints, 1830–1848*, but the only available information is that she was a member of the Nauvoo 3rd Ward. See Black, *Membership*, 2:749.

32. Rebecca Atwood, born October 23, 1825, at Mansfield, Connecticut. Received her endowment in the Nauvoo Temple on January 22, 1846. Married Joseph W. Coolidge. Had a residence in Nauvoo, Illinois. See Black, *Membership*, 2:770.

Levitt[33] <23> [ ] Levitt // <24> [ ] Levitt[34] / <25> Rebecca Wirick[35] <26> Esther Morton[36] <27> Elisabeth Barlow[37] <28> [ ] Hansen[38] / <29> [ ] Hubbel[39] / <30> Elisabeth Chapman[40] / The above names can be changed if best

---

33. Could find no information on Leonora Levitt (Leavette, Leavitt).

34. Numbers twenty-three and twenty-four are both Leavitts with first names left blank. Possibilities include (1) Betsey Leavett, born November 23, 1804, at Staadstadt, Quebec, Canada. She received her endowment in the Nauvoo Temple on January 12, 1846; married James Adams; and was a member of the Nauvoo 2nd Ward. See Black, *Membership*, 27:668. (2) Charolotte (Charlotte) Leavitt, born at Hatley, Quebec, Canada (or Chatauqua, New York), on December 5, 1820 (or December 5, 1818). She married Simon Baker at Nauvoo, Illinois, on April 8, 1845, and was a member of the Nauvoo 2nd Ward. See Black, *Membership*, 27:670–72. (3) Cornelia Eliza Leavitt, born January 5, 1825, at Warren, Ohio. Married Amasa M. Lyman on November 14, 1844. Endowed in the Nauvoo Temple on January 10, 1846. See Black, *Membership*, 27:673. (4) Lucia or Louisa Leavitt. Born August 9, 1826, at Warren, Ohio. Sister of Cornelia Eliza Leavitt. Received endowment in the Nauvoo Temple on January 7, 1846. She was a member of the Nauvoo 2nd Ward. See Black, *Membership*, 27:706. (5) Phebe Leavitt or Phebe Levette. Born July 6, 1794 or 1795. Received endowment in the Nauvoo Temple on January 3, 1846. Phebe was a member of the Nauvoo 2nd Ward. See Black, *Membership*, 27:710.

35. There is no Rebecca Wirick listed in *Membership of the Church of Jesus Christ of Latter-day Saints, 1830–1848*. However, Jacob Wirick and Mary McCoy had a daughter named Rebecca who was born March 13, 1827. This would almost certainly be the Rebecca Wirick listed here by Olney. Rebecca would have been fifteen years old when Olney included her on his list.

36. No information on Esther Morton. However, in Olney's October 18, 1842, list revision, her name is recorded as Esther Martin. I did locate an Esther Martin Reed who was born on December 16, 1832. That would make her only twelve when Olney made the list. Also, there is no record of her ever living in the Nauvoo area. She is probably not the Esther Martin on Oliver Olney's list. LDS Vital Records Library.

37. An Elizabeth Haven married Israel Barlow at Quincy, Illinois, in 1840, which would make her Elizabeth Barlow at the time Oliver Olney created his lists. She received her endowment in the Nauvoo Temple on December 16, 1845, and was sealed to Israel Barlow in the Nauvoo Temple on January 17, 1846. See Black, *Membership*, 21:713–15. If this is the Elisabeth Barlow that Olney was referring to, then she would have been married when he put her on his list.

38. Hansen, no first name given. There was a Mary Hansen, born in Maryland who received her patriarchal blessing from Joseph Smith Sr. on May 4, 1842. This would have taken place in Nauvoo or in the Nauvoo area. See Black, *Membership*, 20:594.

39. Hubbel, no first name given. I did locate a Susan Hubbell who was born on January 9, 1819, at Franklin, Tennesee. However, whether she ever lived in the Nauvoo area or had even met Oliver Olney is not known. See Black, *Membership*, 24:322.

40. The only Elizabeth Chapman that I could find who was a member of the Church of Jesus Christ of Latter-day Saints at the time Oliver Olney made his list was born

Nauvoo June 22 <3> Nancy Rigdon[41] <8> Miss Martha Brotherton[42] < 24> Julia Jinks[43] <28> Abigail Bucannan[44] <29> [ ] White[45]

September 1, 1830, in Ohio. See Black, *Membership*, 9:271-72. She would have been twelve years old at the time Olney made his list. She seems too young to have been on Olney's list. However, Olney did include someone who had died. If he was considering future relationships, then perhaps age didn't really mean anything to him. However, there may have been another Elizabeth Chapman that I have not located.

41. Nancy Rigdon was the daughter of Sidney Rigdon (first counselor to Joseph Smith) and Phebe Brooks. Nancy was born December 8, 1822, at Pittsburg, Pennsylvania. She was baptized a Mormon ca. November 1830. Nancy followed the Saints from Ohio, to Missouri, and to Nauvoo. Nancy became part of a scandal when she refused a proposal from Joseph Smith to become one of his plural wives. See OOP, fd. 3, July 24th, 1842.

42. Martha Brotherton was born at Manchester, England, on May 24, 1824. She was the youngest of the eight children of Thomas Brotherton and Sarah Hamilton. Her family were converted by Mormon missionaries in Great Britain and immigrated to the United States in 1841. George D. Smith, *Nauvoo Polygamy . . . "but we called it celestial marriage,"* 264–65. Martha was a member of the Nauvoo Third Ward. See Black, *Membership*, 6:851. Martha is known for refusing to become Brigham Young's first plural wife and the publicized scandal that followed. See OOP, fd. 3, July 24th, 1842.

43. There is a Julia Ann Jinks in Black, *Membership*. However, Julia Jinks was born April 17, 1824 at Stone, Staffordshire, England. She was baptized in 1840 and was married to John Druce on June 19, 1842—just three days after Olney recorded his first list of thirty women (alternates were dated June 23, 1842). Julia Ann Jinks was married in England and did not immigrate to the United States until 1846. See Black, *Membership*, 27:670–72. Olney could not have met Julia Ann Jinks by 1842. The name Julia Jinks does appear as an alternate on Olney's list. Perhaps a missionary returning from England spoke to Olney about a young British woman who had been baptized in 1840 by Willard Richards. Or there is another Julia Jinks for whom I could find no information.

44. Abigail Buchanan was born on January 9, 1802, at Waltham, Massachusetts. She received her endowment in the Nauvoo Temple on February 3, 1846. See Black, *Membership*, 7:284.

45. White, no first name given. There are a number of possible women by the name of White living in the Nauvoo area, including Eliza White, Elizabeth White, Frances White, Margaret White, Mary White, Melinda White, Ortensia White, Rebecca White, and Susanna White. See Black, *Membership*, 45:674–78. On the October 18, 1842, rewrite of the list, the name of Abby White is written as well as another White with no first name given. There are two women named Abigail White who are possibilities. One Abigail White was born in Vermont on February 15, 1821, and who received her endowment in the Nauvoo Temple on January 12, 1846. The other Abigail White was born on March 30, 1823, in Lawrence County, New York. She was a member of the Nauvoo Third Ward. See Black, *Membership*, 45:662–63. There was also a Lucinda White to whom Oliver Olney sent letters. See OOP, fd. 9, Sept. 10, 1842, and OOP, fd. 11, Nov. 4, 1842. It appears that Lucinda and Oliver may have even discussed marriage.

[Folder number 7] Citty of Nauvoo June 20th 1842

I have lately come from I hardly know whire I take a retrospective vew of things as they pass I have seen much adoing In differant parts, some fidling, some a dansing And a frolicking about. Others Plowing planting and hoing to mature the Comforts of life I se some a Manurfacturing such articles as tends to console and comfort man, and shield him from the storms I se some engaged in Politicks that looks to me Strange why man should contend with his fellow man I hear some a preaching, Of differant sorts, because of their principals of faith, in things that they say to be of God In a word I have seen more than I think it wisdom to speak But suffise it to say I the other day took a retrospective vew of the Citty of Nauvoo Labours in it performed I se men women and Childern All engaged to establish a place of refuge to shield them from the heat and cold Storms I se men of differant qualifications often on the Stand, Some learned some illiterate, By them I was much edified. Again I went down the River some thre or four miles I there met with a people discribe their Looks. Again of their breed I cannot say but they are rather coarse hared and of a dismal look. They are often teaching as they say things of God But in looking at them I have made up my mind that they are not of the rase of man but they are of a link Between man and brute or they have become fallen, That on them is a curse. Whether the latter or former It is about the same They much differ in sise and in looks. Their shades are many, They often are found doting and a telling of what must be don They appear ambitious In their daily moves but their breed I said I could not discribe But their looks denotes the apish kind Some Eyes are black, Others Grisle or Gray They look verry greedy, To arise in the esteem of the leaders of the Church of Latter day Saints but their presant grade Does them forbid to be linked with those, of decent looks But if they of me will receive some advice I will devise a plan That they may arise and possibly make one decent man if not a child they would chance to make that it could gro up from youth and change their degraded State As their is a furnace well under way in the Citty of Nauvoo if they together their would meet and deside to go threw all in a heap I think the product of the pile would produce something If not quite so good if they in this will go a head I think it will stop a fus amongst all around them that if it was not for them would live in peace and harmony I think the bretheren Would gain the time to help them to be thorough in the change But if it should look hard For Eight or Ten Creatures to go threw a firey Flame to be clensed and purified from dross there is an other plan I would devise that Each one plant him self on a good soil and run the resk of the product more or less If its but a grub[46] It will honour its Progenitors Now if they desire an honourable standing in the flesh my advice to them Is to be up and adoing

[Folder number 3] Citty of Nauvoo June 24th 1842

A day of confusion discord and disunion is well known to be a fact amongst the L.D.S. some a rioting and a frolicking and makeing merry on a day set a part To se and be seen as this is a day of Note for many to meet to strike heart and hand in Nauvoo as a loge is formed The Masons meet to prepare for the fulness of the P-hood that will enable them to wind up a senry of wickedness In this age that those of this generation may be left with out exscuse that Zion in prosperity may look down and say to the wicked why did you not fall in with the over tures of mercy that would boy up and strenthen the nacherel mind of man We as a people are much enlightend We have Prophits Priests and teachers and direct Revelations from the courts of Heaven above Thus is your reasonings as you wallow in the mire But as nothing does check you or impede your progress or hinder you on the way but when you look back on your doings when you first with many of us did meet we with open arms did receive you and did cheerfully administer to you that you had our best feelings and property of many that possest wealth You have grone up budded and blossomed I think several times over but blasted[47] in producing fruit You now have ariven as you dote on the stand of being an exated [exalted] people as ever God had on the Earth But in reading my verse remember that your scrub is girdled at the roots by a greedy worm it was surrounded that the top has lost its nourishment that did formerly flow From the roots Its presant moisture is gethered from the mud as mud is of a nachure perculiar to its self when it is dry it brakes esspecially if trod

[Folder number 5] June 24th

A day of confusion discord and dis Union is well known to be a fact amongst the Latter day Saints Some a rioting and a frolicking And makeing merry on a day set apart to come together to se and be seen as this is a day of Note for the Masons to strike heart and hand In theme of their doings esspesially the Citizens of the Citty of Nauvoo Altho I am not with them yet I realise their doings to establish an order of things in the name of the Lord They say by it to receive the Priesthood that will enable them to wind up a senry of

---

46. To dig; to be occupied in digging. *To grub up,* is to dig up by the roots with an instrument; to root out by digging or throwing out soil; as, to *grub up trees. Webster's Dictionary* (1828), s.v. "Grub." Perhaps Olney is saying, "Even if you are just clearing land, it is honorable work."

47. Affected by some cause that checks growth, injures, impairs, destroys, or renders abortive. *Webster's Dictionary* (1828), s.v. "Blasted."

wickedness in this and foren lands That those of this generation may be left without excuse that Zion in prosperity may look down on the wicked And say why did you not fall in with us Our arms was open to receive you in to our Habitations If you had only a ben wise But when it is to late for you to return or well do your duty And fall in with the overtures of mercy that would boy up and strengthen the natural mind of man We as a people are much enlightend We have a Prophit Priest and teacher and direct Revelations from the Courts of Heaven above This is your reasonings as you are a wallowing in the mire but as nothing does check you or impede your progress or hinder you on your way But when you get a reading of your doings when you first with many of us did meet we with open arms did receive you and did cheerfully administer to you that you had our best feelings and property to handle of those that possest wealth You have grone up budded and blossomed I think several times but blasted in producing fruit You now have ariven as you dote on the Stand of being an exalted people as ever God had on the Earth But in reading my verse remember that your scrub is girdled at the roots by a greedy worm it was surroundded that the top has lost its nourishement that did formerly flow from the roots Its present moister is gethered from the mud As mud is a nature particular to it self when it is dry it brakes esspecially if it is trod that the pores become closed That will soon be the case with your platform of which you so much bost

[Folder number 6] Nauvoo June 28th

After an absence of one week I have returned to our noted Citty to se what is now agoing worthy of Note Much smoke is araising on every side that denotes some thing that in my daily moves I will find out Thou I am not perticular to look verry close as I have ben long in hopes to get threw with their ungodly doings but I must give them an other round as I find smoke in volumes is araising all around How long God will bear is unknown to me with such conduct And let his name be disgrased by a fallen people That sits in the Dark But him that has power I Heaven above must speak for him self as he antiently has done He then spoke by Judgments when in to wickedness they ran when they had well fild up their cup of Iniquity But now in the latter times Some light must arize enough to streighten Those caled Latter day Saints as I think they have places That is coverd with snags that will have to be knocked of as they look unsafe as they often speak of power to do as they pleas and it is sanctioned in Heaven above because they hold the Keyes of the Kingdom privelege they possess Of daming or saving as they please forse of which I will speak They cal on the members all as one to come forward and lay down their property at their feet that they may rear up a Citty in the name of the Lord as they say to do to fulfil

Prophesighs that by the Antients was wrote But I think when they look down on the Citty of Nauvoo and hear their names mentiond as being honourd by their doings I think if they have light and Inteligance as we by our teachers are informed that their wisdom far excedes Mortals on the Earth vew of the dark doing of the Leaders of our Church I should like to se their recod If it could be my Lot to se the differance between theirs and mine altho myne with theirs would not compare as I have ben rather parshal towards them in all of my writings But let them snuf up their Nose at what I have wrote I will ask them to look back and se what they have long been a bout

[Folder number 7] June 28th 1842

An abstract of a letter written by Oliver Snow[48]

Brother O. H. Olney

I embrace this opportunity to address you on a subject that has of late that considerbly excited my feelings That of your leaving the Church of L.D.S. aquaintance with you[r] family have enquired of me to know why you have taken the course that you have in leaveing the Church of L. D. Saints

Now sir haveing ben perticularly aquainted with you ~~and your family~~ ever since the latter part of part of your being a school boy to the presant time well knowing the high moral character that you sustained previous to your uniting your self to the Church of L D Saints Also from that to the presant time I now ask your reasons for takeing the course that you do in leaving your Standing in the C of L.D.S— Pleas to be perticular in your communication to me and without delay

O. H. O. Respectfully O. S.

48. Oliver Snow, 1st Ward. See Black, *Membership*, 40:608–10. Oliver Snow was the father of Eliza R. Snow, a plural wife of Joseph Smith, and Lorenzo Snow, the fifth president of The Church of Jesus Christ of Latter-day Saints. Oliver Snow was struggling with his feelings about Mormonism in 1842. "John C. Bennett, a counselor to Joseph Smith and mayor of the city, lost his faith and began delivering a series of anti-Mormon lectures. He also published a history of Mormonism that purported to be an expose of its secret practices. Oliver Snow, who was inclined to be critical of people in authority, decided to leave. He bought a home in Walnut Grove, Knox County, Illinois, some seventy-five miles east of Nauvoo, and moved his family there. Rosetta (his wife) did not want to go, but eventually she acquiesced and went with him." Leonard J. Arrington and Susan Arrington Madsen, *Mothers of the Prophets*, 85. Oliver Snow died at Walnut Grove, Illinois, on October 17, 1845.

[Folder number 9] Extract from a letter from Oliver Snow dated June 28th 1842 to Oliver Olney[49]

Sir having been particularly acquainted with you ever since the latter times of your being a school boy to the present time well knowing the high moral character you sustained even previous to your becoming religious &c &c

Oliver Snow

[Folder number 3] June 30th 1842 Citty of Nauvoo

After a number of days absence I return to the noted Citty of Nauvoo to take recognisance of their doings I have not feelings to use them up at once but let them foam out their shame and disgrace in the eyes of the world I will yet tarry with them, as much is a float In their daily moves They speak of a time that much will be don to honour the day of our independance I suppose if they knew of my doings they would say of me as of others that they would give me a pass down the river on the back of a catfish But I think the poor fish must have a hard job as the story is They have propeld infants down the Rappids of the missippi that the river is so cloged that it is with trouble that the Steem boats gets up or down This is but a story I don't think it half true as it comes in contact with their raising up a A richeous Branch

[Folder number 5] 1842 June 30th

After an absence of about ten days I return to the Noted Citty of Nauvoo to take recognisance of their doings I have not feeling to use them up at once but let them foam out their shame and disgrase in the Eyes of the world I think I will tarry with them untill the forth of July as they speak of a time of much being done to honour the cause Of which our fathers fought But I suppose if they knew of my doings they would say of me as of others that they would give me a pass down the Rappids of the Missisipi on the back of a Catfish But I think the poor fish must be tired of their heavy And weary loads as the storys is they have piloted infants that the river is so cloged that it is with trouble that the Steem Boats gets around The steam boats gets up or down This is but a story I don't think its half true as it comes in contack with their teaching of raising up a Righeous Branch

49. Not written in Olney's handwriting. Likely written by Oliver Snow.

JULY 1842

[Folder number 7] Citty of Nauvoo July 1st 1842

Extract of a letter Written by B. S Walker[1] To O. H. Olney

Broth[er] O. H. Olney I with sympethy of feelings address you at this time as a friend and well wisher Desiring to know of you why you have left the Church of L D Saints We have long ben together In Ohio Missouri that I think we can say that we have bourn the burden in the heat of the day Pleas to give me your reasons for leaving the Church of LDS

O.H.O. Yours in haste B.S.W.

[Folder number 7] Citty of Nauvoo July 1 1842

To the Orthortys of the Church of Latter Day Saints

It is with no ordinary feelings that I address my self to you at this time on a subject of which so much is said. The Periodicals of the day are often crouded with matter that had not orto be speaking of the doings of the Church of Latter day Saints. Now on a principal with out respect to [manuscript torn] party I say to you that you know of Your doings (and I am not altogether Ignorant of them) That you as a people had orto clean your self of the Scandal that has long ben heaped on you you know whether the storyes afloat have a foundation. Now I say to you that I have long ben with you as a Member of the Church of Latter day Saints and have kept a recod of their doings (Tho partial to them) That I feel in duty bound to publish to the world, Unless spedy repentance and acknowledgment to the world of the falts that we know has and does exist I shall publish against you and you may repent at your leisure But if you will go ahead in a reformation and honour [manuscript torn] cause that you have espoused I add no more but will as ever be your Friend

Yours O. H. Olney

1. The only person listed in *Membership of the Church of Jesus Christ of Latter-day Saints, 1830–1848* that would be similar to B. S. Walker is Benjamin Walker. However, Benjamin Walker joined the LDS Church in England and never migrated to the United States. Benjamin Walker is not the B. S. Walker who wrote to Oliver Olney.

[Folder number 8] Quincy July 1st 1842

Mr. O. H. Olney. Sir, I would adress you at this time with the same good feelings that we have ever met in the land of our nativity in Conn. Willington, Windham County. I was there in the neighborhood or within a short distance of your connections and friends and the favorable opinion that I had of your being determined to well do your duty in the attitude as a teacher of the gospel. I am sorry to hear that you have left the Church of Latter day Saints. Please to give me your reasons and you will much oblige me.[2]

[Folder number 3] July 2d 1842 Citty of Nauvoo

After an absence of a few days I return to the Citty of Nauvoo to take recognisence of their doings I have not feelings to use them up at once but let them foam their shame and disgrace untill they make themselves known But I suppose if they knew of my doings they would say of me as of others that they would give me a pass

[Folder number 3] July 2nd 1842 Citty of Nauvoo

Two days past has ben atrayning that has made a dull show as there is much ecitement about John Cook Bennett A noted general as he has had a high standing in the Legion at Nauvoo But because of his doings he has to stop by the way as the officers of the Legion is against him A court marshal was Held his case to deside and the women caled as witnesses against him that is said that he has seduced But as I was not at his trial their testimony I cannot pen But report says he was or must be broken of his office in the Nauvoo Legion So I pas by John C Bennett and let him speak for him self as he carrys the tools with him and are ready for use I will now speak of doings That is said to be kept in the dark But busy boddys cannot be Idle but must speak of doings that now is in voge As a company is a forming in to the wilderness to go as far west as the Rocky mountains and that without delay Yes men women and Childern are all in aray to make ready a voige (voyage) amongst the natives of the far west Let this subject be looked to As this is what they say that they must go whire there is no law to baffle them in their doings We will now use some reason and say shall they go amongst the Indians west and abuse the Inocent And raise a strife amongst the red men of the Forest It is with much feelings that I write If this was not the secret whispering amongst certain ones of the Church of L. D. S. and could be easily proven If man could speak But how is the fact not a man dares to come out in contact with the Leaders of the Church of L D Saints except bearly a case of now and then one that are

2. No name is given as to who wrote the original letter of which this is a partial copy.

so circumstanced that they can speak their minds as it is not only a fine and imprisonment but a man is in danger of his life.

[Folder number 5] July 2nd Citty of Nauvoo

Two days past has ben training that has made a dull show as there is much exitement about John Cook Bennet a noted General as he has had a high standing in the Legion at Nauvo[o] But because of his doings he has to stop by the way as the officers of the Legion is against him A court martial was held his case to deside and the women caled as witnesses against him that it is said he has sedused But as I was not in the office there testimony I cannot pen But report say he was or must be broken of his office in the Nauvoo Legion I again Exspress my feelings as on a high hill it being Early in the morning in the month of May When Flowers is opening in all parts of the land That takes the attention as they pass about I se in a low vally a Horable crime That was performed by a Noted people That said to seve God It was to take the life a free man that spoke for him self But alas he is fallen by the use of a sharp knife I long se him welter in the agonys of death[3] That much excited my feelings to think it possible That I could daily be around amongst such an unwise set but I said in my heart It agrees with the teaching on the Stand that I have herd time and again Yes they cote the Case of Annanias and Sofira that fell dead at the Apostles feet because of Lying about their money as I suppose was a facts that they was inhumanly butcherd by a fallen set That will yet have to suffer the penalty of the Law of God as is the case with some in this age that have taken the lives of some few But as it is in the morning when first lite shines and Early in the Season When flowers show let not nothing hinder The crooked to be made strate and that with out delay As a company now is aforming in to the wilderness to go as far as the Rocky Mountains and that with out delay Yes men women and Childern is now in aray To make read[y] a voiage amongst the Natives of the far west Let this subject be look to as this wot they say that they must go whire there is no Law to baffle them in their doings We will now use some reason and say Shall the[y] go west amongs the Indians and abuse the inosent and raise a strife amongst the red men of the forest It is with much feelings that I wright If this was not the secret whisper-

3. Olney mentions John C. Bennett's case and then refers to a future happening he said to have experienced in vision early on a May morning when on a high hill. He witnesses a future "horrible crime" perpetrated by the Latter-day Saints. Olney is likely foreseeing the murder of John C. Bennett, "a free man that spoke for himself." In vision, Olney views Bennett being killed by someone wielding a sharp knife. In actuality, Bennett was not killed by Mormons. He moved away from Nauvoo and wrote *History of the Saints or an Exposé of Joe Smith and Mormonism.*

ing amongst Certin ones of the Latter day Saints and could be esily proven If man could speak But how is the fact Not a man dares Not a member of the Church of Latter day Saints dares to come in contack with the Leaders of the Church as it is not only a fine and imprisenment but a man is in danger of his life I have continued my writing from time to time because of what is daily agoing amongs a certin few that Leads the Church I soon draw my writings to a close and say from principal I have rote not that they have me abused as I am a fre man at home or abroad I speak for my self In all cases I will again speak my feelings in behalf of the Latter day Saints I will speak my mind Wright or wrong that there is many That use no reason They say Joseph is a prophet of God and his twelve is chosen by Revelation and they can neith[er] say or do wrong Thus stands the majority of the Latter day Saints Again their is other of respectability that have minds of their own but what can they do here is their property and here is there home If they lisp an uneasy feeling a stigma is on them thats not easily got off How is it with my self In my daily moves I am alone Because of engaging in this work. My Companion is dead and my Childern is scatterd one hear and one their untill I get threw with this order of things I am not disposed much more time to spend but to publish my writings to the world I then will settle near some pleasant grove on some rich fertile prairee with my Little family and say I have don all I could to Streighten a crooked set of sticks the sun continued a raising some light on me did shine that I se their doing was so abominable that they was caled to give an act [account?] of themselves As they was about to start amongst the Natives of the west I se they had business to last a few days that caused many to mourn of the Church of Latter Saints

[Folder number 3] City of Nauvoo July 3d Sunday

I to meeting this day went Many came to gether to se and to hear The Prophit Joseph arose in the name of the Lord and coted the teachings Of the ancient prophets that Antient Prophits that Antiently did live He spoke of a time That the saints would be vested with power that the wicked would be come ashes under the soles of their feet I said in my hart whire are the Saints Are they amongst this people If they are we dont hear from them Not on the stand altho it is ocupied by many noted ones that speaks loud and heavy all in the name of the Lord I look at them and judge them by their works that I cal Righeous Judgment as it agrees with the word of God I pass by the fore noon meeting as of not much account This afternoon at 2 Oclock meeting commenced Presidant Hirum Smith arose and commenced to speak about many things He spoke of the Elders being many of the Latter Day Saints that hardly a man But what had the P_hood He spoke of a union amongst them As lying and tatling was the theme he spoke of a plaster for it Altho a mistry he would it unfold They should first meet together all in a mess, and apoint one man as a spokesman for all Then let the rest follow And speak his words and any person coming in contact to discountinance them as of no worth He spoke of troubles That followed the Church that was because of unwise doings of the members That put waddles[4] on their backs I thought of a fuss between a man and his wife that they went to whipping their Childern to hush a dirty scrape He spoke of many things that was desined to lead the minds to put their trust in the Prophit Joseph He spoke of J. C. Bennetts case it being of the blackest die He spoke of the gift of discernment that he well knew the hart of man I will admit the fact And say they and Bennett is all of a Clan as they have ben hart and hand together untill within a few weeks I look at the case of Doct Bennett if their testimony is to be received to be no deeper in the mud Than they in the mire If as they say they can dissern The hart of man if they was not connived with him why have they kept him along with such unwise doings as is in voge

[Folder number 5] July 3d Sunday

I to meeting this day went Many came together to se and hear The Prophit Joseph arose in the name of the Lord and coted to the teachings of the Prophits that antiently did live He spoke of a time that the saints would be vested with power that the wicked would become Ashes under the soles of their feet I said in my heart whire are the saints Are they amongst this people If they are we dont hear from them not on the stand Altho it is occupied by many noted ones That speaks loud and heavy all in the name of the Lord But I look at them And Judge them by their works that I cal righeous judgment as it agrees with the word of God I pass by the forenoon Meeting as of not much account and go back this afternoon that I may hear for my self according to apointment meeting commenced Presiden[t] Hiram Smith arose and commenced to speak about many things He spoke of the Elders being many of the Latter day Saints that hardly a man but what had the P hood He spoke of a Union amongst them as lying and tatling was the theme He spoke of a plaster for it altho a mistry yet he would it unfold They should first meet together all in a mess And apoint one man as a spokes man for all Then let the rest follow

4. Olney may have meant "wattles." A twig or flexible rod; and hence, a hurdle. *Noah Webster's First Edition of an American Dictionary of the English Language—Facsimile 1828 Edition*, s.v. "Wattle." A texture of twigs, osiers or sticks; a crate of various forms, according to its destination. *Webster's Dictionary* (1828), s.v. "Hurdle." It appears that Olney's meaning was that the actions of Church leaders were burdens on the backs of its members.

and speak his words and any person coming in contact to discountinance them as of no worth He spoke of troubles that followed the Church that was because of unwise doings of the members That put waddles on their backs I thought of a fus between a man and his wife that they went to whipping them Childern to hush a dirty scrape He spoke of many things that was desined to lead the minds to put their trust in their spokesman the Prophit of God He spoke of John C Bennets case it being of the blackest die He spoke of the Gift of dissernment that he well knew the heart of man Others of the same grade often dost bost that they well know the hart of man I will admit the fact and say they and Bennet is all of a clan as they have ben hart and hand untill within a few weeks I look at the case of Bennet If their testimony is to be received to be no deper in the mood [mud] Than they in the mire If they have such wisdom and power that they well know of mans works If they was not connived with him why have they kept him along in such unwise doing as is in voge I think I am under the necessity of a vision to exsplain this misterous case As I was a traverling along in the dark or in a dul Moon Shine neer the temple lot I look on the flatts and I se a large Company together in the attitude of holding a Council They some time was in clusters and some time in a mass They desided to be united in what they did They went on a season and in order moved untill ambitious feelings arose that raised exitement from time to time Months past away often with dark shades untill it was desided a Righeous Branch must arise This exited feelings of Jealousy that it made a fus marvelous to relate amongst the leaders of the Church This fuss continued a short time but was finaly looked to by the orthorotys of the State I will now speak of my folly in doing what I have don in takeing a retrospective vew of the Church of Latter day Saints When I first commenced to write I thought I had my match to show them their folly by writing But as I have took the run of my mind I have moved my pen now and then in the channel of their doings that I find no need of calling witnesses as everyone that reads will be a witness for him self Any person that will say what I have wrote is not correct mus[t] be a moveing in dark shades My visions speak for themselves that is according to Scripture Daniel had visions So did others If the Bretheren of the twelve should like to clear up their characters I will help you all I can as I am satisfied If reports is true you have formed a Union to stand by each oth[er] at all hasards and assist each other on their way But I think them that stays to home must have a hard time to se to their own wifes and to the wifes of those that is gone I should advise those that is out to come trotting home as the smoke is fast araising but possibly there is no fire

[Folder number 3] July 4th 1842

This day is spent in trayning amongst the Church of L. D. Saints They mett men women and Childern that made a great show some in high life others in low The Elect Lady waited on her Companion in connection with other females well arayed on horses of life The Brigadeer Geneneral in order moved as Prophit Priest and teacher all in the name of the Lord A few days past much has been adoing to honour the day For which our Fathers fought But if our fathers are whire many suppose and have a vew of things That transpires of both presant past and futer they often must Shudder at the daily doings of the L. D. Saints As between one and two hundred thousand[5] is said to be followers of Joseph Smith said to be a prophit of the Most high God But how is it with him What does he do but like Balam Ass cannot speak the word of God but utter sound of a similar kind[6] that darken Counsil Amongs those that mite be wise We look at his doings on the stand aspeaking of the presant State of man of their degraded Condition now on Earth He as others of the same class speaks of the denominations of the day of their fallen Condition in faith and works But I will draw a contrast Between them and those caled L.D.S. They to be in the same grad as the Apostles do not pretend To be orthorised by the Saviour As was them to cast out Deavils raise the Dead But they say to teach The gospel plan according to the best light they have altho in points They do not agree Yet a sympethy of feeling amongst them does exist that forms a union amongst them of the differant denominations of the day But we look at the Latter day Saints They say to have the P_hood as the Apostles and the Prophits, that lived in the first ages of the world But we look at their

---

5. If Oliver Olney actually heard there were between 100,000 and 200,000 followers of Joseph Smith in 1842, it was an exaggeration. LDS Church membership in 1842 was about 23,500. Church membership did not reach 100,000 until 1873. See "Church Statistics," 529.

6. Olney is making reference to the story of Balaam, an Old Testament prophet. In Numbers, chapter 22, Balaam is requested by the king of Moab to pronounce a curse upon the Israelites. Although God forbids him from cursing the Israelites, Balaam does go with the Moabites. God's anger is kindled at Balaam and an angel with a drawn sword is send to Balaam. Balaam does not see the angel, but the ass he is riding upon does and attempts to stop or turn back. Balaam beats the ass, and the beast is given the power of speech to tell Balaam why they should not proceed. Balaam then sees the angel and is told that had he continued the ass would have been spared, but Balaam would have been slain. Olney appears to be somewhat confused about the story, saying, "Balaam's ass cannot speak the word of God, but utters sound of a similar kind that darken counsel amongst those that might be wise." Although it was not Balaam's ass that could not speak the word of God, Olney's meaning is clear. He is accusing Joseph Smith of being a false prophet who is leading his people astray.

power and works Look back to Kirtland and Missouri Did God move in their behalf to assist them in their troubles No they looked But looked in vain to se some power in their behalf Look at them now, In their presant state Hear them bost of their Military forse Se them Maneuver day after day Hear them defy the powers that be They say by our faith And power with God to brake in pieces the Kingdoms of the World They say the stone from the Mountain that was to be cut with out hand spoken of by the Prophit Daniel has now begun to move. Yet small but well under way to brake in pieces subdue and tread underfoot the wicked of this and foren lands

[Folder number 5] Citty of Nauvoo July 4th 1842

This day is spent in training amongst the latter day Saints They met men women and Childern that made a great show Some in high life some in low The Elect Lady waited on her Companion in connection with other females well arayed on horses of life The Brigadeer General in order moved and stood as Prophet Priest and teacher all in the name of the Lord A few days past much has ben adoing to honour the day for which our fathers fought But if our Fathers are whirȩ many suppose and have a vew of things presant past and futer, they often must shudder at what they daily se Of those Latter day Saints But people in all ages speeck for themselves This has ben the order In this age A people has arriven calded Latter day Saints that I for years have ben Conversant with them I well know of their doings I well kn[ow] of their works I well know that they are a fallen people and reject the Councel of God Altho they bost of their power with him in their daily moves here and there But I look at their doings in differant parts as I have ben a traverling and teaching and ben conversant with all classes of the Church The most of the church is in darkness and know not what is a going on amongst those that lead them Their wise leaders have wisdom to preach and to teach and lay a foundation that looks fair to an observer that feels to boast [boost] them ahead But this kind of Logic is now to be broken up As I have to stand in the name of the Lord to use my influance In behalf of his Law His Law to me is familiar That is said to govern man while passing threw a probationary State After writing what I have written to streighten a crooked mess of Sticks I felt to pass by them As of no worth I count as but Chaff in the wind Altho they by many are boyed up as on Eagles wings. By whom but those, that cannot speak for themselves Yes this People is said to be great between one and two hundred Thousand I[s] said to be on the road with Joseph Smith said to be a prophit of the most high God But how is it with him. What does he do but like Balam Ass Cannot speak the word of God But utter sounds of a similar kind That darkens Counsil amongst those that would be wise Altho in days that is past and gone He, we will say was a man of God But how is it now But a degraded man because of his doings now on Earth We look at his doings on the Stand a speaking of the present State of man of their degraded condition now on earth He speaks of the denominations of the day of their fallen condition In faith and works but I will draw a contrast Between them and the Mormons They to be in the same grade as the Apostles do not pretend being orthorised by the Saviour as was them To cast out Deavils raise the Dead But they say to teach the gospel plan according to the best light They receive altho in points They do not agree yet a sympethy of feeling amongst them doth exist that forms a union amongst them of the different denominations of the day But we look at the Latter day Saints They say to have the Priesthood as the Apostles We have power with God as the Prophets that lived in the first ages of the world But we look at their power and at their works Look back to Kirtland. Look to Missouri and se their doings Did God move in their behalf Did he lisp for them No They looked but looked in vain To se some power in their behalf Threw powers above Look at them now in their presant state Hear them boast of their millitary forse Se them maneuver day after day Hear them defy the powers that be They say by our faith and power with God to brake in pieces, Kingdoms of the World. They say the little stone from the mountain has begun to move In order as spoken of by the Prophit Daniel Altho it was and is yet small but is well underway To brake in Pieces and subdue And tread underfoot the wicked of this and foren lands

[Folder number 7] Citty of Nauvoo July 6th 1842

An abstract of a letter written by Israel Barlow[7] to O. H. Olney

Dear sir having had many years aquaintance with you and your family Haveing had the utmost confidence in you as a Christian I verry much regret to se you situated as you are out of the Ch of L D Saints I hope you will have the goodness to give me your reasons in writing why you have left the Church of L.D. Saints.

I. B.

O. H. O.

7. Israel Barlow was born at Granville, Massachusetts, on September 13, 1806. Israel was one of the first to see what would become Nauvoo in November 1839 when he met with Isaac Galland. He was a resident of Nauvoo from 1841 to 1846 and a member of the Nauvoo Third Ward. He was a member of the Zion and Kirtland camps and served a mission to England from 1853–1855. He was ordained a patriarch by Wilford Woodruff in 1882. Israel Barlow died in Bountiful, Utah, in November 1883. See Susan Easton Black, comp., *Membership of the Church of Jesus Christ of Latter-day Saints, 1830–1848*, 3:562–68.

[Folder number 7] Citty of Nauvoo July 6th 1842 Extract of a letter written by James Cummings[8] to O. H. Olney

Brother O. H. Olney,

I improve a leisure moment in asking you a few questions. First, how do you harmonise your former doings with the presant stand if this work is true as you have said Also you have said there is no salvation for those that comes short of their duty in the service of God Pleas to give me your reasons in writing and you will oblige yours &c &c

O. H. Olney — Ja. Cummings

[Folder number 3] Nauvoo July 7th 1842

As my mind is often a meditateing on what daily transpires I look back to the antient men of God I look at those of the presant age but I se not much resemblance unless it is to imitate Those that are fallen and become rejected In the sight of God I look at the doing of the L.D.S. and se the pains they take to cuver up their foibles I se no time is lost to plaster up sores but all as one are engaged to put on a good out side show to cuver up their iniquity or to change in their doings to suit the times But I look at what is now agoing that is said to be of God But let it be spoken of as wrong they then change their tune for one that will answer the times I have learnt some new rincles that I am satisfied will do them no hurt It is a phrase called Phrenology[9] I know that

8. James Cummings was born January 26, 1780, at Dunstable, Massachusetts. He was baptized a member of the church organized by Joseph Smith in 1837 and received his temple endowment in the Nauvoo Temple on January 3, 1846. James and his wife, Susanna Willard, were residents of Nauvoo. James died in Winter Quarters, Nebraska, on March 28, 1847. The letter to Olney from James Cummings may also have come from the son of James and Susanna Cummings, James Willard Cummings. James W. Cummings was born on March 10, 1819, at Wilton, Maine. James W. was also a Latter-day Saint and was ordained to the priesthood office of Seventy. He would have been twenty-three years old and single at the time the letter was written, making it very possible that he was the James Cummings that wrote to Oliver Olney. See Black, *Membership*, 12:594–97.

9. Phrenology is the study of the structure of the skull to determine a person's character and mental capacity. Also known as cranioscopy, it was based on the belief that there are twenty-six organs on the surface of the brain which are responsible for different mental functions. It was asserted that through the use or neglect of these organs, parts of the brain would expand or shrink, affecting the contour of the skull. Thus, by examining the cranium, a person's intellectual and emotional functions could be determined. The theory was developed by Viennese physician

much of it is said but of its merits and demerits I canot say But I suppose we must say it is correct A gentleman of honour by the name of A Crane M.D. that did officiate in our Citty on some few heads He spoke of their traits being governed by bumps On their heads that much encouraged many because of the good qualities of Joseph Smith He of A C a chart did receive that I find in the wasp at Nauvoo

Amativeness 11 L extreme sussectably Passionately fond of women (Correct)

Philoprogenetiveness 9 L strong parental affection great solisitude for their hapiness

Adhesiveness 8 F Solicitious for the happiness for Friends an ardent desire for females[10]

I mite continue an alegory of the rest of the Chart but I suppose it is correct It speak of bumps As of adhesiveness of being powerful and strong I think he has nothing to fear but to go a head What he looses on one hand if he gains on the other All is well But the gem of Great Price of which he doth so much bost is flead is gone That they have not it got Yes your curses pronounced by the Orthoroty of the P_hood was labour spent in vain but I have feelings To encourage you so go a head in masonry Phrenology Danite Ism and train every once in a few days and bost of your power with God to move in power and wisdom in this and forren lands Also go ahead in Poligemy and raise up a Righeous branch some whire near the Rocky Mountains in the far west, Whire no law can tuch you or hinder you on the way I now say I will draw all to a close by adding some writings of Friends as Friends I have many that doth wish me well But what hurts my feelings is they and I do not se alike They write to me their feelings that is of the best kind To establish my name and their faith in the Prophit J Smith Again I have feelings my self to defend when abused by pettish And course hared pups I will speak of a sett In the form of men that lives down the river Above the steem mill They there have a standing in the name of the Lord as Elders of the Church of L D Saints but their doings does them forbid of being linked with the human race Their

---

Franz-Joseph Gall. Gall referred to the study of the bumps and indentations as cranioscopy. Thomas Foster called the work of Gall and others who advanced the same theory as phrenology. Although it enjoyed early popularity, phrenology has been thoroughly discredited. See Davis Bitton and Gary L. Bunker, "Phrenology Among the Mormons," 42–61.

10. The chart was published in the July 2, 1842, *Wasp*. Olney mostly quoted correctly the portion of the chart he included. He also added parenthetical comments, such as "correct" when referring to Joseph Smith fondness for women.

works denotes A class of beings of which history gives no account but yet on Earth they have a place Thus we must admit That they had a creation one that says to rule the roost I think they cal Ballard An other of a scrufy look they call Eavans and other Big oneyed [one-eyed?] concern Balden by name that denotes a Rough he goat Yet there is more on the wing that speaks much of their power with God I could for them devise a plan that they mite arise from their presant State I would say to eight or ten to form a ring all in a sollid mass and bind with chords that could not easily be loosed Then go threw a firey flam one that would melt lead or sar [?] of any kind and run the resk of the change in states They would run no resk more than a grub that is often found in the root of logs as they in Heaven cannot be known exsept as beings to fill the immensity of space Of course they have no souls to loose or save In speaking of them An other set I will link that I suppose have soles to save as I think they have out stript the Deavil that he with them will not get ketched whire there is so much power of Combattiveness And not Mindyourbusitiveness and such felloniousness and comparativeness and perplexetiveness and Laciviousness Fornicationess, Audultersness And many other Subteranases To numerous to mention But I will fetch them in prose as that of writing I can enlarge as is the custom amongst the Calves I will now draw my writings to a close by subscribing my self a friend to those that can think and speak for themselves when my writings comes to vew But those that cannot may look for themselves Oliver H Olney is my name and English is my Nation[11] I have no a biding place and blest is my Salvation

[Folder number 5] Nauvoo July 7th 1842

As my mind and my person Is roveing about I se much a doing That often makes me look with amasement To se what is a going on I look back to the Antients That once on Earth lived and now and then ask questions How it was with them Did they Labour and toil both by knight and day to cuver up their Iniquity or to change in their doings to suit the times But I look at

11. Historian Dale L. Morgan hypothesized that Oliver Olney was originally from England. He wrote, "From the internal evidence from these papers, it would appear that Oliver H. Olney was born in England." See Dale L. Morgan, *Dale Morgan on the Mormons, Collected Works, Part 1, 1939-1951*, 475. The confusion over Olney's place of birth likely comes from what he wrote as the last lines of his July 7, 1842, entries found in both folder number 3 and folder number 5: "Oliver H Olney is my name and English is my nation I have no abiding place and blest is my salvation." Olney was born in Connecticut. He did not write "England is my nation," but rather "English is my nation." One could surmise that because Olney spoke English and because he was trying to find something to rhyme with "salvation," he chose to write "English is my nation."

what is now a going that is said to be of God But let it be spoken of as wrong they then change their tunes for one that will answer the times But I look at their folly And say in my heart that I think they have about threw with their presant order of things Yet I have learnt some new rincle that I know nothing about But suffise it to say It will do them no hurt But it is a phrase Cald Phrenology I know that of it much is said I suppose we must say it is correct A gentleman of honour By the name of A Crane MD that did of ficiate in our Citty on some few heads He spoke of their traits being governed by bumps On their heads that much encouraged many because of the good qualitys of Josephs He of A.C. a chart did receive that I find in the wasp of Nauvoo

Amitiveness 11-L extreme sussectibilyty of Passionately fond of women (Correct)

Philoprogenitiveness – 9 L Strong parrental affection great solicitude for their happiness (jest so)

Adhesiveness – 8 F solicitious for the happiness for friends And ardent attachment to females I mite continue an allegory of the rest of the chart but I supose it is correct It speak of bumps as of Adhessiveness be bein powerful and strong I think he has nothing to fear but to go ahead What he looses on one hand if he gains on the other all is well But the gem of great prise of which you bost is fled is gone That you have not it got Yes your curses pronounced by the orthoroty of the Priesthood was Labour spent in vain but I have feelings to encourage you on the way Go ahead in Masonry Phrenology and Daniteism And train every once in a few day and bost of your power with God to move in power and wisdom in this and foren lands Go ahead in Poligemy and raise up a righeous branch some whire neer the Rocky Mountains in the far west Whire no law can tuch you or hinder you on your way I will now speak to you of your folly of your with me haveing a fuss What did I do but mind my own business I was caled before the council of 15 men I well knew their weakness and of their weak spots Some fat and Some lean Some high and Some low All moved together in the name of the Lord a padling along in the mud I arose and spoke to them in my behalf and made a comparison That they did not understan but I now will explain it as it spoke for it self They it mite have understood I had tried to get an intervew with Josep[h] and with the twelve time and again Yes I caled on them time and again and was neglected and abused by them untill I said in my heart I will have no more to do with them I said in my heart I will now take my cause and study my own book as I pleas But as soon as they se I could speak for myself they concluded to me arrest But I have soft soaped them from that time untill this by being familliar with them both early and late Yes they have told many of their tales That I have pened without adding but diminishing much O yes I was not worth their notice They to me did look with disdain Now se what you have got by it In plain English I will speak of your standing and doings from this time forth A curse is on you Both heavy and severe and with you will continue untill the Day of Judgment Look back and se your folly of which you have often bost with out premeditating of what you have ben about I could say more to you to encourage you but your works is such that you had orto be damed Look at a female That I have seen this day worn out because of members that with her has daily ben The doings shall be known when her husband returns from a long Mission to palestine[12] I will no more write visions but establish facts As testimony on testimony is a waiting to speak Yes and look at other females that their names are well known that have ben a bused by those say to lead Yes how are they disgrased how was it don It was don by those who say to have

12. The man that Olney was referring to as being on a long mission to Palestine was Orson Hyde. In a conference held in April 1840 at Nauvoo, Orson Hyde was called to serve a mission that would eventually take him to the Holy Land. On October 24, 1841, Hyde climbed the Mount of Olives and there offered a prayer dedicating Jerusalem for the return of the Jews and as a site for a future temple. See Susan Easton Black, *Who's Who in the Doctrine and Covenants*, 143. Hyde returned to Nauvoo on December 7, 1842. In the above document dated July 7, 1841, Olney mentions "a female that I have seen this day worn out because of members that with her has daily been. The doings shall be known when her husband returns from a long mission to Palestine." The female was Marinda Nancy Johnson, wife of Orson Hyde and sister of Oliver Olney's wife, Alice. There is documentation that Marinda Hyde became one of Joseph Smith's plural wives while Orson Hyde was away on his mission to the Holy Land. While there is no question that Marinda Nancy Johnson became a plural wife of Joseph Smith, there are two different dates given as to when. The first date, recorded by Thomas Bullock, is April 1842, which would clearly have been while Orson Hyde was serving a mission. The second date, May 1843, comes from Marinda herself in an affidavit she signed in 1869. See Brian C. Hales, *Joseph Smith's Polygamy*, 1:452–55. If the second date is correct, Orson Hyde would have been back in Nauvoo when the sealing or marriage to Joseph Smith took place. Concerning which date is correct, the question is "Was Orson Hyde aware that his wife was entering into a polygamous relationship with Joseph Smith?" The larger question is "Why was Joseph Smith marrying women who already had husbands, and, in this case, a husband who was a member of the Quorum of the Twelve?" It is uncertain as to how much information Olney would have had during this time. He was not one of the "insiders" who were instructed by Joseph Smith or other Church leaders about plural marriage. Olney had certainly heard rumors that polygamy was being practiced by some leaders of the Church, and there is a possibility that he may have spoken directly to Marinda. Had Olney's wife, Alice, not died before this time, it would have been possible that she could have received information from her sister and shared it with Oliver.

power to do in the Name of the Lord I now say I will draw all to a close by adding some writings from friends that dared to speak to me in the dark I will say I took the advantage of them to establish my name as I exspect to be scandalised and trodden underfoot but I have caled on as good and independant men as the Church affords and I can say I respet them for the faver they have don me in giving me a pass But in speaking of them I will speak of another set That I know of whifet[13] dogs that often does bark They are barking or scowling or making a fus To arise in the esteem of the bawling calves I know of a next that I think have mixed brede with skunks as a sent arises from them that is hard to penetrate Its down the River above the Streem mill a whifit by the name of Ballard is said to rule others is accessary One skunk that badly stinks that they cal eaven a pettish pup He is streaked and speckled with many streaks An other one eyed dog looks large but his breed is such that he stands in connection with a rough he Goat The rist of the mongrel breed that speaks of the folly of man indeed What can be said what can be don with such a set as I have described Under what power will they be ruled as I think they have outstriped the deavil that he with them will not get ketched Whire there is such power of Combativeness and not mind your busitiveness and such felloniousness and comparativeness and perplexitiveness and Laciviousness fornicationess and sellsiousness [salaciousness?] Amurderdeness and many more subirtivenesses[14] to numerous to mention But I will fetch them in prose as that of writing I can enlarge as is the practise amongst the calves I will now draw my writings to a close by subscribing myself a friend to those that can speak for themselves when my writings comes to vew But those that cannot may look and learn

Oliver H Olney is my name and English is my Nation I have no abiding place and blest Is my Salvation

[Folder number 7] Nauvoo July 8th 1842 Extract of a letter from Hyrum Smith to Olivery Olney

Dear Friend and Brother

As the energes of my mind is exited in your behalf I would ask you why you come in Contact with the High Council that you must realise is established by Revelation to try and and put in order wrongs foibles and difficultys that occurs in the Church of L.D.S. You by them have ben tried now do you think

---

13. Olney likely meant "whippet" dogs. A whippet is a medium-sized breed of dog that originated in England. Descending from greyhounds, they resemble smaller greyhounds.

14. Likely referring to "subvert" or being "subversive."

to be justifed in not hearing to their Council There is a rong either in you or them They as a council are to be sustained As they are not inferior to any other council on the Earth You have my best wishes.

O.H.O. Hy. S.

[Folder number 7] Citty of Nauvoo July 8th 1842

An abstract of a letter written by J. D. Parker to O H Olney

Brother O H Olney It is with peculiar feelings that I Address you As we long have ben Acquainted and often together in Kirtland Ohio and in Missour[i] I have noted that you at all times moved in accordance with the Church of Latter D Saints But I understand that you have left them Pleas to give me your reasons for this doing and you will oblige yours J.D.P.

O.H.O.

[Folder number 6] Nauvoo July 9th 1842 ~~Life of Adam~~

A praise and honour to God to be pend [penned] in honour of the sitting of the Antient of days That assembled the 9 10 11 of June that is to be sung in all ages by the Saints in commencement of all Solem Occasions such as thanksgiving and prayers to God Visins and blessings from Heaven is desending by the power and magesty of the most high Let those that have feelings to be up and adoing in the name of the Lord both late and early let man be a doing and well do his duty In times that is to come as the antients is awaiting to be instructing and influenceing those that have feelings to arise and do their duty in the fear of God In honour and riches Let no one bost as it is but by gifts such is received Let mind and boddys that is weak and feble remember that time is but a drug Let all do their duty and trust in God as messengers are assending and desending They have put things in commotion that will cause a Revolution in this and foren lands Much is adoing that speaks of a savior That died that has taken a stand on the Earth A spirit of confusion discord disunion is the theme from this time forth But the time has ariven, That much is adoing to prepare for the coming of the son of man as he is soon a comming In power and Glory and restore all things as at first Let those that have wisdom be up and adoing as the time has a riven For light to shine Dark Shades must be removed in honour of the Saviour, That has took his stand on the Earth A stand he has taken to accomplish his doings as is sp[o]ken of by the Antients that long since lived on the Earth Threw them he has spoken And is adoing to accomplish a work of importance on the Earth

[Folder number 6] Sunday July 10th 1842 Life of Adam

I O. H. Olney being caled by an Angel of power to write the life of the Antient men of God I am first caled to write the life of Adam a noted man with his head Silverd ore [o'er] his locks are long and Curly His frame is Strait and tall with eyes dark and roleing [ruling?] and skin clear and light with stature strong and portly[15] His mind was directly centerd to do the will of God He had a mind for fredom Implanted within that give power to act As an agen[t] for himself Light and dark was set before him that he could plainly se his duty that was due to God Inteligance rold around him that the vision of his mind opened that he se clearly the order of God He thus became conversant With the Father and the Son He by them was instructed and learnt the Law of God As it was plain and easy He did soon understand That he had to use wisdom in passing threw his Probationary State He thus did set a pattern Or led the way for his decendants That should follow him His mind was much enlightend by the Council of God As he was daily conversant about matters and things, He had power given him to roam whire he pleased From East to west The Earth was rich and fertile with rivers brooks and Springs Naught but peace and Harmony on it did rest Beast Birds and fishes and many creeping things was of found in groups and sometimes alone Thus Adam often looked And vewed the senes that often passed around him in his daily moves He at last became uneasy because of his lonely lot And asked the God of Heaven to give him a pardner For life. Thus the Father condecended to grant him his request, That from the side of Adam the Father took a rib. That from it he formed a female that Adam took for a wife She with him was familiar both Early and late. She added much to his Comfort As they traveld about, They had wisdom of God that his atributes they named and a foundation was established for generations to arise As the time had ariven for the Law to be put in forse as the Law was easy And well understood Tho not to be turned to the wright or left Then arises a power That stood in the dark and throwed out enticement On different points that often baffled and decoyed their minds of Adam and his companion That he caled Eave From time to time they were baffled because of the tempter that to them did come The Father forsook them After the Law was given that they stood in the Strength of man By the insinuation of Satan They broke the Law by picking and Eating Fruit That they was forbidden to do Thus a rejoicing then soon ensued by the powers of Darkness That had fallen from Heaven Thus the Ice was broken At the be-

15. The modern meaning of the word "portly" is rather heavy or fat; stout; corpulent. In the nineteenth century the word also had a different meaning: Grand or dignified in mien; of a noble appearance and carriage. *Webster's Dictionary* (1827), s.v. "Portly."

guining of time for Satan to have power over the disobediant for six thousand long years The Father and Son to his childern did return and ask some questions That did them disturb but they acknowledge The wrong they had don and was willing to give Satisfaction to the Satisfaction of the Father and Son But Gods Law was broken And a penalty annext that no shadow of turning would do but man must fall From their present Standing on the Earth

[The following continuation of Olney's "Life of Adam" comes from the July 26 page written upside down.]

Thus a change was predominant all over the Earth The Earth divided into fragments The creveces soon fild with the waters from the north that pored in torents from the North The thorn and the thistle soon came forth that causes sorrow and Lamentation amongst man beast birds and fishes because of the curse that on them did rest Heat and cold in extremes did come Wet and dry was the theme on the Land on which was pronounced a curse that it would not produce in its strength Again death and sorrow soon became the theme because of the degraded sittuation caused by the transgression of Man But this aged Parent looked amased in connection with his partner by his side to se what had took place His eyes was opened to se far and neer And understand the destiny of man

Star Light or twinklin ~~light~~ plain is often vewed by man thats traverling threw a probationary state while threw a vale of tears The time has come for man to arise and show his faith by works Thou man is of a roveing nature He often forgets what is true light Let the mind that would be valient must gain the praise by faith and works as it is a prise of value that of it none but Zions Childern knows Let Zions Childern be united in the theme of right and truth as the theme of truth is Noble It is a praise that but few knows of it because of the fallen state of man But the time is now ariving that the saints must take a stand and persevere in well doing to prepare for the coming of the son of man as he is now awating The time for to arive that he on Earth may have a standing with the saints that long since died The antients long have ben a wating that they on Earth mite take a stand but now they have a theme before them as they on Earth have took a stand Thus they have a work before them that have begun and a foundation laid It is a foundation immoveable Wind and water over it has no power but its on the rock of ages now begun and soon will arise On Zions tower The tower of Zion will arise as light on it will shine no more to be baffled by the folly of Man Let the saints that long have ben a labouring remember well their Saviours Life as he was humble meek and loly That was a pattern for the saints Let the saints be up and adoing As the time is drawing neer for a separation between the tares and wheat

[Folder number 6] Citty of Nauvoo

Dear Sir[16] with feeling of no ordinary kind I addres you at this time Is [I] say in my heart we are far apart that hinders an intimacy that would between us exist I have so much to write that I do not know where to beguin as much is adoing It would make you laugh To se what is adoing in these parts all is in Commotion The old and young is all a talking and looking and gaseing to se what will be don to get things streightend amongst the L— [LDS] Adultry fornication Laciveosesnes is a speaking loud of it doings as The storys is babys is found in the river slily put away that is makeing a disturbance among the boatman because of cloging the boat in passing the rappids Much is adoing that is pleasing At the same time doings that comes under the head of people of God they like the sow have fast ben a wallowing that they are about coverd with mud I have a History of their ungodly doing that is ready to go to the press It will speak to them at the same time raise raise a mist that I shall have a chance to make you a visit I will take the tale with me and give you a correct history of what is and has ben and the situation of our friends

[Folder number 8] Nauvoo July 10th 1842 not read[17]

As much is adoing in the name of the Lord I feel to do as I am shone I often have ben shone my course to take That all mite move in order as is desined by the Antient of Days as this is a time of their sitting I to them draw near As I calt it an honour with them to meet I have by them much instructions received that tends to strengthen And enliven the mind I now am caled on a work for to do that will aid much to the doings of the L.D. Saints A temporal kingdom Is now to be reard by him that has wisdom That is of God that the saints on Earth may have a standing in honour of the Father and Son as was spoken of by the Antients that should in the last days take place Thou art Cald by the Orthoroty of the Council of Heaven to prepare for a new order of things As you have much before you to do that is a wating for you to be about it you have got in a measure threw with the history or foibles of the Church that you now are caled to publish to the world that the secrets in past may be made known of what has took place in this age of time You are now caled to receive and secure the treasures of the Earth to do such things as will establish such things as shone to you to do from time to time Let your mind be to gain information respecting establishing a new stake of Zion at

16. No name given as to whom this letter was written.
17. Unsure as to what "not read" means here.

Squaw Grove[18] and Johnsons Grove[19] as you have ben shone after you have come back from St Louis you then will be caled to go directly and secure the two places get a quit claims[20] deed of all the wrights at both places of timber You are 1st caled to go and do it without being incumberd with your family. You can go as the way opens before you with team or other ways You have much now to do in a short time as you will be directed by me that have taken a stand with you for a short time that I can teach you and se that you make no mismoves in your doings I am Hipsebah[21] one of the Antient of days that have this day sit in connections with others to do and establish certin things that to be don to forward the work of the Lord You are caled on the morrow to receive the treasures of the Earth in gold and silver that was put away by the antient Nephites on the bank of the River below this at a place whire you will be shone you are caled to secure it by digging and receiving it to your care

[Folder number 6] Citty of Nauvoo July 12th 1842

My mind has ben running on things that is past and gone more perticularly from 1839 I then was visited by a messenger from above that spoke his mind to me That did me supprise He told of a work that of me was required to move in connection With the messengers above This to me was supprising As the Messenger I well knew that appeard to me in person and freely spoke his mind. His Name was David Pattin[22] one of the twelve Apostles chosen in the

18. Squaw Grove, Illinois, is a township about two hundred miles northeast of Nauvoo. White settlers began coming into the area and claiming land in the mid-1830s. Squaw Grove is believed to have been the first township settled in De Kalb County. Henry L. Boies, *History of De Kalb County, Illinois*, 506–7.

19. Johnson's Grove was the site where the first white inhabitants settled in that part of De Kalb County, Illinois. It is located within Clinton Township about sixty miles west of Chicago, but there is nothing there today. There is a Johnson's Grove Cemetery not far from Johnson Grove site.

20. A deed of release; an instrument by which all claims to an estate are relinquished to another without any covenant or warranty, express or implied. *Webster's Dictionary* (1828), s.v. "Quitclaim."

21. According to Olney, Hipsebah was one of the Ancient of Days who visited and gave him instructions. There is no Hipsebah in the Bible or Book of Mormon; however, there is a Hephzi-bah mentioned in 2 Kings 21:1. She was the wife of King Hezekiah of Judah and mother of King Manasseh. Hipsebah was not a totally uncommon name during the lifetime of Oliver Olney. A number of people named Hipsebah lived in the nineteenth century, almost all them women.

22. The messenger said to have visited Olney was the deceased David W. Patten. Patten was born at Theresa, New York on November 14, 1799. He was introduced to Mormonism by his brother John, who also baptized David in June 1832. David Patten was chosen as one of the first members of Mormonism's Quorum of Twelve

Last Days to bring about the Latter day Glory in honour of the Son of God My mind was uneasy Because of what I had seen but I took the same course That I hitherto had untill 1840 I was visited again I then was instructed In many things that looked to me strange That I should them receive They daily was with me And with me did freely converse about such things as tended to expand my mind They told me of things that I had to perform and often assisted me In my doings They kept me in business both knight and day that much encouraged me on my way I often was caled a journey to take some business to do That had lain in the Dark I was shone of the power that God would display to establish his name on the Earth I was shone of many things That was to be don by legally orthorised servents on the Earth The Law and the testimony was to be seald and bound up that man on Earth mite be left without exscuse I to the four quarters of the Earth was caled and there was shone what was to be don that the Spirit of God should be withdrawn and the business part of Community broke up as to a prospect of getting rich and that a curse on them should rest that should liberate the opresst I again was caled to take the second round and put on them a tenfold curse that causes confusion discord and disunion in all parts of the Earth As I was often adoing As I was shone it raised excitement amongst the Orthorotys of the Church They soon caled on me To give an act [account?] of myself that I cheerfully did In hopes with them to sympethise But the hand of Opression was on me that I took from them my name and moved in accordance With the Holy Ghost I was instructed in many good things often visited by Angels In Spirit and in person At last the Saviour unto me did come and manifested to me his feelings That was good I then was visited by the Antient of days They freely conversed with me about many good things They spoke of their doings and what must be don first to cleanse and puryfy the church They had shone me from time to time of the Massacre that would follow such ungodly works That a contention would arise first in the Church Then would come in the Orthorotys of some few States that will cause sorrow and sighing amongst men women and Childern of the Church of the Latter day Saints

[Folder number 7] Citty of Nauvoo July 12th 1842

Extract of a letter written by <u>S Stoddard</u> To O. H. Olney

---

Apostles in February 1835. Conflict arose between the Mormons and other residents of northern Missouri in 1838. Patten died October 25, 1838, after being wounded at the Battle of Crooked River. See Arnold K. Garr, Donald Q. Cannon, and Richard O. Cowan, eds., *Encyclopedia of Latter-day Saint History*, 900.

I with sympethy of feelings write to you at this time to know why it is that you do not move as usu[a]l with the Ch. of L.D.S. We have long had an intimacy That is hard to break up I look back at the time that we first met say eight years ago Since that you and I have shared in ups and downs of the Church of L.D.S. pleas to write to me of your presant vews of things

O. H. Olney S B Stoddard

[Folder number 6] Citty of Nauvoo July 12th 1842

My mind has ben a running on things that is past and gone more perticularly from 1839 I then was visited by a messenger from above that spoke his mind to me That did me supprise He spoke of a work That of me would be required to move in connection with the messengers above This to me was suppris-ing as the Messenger I well knew that appeard to me in person and freely spoke his mind His name was David Pattin One of the Chosen twelve to bring about the Latter day Glory in honour of the Son of God My mind was uneasy because of what I had seen but I took the same course that I hitherto had until 1840 I was visited again I then was instructed In many things that looked to me strange that I should them receive They daily met with me and with me did freely converse of things that did tend to enlighten the mind They showd me of a work That I had to do to bring about the order of God as the Law and testimony as is by God decreed that workman of pleasure may move together to form and Create anew The time is at hand for man to arise In honour of God by displaying his power by raising the Dead and changeing the Elements from heat to cold or reverse Also heat and cold will be subject to their word Again as Moses had power over the Egyptians to opress them with plages from time to time so will be the Order of the destruction of the wicked that all may be left without Exscuse against the Comming of the Son of Man as he soon is a comming with his saints in the air

A feast of fat things for the Chosen ones are a prepareing that will enlighten their minds that they may become established in their daily doings as much is adoing and to be don Let those that have feelings Gods will to perform look well to his sayings as he means what he says to bring about his purposes that a rest may be established no more to be changed By sayings or the preceps of Man Let those that have wisdom and say Gods will to perform remember the path of the Saviour while he was a traverlin on the Earth He there set a pattorn for those that with him would coencide of his descendants or friends Was to come to light that the wicked of the land mite be left with out exscuse I was caled to take a Journey to the four quarters of the Earth or so far as the Gospel had ben preached and bind up the Law and seal the testimony The first and second round I was soon caled to take and withdraw the spirit of God in part that a consternation Amongst the people might arise That partition walls might fall between man and his fellow man that the hireling and servent mite be set free To do and say for themselves A famine of seven long years is decreed not only a lack of food But of Coin and of whire with to do business that discord and Confusion mite be the Lot of those that reject the Council of God

[Folder number 3] Citty of Nauvoo July 14th 1842

I yet have feeling my mind to expres about matters and things that transpires I look at the Elders of the L D. Saints as I take a retrospective vew of their doings In my moves about I often se them with each other contend about matters and things and Shamfully abuse the members that are under their care I will mention a case That came to my vew that is not in the dark at all as he and his family has long ben with the Church of L D. Saints They with them in Ohio did unite and from thence to Missouri did go in obediance to the teachings of the Orthorotys of the Church of L. D. Saints They there spent their time untill the Church was driven out They with others Picked up things and started and getherd in the subburbs of the Citty of Nauvoo But because of unwise doings Of the Church he has sold out his possessions and has picked up to clear out As I have kept my eye on the doings I will simply tel the tale how it has ben with him untill the presant time He met with the Church in Union He lent them money in good faith that they was honest upright and just They baffled him in payments from time to time That his feelings was hurt untill he was under The necessity to say that many of the Leaders Had to him lied He received abuse from them untill his patience was gone and said this is not of God or God has changed in his doings from what he antiently did His money he has lost and is about to clear out with what he has got for his possession But what do we hear from those that say to be the watchman on the tower They say he had orto be robed [robbed] on the way as he is about to leave the place Again they say he and his son that has heretofore gone because of such bad works had orto be murderd by being chopped from head to foot This is the destiny of those that say to clear out They have to slip away if they speak of being dissatisfied If not they go and come as they pleas Testim[ony] on testimony Will speak if caled and establish the facts That I have rote His name is Jacob Wirick[23] And son Wm I bearly mention his case

---

23. Jacob Wirick was born May 22, 1787, in Bedford County, Pennsylvania. He married Mary McCoy in 1811 and moved to Ohio. The couple had been devout Calvinists but converted to Mormonism about 1837 and moved to Far West, Missouri, to be with the Saints. Abandoning their farm when the Mormons were

as a sample that whire there is money or goods they contrive some plan to get it if they can They are not perticular in the course they take The story is get it in the name of the Lord and then its theirs And all is well The above case that I have aluded to is bearly one hundreds can speak and tell near the same tale of the advantage being taken of them I now come to a close as ever a friend to wright But discard wrong

O H Olney

[Folder number 5] Nauvoo July 14th 1842

I yet have feeling my mind to express about matters and things that daily transpires I look at the Elders of the Latter day Saints as I take a retrospective vew of their doings In my moves about I se them with each other contend about matters and things and Shamefully abuse the members that are under their care I will mention a case That came to my notice that is not in the Dark at all as he and his family has long ben with the Church They with them united in Ohio and from there to Missouri did go in obediance to the teaching of the Othorotys of the Church of L.D.S. They there spent their time untill the church was driven out They picked up their affairs and stardted because of the fus in that Country and have setled in suburbs of Nauvoo But because of doings and of bad works of the Church he has sold out his possession and has packed up to clear out As I have kept my eye on the doings I will simply tel the tale How it has ben with him untill the presant time He met with the Church in union He lent them money In good faith that they was honest upright and just They baffled him in payment from time to time That his feelings was hurt untill he was under the necessity to say that many of the Leaders had to him lied He received abuse from them untill he got out of patience and said this is not of God or God has changed in his doings from what he antiently did His money he has lost And is about to clear out with what he has got for his possession But what do we hear from those that say to be the watchman on the tower They say he had orto be robed on his way as he is about to leave the place Again they say he and his son that has heretofore

expelled from Missouri, the Wirick family moved into a log school house twenty-five miles from Quincy, Illinois. In September 1841, they moved to Nauvoo. Becoming disillusioned with Mormonism, Jacob sold his farm in Nauvoo and moved to Paw Paw, DeKalb County, Illinois. Wirick died on February 6, 1868. William Wirick was one of Jacob and Mary's twelve children. William was born May 3, 1818, making him twenty-four years old when Olney wrote this. Jacob Wirick is mentioned in *History of De Kalb County, Illinois*. "William Rogers located at what is now East Paw Paw, where he kept a tavern until 1842, when he sold to Jacob Wirick." Henry L. Boies, *History of De Kalb County, Illinois*, 830.

left Because of such works had or to be murderd By being chopped from head to foot This is the destiny of those that say to clear out They have to slip away if they become dissatisfied If not they go and come as they pleas Testimony on testimony will speak if cald and establish the facts that I have wrote His name is Jacob Wirick at home and abroad I bearly have mentioned his case as a sample that whire there is money or goods they contrive some plan to get it if they can They are not perticular of the course they take The story is to get it in the name of the Lord and then its theirs And all is well The above case that is mentioned is bearly one hundred can speak and tell the tale of their propertys being the same I now come to a close as ever a friend to wright but discard wrong Is my theme

O. H. Olney

[Folder number 7] Letter to Oliver Olney from Joseph Smith written by William Clayton

Nauvoo July 15th 1842

Mr O. H. Olney

Yours of today has been received and in answer I have only to say that we request that you would make known to us the matter referred to in your letter, and in order to have a privilege of hearing, we have appointed Sunday evening next at 4 o clock at President Hyrums office, this you will please attend to –

Yours resp- Joseph Smith

By Wm Clayton Clerk

Mr O. H. Olney

[Folder number 6] Citty of Nauvoo July 16th 1842

Thou are caled at this time to prepare your self for what you have to do to bring about the purposes of God You are caled to introduce your self to the Leaders of the Church again as your work is not finished with them they are alooking to know what to do to get an intimacy with you as they vew your daily moves Your are cald to write them and address your Letter to the Leaders of the Church of Latter day Saints and subscribe your name to it O. H. Olney Your are to request of them an answer Whether they will hear you or not if they will hear you you are caled to meet with as many as sees fit to meet togeth[er] to hear you and plainly tel them the course that God has taken with you but not in full say nothing of the P hood or of the famine or of a mobs comeing on them or of Polygemy or their cases of Audultry or fornication Lasiviousness & but speak of binding up the Law and sealing up the testimony and reason with them on the subject Speak of the sitting of the Antient of days and of their doings and the days they set 9-10-11th of June 1842 And show them the order of the days that from this time forth they are to be kept as days of Prayer and Thanksgiving to God That all difficultys shall be Ajusted before these days that no broils shall arise to disturb minds Sho them plainly that the Antient of days have sit and their first business is to clens and purify the Church And have taken possession of the Kingdoms of the Earth and the Kingdom spoken of by Daniel is about to be established on the Earth And that the son of man has come in power and took his stand on the Earth to prepare the way for the Getherin of the saints and his kingdom to be reard in honour of his name That all things may move in order in honour of his name That a Righeous Branch may be raised up amongst the Gentiles that will honour the name of the Lord

I today have ben a looking And vewing things as they pass that comes to my notice in the Citty of Nauvoo This day much is adoing or much smoke does fly that speaks loud of something Not very good A case has come to light that in the absence of one of the twelve That his wife by the Prophit was abused that that has caused disunion That the Elder [was Send? usherd?] out and his wife left alone As much is agoing or much being said I now stand still to se the Salvation of God As much is adoing that speaks of the degraded state of man The boat is a movein and well under way that I se in vision on the Missippi River I se it moveing with the current of the stream that some little excited my feelings As I was in it it moved in good order towards a precipice of about twenty feet It was steadyed by workman That had power to steir the current To the center of the stream I there was amased To se what was to come that we had to go down with the deep waters But in passing down the torrent I safly went threw And safly did land I then had the interpetation That looked to me plain that the boat applyed to the Church of the Latter day Saints and the river applyed to the times and doings of the Church of L. D. Saints They continue on neer the falls that applied to the destruction that was to come I se myself with them all threw the times but was liberated from them by the power of God and left them in the water or mire no more to extricate themselves Thus the vision past away in dismal looks that caused sorrow and Lamentation amongst the Latter day Saints

[Folder number 7] Citty of Nauvoo July 16th 1842

To the Leaders of the Church of Latter day Saints I at this time address my self to you in writing on the principal of thinking it my duty [manuscript torn] not that I desire to croud my self in to [manuscript torn] whire I am not wanted or put myself in [manuscript torn] least in their way But with the best of feelings I write and on the same principal I will [manuscript torn page] with as many of the heads of the Church as [manuscript torn] considered wisdom to notice me as I am [manuscript torn] that I have an actual knowledge of some [manuscript torn] that is for the good and welfare of the Church of Latter day Saints that they know nothing about that is with me a dead secret that I [manuscript torn] willing to devulge to the leaders of the church if they request it of me But if not I am as [manuscript torn] willing to take my own course as usual with the same good feeling To be sure I have had a long standing with the Church of Latter day Saints but the differance Betwen me and others I care nothing about it It is but a speck amongst matters and things altho about it I hear much said But I have before me a senry of things to well do my duty in the fear of God I feel in duty bound to meet with you and I will them to you Unfold some things that is to you in the dark But if you with me desire to converse about certin things That I think to you is dark I am now ready with you to meet or any time between this and Monday morning as after that I shall be oft Remember that I have ben a long steady friend [manuscript torn] am not turned By the folly of man Pleas to write to me a few lines [manuscript torn] how and whire I can you find [manuscript torn] if you with me do not desire of met [manuscript torn] pleas to answer me by putting a letter in the Post office [manuscript torn] soon as you receive this

Yours as ever a friend O. H. Olney

Prest Joseph Smith

[Folder number 7] Citty of Nauvoo July 16th 1842

I of late years have ben a traverling over the American soil I have seen much adoing in differant parts that speaks of the situation of My fellow man I se them of all ages and sises and from the Idiot To the wise man on the tower some in High life Some in low Some well informed. Some illiterate all passing threw a probationary State I say why is it thus With my fellow man Have they not one parent Him that is caled one of the Antient of days Yes this noted Chieftain Has a numerous host that moves under his Observation in the nineteenth Century of time as he on Earth has took a stand in honor of the Father and Son with a number of his decendants a council of twelve Antient

Saints They are arayed in apparel that was made by workman of pleasure that have power to form and Create anew They on Earth have a standing and a Labour are a performing as directed by the Saviour that has with them took a stand to prepare for his coming In the Clouds of Heaven with the Saints A Kingdom of honour a Kingdom of Glory is now to be established Anew on Earth that all things may move in order as was written by the Prophits that wrote as they was moved on by the Holy Ghost They spoke of a kingdom propeld by the power of God that in the Last days Should be established haveing power to rend other Kingdoms that would not submit To the Son of Man The Antient of days have set in Council the ninth tenth and Eleventh of June a day set apart long to be rememberd by those that inhabit the Earth It is to be thre days of rejoicing thanks giving and praying without a foibles being mentioned between man and man But all things must be ajusted previous to coming together in honour of the sitting of the Antient of days They in power and magesty on Earth have a standing and taken posessions of the Kingdoms of the Earth They now are a baffling The powers that be But what shall I say of their first doings as I with them have assembled in a low Mansion In the Citty of Nauvoo They spoke of the Latter day Glory that must soon usher in They spoke of foibles That they first would streighten amongst the Latter day Saints that an honourable people should stand again on the Earth As I have skipted over some noted doings that I have passed threw within several years past I will barly speak of them as I think I have ben much favord by the Messengers above A messenger Came to me And in Language addrest me that he wanted my Labours to assist in Establishing the Kingdom of God From time to time I was juged of my duty that looked to me misterious that I should be thus noticed by a messenger from Heaven that had just took his departer from Earth His looks was familiar his visage plain He freely spoke to me and departed His name was David Patten while on Earth I of late with them have ben familiar as much has ben a doing by them to prepare a rest for the saints of the most high In June 1841 I was visited by an Antient that lived in the days of Enoch by the name of Hipsebah that assended with Enoch Citty

[Folder number 6] Citty of Nauvoo July 17th 1842

Thou art caled at this time to prepare thy self for what is to come as you have before you an order of things that thy hart has not conceived of it is the sitting of the Antient of days and the Saviour in council with them that regulations may be made to regulate and establish a temporal kingdom on the Earth no more to be baffled by the wickedness of man And the presant order of things is to be sunk in to Oblivion amongst the dark shades of the dambed That they may no more disgrase the name of the God of Israel. You are caled to go forward in the way of your duty as you have ben shone and speak frely your mind but be careful and not take up on too many points reason with them if they give you a fair chance by a number to meet to hear from you but if but few meet say nothing to them as they will take the advantage of you by changeing your words or misrepresenting what you say Crowd your self ahead before the Church by degrees that you may get a hearing of them as they will desire to hear from you but I will harden the hearts of those your enemys that they will reject you but not willingly

[Folder number 3] Citty of Nauvoo July 20th 1842

I with feelings of no ordinary kind sit down to write of things That transpires I long have had a standing with the Church of L. D. Saints that I have feelings To do them good and by no means To do them hurt as I long have kept A history of their doings and their ungodly works that is yet lying in the dark I said in my heart if they will reform I will not publish against them but assist in a reformation that their doings may not be known I with the best of feeling To them did write of the Orthorotys of the Latter D. Saints that I with them would meet and convers about matters and things I accordingly met with them but I se them determined in their ways that I soon se that I could do nothing for them I then left them All in a mess the presadancy High councilers and twelve I looked at them And at their works and said to my self They know nothing as they had ort [ought] But they have a law Coming of which they much bost It answers for the presant but it dont reach a head I then said my writings Must speak and unriddle the doings of the L. D. S.

[Folder number 5] Citty of Nauvoo July 20th 1842

I with feelings of no ordinary kind sit to write of things that transpire I long have had a standing with the Latter day Saints that I have feelings to do them good and by no means to do them hurt as I long have kept a history of their doing and their ungodly works that is yet lying in the Dark I said in my mind If they will reform I will not publish against them but assist in a Reformation that their doings may not be known I with the best of feeling to them rote of the Orthorotys of the Church that I would meet with them and freely converse About matters and things I accordingly met with them but I se them determined in their ways that I soon se I could do nothing for them better than to brake them all up Yes I look at them and how they are combind a power establishing In the name of the Lord that will yet rule all other powers

[Folder number 6] Nauvoo July 20th 1842

Thou art caled at this time to take a retrospective vew of things that transpires in and about the Citty Of which much is said As much is adoing by those that usurp power I will write of their folly and of their works that they have wholy discountenanced me that I with them can do nothing but leave them to their own destruction I now am ready them to leave in chains of Darkness of things of God I have met with the Leaders of the Church and freely spoke to them of things that has ben but they arose against me and reasoned and endeavored to cuver up light But I look at the God that rules above and say in my heart let his will be done I look at the doings of the Latter day Saints and say nothing can help them because of their depths of Iniquity as this day the Chieftains have took a stand to commence to purify and make clean They on the Church have desided as no reformation can be got to establish an order of things that will brake up the Latter day Saints First a division amongst them will arise that will cause sorrow and Lamentation amongst those of the Lay members of the Church Then will follow after a senry of things that will cause a Union in the Church It will be the movements of the people both far and neer That will say we will no more bear with them as they are not fit to live And in honour of our Country of which we have much reason to bost we will arise to a man and cut them of Thus men women and Childern all in a mass will meet together each other to defend. But the weapons of war on them will fall that will cause a destruction amongst the Latter day Saints Those that have lead in to bondage and the poor much opprest will reap the reward of their Labours by being brought to Justice They will have to suffer the penalty of the Law of God that they shall be disgrased from this time forth In an unexspected way Testimony on testimony against them will speak that their doings shall be unridled in the eyes of the world

[Folder number 7] Quincy July 20th 1842

As I of late have vewed The Periodicals of the day one our

[Olney began the July 20th entry, then drew a line and wrote the second page of the first entry for July 22.]

[Folder number 7] Quincy July 20th 1842

As I of late have vewed the Periodicals of the day I have vewed many that is printed in Nauvoo I look at them with amasement because of the matter in them contained that say to come from a people of God Do they write by inspiration as did the Antient men of God Or how is it with them From whence do they receive their Istructions Is it from the powers above or is it from the powers of darkness that is said to lead man astray into by and forbidden paths Either the former or Latter I very much doubt As such degrad writings woul[d] dis honour either of their names if their writings and doings is dictated by their God He must be a being of business As we find much is a going on I will pas by perticulars and speak on general terms and of you request an answer that I may know what being you serve You may think strang[e] of my writing to you but I will write the run of my mind as my information I have received from your members That does for you contend they say you have power to do as you pleas He must be verry liberal with you if what I learn is correct and as I am an enquirer after truth I would like to fall in with a people that has some Light as I have ben informed by the members of the Church of L D Saints that you are to receive of your sisters in the Church a plurality of wives as they say is of God in order to raise up a righeous branch They say you have power To make Laws that your God will sanction In a futer day They say if you have no accusers amongst your selves you will not be accused by the God that you serve when caled to give an account of your selves They say with your numerous wifes and maidens you are about to start west as far as the Rocky Mountains whire you will raise up a Righeous Branch without being molested by the Laws of the land As I stand nutral and a looking about I would like to use all the wisdom I can and get my mind setled in something that will now and then cheer up my drooping Soul If you with me will freely write and explain to me of the God you serve and whether the information that I have got from your members is correct and send to me by Letter if you have not room to put it in one of your Valuable Periodicals of the day Yours ~~with the best of feeling~~ a seeker after good A. O. Carpenter[24]

[**Folder number** 7] Citty of Nauvoo July 22d 1842

It is with no ordinary feeling that I at this time Address my self to the Orthorotys of the Church of Latter day Saints on a subject that is arousing the attention of almost every freeman as far as the name of Mormonism is known As I long have had a standing with them I have ben prejudised for them but at the same time I have kept in vew Wright and wrong and have a recod if partial it is in behalf of the Saints As When I united [manuscript torn] to united with a people of God, but from that time untill this I have took a retrospective vew of things that have transpired and have it in writing at my Command now As a friend to man and a friend to the Latter day Saints

24. Could not find any information for A. O. Carpenter. I did locate an Alan Carpenter (born July 1813), who was a member of the Reorganized Church of Jesus Christ of Latter Day Saints. There is a possibility that he had been a member of the Church prior to the reorganization.

called [manuscript torn] freely speak to you my mind That as you say to be a people of God and a people that receive direct Revelations from Heaven and are governed by them this you know to be the theme. At the same time you know what is afloat at this time and has ben from time to time Now you know and I know how things have ben and now is Now I will say to you with the best of feeling that unless you speedily repent of your doings that [manuscript torn] and streighten Crooked and rough paths and that without delay I shall move against you threw the medium of the press I know that I am not at this time a member of the Church Why because you found I was a writing what you knew not [manuscript torn] You demanded my writings I caled them my own and kept them You withdrewed from me the hand of fellowship I then took my name from the Church all don in good feeling But now a thourough Reformation must be or I will unriddle your doings on the house tops I deni being of any party feeling either for you or against you I move as I think [manuscript torn] a duty that involves on me for your good and the God of my fellow man Now if you will be thourough in a Reformation and acknowledge your falts to [manuscript torn] world threw the two Periodicals of your Care. I have no more to say but be as ever a friend to you and my writing shall lie in the dark If not speak of the foibles of the Church of Latter day Saints that is extant on the Earth I have seen of their doings I have seen of their works untill I say they are dangerous people to be together on the Earth If they was to the rocky mountains as they are there desined to go what would be the consequence If they there should form a home I will reason some little as I know of their plans A few first will start And go out by degrees untill all will follow That has in them faith They will there form a Union as is directed by a few Others move in order untill they become a powerful people They will unite with the Indians as this has long ben the theme by them of the Leaders of the Church. That they will lead them over the American soil In the power of God I long have ben a writing And kept a close mouth in hopes of a change for the better But what do I se that causes me to mourn It is that this people gets worse and worse They are deep in iniquity of the basest sort all don in the name of the Lord I again draw my writings to a close by subscribing myself. O. H. Olney

[Folder number 7] July 22d

I now draw my writings and doings all to a close And leave the Citty and them in it to foam out their Shame I will start down the rappids on the Rivers bank without troublin the Catfish that have long had a hard time as is of them said When storys get a going thy find no place to stop But I will put a veto on one that is afloat. Respecting The rivers being closed but barely a wink give the Story a start as neer as I can learn only one infant has ben found in the river They say sewed up in a bag Of what is a going and of what is said I am sorry that the females have to be named as I am satisfied there is but few of il fame But because of the few we have to use the name Yet a sosiety is formed that says to be good to assist in helping the poor and recomending good morrals In going thus far they have honourd themselves The trap that is set for them they are entirely ignorant of but when a Revelation does come its of God and cannot be turned Thus a trap is set for them by and by when they get whire the law can have no effect Amongst the natives west But at presant nothing can be said derogatory to the Character of Our females except a certin few In the Citty of Nauvoo I have not feelings the honest to abuse but whire names Are known names must be spoke Thust amongst Male and Females They now suffer approach untill they singled Themselves out There fore let such as have wisdom clear out of the Citty of Nauvoo and make themselves homes whire they can situate themselves by being industrious to do well A word to the wise is sufficient Let the Ignorant Stand and look and Learn by sad experiance their futer destany Look around and se the greedy dogs Alooking to take your effects by saying Thus saith the Lord Look at the power [poor] and destitute of the place No money no provision coverd with rags Look at their habitations being from one hundred to two thousand dollar lots that of which is said to be a fact that but a few legall titles can be given Look at the thousands around that stand as minetmen to move as is said by the orthoroty of the Church What does this Lead to But to establish a king in a Country of fredom that much blood has ben lost To gain I write my feelings on a principal and good will to man and in the fear of God that if they put their plans into practice whire will they soon be but on their way to the Rocky Mountains A chosen few say fifty in number that would not be noticed on their way Otherers would follow as the way opened that they would soon use up our Frontiers as of it they long have bosted Look at Missouri of which much is said Let from fifty to a hundred thousand Natives with a Leagion come on them as they say this is one way to suck the milk of the gentiles The other ways I will mention when they put on me their slang but if they keep silent towards me what I have rote they acknowledge is corre[c]t So act your feeling as after I go out and breath fresh air a spell and se what is go in and about the Country I had as lives write a little in prose as I can tell the story more [free?] especially in speaking of facts

Yours as you find me every day alike

O. H. Olney

[Folder number 3] July 24th 184[2] Citty

This noted place speaks loud of doings that has long lain in the dark as hoops are a bursting And casks falling and their contents a fermenting it raises a mist in the Citty of Nauvoo Much is adoing And all a saying what can be don That all may be well as our leaders Arise in contention and do with each other twit[25] on facts They accuse Each other of being guilty of Crimes that speaks loud of a degraded people ~~that lives in the~~ Citty of Nauvoo A fuss is a raising That speaks of doings that must be degrading In the sight of God To tell the tale more clearly I will speak a vew I had of them that will unfold a mistry That lies in the dark that speaks of a clan That has moved together to establish certin things Or principals that has broke a felm[26] Or renewed a mist that many dark things Is comming to light As I passed by the temple I herd some say that such and such ones Was much engaged to go a head I looked at their movements to be mostly in the dark They often meet together At late hours of knight and spied out Each others doings that they well knew of each others ~~works~~ From time to time Feelings a rose that many became exited lest they should be undervalued Many names I mite mention that come to my vew That looked to me strange to think that they should stoop so low as to be roveing around houses of ill fame at late hours in the knight when the saying is Honest men should be a bed I se their ambition to move a head untill an unfore seen trouble arose that caused a split amongst The Church of L. D. Saints A noted one caled Doct. Bennett got far on the lead that many moved Against him to distroy his influance But Benett looked amazed to be thus approached And take from him priveleges that caused him often to mourn He with feelings Of no ordinary kind took a stand him self to defend He spoke of things that had actually ben and continued to devulge from time to time His former assosiutes against him did arise and did Scandalise him at home and abroad Again others arose and spoke of doings and bore testimony of to the Church of L.D.S. Testimony after testimony began to speak that unridled much Iniquity that was agoing amongst the Church They arose against their accusers with a determination Their influance to distroy Many they abused That had characters fair that has had to suffer their approach because of fear of truth comming to light Some names I will mention of females that of them much is said to distroy their testimony and influance that they had tried to seduce by sayings of thus and thus saith the Lord With one I have

25. To reproach; to upbraid; as for some previous act. He *twitted* his friend of falsehood. *Webster's Dictionary* (1828), s.v. "Twit."

26. Olney likely meant "broke a film," which could mean to break through a veil or to uncover something that had been hidden.

ben aquainted from youth up to the age of eighteen Nancy Rigdon[27] by name Her character is good at home and a broad Another altho a stranger to me but I am Credibly informed that she is a person of respectability by the name of Martha Brotherton[28] that they tried her to seduce S[h]e with her friend From England did come because of principals of doctrin and faith They with the saints did Assemble in the City of Nauvoo She there was salluted in the name of the Lord To be a second Companion to one of the noted leaders of the Church She was enticed and perswaded In the name of the Lord by several that said to have influance with God They first took the advantage of her by getting her in to a room by her self and then makeing use of the name of the Lord to bring her into subjection for their use But bearly a youth had the presance of mind to clear her self from them in an honourable way What

---

27. Nancy Rigdon was the daughter of Sidney Rigdon, counselor to Joseph Smith in the First Presidency. In April 1842 Joseph Smith proposed marriage to Nancy Rigdon to have her become one of his plural wives. Nineteen-year-old Rigdon was reportedly outraged and rebuffed his proposal. Within a few days, Joseph sent a letter to Nancy, explaining the doctrinal teachings that he hoped would persuade her to change her mind. Although the letter was intended to be private, it ended up in the possession of John C. Bennett, who had it published in the *Sangamo Journal.* Joseph visited the Rigdon home several times and, to some degree, smoothed things over with the Rigdon family. However, the rift between Joseph and Sidney Rigdon, only in part a result of Joseph's proposal to Nancy, widened. After Joseph Smith's death and Sidney Rigdon's failed attempt to secure leadership of the church, Rigdon was excommunicated, moved back to Pennsylvania, and started his own church. On September 13, 1846, Nancy Rigdon married Robert Ellis, a member of the grand council of the church Sidney Rigdon founded. Disaffected with the Latter-day Saints, it is likely that Nancy was involved in her father's church. The Ellises lived the rest of their lives in Pittsburgh, Pennsylvania. See Hales, *Joseph Smith's Polygamy*, 1:477–84; Richard S. Van Wagoner, *Sidney Rigdon: A Portrait of Religious Excess*, 290–93, 394n2.

28. Martha Brotherton was from Manchester, England. She, her parents, and two sisters converted to The Church of Jesus Christ of Latter-day Saints and immigrated to the Nauvoo area. Brigham Young had known Martha Brotherton while he served as a missionary in England, and she became the first woman that Brigham Young approached to become his plural wife. Martha rejected Young's proposal and reported the encounter to her parents. Already struggling with their beliefs in Mormonism, Martha's ordeal was more than they could endure. John C. Bennett, by this time a bitter enemy to Joseph Smith, met with Martha to hear her story firsthand. Bennett helped her draft an affidavit of her experience on July 13, 1842. She allowed Bennett to publish the affidavit and her story in a series of exposé letters. See Hales, *Joseph Smith's Polygamy*, 1:489–95. Richard S. Van Wagoner wrote: "According to Salt Lake Endowment House Records, Brigham Young was sealed to [Martha Brotherton] by proxy on 1 August 1870." Richard S. Van Wagoner, *Mormon Polygamy: A History*, 26n7.

has since ben the theme Her character has ben defamed To the lowest[29] This is the course that is took to abuse those that is likely to speak In contact to the Leaders of LDS The names of more females I mite mention but I speak of the above cases as a sample of the doings of the Leaders of the C. of L.D.S. As much is a saying and adoing and smoke araising By Bennett and others yet much is in the Dark I will speak of a whiproe they have to cloak sin that when they do wrong They get rebaptized They then stand fair in the sight of God altho they have done ever so bad This is the theme amongst those that are a wallowing in the mud It is but seldom a sacrifice is offerd on the alter except in behalf of the P hood that was according to the Law of Moses

[Folder number 6] City of [Nauvoo] July 26th 1842

I still continue a moveing about that I am priveleged of knowing of the doings of the Latter day Saints High winds are a blowing on every side that speaks of the folly of those caled saints I look at them And look at their works and hear of their contentions and Opressions That they on each other heap They arise with a determination the powers to baffle that does with them come in contact They arise with feelings To go a head and put in to subjection all powers or persons that does with them come in contact They speak of their power with God to do They speak of an endowment that is now to be that they must meet together and prepare it to receive By being baptised for a remission of sins that all will be well with them in a futer day as their sins is many And of the blackest die they use means to pass by them that God may

29. The Martha Brotherton affidavit and exposé letters were first published in various Illinois newspapers on July 16, 22, 23, and 25, 1842, and in other newspapers in the days that followed. The Latter-day Saint newspaper published in Nauvoo, *The Wasp*, retaliated in the August 27, 1842, issue, referring to John C. Bennett as "the pimp and file leader of such mean harlots as Martha H. Brotherton." "Remarks," 2. Olney's comment, "Her character has been defamed to the lowest," is dated July 24, 1842, prior to the negative comment found in *The Wasp*. He is either referring to gossip and comments circulating Nauvoo vilifying Martha Brotherton or he wrote this entry after the August 27 *Wasp* article. Olney wrote several drafts of much of his writing. It is possible this manuscript dated July 26 was written later. Nancy Rigdon also had to endure denigrating comments. For example, a broadside published in Nauvoo on August 31, 1842, included the affidavit of Stephen Markham stating that "he saw Miss Nancy Rigdon laying on a bed, and John C. Bennett was sitting by the side of the bed, near the foot, in close conversation with her; deponent also saw many vulgar, unbecoming and indecent sayings and motions pass between them, which satisfied deponent that they were guilty of unlawful and illicit intercourse, with each other." "Affidavits and Certificates, Disproving the Statements and Affidavits Contained in John C. Bennett's Letters," Nauvoo, August 31, 1842.

not look on them with disdain They on the alter offerd a Lamb without spot or blemish as did those that kept the Law of Moses[30] Thus we se their folly in doings and works as all such things was finished at the death and resorection of Christ No more offerings was needed to tel the tale of wrong but the sacrifise of a broken heart and a contrite Spirit of man to become exceptable in the sight of God Again rebaptisms is but a curse as by it man takes libertys in doing wrong that tends to encourage him in wicked ways Let those that have feeling both say and do by being obediant to the commands of God

[A section on this page written upside down is the concluding part of Olney's Sunday July 10th writing. It appears that Olney either did not have paper at the time or there was a large part of a previous page left blank and he used it to conclude the July 10th thoughts on the life of Adam. He likely wrote upside down on the page so he would know that it was not a continuation of the writing labeled July 26. The upside-down section had been added to July 10th where it belongs.]

[Folder number 3] City of Nauvoo July 27th

I long have ben a writing of the doings of the L.D.S. untill I am weary Of seeing their works As it is a day of note amongst them for all to come together And be baptized anew for the remission of their sins[31] I look at the principal of such

30. The July 15, 1842, issue of the *Sangamo Journal* contained several letters written by John C. Bennett, the recently excommunicated Church leader. Bennett claimed he witnessed Sarah Pratt (wife of Orson Pratt) reject Joseph Smith's advances to have her become one of his "spiritual wives." Bennett reported that after Joseph was rejected, the following took place: "'Well, sister Pratt,' says Joe, 'as you have refused me, it becomes sin, unless *sacrifice* is offered;' and turning to me [Bennett] he said, 'General, if you are my friend I wish you to procure a lamb, and have it slain, and sprinkle the door posts and the gate with its blood, and take the kidneys and entrails and offer them upon an altar of twelve stones that have not been touched with a hammer, as a burnt offering, and it will save me and my priesthood. Will you do it?' I will, I replied. So I procured the lamb from Captain John T. Barnett, and it was slain by Lieutenant Stephen H. Goddard, and I offered the kidneys and entrails in sacrifice for Joe, as he desired; and Joe said, 'all is now safe—the destroying angel will pass over, without harming any of us.'" John C. Bennett, "Further Mormon Developments!!!," 2. Olney got the information for his July 26, 1842, entry from Bennett's article. See OOP, fd. 3, August 13, 1842.

31. Baptism is an ordinance performed in The Church of Jesus Christ of Latter-day Saints for remission of sins and for Church membership. Olney is troubled that rebaptisms were taking place in Nauvoo. His argument is that Church leaders and members commit all types of iniquity and then are simply rebaptized to have those sins forgiven. He views rebaptism as a substitute for sincere repentance and as an easy

doings and se the degraded traites to which it leads as Iniquity is the theme and upheld by the leaders of the Church in the name of the Lord They acknowledge Their foibles being many but they yet of them a permit by going in to the water as did the Antient Saints For remission of sins This is the teachings And well understood that when they have ben in Iniquity if ever so bad They have a remady for it by being baptised In the name of the trinity Father Son and Holy Ghost amen by one of their clan Thus they take lenity and continue their doings Both early and Late Again we have an Institution amongst us set up that of it I have not much to say but our leaders say threw it the Priesthood to receive I now ask a question does God work In the Dark Are his ways unequal that a few is priveleged and others not A theme is a raising Of which much is said It is an institution amongst the females caled a degree of Masenry for them to receive They say by it much light to obtain and arise verry high In the esteem of God They have a picked Company all in aray They often meet together as Friends and receive instructions From one another Also from the Orthoritys of the Church They are mostly honest in their doings All but a few are in the dark of its designs But as people is often a talking when excited for good things to come many now is a speaking of going to the Rocky Mountains while God shall distroy The wicked of the Land It will be with them As with Lot and his daughters as they went out of Soddom They will say to be the only people on the Earth Thus chords is a drawing That many is a saying of the fair sex That they will leave their Companions rather than to stay While scourges pass over the soil Thus a trap is set That will brake up many families that are of Respectability if they was left to take their own course But the modern teaching Is such that it leads the mind In to bondage as they all as one say we have a Prophit to lead

---

way out of transgression, ultimately making iniquity of no consequence. Beginning in 1840, Joseph Smith taught the principle of baptism for the dead, an ordinance whereby deceased relatives and friends who had not been baptized could receive that ordinance necessary for salvation. Olney may have been referring to these proxy baptisms performed by Church members. More likely, Olney was writing about rebaptisms performed for living members of the Church. Rebaptism is not practiced today in Mormonism and has been relatively rare throughout most its history. However, during the Nauvoo era of Mormon history rebaptisms were quite common. In 1842 a call for reformation had come from Church leaders. As part of that reformation rebaptisms were performed to demonstrate a renewed commitment by the Saints and for remission of sins. D. Michael Quinn wrote, "Most of the Latter-day Saints who were rebaptized for remission of sins during the Nauvoo period were not receiving this ordinance for what was regarded as gross misconduct, but instead for a personal reformation and remission of those sins which the ancient apostle John said were part of the human condition." See D. Michael Quinn, "The Practice of Rebaptism at Nauvoo," 228.

and direct us in the path of wright They say our Antient teachers instructed a people That lived In an early day

[Folder number 8] July 27 1842 Nauvoo Citty

This noted place speaks loud of doings that has lain long in the dark As hoops are a bursting And Casks falling and their contents a fermenting it raises a mist in the Citty of Nauvoo Much is adoing And all a saying what can be don That all may be well As our Leaders arise in contention and do with each other twit on facts they accuse each other of being guilty of Crimes that speaks loud of a degraded people cald Latter day Saints A fuss is a raising that speaks loud of doings that must be degrading in the site of God To tel the tale more clearly I will write a vision that will unfold a mistry that lies in the dark that speaks of a Class that has move together to establish certin things or principals that has broke a felm or removed a mist that many dark things is a comming to light As I pased by the temple lot I herd some say that such and such ones was much engaged to go a head I looked at their movements to be mostly in the dark They often met together at late hours in the Knight and spied out Each others doings that they well knew of Each others falts From time to time feelings arose that many became excited lest they should be undernoticed Many names I mite mention that come to my vew That looked to me strange that they should condesend To stoop so low as to be a roveing around houses of il fame at late hours in the dead of the knight when the saying is honest men should be asleep I se their ambition to move ahead untill an unforseen trouble arose that caused a split a mongst the Church of Latter day Saints A noted one caled Doctor Bennet got far on the lead That many moved against him to distroy his influance But Benet looked amased to think that they should him abrubtly aproach and take from him his priveliges that caused him often to mourn he with feelings of no ordinary kind took a stand him self to defend He spoke of things that had actually ben and continued to devulge from time to time His former assosiates against him did arise and did scandalize him at home and abroad Again others arose and spoke of doings and bore testimony to the Church of L.D.S. Testimony after testimony began to speak that unriddled much iniquity that was agoing amongst the L. D. Saints They arose against their accusers with a detirmination their Influance to distroy Many they abused That had Characters fair that had to suffer their aproach because of fear of truth comeing to light Some names I will mention of females that of them much is said to distroy their testimony and Influance that they had tried to seduce by saying thus and thus saith the Lord With one I have ben aquainted from youth up to the age of Eighteen by name Nancy Rigdon Her Character is good at home and abroad Another altho a stranger to me but I am Credably informed that she is a person of respetability by the name of (Syntha Brotherton) that they tried to seduse She with her friends From England did come because of principals of doctrin of faith They with the saints did assemble in the Citty of Nauvoo. She there was saluted in the name of the Lord to be a second Companion to one of the noted Leaders of the Church She was enticed and perswaded in the name of the Lord by more than one that said to have much influance with God They first took the advantage of her by getting her in to a room by herself and then makeing use of the name of the Lord to bring her in to subjection for their use but barly a youth had the presance of mind to clear herself from them in a honourable way What has since ben the theme Her character is defamed to the lowest This is the course that is took to abuse those that is likely to speak of the doings of the Leaders of the Church of L D Saints Many more names I mite mention but I forbear And let males speak for themselves As I se by the doings they will soon have a chanse as much is adoing and saying and smoke ariseing by Bennet and others yet much is in the Dark I will speak of a whiprow They have to cloak Sin That is if they do wrong they can go forward and be baptised anew they then stand fair in the esteem of Heaven This is the theme now amongst those that are a wallowing in the mud It is seldom a sacrifise on the alter is offerd except in behalf of the Priesthood that was according to the Law of Moses I look at the weakness and meanness and the unholesome doings and say how is it possible that a community like this can be daubed over and be satisfied with such ungodly and unwise works Since on a principal I rote the first page that spoke of the doings of the Church of L D Saints if I could be releived And things made streight I would freely stop my history of the doing of the Church and let it by as usual in the dark but what can I say what can I do but Carry out the Principal as I said to do when I commenced to write

[Folder number 8] Citty of Nauvoo July 28th 1842

I of late have ben adoing much that has looked to me strange but as I was caled upon I performed I was traverling and a preaching the word when a messenger Came to me and said the time had ariven For me to change my work I gave head to him, And from him received much light Him in connection with others Has ben with me from that time untill this I have ben much delighted with them as they have with me ben free to teach me and Instruct me about many things. They first told me of doings that soon must be to bind up the Law and seal up the testimony that the wicked mite be left without exscuse I was shone of a work that was to be done to prepare for the comming of the son of man but the power of God must be displayed threw man on the Earth

By raising the dead and other things marvelous to relate Being caled on by the Spirit this work to do I cheerfuly Labour it to perform I willingly do I willingly perform my duty as to me shone Or stand still and se the Salvation of God I now am caled thre days to stand still and do up some writings as I am shone then prepare for a voige to St Louis and publish the foibles of the Church and then scatter them in all parts In the round I am caled a Journy to take in to the Eastern Country At Boston and there from the Tomb And raise up S Adams[32] and take her to her parrents and leave her untill some futer time I then am caled to take my course home and take an other retrospective vew of the L.D.S. as a scourge on them soon will arise that will speak louder than peels of thunder in the Eyes of the world As much is adoing and much is afloat a general gethering soon will be caled to meet together that the Saints can Stand in their own defense as spirit of war soon will arise in the breast of all In differant parts some for some against The L. D. Saints The spirit of contention will commence to arise at the time of my writings comeing forth A spirit of confusion discord and disunion will soon be the theme In all parts that a contention will arise The Latter D. Saints will be over powerd because of their wicked works I se a contention follow my writings Some said they was correct others fals that caused a confusion that caused a division That many cleard out Coming and going was the theme both day and knight the time was used untill a contention did ensue between the Church and the world around

[Folder number 8] Citty of Nauvoo July 29 1842

I long have been a writing of the doings of the Church of Latter day Saints untill I am weary of seeing their works This is to be a day of Note amongst them as it is a day set apart for all to come together and to be baptised for ther sins I look at the principal of such doings and se its degraded trates To which it leads As Iniquity in this place is the theme and upheld by the Leaders of this people and in the name of the Lord They acknowledge their foibles being many but they get of them a permit by going into the water as did the antient Saints For remission of sins This is the teachings and well understood that when they have ben in iniquity if ever so bad They have a remedy for it by be-

32. Olney reports that he has been called by the Spirit to travel to St. Louis and then continue his journey to the East. At a tomb in Boston, he is to raise a female (S. Adams) from the dead and return her to her parents. The identity of S. Adams in unknown. Earlier, Olney did missionary work in the East and was for a time in Boston. See letter to Orson Hyde in OOP, fd. 11, February 5, 1843, and February 6, 1843. It may be that Olney became familiar with a family named Adams and their daughter while he was serving as a missionary. Olney mentions nothing else about S. Adams or any attempt to raise the dead.

ing babtised for it In the name of the Trinety Thus they take lenity from time to time and continue their doings That is unrigheous and not sanctioned by those caled wicked of the land Again we have an institution amongst us set up that of it I have not much to say But our Leaders say threw it The Priesthood to receive I now ask a question a question Does God work in the Dark Is his ways unequal that a few is priveleged Others stand back A theme is a raising of which much is said in an earlyer day than this Thus we will reason some little of the presant doing of the Church of L D S They say to be the chosen people of God and are to be governed by his prophit that he has raised up in this age When his word is spoken Its not to be broken but carryed in to effect by his aids He has a life gard[33] attends him by knight and by Day There is a penalty annext[34] on anyone that shall lisp against him or against any of his chosen ones of the ~~church of~~ L D Saints I again close my writings and say I am weary of what I daily se agoing on

O. H. Olney

[Folder number 3] July 30th Citty of Nauvoo

Much is adoing as well as to say that speaks louder than words of the people of Nauvoo They long have ben a doting of their power with God that they could put to flight their opposers by merly a nod They have doted and bosted of their strength and power and long have ben makeing in case of an attact But after doting trayning and fixing and a makeing ready to contend they hear a sound of dissatisfaction because of the storys afloat that brings to their minds fearful looking objects A Spirit of consternation on them does rest that they are often alarmed lest they are looked to by the Orthorotys of the State

33. Because of persecution, arrests, attempted kidnapping, and the possibility of assassination, Joseph Smith had bodyguards during most of his years as the Church's leader. The best-known bodyguards are Orrin Porter Rockwell and Stephen Markham. Many Latter-day Saints take great pride that their ancestor was a bodyguard for the Prophet Joseph. It should be noted that many men were asked to guard Joseph from time to time. A cursory investigation into published histories, journals, and recorded family lore produced over eighty names of men who are believed to have been Joseph Smith's bodyguards. The Nauvoo police force and the hundreds of men in the Nauvoo Legion could be assigned as Joseph's bodyguards. Olney mentioned that Joseph had a "life guard" with him day and night. The pin worn by Nauvoo Legion members had a beehive in the center with the initials N. L. underneath it and the words "Life Guard" above.

34. To unite to something preceding; to connect with; as to *annex* a penalty to a prohibition, or punishment to guilt. *Webster's Dictionary* (1828), s.v. "Annex."

They have just sent to the Governor with a cataloge of names By females[35] that they may gain his applause We see them mixed up in doings some of the time a doting and defying at other times a pleading for mercy at the feet of the rulers of the Land Why not keep a steady course of doings without abusing The priveleges of a free Constitution that our Fathers fought and gained by the Shedding of much blood

[Folder number 8] July 30

I again have feelings My mind to exspress about matters and things that daily transpires in and about the Citty of Nauvoo Much is a doing as well as to say that speaks louder than words of the doings of the people of Nauvoo They long have ben a doting of their power with God that they could put to flight their opposers by mearly a nod. They have doted and bosted of their Strength and power and long been makeing ready in case of an attact After doting and braging and fixing and makeing ready to contend they hear a sound out of dissatisfaction because of the storys afloat that brings to their minds fearful looking objects A Spirit of consternation on them does rest that they are often alarmed, lest they are looked to by the Inhabitsants of the Land They have just sent to the Govenor with a cataloge of names By females that they may gain his applause We se them mixt up in doings some of the time a doting and defying Other times a pleading for Mercy at the feet of the rulers of the land Why not keep a steady course of doings without abuseing the priveleges of a free Constitution that our Fathers fought and gained by the shedding of much blood I look at them in Their daily moves they appear like Childern in the sand Some a playing some a contending others looking and know not what to say or do Thus I speak of their doings In the Citty of Nauvoo They together here have getherd untill the place is a running over Yet they are a calling Loud and Heavy together to gether from all parts Whire is their reasen

35. Joseph Smith was accused of being complicit in the assassination attempt on Missouri Governor Lilburn W. Boggs. Thomas Reynolds, the new Missouri governor, sent a requisition to Illinois Governor Thomas Carlin. Carlin issued arrest warrants charging Orrin Porter Rockwell with shooting Governor Boggs and Joseph Smith as an accomplice. Both Smith and Rockwell went into hiding. Joseph's wife, Emma Hale Smith, began a communication with Governor Carlin in an attempt to convince him of her husband's innocence. As president of the Relief Society, Emma spearheaded a petition signed by approximately one thousand women to be sent to the Illinois governor. The petition stated that although "it would be more consistent with the delicacy of the female character to be silent," they were seeking protection from the Missouri mobs. It also requested that Joseph not be extradited to Missouri because the women believed Joseph to be a man "of integrity, honesty, truth, and patriotism." See Linda King Newell and Valeen Tippetts Avery, *Mormon Enigma: Emma Hale Smith*, 122, 127.

whire is their wisdom to call together a set of Farmers and mechanicks that have but sçanty means to live Look at the principal of comeing together and se the result of such doings Their means is squanderd in differant ways that they become disconsolate and know not what to do for to gain the comforts of life At the same time they say to be a gaining because of the rise of the Citty lots that they eumer themselves daily in hopes of better times But the times is getting harder Money for Labour is hardly got Altho lots are caled of value by none but the Latter day Saints they have raised them to an unmeasurable prise that has took the means of many that they no title of worth can give Thus they are a padling and poking in the sand Their move to me is much disgusting those that say to lead the Church If a man or woman Lisp an uneasy feeling their character is riddled on the stand and those that speak in their behalf I now will speak of a noted Couple that lives in the city of Nauvoo It is Professor of Law Orsen Praat and Lady They now are run to the Lowest As for Mrs Pratt I am not aquinted altho of her I much do hear Some say she is a respectable Lady. Others say not But I will speak of the storys with feelings not to use any person wrong Its well known That Pratts has ben to England apreaching and proclaiming the word and Mrs Pratt has ben to home alone Now if there is any thing wrong I am satisfied it is as it was with a Gentleman and his servent maid As she was young black and airy she was looked upon by Coulerd males around By scores they often getherd around her that her Master se the danger she was in He caled a servant Sambo up before him and says Sambo Take care of Nan Keep them lads from her Sambo says well Masser I do it Sambo then went in to business and clerd the Ground of all the blacks But by and by a tale arose that something must be the matter with nan Sambo was caled on by his Master to know why it was thus with Nan Sambo says master you know the siteation that so many lads was around To do anything for you I had to se to her meself Testimony on testimony comes that J C Bennet was at Pratts at a late hours in the knight But we find he Bennet helped her to a home and borded with her If what I hear is correct as Pratt was gone If Bennet volenteerd his servises to keep of scores That moved around I think Pratt may think he is well off and consider it a kindness from Bennit I will reason from their testimony as the testimony is that many has come forward and said that at a late hour in the knight they found Doct bennet there in the house with her what was they there for eaven if Bennett was in the wrong what should cal so many as has bourn testimony against her that they was there twelve and one O clock at knight It appears by her testimony and faces Joseph Smith down in it that he has used the name of the Lord to seduce her several times (In company) She declares it to be a fact I know not of the virtue of Mrs Platt but suffise it to say If Bennit has took charge of her and don by her as Sambo did by Nan Elder Orson Pratt may think himself well ~~used~~ of considering what mite a ben as from testimony and storys afloat I think Benet had enough to do away from home to use the family well that he lived with I think as the story is about the hogs that Doct Bennet has for Months ben in the Clover up to his eyes amongst women that think they have ben abused by their Husbands

[Folder number 3] July 31st 1842 Citty of Nauvoo

For several days past Much has ben adoing to prepare for the Election that is now at hand Stump speeches[36] have ben frequent by the two parties That many does meet to se and to hear what is afloat The candidates spoke freely their feelings in hopes of a liberal support of Patronage But to close up a senry of doings the presidancy arose With good feelings and says Bretheren we want you to meet tomorrow and then we will tell you what is for your good On Saturday 30th they came together and received the mind of the presidancy that established a Political Union in favor of the dimocrat party in the name of the Lord They in union moved together to lay a foundation To put into office such men as they pleas They say first to rule the County by going with one of the established partys By thus doing they have much strength besides their own They each other umer that the time is not far distant when they will sway the cepter over the American soil

[Folder number 8] July 31st 1842 Citty of Nauvoo

For several days past much has ben a doing to prepare pare for the Election that now is at hand Stump speeches have been frequent By both partys that has brought together to hear what was said They expostulated much on doings The candidates spoke freely their feelings in hopes of a Liberal support Amongst the L. D. S. But to close up a scenry of doings the Presidancy arose with good feelings and says Bretheren we want you to meet tomorrow and then we will tel you what is for your good On Saturday 30th they come together and received the minds of the presidency that established a political Union in favor of the Dimocrat party in the name of the Lord They in Union move together to lay a foundation To put in to office such men as they pleas

36. Speeches made by political candidates. The term "stump speech" originated from "a time when candidates would travel from rural area to rural area, stopping to speak wherever they might find a group of people large enough to constitute a crowd. Because stages, halls, and auditoriums were not in abundance, candidates would often stand on the highest ground to address crowds with their political rhetoric. In many instances, that highest ground might have been the flat-topped stump of a recently felled tree—hence the name *stump speech.*" Joseph S. Tuman, *Political Communication in American Campaigns*, 47.

They say first to rule the County by going with one of the regular partys By thus doing they have much strength besides their own In the round they eumer each other that the time is not far distant when they will sway the cepter over the American Soil Much is a doing Much a saying that I say there is a confused mess of stuff I long have ben a writing of doings untill I am weary of what I se and hear in my daily move Testimony on Testimony can be brought If the way opens that people in safty can speak I again draw to a close and say I have wrote as I have written Without respect to feelings but have not enlarged on tales as Is the custom with our penmans in Nauvoo

O. H. Olney

AUGUST 1842

[Folder number 7] Citty of Nauvoo August 3d 1842

Dear Sister Phebe M Wheler[1]

With feeling that is of the best kind I to you write my mind Tuching on matters and things <illegible> of the doings of the Church of L D Saints that they are like an old Cole pit that you have often seen smokeing in the east Much smoke is a riseing day by day that plainly show some fire is a burning To stop the smoke a short time I think would cause an exsplosion that would be marvelous to relate As much seed was sone before you went away You must say it will come to maturity in the due time of the Lord Sister Wheler I again will say to you live [manuscript torn] to God that you daily receive his spirit to lighten up your path Much I mite write but you know my mind (and look) back that I do not put my hand to the plow I will say to you we have a confused <illegible> Man is of a roveing nature He often wanders in the dark

---

1. There is little question that Oliver Olney was very interested in Phebe Wheeler. She was the first person on both his June 1842 and October 1832 lists of women. See OOP, fd. 10, October 18, 1842, for both lists. In the book *Women of Covenant: The Story of Relief Society*, it appears that they have mistakenly listed Phebe J. Wheeler as assistant secretary in the first Relief Society. However, in their list of charter members of the Relief Society, there is a Phebe M. Wheeler but no Phebe J. Wheeler. See Jill Mulvay Derr, Janath Russell Cannon, and Maureen Ursenbach Beecher, *Women of Covenant: The Story of Relief Society*, 27–8, 30. The Nauvoo Relief Society Minute Book lists Phebe M. Wheeler as the assistant secretary of the Relief Society. See *The Joseph Smith Papers*, "A Book of Records, Containing the proceedings of The Female Relief Society of Nauvoo," Nauvoo Relief Society Minute Book, March 17, 1842–March 16, 1844. There was likely only one Phebe Wheeler in the Nauvoo area at that time—Phebe M. Wheeler. There is little information available about Phebe M. Wheeler. In a letter to her aunt and uncle, Phebe reports that she has married Oliver Olney. She writes that Olney is five or six years older than she. Oliver Olney was born in 1796. If she is correct about Olney being five or six years older, that would put Phebe's birth about 1801–1802. She would have been about forty when she married Olney. At that age, Phebe easily could have been married before and widowed. However, only in *Women of Covenant* do I find any mention of her being a widow. In an 1842 Nauvoo Stake Census, Phebe is listed as one of six females living in the house of Joseph Smith as house servants. D. Michael Quinn, "The Culture of Violence in Joseph Smith's Mormonism," 36n135. Also see Lyman De Platt, *Nauvoo: Early Mormon Records Series*, 86. Of note is the fact that, of the six women listed, Phebe Wheeler is the only one who did not become a plural wife of Joseph Smith. George D. Smith, *Nauvoo Polygamy . . . "but we called it celestial marriage,"* 621–23.

because of besetments That does him beset Let the mind that has wisdom put their trust in God above as he has power he has wisdom to expand the mind of fallen man From my youth I have ben conversant about time matters and things I say in my hart when shall I get threw with the presant order of things I am weary I am lonesome I hardly know what to do as the hand of Opression is on me I have but few friend and no home I am daily a roving too and fro on the Earth I see but little chance of saving but few of the Latter day Saints alive but because of the sealing power that I have on them heretofore pronounced they in Heaven will have a standing altho they foam out their shame and disgrase but the mind that has wisdom may steady their bark safly threw by going out in to the Country or living neer to God in the Citty of Nauvoo Let the wise have wisdom to move in order Let the wicked stand and look as a day of trail is approaching that the Latter day Saints must look about

[Folder number 6] 4 sitting

Citty of Nauvoo August 4th 1842

As I often am a writing Of things that daily transpires I write as instructed By the A. of Days as they have in part meet with me some business to transact as they have meet in Council Gods purposes to bring about I now write of their doings and what is to take place A temporal Kingdom is to be reard in honour of the Antient men of God as they will give directions the work to do as Is directed by the Saviour to be don in this the nineteenth Cen. of time As I am caled an agent For them to act I cheerfully do as directed by them in pasing threw a probationary state As this is a day of business set apart they together in Council have meet to do such business as is to be don As I am caled on a work to do as I am seited in a low mansion in the Citty of Nauvoo A council meet and Ordained me to the orthoroty of the High P hood after the order of the Son of God to administer in temporal Concerns They spoke of a Company That with me should meet and receive ordinations that would form a coram of twelve that they would be caled by Revelation to Labour for God and move as volenteers in honour of his name as is directed by the Antient of Days As all other Kingdoms must to them submit the way must be opened it to be don Let those that are ordained to this power look well to their duty and manage as is directed by the Antient of Days As power will be given them to move in aray By being one in spirit and mind they shall receive power From on high to move in the doings of the world and baffle them in all their ways that they shall excede them In wisdom and doings to sho them their folly by being outdon in strength and activity They far shall excede the doings of the world that they shall baffle The powers of Darkness Let those that volenteer and are caled look well to their duty In honour of God as in cases of transgression or apostasy use no intrige to disharten those by takeing from them their wrights or a makeing use of their means by saying thus and thus saith the Lord Let each one do as seemeth him good that he may be judged on his own merits Let him that has property remember that the Earth is the Lords and the fulness thereof that he give and receives as he pleases Let him that has not set reason to work and remember That was his choise in takeing on him a probationary state while others said riches we will have and others said we will become a fool for Christ sake Again it is to reverance God and [a]cknowledge him in and over all in both Heaven and on Earth Alłso to set out a voluntary act to move in the path of duty as the Saviour and Antient saints have marked out By sayings and doings from the first age of the world

[Folder number 7] Citty of Nauvoo August 4th 1842

Being previously caled upon by the Antient of Day With them to meet in council I with them take my stand and keep a recod of their doing as I by them am shone as I often am writing of things that transpires Being an Inhabitant of Illinoi on the Missipi River bank I se and hear much a going in differant parts Some things of Note has come to my vew Above the Rappids in the Citty of Nauvoo. I hear much of them and of their works I now ask a question and desire to know If what I hear is correct They say the Mormons have power with God to make and establish his Laws and by him they are sanctioned that is desined to rule man I hear they are a people set apart that is much eumord in their doings because of their works I hear of their works being many such as Laciveousness Fornication and Audultery Poligemy or Certin ones haveing a plurality of wifes I hear A righeous Branch that they are about to rais[e] up that they may have faith to bring about the purposes of God I hear of a Nauvoo Legion that often does meet all Equipt to menouver to propel the Kingdom Spoken of by Daniel that is said to arise And brake in pieces all other Kingdoms of the Earth Many more questions I might ask but I first want to have answered by someone that is aquainted and is free to answer the above questions

[Folder number 8] August 4th 1842 City of Nauvoo

In my daily a museings I had a dream that spoke of the Standings of the Latt. D. Saints I had a vew of a key That wound up my watch that commenced to brake of by pieces untill it was all broke up I se it was long a brakeing before it was unfit for use It much exsited my feelings to se why Iron should so easy brake I asked the interpretation of the dream. I was answered by being shod [showed] that it applyd to the P_hood of the L D Saints I looked back to the time That I was caled to withdraw the Priesthood from the Latter D Saints and se by degrees it from them was took untill they was of it Completely stript

I se from the Commencement of the year 1842 that a change Commenced and Continued untill 1843 That much was don to bring dark to light By the Orthorotys of Heaven I se within the time a contention arise between Brother and Brother In the Church I se much adoing that looked to me bad to be don by a people That said to serve God I se because of wicked works That they the P hood lost That was took by degrees I se as the P_hood did them leave that their iniquity was devulged in many differant ways I se them look I se them Gase in hopes of power in their behalf but alas did I se pass a way 1842 with many yes many sorrowful looks I se 1843 Come in with prospect fair with prospects fair To do some good I se a Kingdom then set up In power that Commenced to baffle others, And continued untill they was finly [finally] laid low in the dust I se a kingdom by God devised That moved in power propeld by the Saviour threw the Antient of Days as they on Earth have took a stand to prepare a people to do Gods will

[Folder number 8] City of Nauvoo August 4th

As I, often am a writing of things that transpires I now write of things That comes to my vew I write as instructed by the Antient of Days as they have in part met with me some business to perform as they have met in Council Gods purposes to bring about I now write of their doings and of what is to take place A temporal Kingdom is to be reard in honour of the Antient men of God They will give direction The work to do as is directed by the Saviour to be don in this the nineteenth Century of time As I am caled an agent For them to act I cheerfully do as directed by them as I pass threw a probationary state As this is a day of business Set apart they to gether in council have met to do such business As is to be don As I am caled on a work to do As I am seited in a Low Mansion in the Ciyty of Nauvoo A Council met and ordained me To the orthoroty of the High P.hood after the order of the son of God to administer in temporal Concerns They spoke of a company that with me should meet and receive an ordination an Ordination that would form a Corum of twelve that they would be caled by Revelation to Labour for God And move as Volenteers in honour of his name As is directed by the Antient of Days As all other Kingdoms must to them submit the way must be open it to be don Let those that are ordained unto this power look well to their duty and manage as is directed by the Antient of Days As power will be given them to move in aray by being one in Spirit and mind they shall receive power from on high to move in the doings of the world and baffle them in all their way They shall excede them wisdom and wit to sho them their folly by being outdon in strength and activity They far shall excede the doings around that they shall baffle the powers of darkness Let those that volenteer And are caled look well to their duty in honour of God As in cases of transgressions or apostasy it shall not be known as God will take the offender from the eivel to come that is caled by Revelation his will to perform

[Folder number 8] August 5th 1842 Citty of Nauvoo

I long have ben a Member of the Church of L.D.S. Much has come under my observation of which I have not wrote It is principals and doings that is disgusting in the site of God It is takeing the advantage of the jentiles or the unbelieveing part of Community by cheating and defrauding by lying stealing and getting in debt to them without a disposition to pay Such reasoning and teaching altho it lies in the dark to many yet it is principals held to by the Orthorotys of the Church of L. D. Saints saying to suck the milk of the Jentiles The jentiles as a people are Corrupt but yet there is honest good amongst them yet to be severd out They as a people much have erd and become fallen that on them is a curse but the curse can be moved from those that well do their duty and submit to the Law of God and move in accordance with his word An order of things long since was establised that brought forth much light such as the book of Mormon and Covenants as the Original was wrote But it has since ben alterd by the folly of man[2] That is not wright in the site of God The P_hood in past was established At the Arise of the Church of LDS that many have ben enlightend and brought forth fruit to the glory of God But the day has ariven That the Saviour has on Earth took a stand To put things in order agreeable to his will Let those that have feelings with him to coencide Look well to their duty as much depends on their work As an order is a raising Again on the Earth that will boy up and enlighten the mind that is wise But those that takes the downward road Their doom is seald For the want of Faith and works they must suffer the Penalty of the Law of God

[Folder number 8] Citty of Nauvoo August 9th 1842

I today had a vision that I looked with supprise to se a gentle man and Lady walking in differant ways I said to my self what does it mean that a couple should appear engagaged I enquired of the Lord the Interpetation to know

2. It is not clear what Olney meant by "altered by the folly of man." It may have reference to wording changes in the Book of Mormon and the Doctrine and Covenants, although the majority of changes made had to do with punctuation, grammar, and minor errors made in copying. Book of Mormon scholar and expert on editions and manuscripts, Royal Skousen, wrote, "[O]nly a small percentage of these changes make any difference in meaning." See Arnold K. Garr, Donald Q. Cannon, and Richard O. Cowan, eds., *Encyclopedia of Latter-day Saint History*, 120–21. It is more likely that the alterations made "by the folly of man" were Joseph Smith's changes and additions to doctrine that were different from what Olney saw in the 1830s.

I directly was shone that the man and woman that antiently lived Had on Earth took a stand to bring about the purposes of God The gentleman and Lady that to me appeard was caled Elijah and his Companion that had come to tirn the harts of Childern to their Fathers and Fathers to Childern lest Gloominess and sorrow should cover the Earth

[Folder number 3] Citty of Nauvoo August 10th 1842

As I spend my time in and about the place I get the daily news that is agoing As a story arose That Ex Gov. Bogs of Missouri was shot By some villin or Assassin in the knight it went threw our Citty like electricity Many spoke of the deed as a Noble act that who ever did it Was entitled to the P_hood after the order of the Son of God Many continued talking About matters and things that I became satisfied That many knew who shot Ex Governor Bogs I mite say much of the low Cunning of which the Latter D Saints much bost but I pass by perticulars and speak in general terms and say that the presant doings must be an abomination in the sight of God

[Folder number 8] Citty of Nauvoo August 10th 1842

For some days past I have ben a vewing certin things amongst the doings of the Latter day Saints as their doings to me is familiar I well under stand their moves as they are free to converse with me about matters and things As a story long since arose that Ex Governor Bogs what shot by some villin or Assasin In the knight It went threw our Citty like Electricity Many spoke of the deed as being a noble act and for doing it they was entitled to Priesthood after the order of the Son of God Many contined talking of matters and things that I became satisfied That many knew who shot Ex Governor Bogs To tell the story more clearly a vision I will write On certing points that have come to my vew At the same time I have fears of being caled a visionary man as in past time they often was hung for witches But I think the presant one will me suffice so I will write what I se on a high hill I looked in a low vally and se chaps in the mud conversing about Certin things They spoke of trials that they had undergone by being harrased and driven time and again They spoke of what they had to endure while in Missouri because of Ex Gov. Bogs as his doome had ben seald from time to time by differant ones that held the P__hood that he on Earth should not live but should die an untimely death and his wife left a widow and his Childern fatherless They in a mass together decided that the set time had come for their prophesi to be fulfild They made a contrebution some money to raise to defray exspences for some one to go and assasinate Ex Govenor Bogs They agreed on a person The act to perform He soon started by being offered a hansone [handsome] reward As soon as the act he had

~~performed~~ don he continued his Journy By knight and day down the Missipi and Up the Missouri untill he arived at the residance of Bogs He directly said the act to perform but faild in accomplishing the deed But he made a wound Both deep and severe that caused an exitement soon to be herd Much was said respecting the act by all classes In differant parts The news came to our Citty of fame that caused a rejoising amongst the L D Saints Many spoke of the trates of the man that had the act performed in fulfilment of Prophesi That could not be void All lay still a certin time but at last fears arose lest the truith mite come to light They sent out some aids the story to quill[3] that visited and Laboured in behalf of the Accused They went to missori And with the Governer conversed that unfolded a secret that they was in the gilt or that they would not have taken so much pains to clear up their Characters They freely conversed about matters and things and returned home with feeling that all was well But by and by a sound arose by the Orthorotys of the State that the case must be enquired into They sent officers the men to arrest that said to be the ones that was gilty They arrested Joseph Smith and P Rockwell[4] but of their gilt I have nothing to say but am satisfied that Joseph Smith was at home at the time the deed was done Many is a talking and much adoing that speaks loud of doings at this time Again I passed over an other moun and had a vew of things that looked to me strange I se an apregation[5] or likeness of the form sise and looks of P rockwell and by his side on the ground a pistol drawn in honour of his shoting of Gov Bogs All at once I se him arayed in riches because of the deed he had don to take the life of a free man as he by a number was hired As I got threw with my vision I enquired after the two Prisoners I was told that Joseph

---

3. Olney likely meant "quell": To crush; to subdue, to cause to cease. *Noah Webster's First Edition of an American Dictionary of the English Language—Facsimile 1828 Edition*, s.v. "Quell."

4. Orrin Porter Rockwell was born June 28, 1813, at Belchertown, Massachusetts. He was a friend to Joseph Smith from his childhood. Rockwell was baptized on April 6, 1830, the very day the Church was organized, making him one of the first members of the Church. He served as a bodyguard to Joseph Smith and later to Brigham Young. Rockwell was accused of the assassination attempt on Missouri Governor Lilburn W. Boggs; he was arrested and spent nine months in a Missouri prison. He was released after the Grand Jury declined to indict him. After Joseph Smith's death, Rockwell traveled west with the majority of the Saints. He served as a peace officer in the Utah Territory until his death in June 1878. A colorful figure in Mormon history, he has become legendary and something of a folk hero, and has become the subject of biographies, novels, and movies. See Garr, Cannon, and Cowan, *Encyclopedia*, 1038; Donna Hill, *Joseph Smith: The First Mormon*, 106.

5. Unable to locate "appregation" or any similar words in several unabridged dictionaries. Perhaps Olney meant "apparition." In context, it would then read, "I saw a strange apparition or likeness of the form, size and looks of Porter Rockwell."

Smith had gone to Washingten to se what could be don and P Rockwell had gone to missouri after witnesses To speak in his behalf Thus the Prisoners give them the slip That caused a rejoiceing amongst the Saint In writing my vision I have rote the tales that daily is told but will not vouch for the truith of what I have written as I find I am amongst a Lying set

[Folder number 8] Citty of Nauvoo August 10th

Being caled on by the Messenger from on high to take my course down the river about thre miles I was there visited by the Antient of Days and shone that there was an innumerable sum of money to be got by me at some futer time to establish a stake of Zion build dwellings places of worship and prepare for a famine against a time of need

[Folder number 8] Citty of Nauvoo August 11th

I still continue my writings of things that daily transpires In our Noted Citty as many is a talking and much adoing that speaks louder than words As a theme of doings has long ben spoken of for the Saints to arise And extricate themselves by going in to the wilderness with the Natives west As a way is opening for many to start To the Rocky Mountains in order to raise up a Righeous branch the two Prisieners are in alerk [alert?] awaiting the time that they can move together as is said to be the theme For a Company to start in fulfilment of Prophesi to the west whire no power shall oppose them or turn them to the wright or Left I still have feelings my mind to express about the Church of Latter day Saints and they to a member will agree with me that any move that is made by their Leaders they as a people will all go for it Let be it right or rong This fact Has put many to shame That mite have ben decent men A word from their Prophit J Smith by the way of prophesi Is sanctioned and must to the Letter be fulfild The case of Ex Gov Bogs made a slip but yet their is a remady for it that the Prophesi of many may come to pass Tis when they get setled in the west and form a Union with the Indians they then can move on the wicked world and put to flight those that have oprest them As this has long ben the theme that the Indians as them have ben abused to be sure the Indians have ben driven or they have sold and moved from East to west Why in fulfilment of prophesi on them is a curse that their skin is changed to dark shades and they an idle loathsome people[6] and will continue

6. The Book of Mormon was published in 1830, proclaimed by believers to be a translation of an ancient record of people who lived in the western hemisphere. Early Mormons believed that the so-called Indians of the Americas were direct descendants of a Book of Mormon people called Lamanites. This is still a common belief within The Church of Jesus Christ of Latter-day Saints, although there has been a pull back

untill God se fit to chance [change?] their state As God has always worked by means I think He will not make use of means such as is in aray to go amongst them at this time No when the curse he does remove if he makes use of man he will take some besides Murderers or the wickedest part of Community I have now come to a close and say I add no more O. H. Olney

[Folder number 8] Citty of Nauvoo August 11th 1842

This my birthday I sit down to write of things as I am caled to perform I am met by the Antient men of God that now and then meet in council some business to perform as this is a day of business with them I write of their doings as to me is shone that speaks of what is soon to be don They instruct me in business that soon must be don by me and others that is caled Gods work to perform A temporal kingdom is soon to be set up by order and direction of the Antient of Days As I am caled by them and set apart I depend on them to direct me in my daily moves about By them I am instructed some business to do to bring about certin things that to me has ben in the dark It is up the river not far of that a building was established by the Jaredites and new vamped over by the Nephites That reard a Citty here I have orders to visit the Noted

---

from earlier declarations. The introduction of the current copy of the Book of Mormon states that the Lamanites "are among the ancestors of the American Indians." Whereas, it used to read that the Lamanites "are the principal ancestors of the American Indians." Among early Mormons there was an even stronger feeling connecting Lamanites and American Indians. Olney's reference to a curse, dark skin, and idle, loathsome people comes from the Book of Mormon. 2 Nephi 5:20–24 reads: "Wherefore, the word of the Lord was fulfilled which he spake unto me, saying that: Inasmuch as they will not hearken unto thy words they shall be cut off from the presence of the Lord. And behold, they were cut off from his presence. And he had caused the cursing to come upon them, yea, even a sore cursing, because of their iniquity. For behold, they had hardened their hearts against him, that they had become like unto a flint; wherefore, as they were white, and exceedingly fair and delightsome, that they might not be enticing unto my people the Lord God did cause a skin of blackness to come upon them. And thus saith the Lord God: I will cause that they shall be loathsome unto thy people, save they shall repent of their iniquities. And cursed shall be the seed of him that mixeth with their seed; for they shall be cursed even with the same cursing. And the Lord spake it, and it was done. And because of their cursing which was upon them they did become an idle people, full of mischief and subtlety, and did seek in the wilderness for beasts of prey." Early Latter-day Saints believed that one of their responsibilities was to take the Book of Mormon to the Native Americans and convert them, fulfilling the prophecy, "And then shall they rejoice; for they shall know that it is a blessing unto them from the hand of God; and their scales of darkness shall begin to fall from their eyes; and many generations shall not pass away among them, save they shall be a pure and a delightsome people" (2 Ne. 30:6).

place and go in and out and find paster [pasture?] or to be administerd to In temporal concerns I am now caled to withdraw from the Church as a spirit is ariseing each other to opress and a spirit of war will soon be the theme on men women and Childern as it God has decreed

[Folder number 8] Citty of Nauvoo Aug 12th 1842

I am write of the doings of the C. of the L.D.S. as much excitement is in voge Much is a saying as well as doing to prepare for the Coming of the Son of man A union is established Amongst the Church of Latter Day Saints that they will stand by each other at the exspense of their lives Its because of visitors That has come in with orthoroty And writings Greeting that cals for two men of the place but they yet come up missing or are not to be found By the Officers that for them has come I think fair weather with them would fetch them to light that they would arise with the sun amongst us If what I Learn is correct as many say bearly the sound of a traump by them would be herd that they could speak for themselves

[Folder number 8] Citty of Nauvoo August 12th 1842

I this Morning sit down to write of things that comes to my vew. And speak my feelings about matters and things I look at the sun as it a raises in the East I se its colour form and sise as it appears to me And the velocity of the Earth on which I stand And say Who can Fathom the power of God Who has wisdom to know of his works as we se the revolution of the Earth once in twenty four hours in Obediance to the King of day We look at the Earth in the form of a ball placed on a Crank and turned from age to age We look at the power by which it is don We se no foundation To commence to build We know not of the materials That supports the earth and keeps it daily in its place We know not of the power By which it moves or why it is that we move with such velocity and seem to Stand Still We look at the days some Long and at another time short and say why is it thus Why are not the days all of a length We look at the seasons of both heat and Cold and say why does weather so soon change We look at the Mountains hills vallys and Lakes and say why was it not made Level with small rivulets to flow We look at the rivers both Large and small and say how are they supplyed at the fountain head We look at man as he was made upright and Just and at his presant condition now on Earth We se them towards Each other move in contact that looks to me strange Why they with each other should contend I look at the beasts of the fields And Fowls of the air and se a spirit of Contention As with man I look at the Flowers and lillys of the Fields I se nothing but buty and Harmony amongst them I look at the degraded state that I se man and beast Birds and fishes And the Earth and say it was occasioned by sin that man became fallen because of doing wrong that has revolutionised the Earth and plased things in their presant state If I had Faith and could Comprehend the glory of God And his magesty power and dominion I would answer the rest of my questions that for the presant would satisfy my mind But as I am a Lacking I am willing to wait a move in accordance with my fellow man

[Folder number 3] August 13th

I still have feelings my mind to express I se their is much a going at home and abroad That daily salutes my ears that takes the attention of many I look at the doings That gives The storys a start and se them mostly Founded on facts The Sayings of J C Bennett is by many hardly received but I am satisfied That he has not half told the tale At the same time he has wrote things that is not correct yet mutch in the dark He spoke of a Lamb That on the alter was offerd to fasten the P hood lest it should be lost that I suppose was correct as blood was found on door and posts that of it at the time much was said[7] But I think of the P hood they need not a lost if they can make it up other ways I have no more to say I cannot yet pass by Doct Bennett Altho he is a stranger to me yet I have often seen him about Bennett had a long and high standing In the Church of L. D. Saints was extolled to the highest by those of the first He was put forward as a man of God that his council was received by the most of the Church But all of a sudden He gave up his post as mayor of the Citty and stood a looking on that caused much to be said about J. C Bennett I have ben impartial in my moves I am satisfied They are all of a mess I se they all moved to gether hart and hand untill the difficulty arose and J. C. Bennet left the Church I well know of the affidavits that is afloat and know they are obtained Some one that wisdom to write such and such articles as will back the case some lacky is ready to sware to them Thus they can get as much testimony as they pleas They can build up or put down at leisure As I find my self engaged with feelings good I to do justice between man and man I will only write the simple truth and leave much That wisdom says keep back

[Folder number 8] Citty of Nauvoo Aug 13th 1842

I still have feelings my mind to express about matters and things that daily transpires I se there is much agoin at home and abroad that takes the attention of many I look at the doings that gives the sayings a start And se them mostly founded on facts The sayings of J C Bennet is by many hardly received but I am

7. Olney states that his information about the sacrifice of a lamb comes from the sayings and writings of John C. Bennett. He does add the "blood was found on door and posts that of it at the time much was said." Other than Olney and Bennett, I have found no mention of the sacrifice of a lamb in Nauvoo.

satisfied he has not half told the tale At the same time he has wrote some things that is not Correct And left much untold He rote of a Lamb that on the alter was burned to fasten the Priesthood lest it they should loose I will speak in behalf of Doct Bennet As I se much a float To distroy his influance by the Leaders of the Church of the L D Saints As for J C Bennet I have bearly to him spoke but he has ben put forward in the Church and extold to the hiest untill within a few weeks I se they of the Church turn against him and Slander him as is their way to do when a member does them leave As for Bennet I think him much exited to use them up at once If he will let them alone they will use up themselves As I daily have ben with him and with them I have looked at them to be all of a mess If he had any advantage It was because of his skill of being a noted Phisitian [physician] And could feel their hurts But the time has ariven that the orthorotys of the States has said to enquire into their doings of the Church of Latter day Saints I look at the course that they say to take I see them determined to go a head and streighten a crooked mess of sticks The Sherifs first came to the place with writs to take two of our Citty and try them by the Laws of the land The two they soon took. The Citty council meet and by a writ said to take them out of their hands The officers for fear of doing wrong left the Prisoners and went to the Governor and enquired into the affair They soon returned The Prisoners to take but to their supprise was a missing The Governor soon came And Enquired for those named in the writs <last line of the page cut off> I pass by perticulars and speak on general terms and say I am disgusted at what I do se as I am a passing and repasing amongst the members of Latter D Saints They bost of the power of God in their behalf and say Brother Joseph has wisdom to out wit the doings of the world They say God will direct him in his way altho he has ben much out of the way They say we as a people have influance with God that he will preserve us protect us that all things will work for our good They speak readily of the Iniquity of the place but pass over it as of no account They say such men as the Presidancy and Gods Chosen Apostles of the twelve and many other leading characters that leads the Church Would not do thus and so unless they knew it was wright Thus they reason that I count them about all of a mess If not all in it they have not a mind to do or act for themselves But bearly a few In the City of Nauvoo can open their eyes enough to think or speak for themselves The more I se of them The less of them I think They receive all that is said by many to be the word of God Altho they are in iniquity ever so deep How long God will bear with such a set I cannot say but suffise it to say if they are wright and go to Heaven as they now are between them and the Antient saints in Heaven will be a fuss Before they can unite I again draw to a close and say if I any more write I shall do it against my feelings as my feeling is troubled To se so many unwise Cretures together on the Earth I am a friend to nobody hardly to myself untill I can git in to differant Company and whire I can breath air in some decent place I am as ever

O. H. Olney

[Folder number 3] Citty of Nauvoo August 14th 1842

Again I have feeling that is not of the best kind when I look at my self and the people with whom I am daily conversant They say to be a people that lives near to God They say to blest with Revelations that directs them in their ways This sound has gone forth to the Nations of the Earth that the Latter day Saints are much faverd of God In will ask them a question In earnest and let them answer it themselves if the name of God is not disgrased by the people caled L D Saints Look back on your doings with supprise to think that God would suffer him self to be mouthed by you to Carry on your ungodly works I have skipt ore many Items that I hither to have pened I shudder for you When I think of your end I can quote the words of an Antient that you had better not a ben born than to a don as has ben your course in passing threw a probationary state By you the Law of God is broken and fairly underfoot trodden and of course the penalty will be annext

[Folder number 8] Citty of Nauvoo Aug. 14th 1842

I again have feelings to write that I will say is not of the best kind Whire am I but amongst a people that say to do Gods will And receive Revelations to govern them in their daily moves They say to be the chosen people of God and are daily instructed in things of God I ask of the Character of God and his condesention to man that he at the meridean of time condecended to take a tabernicle of flesh and take up his abode on Earth What was his doings What was his works Did he Lie cheat Decieve and defraud and take every advantage to gain his points Or was he open free and familiar in his daily moves Without a shadow of turning because of the unwise doings of man Did he not set an example for man to imitate by being honest and upright in all his doings Was not his life for an exsample to be followed by those of the creatures of his care Did he not give a Law to govern man Was it dark sayings Or was it easy to be understood We find it was easy As he marked the way and well in structed his apostles in the course that they should take day by day We thus have his teachings In connection with his life that lays a foundation to move in the order of God But in looking at the doings of the L D Saints what do I discover amongst them but Iniquity a low mean order of things The pattern is set by those at the head that the system is well <illegible> With the pattern set There ways and doings is now to well known For them to be caled or have the name of being a people of God I now draw to a close and say to those that has wisdom to think and speak for themselves to be up and adoing and no more be daubed over with the said Prophits in Nauvoo As a new one has arose[8] In the place of the one gone as he said on the stand to Washington from thence to England to be gone for years Whire is he but in the Citty of Nauvoo Is it now well known that J Smith is now in the Citty of Nauvoo by many Why need his Brother Hiram say that he has gone to such and such places when he is conversant with him every day As for P O Rockwell I know not of him but no doubt but he is gilty of the Crime that to him is alleged If Joseph is clear why not come forward and speak for him self Or why need so much deception be used to say thus and so When it is not a fact That is calculated to keep the members in the dark respecting things that they had orto to know But as a new Prophit has took a stand and set apart by Revelation and ordained to fill Joseph place in case that he should fall As he has fallen and well underfoot its hopeful that Hiram his Brother will honour him self by doing well But he has a snarl to beguin on But he must be aversed[9] in the way as he has had a hand in the doings from the arise of the Church untill now I now draw to a close as usual.

O H Olney

---

8. A revelation dated January 19, 1841, directed that Hyrum Smith become Patriarch to the Church. It also stated concerning Hyrum: "And from this time forth I appoint unto him that he may be a prophet, and a seer, and a revelator unto my church, as well as my servant Joseph; That he may act in concert also with my servant Joseph; and that he shall receive counsel from my servant Joseph, who shall show unto him the keys whereby he may ask and receive, and be crowned with the same blessing, and glory, and honor, and priesthood, and gifts of the priesthood, that once were put upon him that was my servant Oliver Cowdery" (D&C 124:94–95). This unusual office in the First Presidency was first held by Oliver Cowdery, who by this time had been excommunicated. Hyrum Smith replaced Cowdery as Associate President of the Church (a term not used during Hyrum Smith's lifetime but applied later by historians to describe the office held by Oliver Cowdery and Hyrum Smith). Olney writes that "a new [prophet] has arose." This statement was made when Joseph Smith had gone into hiding and Hyrum was leading the Church in Joseph's absence. On August 8, 1842, sheriffs arrived in Nauvoo and arrested Joseph Smith and Orrin Porter Rockwell, who had been accused of the attempted assassination of former Missouri governor, Lilburn W. Boggs. The prisoners were taken to a court in Nauvoo and both were released on writs of habeas corpus. When the sheriffs returned a few days later, they discovered that Rockwell had fled to Philadelphia and Joseph Smith had gone into hiding. Rumors circulated Nauvoo that Joseph Smith had gone to England or to Europe. It was reported that he had been seen on a steamboat going toward Canada. See Hill, *Joseph Smith*, 311–12. The false rumors were likely spread to dissuade the sheriffs from continuing the search. Joseph remained in the Nauvoo area.

9. Disliking; unwilling; having a repugnance of mind. *Webster's Dictionary* (1828), s.v. "Averse."

[Folder number 9] Citty of Nauvoo August 16th 1842

Being caled on by a Messenger from above, to meet in Council, With the Antient of Days, on this the sixteenth day of August 1842. With them I meet And with them I Sympethise of things that is about to transpire, amongst the Church of Latter day Saints. The leaders of the Church is first in voge, that a decision on them is past, that because of their works being unjust, and rejecting the Council of God; and putting To defiance his power and araising up In their Own strength, that from them, Is now to be taken, their gifts. And they left in their own strength altho many to them is a looking—and cheerfully moves under Their watch care, But the anger of the Lord is kindled, at what is and has ben daily a goin on. Because of such doings, In his name; he of late has visited, And vewed them, and given directions what to do, to those of this Servents, The Antient of Days, as they now have mett in Council, a decision by them is made—That a scourge must chasten them, untill they se the folly of their doings. Their destiny is determined by the Council—That has on Earth took a stand, that their folly is first to come to light, by being published, To the world. At the same time A confusion- amongst them, Is decreed, by the order of Heaven, that will cause an excitement- amongst those that do not with them coencide A war of Extermination[10], is also decreed, That will usher in, as soon as their works is known. Then a work of Importance is to

10. Several times in Olney's writings he states that a war of extermination is decreed against the Saints because of their evil doings or bad works. His use of the phrase "war of extermination" is interesting. Amid the hostilities between Mormons and non-Mormons in Missouri, on July 4, 1838, Sidney Rigdon, counselor to Joseph Smith, gave a sermon in Far West, Missouri. It was a fiery sermon which included the following statement: "Our rights shall no more be trampled on with impunity; the man, or the set of men who attempt it, do it at the expense of their lives. And that mob that comes on us to disturb us, it shall be between us and them a war of extermination; for we will follow them until the last drop of their blood is spilled; or else they will have to exterminate us, for we will carry the seat of war to their own houses and their own families, and one party or the other shall be utterly destroyed." Peter Crawley, "Two Rare Missouri Documents," 527. The speech given by Rigdon was published in pamphlet form and picked up by several Missouri newspapers. See Crawley, 517–27, for the document in its entirety. On October 27, 1838, Missouri Governor Lilburn W. Boggs issued what has become known as the "extermination order." Using words similar to Rigdon's July 4th oration, the order stated that the Mormons "must be treated as enemies, and exterminated or driven from the State." See Garr, Cannon, and Cowan, *Encyclopedia*, 351. Olney would have experienced the persecutions suffered by Mormons in Missouri and was driven out of the state as a result of the extermination order. Yet, in this entry of his writings, he also uses a comparable phrase, stating that "a war of extermination" had been decreed "by the order of heaven."

arise, that will call for valiant Labourers, to come forward As volenteers. As a work is to be don by the- Antient of Days, That will be- marvelous in the Eyes of the World. It will be don by the wisdom, And power of God, threw chosen vessels, on the Earth, The gifts of the Gospel, on them will rest, that wisdom knowledge and Dissernment will expand the mind, That Iniquity by the Saints will be siverd out as the teachings of Elijah will be the theme or they an other Comforter will receive that will direct them In their daily moves

[Folder number 9] Citty of Nauvoo August 16th 1842 not to read

Being caled upon by a messenger above to meet in council with the Antient of days on this the Sixteenth of August 1842 With them I meet And with them I sympathise about things that is about to transpire amongst the Church of Latter Day Saints The Leaders of the Church first is in voge that a decision on them Is past that because of their works being unjust and rejecting the Council of God and putting to defiance his power and araising up in their own strength that from them Is now to be taken their gifts and they left in their own Strength Altho many to them is a looking and cheerfully moves under their watch care But the anger of the Lord is kindled at what is and has ben daily agoing on Because of such doings In his name he of late has visited and vewed them and give directions what to do to those of this servants The Antient of days As they now have meet in Council a decision is made, That a scourge must chasten them Untill they se the folly of doing as they have don Their destiny is determined by the Council that has on Earth took a stand that their folly is first to come to light by being published to the world At the same time a confusion amongst them is decreed By the order of Heaven that will cause an exitement Among those that do not with them Coencide A war of extermination Is also decreed that will usher in as soon as the their works is known Then a work of Importance is to arise that will cal for valiant Labourers to come forward as Volenteers As a work is to be don by the Antient of days that will be Marvelous in the Eyes of the world It will be don by the wisdom and power of God threw chosen vessels On the Earth The gifts of the Gospel on them will rest that wisdom knowledge and desernment will expand the mind, That iniquity by the Saints will be severd out as the teachings of Elijah will be with them or they an other Comfurter will receive that will direct them In their daily moves

[Folder number 9] Citty of Nauvoo August 16th 1842

Again I am caled my mind to prepare to [receive?] such things as will satisfy my mind As I long have had before me a senry of things That has ben to me a trouble time and again I[t] was shone to me some twelve months ago but have toiled for it but not got it as yet But its now said to me the prise to receive of hidden treasures that have long lain in the Earth It was hid up by the Nephites many hundred years ago desined to come forth In time to establish a work thats now in voge Its barly Commenced and on the move altho in the dark to man except a few that knows not what to say or do But its rise is determined and on the move as is spoken of by The Prop[h]et Daniel and is no more to be baffled or trodden underfoot of men but is to be reard by the power of God and He honoured by it, because of their doings Its now to be established Routed and grounded with light Knowledge and wisdom not lacking in things, Such as money Goods and chattels To move it a head As money is a waiting To give things a start that is hid up in the Prese[r]ved by a messenger that over it has power That holds it untill it is caled for in a legal manner His name is written And known by the messengers above As Thomas[11] that live at the meridean of time By that name he will answer when legally caled on And will open a door in to the bowels of the Earth whire much is arayed of different kinds of immens value; When put use The time is fast approaching the treasures to obtain As the treasures is many thou art first caled To enter the mansion and take out some little or what will do the for the presant say five hundred dollars Then leave the Mansion as it you find and do as you are shone to bring about the purposes of God You will first visit the mansion ~~to enter the house~~ day after day and when the time comes the door to you will open That you can go in By calling on Thomas and ask a permit you will know him when you se him as He will sit clothed in black and arayed in dark shades So untill you meet with him the time has not come to enter the the mansion in the name of the Lord But you daily are caled to go there unless you are other ways shone

[Folder number 8] August 17th Citty of Nauvoo

This noted place speaks loud of doings as many is combined together to bring about the purposes of God Some is a writing And a publishing to cuver up old sores but the sores are open and the filth a getherin And a running out altho they have many nurses that spends all their time to daub over with a plaster of something that will cover up a dirty mess I look at those of the Leaders of the Church and daily vew their doings that they say is of God That they are his agents to administer in his name That they have power with him

11. Olney was likely referring to Thomas, one of the twelve apostles chosen by Jesus (Matt. 10:2–4). Thomas, also known as Didymus, which means twin, was not present when the resurrected Jesus first appeared to the apostles (John 20:24). Because he said that he would not believe Jesus was resurrected until he did personally "see in his hands the print of the nails, and put my finger into the print of the nails, and thrust my hand into his side" (John 20:25), he is commonly known as "Doubting Thomas."

as did the Antient men of God to build and establish in his name I look at their doings I look at their works I look at two foundations That is begun to build in the name of the Lord The first is the temple or house of the Lord that was commenced neer two years ago It now as high as the Abasement story and barly commenced on that to build I then look at the Nauvoo house that is said to be an Inn in the name of the Lord that has ben a going or building about in accordance with the temple I look at the means That has ben used to build I look at what is don And say to those that take charge of the work that there is somewhire a wrong Has there not ben men set apart that have spent their time in collecting fund from East to west and North and South As far as the name of Mormon is known Yes I well know of many that have spent their time and agetherd much to assist in building the houses In Nauvoo Much from foren Countrys has ben brought in connections with funds getherd in our own Country to build the temple and the Nauvoo house All in the name of the Lord Many thousands has ben brought in as a fre gift to help on the work Much in tithing has ben paid The Consecration Law has brought in much We in safty say in all – enough Enough to build or put up and inclose both of the houses But instead of that what is don Barly two foundations is begun and one the sleepers[12] hardly placed for the first floor The other not a sleeper laid But hands to work that say that they do not get enough to sustain them but suffer for the want of pay for their work It is the same with those that on the temple work They merly get enough to bearly get along And keep to work Thus they get along with the work Two thurough men With a few thousand dollars would a don more in Sis months than has ben don to a built the two houses I look at the course that they have took and se what they have ben about in Opressing the poor as they have don that hundreds of familys is a suffering because being caled on In the name of the Lord by those that take charge of the work Yes thousands after thousands has ben paid in To do the work but not put to the place desined Neither have hands ben paid or half paid for what they have don One tenth of every mans time is required that would have don If half worked their time more than what is don I dwell in facts and not on tales As is the case with those that spend their time, A plastering up old sores But as they are aversed in plastering I will admit the fact That they have wisdom to write in their own defence if the language they make use of is ever so low and mean It well answers their purposes as all they say and do is verry Cunning in the estimation of their friends The lower their doings the better for it better by them understood as they have got their faces

12. In building, the oblique rafter that lies in a gutter; a floor timber. *Webster's Dictionary* (1828), s.v. "Sleeper." Because Olney mentioned sleepers placed on the first floor, he was likely referring to floor timbers.

downward and a padling in the mud They speak of useing up Editors in differant states They say we have tools to do it But their tools are of a slippery kind They are often on the Alert They are not often found among what is wright They often are in Company a speaking of great things But when we come to sound them we find them still in the mud If they have feelings When my writings comes from the press say about one hundred of them with me to coencide I will assist them to get out of their presant state as it must to them be degrading to allways be a nusling in a nasty mess of mud If I have time I will assist them to get out of their degraded state The plan I would devise is to put them in hill of burning lime some eight or ten together as it should seem best and let the fire Clense them It mite save the Deavil the trouble of popeing[13] them about But if it should look hard for ~~them~~ some over one hundred Cretures to go threw a firey smoking hill to be cleansed and purified from filth there is an other plan I would devise that each one repent of his ungodly works and reform in every sence of the word Stop writing preaching teaching and go to work and be honest men and scatter to the East and west and North and south And no more be ketched to gether in dirty scrapes But if it should look as hard to part as burn, There is another plan I would devise that Each one plant himself in a rich Prairie Soil And say to come forth in the name of the Lord Perchance they may Cheat old blackfoot out of picking their bones for doing what they know is wrong and disgusting in the site of God I now draw my writings to a close with feeling as ever of the best kind

O. H. Olney

[Folder number 9] Citty of Nauvoo August 17th 1842

Being caled on by a Messenger of power I take my seit in Low Mansion in the Citty once caled Desolation[14] because of the many destructions by wars But

---

13. Olney is accusing the leaders of Mormonism of being led by the devil. His use of the word "popeing" is likely a pejorative comment about Catholicism that was common among Protestants at the time. He is saying that the "pope" of the Mormons is the devil.

14. The Book of Mormon refers to the "land of Desolation" and the "city of Desolation." In the sixteenth chapter of Alma, the city known as Ammonihah and every inhabitant of the city was destroyed by a Lamanite army. "Behold, in one day it was left desolate; and the carcases were mangled by dogs and wild beasts of the wilderness. Nevertheless, after many days their dead bodies were heaped up upon the face of the earth, and they were covered with a shallow covering. And now so great was the scent thereof that the people did not go in to possess the land of Ammonihah for many years. And it was called Desolation of Nehors" (Alma 16:10–11). The land of Desolation is mentioned a number of times during the remainder of the

I write of things That comes to my vew and speak clearly my mind on principals that lies in the Dark I look at the Sun at noon day I look at the Earth on which I stand and say how is it possible That from morning till noon Can be such a change I look at the Earth, in the shape of a ball I look at the power By which it is governed I look at the Sun from morning till knight and se it arise in the East, and set in the west I vew the Earth That appearently stands still I look at the planits in Connection with the sun I se a Combination of matters and things I look at the Sun at a distance of that it appears to be small at sight I look at the Stars As inhabited worlds being far this side of the sun and yet appear but a speck I look at the Earth on which I stand and se it to be in connection with the planit of the Stars That revolves once in twenty four hours In honour of the sun I look at the foundation on which they stand and at the foundation of the Sun I se it has pillows[15] on which it rests that a tower is raised In honour of God I look at it sise far to supersede all other planits in the immensity of space I look at the power By which it is governed I there se the habitation of God, a home and a rest for him and his Son both in person in power and glory with their aids around them that goes and comes at their Command They have power invested in them that they move in the power of God and put things in order, Agreeable to his word They have power to form And create anew They have power to add Or diminish and to govern and rule the planits that revolves In honour of the Sun They by fixed principals is governed from age to age by hands of power that centers to the planit of the Sun Thus a foundation is laid that rules the Earth that it raises it lowers And revolves in obediance to the Law of God That its work is performed agreeable to the Law of God Its work is daily to be don Without a shadow of changing to suit the times Or those that on it dwells As there is cretures of differant grades from man to the Lowest insect that are for a wise purpose Created Altho there is many That are obnoxious in the site of man yet they for a wise purpose are on and in the Earth altho the resorecting power will not bring them forth No none but the sensitive and harmless will be raised to Come forward with the Saints at the first resorection In the melineum morn

---

Book of Mormon. In the latter part of the Book of Mormon a city of Desolation is referenced, again in connection with war. "The Lamanites did come down to the city of Desolation to battle against us" (Morm. 3:7). "The Lamanites did take possession of the city Desolation, and did slay many of the Nephites" (Morm. 4:2). Olney appears to be saying that Nauvoo stands on the site of the Book of Mormon city of Desolation, so called "because of the many destructions by wars."

15. Although it is possible that Olney was making reference to "pillowy" clouds that the sun appeared to be sitting upon, it is more likely that he meant pillar. For example, in his November 13, 1842, writing, Olney refers to "a pillow of fire." See OOP, fd. 10, November 13, 1842.

Again their is many That will come forth with the rest of the dead That have ben with them threw the thousand years of the melineum of the obnoxious kind On their planit of destiny whire they reap the reward of their Labours for doing wrong Or rejecting the council of God They then come forward With natures changed in honour of the God above and have a standing on the Earth In peace and Harmony they will meet those that come forward at the 1st Resorection They then will have a pleasant home In honour of the Father and Son they will have a place of high renown that will be satisfactory to them but not on the planit with the Saints

[Folder number 8] Citty of Nauvoo August 18th 1842

As I have often ben Assaild by the people caled the Latter day Saints I have bourn and bourn with them untill I am weary of their works I first met with them with feeling that was good and was submissive to them untill I was weary of what I daily se and herd I first meet with them saying to serve God but what did I se and what did I learn that turned my attention but wicked works I often looked I often gased on things that we was taught by those that said to lead the Church of Latter day Saints With their doings and ways I did first Conform as I supposed and verrily believed that I was to be governed by a Prophit of God But from time to time I have ben assailed by them that I bearly said I from them would take my name It I did threw the medium of the press And bearly hinted that by them I had ben abused Now in return they have commenced again on me threw the medium of the wasp As the Wasp is by many propeld and has commenced on me without a just cause I now do fell to take a stand and write from time to time with the best of feelings of the doing and motives of the Latter-day Saints on a principal of Honour and good will to man I take a stand without respet to party or friends or foes I will of things that I actually know and of things that I verrily believe and of things that I can prove I will give my reasons As I have long ben with them and ben conversant with their ways I well do understand their course What a person speaks in their own behalf They in a mass will all arise say fifty or sixty and put on their epothets first in the Church They then will publish to the world by slandering Abusing misrepresenting them to the loest Now if the Editors of the day will give heed to my writings I will tel them about the people caled Mormons or Latter day Saints weekly as I feel it a duty on a principal of Righteousness Now to take a stand and expose them with feeling to do them good as a people I consider them a dangerous people and an ungovernable people or a people that are ~~in the round~~ determined in the round to put to defiance the Laws of the land I now draw to a close by subscribing myself as a well wisher to well doers

[Folder number 3] City of Nauvoo August 19th

As time passes much is adoing that daily takes my attention of the doings of the Latter day Saints As much is agoing Old sores a running that long have ben exsposed to the air its contents a fermenting Plasters cannot be found to cover them up Altho many is a looking a multitude a talking many a writing but its Labour spint in vain As the chose[16] is affected it has become rotten harted and the skin fractured because of the filth That it contains So I pass by them as of as of not much account Again I look at their doings as being Birds of a feather some wet and muddy Without Conveniences to rinse of the mud But I look at them and se the pains taken and say it is harder Than to do wright But a pattern is set By the leaders that no shadow of turning will be received I look at their doing And their works also two foundations That is begun to build in the name of the Lord The first is the temple or house of the Lord that was commenced Near two years ago It now is as high as the abasement story and bearly commenced on that to build I then look at the Nauvoo house that is said to be an Inn In the name of the Lord that has ben a going or building About the same time

[Folder number 3] The absurdities of Mormonism[17]

Portrayed By O. H. Olney
Nauvoo Hancock County Ill
An introduction

The desire of the Orther in publishing the following pages is to show the Absurdities Doings Trates Of certin ones who profess to be led by the spirit of Revelation from God that stand as leaders of the Latter Day Saints I pass by Doctrinal points, Wholy and speak of the doings of those That are looked too as Infalaible men of God. My design in publishing this work is more perticularly, To open the Eyes of many, That have not had the privilege, That I have to know of their doings of the Church of L.D.S.— I have ben with them Above eleven years, not at a watcher after Iniquity, But as an impartial observer, And have an impartial record of the doings of the Church of L.D.S.— that will speak for it self in due time. On a principal I have rote these few pages with

16. *Chose* being derived from the French *chose* and Spanish *cosa*, meaning suit, cause, thing. See *Thing* and *Cause. Webster's Dictionary* (1827), s.v. "Chose." Olney was likely referring to the symbolic sore or "thing" that had become dirty or infected. He was writing about past wrongdoings of Latter-day Saints that had been kept hidden and were coming to light.

17. In March 1843 Olney published a booklet entitled *The Absurdities of Mormonism Portrayed*. This entry appears to be the beginnings of his first draft of that publication.

much reluctance, But not knowing of any other person, About to devulge the Iniquity I commenced last April and have bearly tutched on the doings of a certin Company, That I feel in duty bound To wield my pen against them To show to those, that move under their watch care, the Iniquity of those that lead them I add my own testimony And the testimony of others Of the truth of what I have wrote It is those that are aquainted with the doings of the L.D.S. That are not aferd That are not aferd to speak for themselves with characters Unimpeachable

Again I will add some letters That have ben written to me by friends (That I will venter to say as good men as there is in society) To know why I have left the Sosiety of the L. D. Saints, I have I think twelve of them I add all or a part That will establish two points as they are mostly in ful faith With the presant doings of the Leaders And their confidance in me As to morality

[Folder number 4] Citty of Nauvoo August 19th 1842

I again write of things that comes to my vew As many is a talking some few adoing in our citty of Refuge as the story goes freely The rounds that a company is a fixing to go some whire near the Rocky Mountains whire no Law will disturb them or they can make Laws of their own to gain a place of rest A rest to them that will be of value In their daily moves As much is on the wing to be don or this presant Jentile Nation as they would say must be damb for the want of the Royal Blood to arise and Preach to them Men women and Childern all as one are engaged To commence a work of importance that will reach to the fore quarters of the Earth As fishers and hunters Is soon to be cald to scour the Country Both far an neer Altho there is many daily agoing out but they are not of a class that is desined To do the great work that will usher in the Latter day Glory Those that are gone of them I forbear to speak as some of them hinted to me any thing to get away from the doings of the City of Nauvoo With but few exceptions its rag Shag and Bobtail that is daily on the move to go forth to bind up the Law and seal the testimony of this gentile race This is not all that of them is required as excitement arises about Ex Gov Bogs as the othorotys of the of state has cald for President J Smith and O. P. Rockwell as being Accessary to the Crime as they keep housed or holed up or split up that they are not to be found It raises much excite ment around with other facts that takes the daily rounds that Zions Watchman Is cald to put down or pronounce them all lies or Persecution for Christs sake I could add more if I thought it best but I don't wish to hurt there feelings for old aquaintance sake It is supposed by many That Joseph Smith is the only big man in the Church but I can mention numbers at the same time he says to lead but they are as geese and goslins full grown it is hard to tell the differance Yet

Joseph has the Preeminance amongst about fifty or sixty The rest are of the lesser grade They mostly do for Lackys They are ready to do or say as orders comes from the more worthy ones I have often shudderd at their teaching on the stand One case I will mention neer the temple North west By Brigham Young in February or March last in teaching or lecturing on Sunday said to be in honour of the Son of God He spoke of those That left the L.D.S. that if he had power he would cut their guggles[18] The third time he did it repete but lest it they should not understand he repeted it By saying he would cut their throats if God would give him power I look at his agency And Danite oath and said who is safe in their hands well knowing That several hundreds are in aray To put into execution their degraded trates I look at the colloms of the Wasp and read a clause of the Danites put in by the Citty Council They say they know of no such Clans but I look at the whiproe they take and se them shift names to carry on their ungodly trates As much is a doing amongst us an Institution is established Cald Masonry The Danites have come forward and united with them fre of expense As Masonry is all the theme they enter thre a day I have often wonderd why they dont all go at once if it is a good institution As many to me says It must be much disgraced such a set as has to it conformed in the Citty of Nauvoo I[t] has made me think of a story that I long since of the death of Morgan[19] As the story was he by the Masons was kild I know nothing the tale but the late doings brings it to mind I look at the case of J C Bennett and hear much of him said that he had orto a ben put into the river or put out of the way Before he left the place from men women

18. Under "guggle," *Webster's Dictionary* says "See gurgle." Under "gurgle" it says, "the throat." *Webster's Dictionary* (1827), s.v. "Guggle." Olney was reporting that Brigham Young had remarked that if he had the authority to do so, he would cut the throats of apostates.

19. William Morgan was a Royal Arch Mason. He signed a petition seeking permission to organize a Royal Arch chapter of Freemasonry in Batvia, New York. After his name "was removed from the petition and he was denied entrance into the chapter after it was organized," Morgan became a bitter enemy of Freemasonry. He threatened to expose the Masonic rituals. Even though a number of Masonic ritual guides and exposés had been published for many years, local Freemasons were outraged by Morgan's deliberate disregard for the oaths of secrecy he had made. On September 12, 1826, Morgan disappeared and was never heard from again. It was presumed that he was abducted and murdered. Many suspected that Morgan had been killed by Freemasons for publishing *Illustrations of Masonry by One of the Fraternity.* Interestingly, William Morgan's widow, Lucinda, became a member of The Church of Jesus Christ of Latter-day Saints. She was married to George Washington Harris. After Joseph Smith's death, Lucinda was sealed to Joseph Smith by proxy as one of his eternal wives. See Michael W. Homer, *Joseph's Temples: The Dynamic Relationship Between Freemasonry and Mormonism*, 51–55, 234.

and Childern The tale has gone by many of the place I look at the people cald LDS esspecially their Leaders And many others that would be great and say is it possible That the nineteenth Century can produce such a set in a land of liberty Of which our fathers gained by a long an slaveish war to gain their wrights I has over Items of which I mite speak but let wisdom dictate And in silence look I look at the Arabs The Hotentots the natives in differant parts They have a law implanted within to do violance to know man except an actual enemy No none but the Robbers with them will coencide alth[o] many of the LDS would Blink at the thought of being linked with such a set But if they will open their Eyes and se the daily moves that is they need no more query But say that all the Leaders of the Church are deep in Iniquity or sanction it that they all move in a mass at the same time there is a few that Stands looking And know not what to do. I have spent time and feelings for months past and gone in hopes of a change of doings but the daily moves is such I have no hopes of a Reformation As much is adoing And much don I some time have feelings to look ahead and se what ten years would bring about I look at them far from this some whire in the Rocky Mountains in the far West Men Women and Childern all in aray with many Leaders of both Prophits and Prophitess that would say in the name of the Lord They would move in a oneness togethor asaying to lead Those of less note Would follow after a saying to be much blest of God

[Folder number 8] August 19th 1842 Citty of Nauvoo

I again Commence writing About matters and things and that speaks about the foibles of the Church of Latter day Saints as much is daily adoing in the name of the Lord Many Noted Familys is a fixing to move to the far west They fast are a makeing ready a voige to take As far as the Rocky Mountains to gain a place of rest A rest that to them will be of value In their daily moves to establish a foundation whire they can live They have long ben a fixing that much as in store such as money and goods that has ben donated in the name of the Lord that is carefully laid away in boxes to be ready to load when the way opens to go to the Rocky Mountains Men women and Childern are in aray fast a fixing to be under way with their Prophit Joseph That is daily a looking and anxious by awaiting to be at liberty that he can speak for him self Altho he has a Company That is under oath to do as he says At the Expens of their lives yet there is a veto on them at this time because of what they have don As much has ben agoing in the name of the Lord That is in part known by many around They se it wisdom to stand still untill they can extricate themselves by darkening the Storys that is afloat But their wisdom to darken looks dim as they have so many to talk They unriddle their works like the story of Joseph Smith going to Washington and Europe to be gone several years at the same time say he is nearby on in the limits of the Citty of Nauvoo As for their doings I bearly speak my mind that nothing is to bad for them to do to gain their purposes In the name of the Lord As this is the theme with them when caled on by many that says to lead that speak by the way of Prophesi that they say must be fulfild It is supposed that Joseph Smith is the only big man, But I know to the Contry [contrary?] I know of many About ready to burst unless something happens to them I think there will now and then be an Explosion Marvelous to relate I often think of their discourses or Lectors that I have herd by those that stands high amongst the Latter day Saints I herd him say in public That if he had power that he would cut the guggles of any one that would apostatise or leave the Church of Latter Day Saints He repeited it several times ove At last that we might understand him he said that inasmuch as a person should fall away or leave the Church if God would give him power he would cut their throat I look at the oath of those of the Danites that the Citty council publish in the wasp that they know of No such Clan But I look at their whiproe or turn I am satisfied they changed their names as their names are changable as well as their ways If what I Learn is Correct they have taken the oath of Masonry and enterd the Institution fre of expins As Masonry is all the theme they enter thre a day And have regular since the Institution was set up last winter To speak of masonry I forbear but if it is a good Institution as many to me has said it must be much disgrased by such a set as has to it Conformed that I know of in Our Citty of Nauvoo It has made me think of a story that I long since have herd that said Morgan by the Masons was murderd I know nothing of The truth of the story but I know of a set That could work at it if what they say is correct They speak of the life of a man of less note than a visious man would of the life of a dog I look back at the course of Doct J C Bennet And say that he has ben shamfully abused by the Church of Latter day Saints He first fell in with them and to them Conformed and then some difficulty arose in the summer of 1841 and asked to be dismissed by them They heaped epothets on him that I am informed untill they pervailed on him to stay He has continued with them untill of late and his name is skandalised to the lowest in their Publications of the day But what do I hear said by the many of the Church of the Latter day Saints Yes Men women and Childern I can almost say as one that J C Bennet had orto a ben kild or a ben put into the drink or sent down the river on a catfish Such preaching lecturing teaching and such talking often makes me stare to think of what a people lives in a land of liberty For which our Fathers long since fought to take the lives of freman in this American soil of Independance of which so much is said Look at the Arabs The Hotentots the Natives In different parts They have a Law planted within to do no such Act Whire is the pattern Its not to be found But amongst Robbers that move in the dark They ways and their doings with the Robbers will coencide altho many of the Latter d S would blush at the thought of being linked with such a set But if they will open their Eyes and se the daily moves that is they need no more query But say that all the Leaders of the Church are deep in Iniquity or sanction it that they all move in a mass At the same time their is a few that stand a looking on And know not what to do I have spent time and feelings for months past and gone some of the time looking about then a waiting again to work and some of the time adoing nothing but getting hold of their eavil deeds I have looked for their good deeds but they keep out of my sight or they have known[20] that comes to light But I understand their is some underway that is soon expected in due time I am in hopes that neither the sad or [siner?] will hide away any more as has ben the case If the tale is correct that has taken the daily rounds I would say to those That has a mind to go ahead to be up and adoing In the name of their God as he is liberal with them in their Daily moves about As a Righeous Branch is the theme they must be up and adoing as many is a suffering for the word that is waiding in darkness at noonday Let childern be matured And instructed in the name of your liberal God that will admit of Murdering and every other vise That of is spoke and give them the orthoroty of the P_hood that you receive from your liberal God and they must be men of works if they take after their progenitors and follow on in the name of their Lord As much is adoing and much a ben don I some times have feelings to look ahead and se what the Common course of things in ten years would fetch about I look at them far distant from this Some whire near the rocky mountains in the far west Men women and Childern all in aray with many wise leaders of both Prophits and Prophitessis that would say in the name of the Lord They would move in a mess together asaying to lead Those of less note would follow after saying to be much blest of God They would receive Instructions from time to time that they would say they was the only people on the Earth They thus would move with one at the head and others accessary Untill they had well fild the western woods As a Company would be left to tale along as fast as the members got ready to move They in aray would meet with the red men of the forest and condecend to them To gain their strength In this order their Kingdom will as they quote the teachings of Daniel That it will brake in pieces all others. Thus a Plan is laid A prophesi to fulfil that not not long since was deliverd by the new Prophit that is set apart that in ten years they would be six hundred thousand strong In the name of the Lord Thus in aray being united to be revenged on the Orthorotys of the land Not to subdue but to disturb the frontiers now and then and lead in

20. Olney wrote "known," but likely meant "none."

Armies and take them as they say by proxy Thus is the theme with our noted leaders That would stand and say to others to go a head in aray they would move in accordance with Joseph Smith at the head and no man would dare to lisp against him lest the new fangled Masons should light on them in the dark I am not a sworn member to them but by information I know of their works and how they say to do in case of an attact They say first to form a Company of all their males And those that do not coencide to feed them to the Catfish that they may know on whom to depend This has long ben the talk an order of the Danite clan That they are a teror to all that comes under observation Amongst us eyes are open on the clan but none dares lisp against them or against the Leaders of the Church except some that would be looked to if they was a missing I now look at them with feelings to do them no harm but say they are a dangerous people now in weakness and together But many of the leading ones will move in aray In the dark untill they get out of reach of the Laws of the United States They will leave the road behind them that others will follow on after those that goes out and forms a new Stake of Zion as this is the theme

[Folder number 9] Nauvoo August 19th 1842

Ode to contentment
The mind that would rest
And become as fre as the air
Must move in accordance
With the smiles of God
As his word is given That Comprises his Law
No shadow of turning to the wright or left
Will answer his doings In the least
As his Law is easy simple and plain
All can understand it That can read
And if not Learning Its implanted within
That the mind is governed by the Spirit of God

As many is a looking To know of Gods will they have a theme before them that will daily improve their time Its a mind to arise in the name of the Lord by faith words and doings Agreeable to his word As his word is Spoken Its by man to be understood that from choise are passing a probationary State A state of trials that is by few understood But yet it is of Importance to prepare the mind of those to arise that have from choise took a stand on this the lowest planit beneath the Heavens But still its desined The mind to arise by changes that is often the theme Tho troubles and trials by many is counted to be hard To endure but its the order of Heaven To prepare the mind that it may expand In the things of God As God to man is a looking His will to make known they of him receive inteligance according to their works So those that are slothful or Idle on their way losses by their negligance in the performance of their works But those that are up and adoing in the servis of God Has daily Instruction that they become well informed They arise with the gifts of the Gospel that establishes their faith on the rock Christ Jesus in defens of the truth

[Folder number 9] Knoxville[21] August 20th 1842

I of late have ben a traverling threw the western states I hear se and read much that I get news from differant parts I find the excitement is over at presant that not much is said Except it hard times as money is scares. That causes some to mourn because of living in debt to one another As politicks is at rest Mormonism is in voge that take the attention of many that has time to read As much is published in the Periodicals of the day That excites Curiosity amongst those that has an ear to hear As I the tales have perrused on both sides I hear and se much In my daily moves I look at the Writings of John Cook Bennett that takes the daily rounds I look at the writings against him published by the mormons as is said I look at their doings and sayings as with them I have had some chance to learn of their ways I look at them and at the doing of John Cook Bennett Between them I draw the Contrast and say that J C Bennett has gaind the Ground as he has stemed the torrent alone against a multitude Altho they on him have lit like a hawk on a hen yet he flutters and works the [Card?] well I defy anyone to say or prove which is most in the falt Bennett or Josy[22] and his Clan that would be Prophit of God But as Joseph and his clan are all in aray to meet anyone that will speak in behalf of them selves that comes in contact with the Mormons as they in aray have took a stand no more to be baffled the[y] say by the folly of man But I look at them And with them Converse about matters and things that is afloat I vew them as a community to be corrupt If their own teachings to me is correct they speak of their power with God that he with them doth Coencide In all their doings He instructs them that they are a blest people of God They speak of their doings Such as bringing in to subjection The laws of the land Also of becomeing a terror to the Nations of the Earth I look at their Editoral department and say What God do they serve if as they say he instructs them in their daily moves He must be liberal as they have mutch afloat To tell of their doing would now be in vain but suffise it to say J C Bennett has not half told the tale

21. Knoxville, Illinois, is a small community located about eighty-five miles northeast of Nauvoo.

22. Joseph Smith Jr.

But for me to write of their doings it is a hard round to take because of the hedges and ditches and hills and vallys that they pass by to track them in their windings and unlawful doings is no small job But I think I will beguin and track them and run the risk of comeing out But if by the by they on should light all in a mass like a hawk on a for the lack of claws they may slip off

[Folder number 9] [Letter from Phebe Wheeler to Oliver Olney]

Friendship Knoxville August 21st 1842

Dear Brother in tribulation and patience,

Yours of August 3d came to hand the 16th and being out of Knoxville 6 miles could get to no post office until today; I learn your Coat Pit if fast progressing – I hasten to write you; Thank you for your very acceptable letter; for your kindness proffer,d me; "friends" in these days are "rare pearls" I am in good spirits cordially received by my friends who will rejoice to have me stay with them My things you will please take care of them as you said you would Protect me;- when you may deem it necessary; I can see no harm it I know of no opportunithy to get them myself When you think proper go and take them and take care of them Will you get an umbrella & parasol which I had forgotten to bring with me— Also I left out of my Box for Sidney's use a brass fire shovel and blue and white bed blanket <u>both</u> valuable; I fear I may meet trouble in getting all my things I have a Band Box[23] with 2 hats or Bonnets which are valuable; 2 Boxes remmember!! Should Sidney object; regard his feelings and remove his groundless fears as much as possible My heart is with the Church and people Of Sidneys manouverings I <u>feel</u>, yet forbear to speak except that you and me may find in the Sequel "it is all for the best"— I have just written them & several others I write favorably as possible as you advised me I have ever found your advice wholesome & Salutary; altogether to my advantage. let me have your Prayers you may rejoice and I too— for your deliverance is near at hand I was supprised to hear of Bishop V Nights[24] Death

23. A slight paper box for bands, caps, bonnets, muffs, or other light articles. *Webster's Dictionary* (1828), s.v, "Band box."

24. Vinson Knight was born March 14, 1804, at Norwich, Massachusetts. In March 1834 Vinson and his wife were visited in their New York home by Joseph Smith and Parley P. Pratt. The Knights believed the restored gospel message taught by these two missionaries and were baptized a short time later. Vinson sold his New York home and the Knights moved to Kirtland, Ohio, to be with the Saints. Later, Vinson moved to Missouri, where he was selected as acting bishop at Adam-ondi-Ahman. Moving to Illinois, Vinson served as bishop of the Lower Ward in Nauvoo. On January 19, 1841, he was designated Presiding Bishop of the Church (see D&C

Of the prophecies against me of which you speak I wonder why it should be; Sister Emma Sister Marks Whitney & robinson and many others were my permanent friends I wish you to pray for me I can not believe that I will loose the Confidence of the people I recollect you told me in reference to my coming to Knoxville that if came I should avoid much trouble should come and return with the Confidence of the people this I still believe bear ~~in~~ me in the arms of faith to God Today heard by the "Peoria Register" that the Mormons & Anti Mormons have come to Battle 40 kiled & wound Please give me inteligence soon, of this and other matters I am surrounded by my sectarian friends on all sides if I had a shade or grove I almost think a cave or cell where I could retire to and be alone I could be happier Friends are kind, but they control me and talk to me taking advantage of rumours protesting against the Church doctrines &c &c If I am silent they Interogate me that I must decide & answer in favor of the Church I look to you for advice I am come here away from all the Saints and shall look to you for the watch word when I shall return You say no return; I suppose you mean to Nauvoo But the Lords own work will roll forth for [Savoir?] God is near;!!! Let me hear from you Let me hear inteligence of the doings and tell me <illegible> the similitude of the coal pit if you please Be of good Courage for you will soon see that God is in the storm Now is the trial of my faith I can not enter in to the Sectarian Spirit nor deny the faith & doctrine of the L. D. Saints - No Sir, I sometimes think I can not stay long here Because all are so united in putting down this gospel & the power of it & take Smith as a Speceman of the whole yes a sample of Mormonism Think of this and tell me your mind & advise me if you can what I had better do; I am worried sometimes but please keep this in your own mind communicate it to no one

You spoke of coming to Knoxville; I would be very glad to see you but you will be interrogated that you will have wisdom to answer probably better than I can All about the combustibles of the coal pit They are making a desperate effort to save me from what they call the whirlpool of destruction Delusion!! A protracted meeting is in progress But I will venture it yet While the Lord is near I think to go tho <illegible> times <illegible> Galesburg[25] I think I should prise a time of rest from anxious friends Many are so exceedingly concerned for me that may employ every means to accomplish their purpose you have blessed me - prayed for me and I have been blessed and asstonishingly provided for and I feel that God will continue to keep hold and guide

124:75). His health began to fail, and Vinson died July 31, 1842, at the age of thirty-eight. See Susan Easton Black, *Who's Who in the Doctrine and Covenants*, 172–74.

25. Galesburg, Illinois, is a city located about seventy-five miles northeast of Nauvoo.

me to the end you too are favord "Oliver" tho fortune frowns and tho friends forsake yet let us hold to the "word of Truth" cling to the doctrines of Jesus abide in the faith and patience of Jesus until the Lord should come with a recompense May you be comforted I have prayed for you that your faith fail not I often pray for you that you may find a happy issue out of all your perplexities & sorrow You will reccollect as a child I look to you for advise I do indeed. May you be kept stedfast in the Truth & may you walk in the Light and by that Light lead me until we get thru this slicory[26] intricate Maize I can not see much ahead except I see that the Saints will soon sit upon the ground Any truth is good have heard from Conn my friends are well concerned for me hear the News of the day request an explanation Yours with sentiments of Respect

Phebe M. Wheeler

Mr O H Olney

[Folder number 8] Greenfield August 27th 1842

I of late have ben a traverling about and a takeing a vew of things That comes to light I say often to myself What can be don to open peoples eyes to se for themselves Testimony in differant ways appears of the unwise doings of the Elders of the Church of Latter day Saints What more can be said What can be don to satisfy a community of bad works I look at them as a people and deside in my mind That dark shades is over them that they know nothing wright I look back to the Antient Prophits of both Moddern and divine and se the attraction of power that their followers did to them give heed I looked at their usurped Orthoroty that lead in to bondage The mind of those that said to be their followers They with their would arise or fall with them as the boddy of a Brute that we find in all cases follows the head Thus it is with the members of the Church of Latter day Saints They say Joseph is Our Prophit and teacher We with him are willing to arise or fall after as plain testimony As could be asked to substantiate a fact to hang a man for his unlawful doings Testimony on testimony has come to light of Crimes that must be abominable in the site of God But what is the theme but for them to arise and scandalise any one that would bring Iniquity to light A big dog will arise and bark that will roust up a set of peevish pups that will make such a yelping whining and strapping that a fellow is in danger of getting his shins barked by them if he gets within

26. "Slickery" is a combination of slick and slippery. It means the same thing as slippery (a surface that is difficult to stand on or an object difficult to hold firmly because it is smooth, wet, or slimy). It is not uncommon in some parts of the country to hear the slide on a children's playground referred to as a slickery slide.

their reach In speaking of the Foibles of the Church of Latter day Saints I freely speak my mind of their doings As their doings are daily before me Much is said and written By John C Bennet He has had a chance to know of their doings and secret works as he has long ben with them familiar That their doings to him is known that he now appears to be divulging. Why because he says by them he has ben abused Many Could speak and bear testimony in connection with Bennett Of the most of his writings But their Presant situation forbids As they with familys and home keeps them in an attitude that the daily threats puts on them dread to commence to devulge Bennett well knew his destiny if the staid in Nauvoo I have often herd said by many that he had orto a ben put into the drink (meaning the Missippi) before he was sufferd to leave the place Such epothets is daily throwed out That a silance has to be but in favour of the Church of L D Saints They say the shooting of Ex Governor Bogs was a noble act that their name had orto be immortalised that did it. Such insinuations are thrown out by many of those that stand as teachers in the Church That the Youth and mid-aged are a ketching the sound That I find falt with thats leading minds in to the path of Iniquity that if other wise was centerd would become worthy Cittizins. But the presant teachings is such as tends to degrade the mind of those that come under their watch Care of the Leaders of the Church of ~~Latter~~ D Saints. They say our recent Revelations is desined to govern us And we have power with God as had Moses and Aaron. Also we possess as did the Apostle Peter the Keys of the Kingdom They say if Joseph is gone God has apointed an other in his stead to lead us That is his Brother Hiram. Thus a door is opened for to lead them along step by step It is said that Joseph[27] but the secret whisperins is that he is in the Citty of Nauvoo Amaking ready to start to the noted boiling springs amongst the Natives neer the Rocky Mountains. I shudder at the thought of an established stake of Zion as they cal it Amongst the Natives west As I know of the course that has ben taken with them They have ben ensnared by presants and smooth words for years to to gain their applause that in a case of Imergency a door mite be opened to go amongst them. I am informed that fifty familys is now a makeing ready to be on their way They with the Prophit Joseph leaveing Hiram to take the lead home And send on familys as they pleas But let the first Company start with fifty familys or less and get one hundred miles on their way With Joseph and Lyman White Some few others The story is at once told, As the rest would follow on by degrees Without being noticed

27. There are no lines missing and the pages are in order because they are bound. It appears that Olney did not complete his thought, which might have been something like: "It is said that Joseph is gone, but the secret whisperings is that he is in the city of Nauvoo."

Untill they would get an innumerable company together not only of our own Country but from foren lands. Then add the Lamanites as they are caled and who or whire is the people that would [want to?] If they should come upon our frontiers as this is their theme to be rivenged on our goverment for their wrongs, move against them and follow them on a retreat in to the wilderness west Untill as they say by proxy to surround any Company that was fatigued and worn out a traverlin Is it not better now in their weakness to look to them If their is some wrongs bring them to Justice in an honourable way Brake up the Community by giving them a chance to scatter in differant parts In this way they will soon become disorganised and many that is bourn down in sorrow would arise and become an honour to our state or the state in which they should reside I have looked at the Course of Doct Bennett and many others that have come out against the doings of the Church. It is said by those of the Church that they ware treacherous unholy dishonest Brothers Doct Bennett mite a gone along in his doings in the Church if he had a ben a little more careful but a jealousy arose that an exitement was raised against him that he spoke of others falts That they tried to hush up and all move in accordance But but the bag strings slipt of and the Contents began to run out that caused a stench not to be compared to dirt. Such and such doings only tends to bind the members stronger together as they cal it percecution for Righeousness sake. Thus his sayings Writings and doings is calculated to bind them together instead of weakening their bands But as much is adoing amongst them that is supposed by them to be in the dark yet it is unridling from time to time that they have no secrets to keep They have said to send away their Prophit but we find he is still with them hid away in a Loof[28] But as for Rockwell we do not hear much of him said but it is likely that he will be ready to start to west with the Clan as they are fast a makeing ready this Journey to take Lead by Lyman Wite as he is a bidding up for volenteers this Journey to take. No doubt but this Company will soon be on the wing To the far west that will Liberate the oprest that long have looked to be set free from the Laws of the land of Independance for which our Ancestors bled by contending for their wrights on this our american soil O H Olney

28. The 1828 *Webster's Dictionary* defines *loof* as "The after part of a ship's bow, or the part where the planks begin to be incurvated, as they approach the stem." *Webster's Dictionary* (1828)., s.v. "Loof." However, it is unlikely that Olney was referring to this type of loof. It is possible that Olney was referring to a "loft" or room directly under the roof of a house.

[Folder number 8] Citty of Nauvoo ~~August Sept~~ August 29 1842

I yet continue my writings as much is afloat I se no place to stop Unless I go to sleep That would be easy for me to do as I would find Company on every side I of late have ben a journy of some sisty miles of and on my return I found a Company that had met in aray To hear from the Prophit that they said had ben far away He Laboured to show them The order of God and the influance he had with the Father and Son He spoke loud of our land of wisdom and light He spoke of the rulers at large that they ware unwise and wicked and stood rejected in the site of God He spoke of with them as haveing a fuss that he had gaind the Ground of them because of his wits He spoke of Laws in general that he with them was willing to move and be judged by them In the Citty of Nauvoo according to the Charter of the Citty Of it he much did bost As being liberal also the liberality of those that did it grant He spoke highly of his power with God to topsiturvy turn things that moves in contact with the L D Saints He spoke of the Priesthood that it he had and by it to remove Hills and fill vallys cut in sunder armies That should Come in Contact with him Or say to take his wrights He caled on many of the Elders to be ready to move amongst the wicked of the land as an eventful door was open to preach in differant parts He gave them a text to dwell on It was the abuse That has ben received from the Governors of Missouri and Ill that because of their unlawful doings the Latter days Saints had much bourn that was more than God of them required The Elders or all from the Presadency down that say to hold the P_hood are caled to go out and streighten Crooked places in the Church They in aray will move to reason in behalf of the oprest That they say is much abused by Orthorotys of the States They speak of the Governors of the two states that have issued writs to take Joseph Smith and Porter Rockwell for shooting ex Gov Bogs I have nothing to say further than I believe That Joseph Smith is as clear as many others in the place as he was here and attended trayning on the seventh of May And Bogs shot the sixth as we hear. But I look at the Cloak or the Mantle that is made to cuver works and speak of their course of doings that I think is unwise And unrigheous to take It is the dealings with the members of the Church of Latter Day Saints They speak of letters that to them has ben sent a ben sent a begging their Pardon for Illegal doings They say several letters has ben wrote by those of Influance one by Governor Carlin That all their doings was wrong Why have they not a shone the letters that others mite se for themselves As well as to be daubed over with soft soap by the Leaders of the Church of L D Saints They dout much of their Charter that it is to them of much worth because of its priveleges and its lenity that it admits of many Citty laws But I ask a question and it solved Would the state of Illinois give more than they have got themselves Would they give a Charter And their own ways to abuse If not why do a handful Take such libertys as the orthorotys of the Church of L D Saints as to take Prisioners out of the hands of the Orthorotys of the officers of the state How did they do it but as they say by proxy They are not to be blamed For the cours they took but they had orto be dambd for their lies that they daily are a telling to soft soap But they have got In a way of it that it to them is a secont nature If I could be permited To fully speak my mind I would speak of their folly of Lyining I think it is a distemper that is ketching as it has much absorbed the lump It moves as the blood in a person being propeld by the Heart So it is with the lies They from the heart of the Church of Latter D Saints start that causes a quick beating of puls As for me any more to write of them I will do as J C Bennett but half tel the tale Altho myself with J C Bennett I will not compare as I have rote on a principal of duty and with the best of feelings and Bennett wrote because he was mad[29] But I think their is not many to blam him as he met with such a charge to be turned out of a rowing lot in to a rough dry field No doubt but that he often looks back and mourns in certin plotting on what good things he left But to Comfort him on his way I will say to as the western phrase is we have a heap of faat fellows that no doubt has made his place good I will speak of the Elders That is agoing out I laugh in my sleves[30] to se the trap that is set to baffle they say by proxy their opposers of the land. Their text is given It is to be first Bogs and then Carlin Governors that have sent out the writs They will move in order And make a sweeping move by Daubing soft soap on the Succors Wolverenes and huskers The buckeyes will have a round and soon clear down East to the ocean I suppose as they like the Apostle Peter the keys of the kingdom they say to possess They will bind up the Law and testimony as they pass But with the suckers I am some aquainted They think and speak For themselves also the Whosers as well as the wolverenes The buck Eyes are sharp shoters They

29. Olney writes that he and John C. Bennett are unveiling similar dark deeds and secrets about Mormonism, but Olney sees himself writing for a higher purpose or motive than Bennett, who "wrote because he was mad." Although Olney does not totally condone or agree with Bennett, he appears to be very understanding of Bennett's situation. This seems somewhat strange because it was Bennett who preferred charges against Oliver Olney for "improper conduct—for setting himself up as a prophet & revelator in the Church." John S. Dinger, *The Nauvoo City and High Council Minutes*, 407.

30. Laugh up your sleeve: "To be amused or to gloat a bit without giving it away. It was easy to conceal a laugh or a derisive smile in a sleeve when people wore loose and flowing garments, so the expression probably had a literal as well as a figurative meaning in the 16th century and quite likely earlier." James Rogers, *The Dictionary of Cliches*, 152.

are not to be turned by a wink or nod[31] Our downeasterners are a people that have ben to mill and to meeting from their youth up That I think they will have their match in the Older States To daub with soap But now comes the nub of the story that is said by wisdom is laid that an exitement may be raised out that a Company Can Clear out without being noticed I would say as once before that when they beguin to teach proffer them with a Jack nife If they take the hint let them go If not give them a pass to Come back and form a reformation amongst the Church of L D Saints I with good feelings draw to a close The Lord only knows what will be next so good by brother Mormons

O H Olney

---

31. Olney sets forth his belief that the Mormon leadership intends to take over the nation step by step. He uses the nicknames of various states to describe into which areas the Mormons would likely attempt to move next. Buckeyes are used to designate the people of Ohio. The state of Ohio is commonly referred to as the Buckeye State because of the prevalence of Ohio Buckeye trees within its borders. Wolverines is used as a nickname for the people of Michigan. There is a belief that people from Ohio gave Michigan the nickname "The Wolverine State" around 1835 during a dispute over the Toledo strip, a piece of land along the border between Ohio and Michigan. Rumors in Ohio at the time described people from Michigan as being as vicious and bloodthirsty as wolverines. It is probable that Olney uses the word "huskers" (short for cornhuskers) as a name for people living in what would become the Nebraska Territory. The term "cornhusker" comes from "husking" or harvesting corn by hand, which was common in Nebraska prior to the invention of husking machinery. For much of the nineteenth century, Illinois's nickname was "The Sucker State." The origin of the name is still the subject of debate. According to one researcher, "Probably the most popular explanation of how Illinois came to be known as the Sucker State involves the state's first lead mine, which was opened in 1824 near Galena. . . . Because the Illinois workers traveled up and down the Mississippi on steamboats to get to and leave Galena, their migration pattern became a matter of note. Specifically, Missourians jeeringly referred to them as "suckers" in recognition of the fish by that name that migrates upstream each spring." Dave Koltun, "The Sucker State?" Olney similarly appears to refer to the citizens of Illinois as suckers. Indiana is known as "The Hoosier State." The word "Hoosier" was widely used by the 1830s. In 1848, John Russell Bartlett's *Dictionary of Americanisms* defined "Hoosier" as "A nickname given at the west, to natives of Indiana." Although there are a number of theories, no one seems to know how the word "Hoosier" came to be. Olney appears to believe that the citizens of Ohio, Nebraska, Illinois, Indiana, and Michigan would not be taken in by what he believed to be a Mormon plot of domination.

SEPTEMBER 1842

[Folder number 8] Citty of Nauvoo Sept 1st 1842

I still Continue in busines both early and late tho some speak of my way of living as easy but with such I do not at all with agree as I have to pass over many rough places that seems hard to pass threw But if the weather was fair and eaven my way would be clear And business differant that it would be with me as with others that attend to their Common Concerns But my concerns is uncommon unnatural uncaled for ~~unconstitutional~~ and disgusting to wright of think of or speak of But as I have begun I move sloly a head If slow my course is sure as I move with the tide on the big waters when the wind blows The tides run high Because of the power of the air that will compare with the doings of the Church of Latter day Saints as they often are a medling with things that raises exitement Amongst the people that their doings is daily noticed that the sound as the waves of the sea comes to an Iron bound Shore that I think there must needs be a vision to unriddle the fact But of visions I am aferd as I often have learned That in ages past they in all cases hung those that had them for witnes But as I have muscular power I shall be apt to defend myself esspecially If I am ketched amongst the new fangled Mason, As threats is out on any one that does not with them move Also they say to have their tools ready to do to bring those in to subjection as they please As I yesterday was a traverlin in the lower part of the place I had a vew of things strange to relate It was done and performed because of mismoves to get things in order and put exitement down I se noted ones that had moved in aray all meet together and deside what to do They agreed on a plan to extricate themselves by arming and equipting the females with swords pistols Rifles and guns Some few was instructed That was desined to lead that they could move at the head of a host I se their plans was simple and plain that much excited my feelings to se them move I looked at the Nauvoo Legion all in aray and said why do they cal on the women to fight I inquired in to the affair of a man of fame why the Nauvoo Legion should clear out and the women arise and fight in aray He showd me the plan That because of bad works the excite was aut that That they feard of being looked to by the Orthorotys of the States They desided the men to send away Many a preaching and others of to work That barly women would be left to take charge things to home I se the women mostly understood the plan that much excited their ambition because of thinking of being honoured Again they looked at the falts of the men and desided that this course would save them from bonds as this was their teachings That they only would stand and their Looks would dis-Harten their opposers that if they come in they would go of ashamed rather than to come in contact with females as that would be a disgrase for men of worth to move in contact with the weaker Class When I say weaker I would not be understood that I would apply it only on general terms as I am fully satisfied that the females of Nauvoo are better informed And have courag far to Exscede the men I se the men scatterd all but a few to fix to be of in a company to a Noted place west the tim for to start I did not learn But it looked to me neer at hand as I se many busy a fussing and fixing to be of before the Cold fall storms I mite write much more but perticulars I pass by only tel in part the tale as does Bennett As my vision is ended I will speak of facts that looks to me strange for people of God As Joseph has returned he is all in aray a teaching and telling of the visions of heaven that came to his vew as he was a dodgeing from place to place He spoke of being in differant parts of the Citty At the time that the New fangled Prophit said he was gone to Washington and Erope Who ask of him a lie Again the case of Rockwell I am informed by a new fangled Mason that he was all the time in the place Whire is the God that rules above Whire is his power on Earth displayed Is it in dark sayings and doings on Earth No but in wisdom he always does moves and often leaves a community to themselves to fill up their cup of Iniquity On his footstool As his name is much degraded Reason does speak and say God will not much longer bear with such unwise teachers to dishonour his name They speak of being persecuted for Righeousness sake But what did Joseph say on the stand but caled on his new fangled Clan to Tar and feather any one that should them oppose He said the materials is ready to be used therefore deal thus with them. Thus saith the Lord Eeys are a watching on every side that would not wait for Tar and feathers as I well know the fact that a mans life is considered by them of No value For months I have well known the fact that I have ben watched both Early and late by them that I have ben on my gard But I have friends in all parts of the place but I keep them in ignorance of what I am about so my writings are a dead secret to those of the Church and will be untill they come from the press I long have ben a writing of actual facts and before I would add I should diminish much as I am tired of what I se and hear as I am about that takes place amongst The L D Saints I now draw to a close and fix to Clear out to be gone a few weeks Then return and se what is afloat as I am weary of their works

O. H. Olney

[Folder number 9] Sept 1st 1842 Citty of Nauvoo not read

Being caled on previous to this time to meet in Council with the Antient of days in obediance to my duty I move to do as I by them am shone without fear or regard to Mortal man I move in accordance with the Antient of days as they on the Earth have took a stand to Liberate the Captive And opress the Ignoble that binds hard burdens on the weak As much is adoing and much to be don a temporal Kingdom is now to be established commenceing at the North East part of Ill. The place is desined a Citty to build in the name of the Lord by faith and good works Thou art now caled thy mind to prepare to move in order As directed by a messenger of power Thou art caled of a messenger of power as thou art this time Ordained by the Prophit Judah to activity and strenth that no power shall baffle the or turn the to the wright or left The life of Judah and his doings is a tipe of thy work as strength and inteligance shall not be lacking Thou art cald Gods will to perform as the order of Heaven is againing Ground Gods ways are Equal Altho man turns Gods plan was established at the beguinning of time A Law was established to govern the race of man Much more I mite write but suffise it to say God word is given and all to it must conform As this is a day of business set apart the time has arived For something to be done As the blessing of the Earth has long ben conceald A door opens to them from this time forth no more to be shut As treasures will beget treasures untill the riches of the world is in the hands of The Saints The Saints are a people that have Always ben Oprest But the day has ariven That they are to be set free on the Earth Thou art now caled In thy poverty to arise and take a retrospective vew of the treasures that thou has been shone in differant parts But thou art first caled To enter a room on the Coming Saturday that thou hast ben shone There is money and Jewelry of much worth and other articles of much Note that is ready and awaiting to be used by those that have Influance with God Thou art caled to be ready next teuesday to start to the new Stake of Zion That is set apart Thou art there caled to beguin to purchase to establish a home For the Latter day Saints that will soon be agetherin in to take up their abode

I will Now chang the subject and write of the doings of the City of Nauvoo as wisdom directs me Of things that I daily se and hear All is in aray to know what to do As they say all ant [ain't] well One hear another their all in aray to get things Streightened In the name of the Lord Many is alooking to se the turn of times in hopes for the better As they say that they cant be much worse Men women and Childern is all in arms because of the daily news or storys that they say is all lies That speak of audultry poligemy fornication Laciveousness and the Orthorotys of the Church a clokeing iniquity under a garb of Religion that is well known to be a fact Their doing I have undertook to pen but I have my match to keep up with them because of their qu[i]ck moves But I will warrent them a hearing at some futer time To their Shame and Disgrace That on them will come I look at the Smith family with supprise and say what can they think for them selves I look at the most of The twelve and say that I have never seen their equal for abominations I look at others of the same grade They move together in their daily move I look at the new fangled Masons in their daily moves and say There day mus[t] be <illegible>

to move in this career as God on them is a looking that he knows of their works And his name disgraced

[Folder number 7] City of Nauvoo Sept 4th 1842

I often am writing of of things That comes to vew and as I se much adoing I speak for my self as I am familiar with much that is on the wing I say let Gods will be don If man finds falt I look at the doings of the Latter day Saints and se their daily movements That take place I se for the Lack of wisdom much is in voge that speaks of the unwise doings of the L D Saints They as a people are on the Alert down to an untimely end an end is desined soon to be that will baffle doings of many that is now in High life That cal on the Saviour in differant ways but not exceptable to him as he well set a pattern that all of him mite know by following his Example As is written in his word His word is writen on tables of stone It was don by Moses that is yet preservd It is yet awaiting for the time to arive That they may come forward as a testimony of antient work It will be a work of Importance to those that sits in Darkness governed by the man of sin Many is a looking to know what to do To extricate themselves from their presant degraded state They look at the sun That they suppose is a ball and moves by its own power as they cal it God They look at the moon as its accessory bride and the Stars as specks of dimons in a wall They look at the Earth on which they stand and say it rests on pillows not made with hands, but is governed by a roleing sun They se it set and arise both morning and knight to their supprise They look at the rivers seas and Lakes and say from whence do they arise It they cannot Comprehend They look at the showers that from Heaven does flow and moisten the Earth They look at the heat and Cold and se days lengthen and shorten And say why is it so In a word they are in darkness Because of bad works that they are under a Curse and in the Dark x x x Because of certin things that was wrong in the site of God that amongst the Saints a union of spirit did not exist more perticularly amongst the leading ones as I was shone it had become my duty to warn them of the fact that it was not pleasing to God I was shone that a union must needs be and it would be required at my hand to unriddle this truth When the word of the Lord was received Threw Joseph Smith that would unfold my mission[1] That I mite be known in Christ But because of his not a doing I had to stand still and se the salvation of God I often have mourned at what I have seen from time to time I have seen as I was shone That a reformation must be Instead of a scenry of things that caused sin

1. Olney believed that he had a special calling or specific mission to accomplish in the Church. He expected Joseph Smith to make this special calling known to the membership "that I might be known in Christ." But Joseph Smith did not do as Olney had hoped, which caused Olney some consternation.

to sin that comes in contact with the Law of God I have seen that Gods Law was broken that was said to be given to govern man that has caused Sorrow and Lamentation to rest often on my mind I look back at the time that it was easy for them to a reformed but when they pased by me Their doom was decreed that an utter destruction would eventually be I Laboured I sought some few to save by showing them the order of God I for my doing before the council was cald that they took from me my standing in the Church that I have long a ben looked at as an enemy to the Church of Latter day Saints yet I have feeling to do them [manuscript torn] But their day of reform is over And not to be recald they have moved with their Eyes open [manuscripts torn] they are left without exscuse [manuscript torn] are in Iniquity and others coincide [manuscript torn] forms a Union That they move in a mass iniquity doth abound The love of many does wax cold [manuscript torn] an utter destruction is decreed in the Citty of Nauvoo I have ben with and with them [manuscript torn; likely "would" or "could"] have sympethised but I am wholy rejected by them [manuscript torn] with them I have no home But I have a recod of them as a fallen people that have violated the Law of God that will be handed down to futer ages that their works may be known They often in aray assemble in Gods name but whire is their union but flead disorganizeation is decreed That is a ushering in because of bad works As their works is many they think in the dark but it is written and they will be exposed on the house tops The sin of Ignorance is not in their behalf because of what they have done from time to time

[Folder number 8] Sept. 4th 1842 Nauvoo Citty

Yet much is a doing That is said and don as much is afloat In this realm The sound has gone out for all to come in that a general getherin soon may be The twelve in aray have took leave and a gone out to hush up the storys That take the rounds But if there is not a change in their doings the smoke from them will arise as they think to be herd to whirever they go I will admit they have wisdom to tell a smooth tale as they long have had experiance it to perform Many more is a starting To follow on that can say they know the storys to be fals Those that cannot are forbidden to go out but stay to home and keep still and se the salvation of God As god is a looking as they say his power to display in behalf of the Church of Latter day Saints As much is a going at this time the Sherifs after the prisoners have returned but when they got whire they was They was gone that no Josy and Porter R Could be found At the moment before They was in aray to soon establish an order of things to outwit the Pukes and succors[2] at once But as the story is of the Indians that when they

2. Again, Olney believes that the Mormons have a scheme to take over part of the country. Here, he claims that they are prepared to "outwit the Pukes and Suckers."

in a mess get drunk they keep one sober man to look out Thus it is with the Latter day Saints They say to be watchman on the tower and can do as they please as the world around them is in darkness no more to be a waked untill they wake up at the day of Judgement as they have stemed the torrent untill they say the kingd[om] spoken of by Daniel is established and the antient of days they say has set At the time Joseph and P Rockwell was hid away from the Sherifs That they with old father Adam and two of the Nephites met and held a council and desided on what should be don I look at their weakness In their daily moves and say how is it possible that a community can be sedused as to receive their testimony and say all is well after testimony on testimony has ben that many of our noted leaders Has ben deep in Iniquity of differant kinds But I look at them in their daily moves and say they are all of a mess exsept now and then are Those that are not in it sanctions it And says that God rules through our Prophit Joseph Smith that all are in the mud alike In or neer our Citty and the saints are no more to be trodden underfoot but they the kingdom now possess that all things will move in the order of God But I for them could speak a word and tel them of some solem facts I by the by will say to them That God does not move in unholy temples I will no more mention over the Crimes that the mormons is guilty of time and again and instead of repenting of them undtake to cover them up by Lying This is not the path the Antients trod or marked for their followers to travel in But each leader has his band In all ages it has ben the same That they would follow in his tracks whether he arose or fell its all the same Thus its with the Latter day Saints in a mass they move in acordance with their fallen Prophit I now to a close my writings draw and wait to se the turn of times As times is changable because of moves That of often made by man to accommodate themselves But as now to me a peculear time as I am looked upon by many squinting eyes and minds that not above aspaniel As aspaniel dog is said to be good to watch and bite so it is with the Latter day Saints If they do not bite a peevish sound they continually make that keeps a fuss all about

---

As previously mentioned, "suckers" was a nineteenth-century nickname for the inhabitants of Illinois. Olney similarly calls the Missourians "pukes." According to an 1890 newspaper article published in California, when lead ore was discovered in Illinois, a great number of people from Missouri flocked to the area, hoping to profit by being early in the mining districts. "They were successful in their expectations, and occupied many of the best claims, and so numerous were they on the mining grounds that men from the East, finding themselves shut out, declared that the state of Missouri had taken a puke and emptied all the population into Illinois." See "Why Are Missourians Called Pukes?," 1.

[Folder number 9] A Lamentation Citty of Nauvoo Sept 4th 1842

I now have feelings my mind to relate as one year ago today I returned from a long mission in the Eastern States I arived with feelings of no ordinary kind because of the Loss And sickness of friends[3] I looked to them both Early and late that I was much reduced Both in boddy and mind As I had ben Labourd with By a a messenger above that I mite move in accordance with the Church I went to the first Presidancy of the Church that my case might be known that I could move in accordance with the Church of L. D. Saints He first said to do for me, But stopt by the way that caused me to mourn time and again as by thus doing It left me in an uneasy state as I had ben caled on to do certin things for the good of the L. D. Saints because of Certin things That was wrong in the sight of God That a union of spirit Amongst the saints did not exist more perticularly amongst, The leading ones As I was shone that it had become my duty to warn them of the fact that it was not pleasing to God I was shone that a Union must needs be and It would be required at my hand to unriddle this truth When the word of the Lord was received threw Joseph Smith that would unfold my Mission that I might be known in the Church But because of his not doing I had to Stand still and see The Salvation of God I often have mourned, At what I have seen from time to time I have seen as I was shone that a reformation must be But instead of it a senry of things that added sin to sin that come in Contact with the Laws of God That comes in contact with the Laws of God[4] I have seen that Gods Law was broken that was said to govern man that has caused Sorrow and Lamentation to rest often on my mind I look back at the time that it was easy for them To be reformed but when they passed by me their doom was decreed that an utter destruction would eventually be I Labourd I sought some few to save by showing them the order of God I for my doings before, The high Council was caled that they took from me my Standing in the Church that I have long ben looked at as an enemy to the Church of L. D. Saints Yet I have feelings to do them good But their day of Reformation is over And not to be recaled They have moved with their eyes open that they are left without excuse Some are in Iniquity, Others Coencide that forms a Union That they move in a mass As Iniquity doth abound The love of many doth wax cold that an utter destruction Is

3. There is no way of knowing who the friends were who had suffered illness or passed away while Olney was a missionary in the East, except for his wife, Alice Johnson Olney. Alice died July 16, 1841, at Nauvoo. Her obituary in the *Times and Seasons* reported, "Brother Olney is absent from home and probably knows nothing of the afflicting occurrence." See "Died – In this place July 16th, Alice consort of Oliver Olney," 501.

4. Olney began the next page of his writing with the last line of the previous page.

decreed in the Citty of Nauvoo I long have ben with them And with them would have sympethised but I am wholy rejected by them that with them I have no home But I have a recod of them as a fallen people that have violated the Law of God that will be handed down to futer ages that their works may be known They often in aray assemble in Gods name but whire is their Union but flead A disorganisation is decreed That is ushering in because of bad works As their works is many they think them in the Dark But are written and will be exposed On the house tops The sin of Ignorance is not in their behalf because of what they have done from time to time

[Folder number 9] Dear Sister L White[5]

As time passes Things comes to mind that has happend From my boyhood Friends and Connections Is often on my mind as by them I have often ben cheerd in my lonely moments They twine around my past Why can I not se them Reasons are many Some is far in distant lands Others are scatterd In differant parts that I have not time to look them up Again I have business that must be don that wisdom says I must stay at home as I have those that is dependant on me for the necessarys of life that I feel in duty bound to support They are Childern That is often by my side from four to fourteen We as a family together reside but what shall I say In addition to that No less than one is a lacking to form a family circle When I was a boy I learnt to talk and since have in all cases spoke for myself that it has become a principal that is implanted within that I must say it is a trick of youth if I have sufferd again By saying that I did as I pleased Let this principal cherished amongst the youth That is agroing up their mind would expand and they would know something for themselves But those that looks to pappa mamma to be told what to do They can talk about their Domestic concerns That moves before their eyes because of their contracted vews of always being swayed by the older Let there be a principal cherished to set reason to work and move in wisdoms ways being governed by the principals that is just Let such minds dwell on matters and things their minds will expand that they will be an honour to themselves and to all That to them pertains

Miss L White I have rote to you a number of times but received no answer from you I well know your situation That you can hardly stir but what you are looked to If you have friend amongst your own kin and aquaintace they are scarse I visited you when you was sick and was satisfied that you was in cold hands or amongst those That did but little regard you Respecting our selves I have but little to say we both have minds to speak for ourselves and in a word

5. Lucinda White.

if we act as wisdom decrees we can do as well as we are a mine to You have had my best feelings since I first meet with you Since we have concluded to live together[6] I have ben decidedly the same mind since But if your mind is changed it would change mine I will propose to you that I will make you a visit and ask you to take a ride to our Citty of Nauvoo if you comply be assured I will use you well both in coming and agoing You can then se my Childern and do as you pleas pleas to make up your mind and I will cal on you as soon as the way opens and take you to any of your friends in this place I will se used well as I dispise the mind that would a female abuse and a youth to That lies near my heart My mind from you is not easily turned as I look on you a gift from God

[Folder number 9] Sycamore Sept 10th 1842

Dear Sister Lucinda White[7]

As this time presents an opportunity of addressing you in writing I with the best of feelings in close you a few lines that you may know my mind As we have formed a short acquaintance and both ben fine in conversation and have ben agreed as far as we have we have Conversed I will say to you that you took my attention That was why I took the pains that I did to visit you Now I have nothing to say but let the will of God be done if it is not wright for us to live together I am glad to know it but as for me I had that light of you that I was more bold in conversing with you than I should have ben had it a ben otherways The remarks of your haveing a vew of me Strengthend my testimony Now Sister Lucinda if it is wisdom in God that we should move together the way will open in the due time of the Lord and we shall se our way clear But if not let us continue our friendship as I think much of a friend

As a friend to me is Always Dear
As I by them am often cheerd
For them will I do when I have a chance
To encourage them in their daily moves

---

6. Evidently, Olney and Lucinda White had discussed getting married. Olney wanted to go ahead with their marriage plans but wrote this letter to determine if she has changed her mind.

7. There is a record of a Lucinda Emily White born in 1825 at Parishville, New York. She is only listed in *Membership of the Church of Jesus Christ of Latter-day Saints, 1830–1848* as the daughter of John Griggs White and Lucy Amanda Bailey. John was a high priest in The Church of Jesus Christ of Latter-day Saints and died in Utah. It is likely that Lucinda was also a member of the LDS Church, but there is no record of her baptism. Luncinda died in Missouri in 1894. See Susan Easton Black, comp., *Membership of the Church of Jesus Christ of Latter-day Saints, 1830–1848*, 45:694–95.

My mind for you is well inclined
I with you would like to spend my time
But if it should not be my lot
<bottom line of the page cut off>

The cause that I have took of Late is supprising to me to think of it I have long ben a member of The Church of the L. D. Saints but because of reasons to me known I from them have took my name It was because of a work that I had to do That I would a pased by if I could have had my chose But the work to me was plainly shown that was required to perform It was to keep a recod of the doings of the C L D S As impartial recod I was caled to keep as was ~~by~~Josephus ~~History~~ of the Jews I kept a recod of of their good and unwise doings untill they caled me to an act the[y] demanded my writing But I to well knew my duty to give them up As it was wright my writings to keep I told them plainly That they could not have them That has raised an excite against me that I have to bear the frowns of some that does often hurt my feelings But I am in hopes The time is at hand when what I have ben adoing will be knowne As I long have ben daily on the move to keep an account of what has transpired I feel that by many I have ben abused jest enough to pen the truth If you should hear from me by the way of the prints <last line partially cut off> not at all think <last line cut off> in a pamphlit It will tell the tale in black and white of the unwise doings of the L D Saints If I with you had a met again I should spoke to you of these things but I for you have feelings good and say to my self That the time will be that we will meet and no one to oppose Thus being agreed we will spend our time in wisdoms ways In honour of the God above and when we get threw with this toilsome and weary life we will go to God that gave us breath And when that time is past and gone we have but barly begun to live We to another world will go whire light onour and Glory is the theme We will then look down and se the contracted minds of those that minds the business of those that does not them Concern I now to a close my writing draw and say if it would meet your feeling I should like to have you write to me as I have a friend That will hand you this You by him can convey to me without a word being said to friend or foe So goodby for the presant

O. H. Olney

[Folder number 9] Lamoil[8] Sept 15th 1842

As time passes I still have to write now and then a little to keep a run of the Church of L D Saints I se much a going at home and abroad that I think it

8. La Moille, Illinois, is a small village in Bureau County. It is located about 160 miles northeast of Nauvoo, Illinois, and about 100 miles west of Chicago.

my duty to pen that not to much may lay in the dark As I of late have ben a traverling on business in differant parts I se much a going in my traverling about The watchman of Zion I often meet that have latly ben sent of out from Nauvoo I find them to be true to their trust as they actually say the reports are fals that is afloat of the doings of the Latter D Saints But in conversing with them I have to say that I pitty them because of their lot They well know their destiny If they stop by the way or admit a shadow of foibles in the Leaders of the C of L D Saints Their destiny is a veto on them and they caled to an account Then if they do not submit are published abroad Again I look at their minds so contracted that they Cannot speak or think for themselves but move in accordance with those that send them out Again such is caled And others left to home that does not say to speak That all is well and move in accordance with the Leaders But as I am on my way to the City of Nauvoo I will soon yet get a run of their doings as every week brings about something of note I patiently wait Untill it comes to light The shape Looks or form I cannot say but I think it will be formed by the time I get back

O. H. Olney

[Folder number 9] Lamoil Sept 16th 1842

The mind of man is wandering
It raises high and low
As [ponds?] is often [foaming?]
When er the winds do blow

It is thus with the mind of those that are wandering in the dark because of their fallen Condition The man of sin does move that their minds are often ensnared in their daily moves But their is a plan devised altho to such in the dark Yet it is plain and easy to those that are upright as they drink into the fountain of the treasures of Heaven above that their minds become enlightened in things that be of God As in him they have an Interest while passing on their way that they become established that they are not turned or led astray As the testimony of Jesus is their theme that they daily are enlightened to well perform their task Their task is plain and easy its bearly for to do As the Saviour did direct at the meridean of time He then laid a foundation on which the saints must build and set up a Standard, To govern man that they mite do their duty He to them did <bottom of page cut off>

[Folder number 9] Citty of Nauvoo Sept 22d.

As I have returned from abroad I find much a going in the name of the Lord Much is a saying of the times because of excitement afloat All is enquireing to know what is said out in the Country around Altho they have orders to stand still and let the orthorotys of the Church move agreeable to their minds but I find they are in trouble and know not what to do to clear themselves of the doings that takes the daily rounds Joseph is yet housed up and P O Rockwell[9] on the wing that much excites the feeling of many that causes them to mourn because he is not about The Elders is much engaged both high and low To put things to wrights that nothing more may be said They look back at their doings but alas it is to late to retract their unwise steps Their steps have ben many altho in the dark to many Yet it is fast a leaking out Many is suffering because of what they have don that they are bourn down in rags and have scarsly a morsel to Eat Whire is their means but in the hands of men that have taken the advantage of many That if it had not a ben for them they would now a ben well of They have said to build a Temple and an Inn, all in the name of the Lord that it became an established Law of God Tho time by many is spoken of that it has neither Beguinning or end As we become enlightend and better understand we find that time commenced at the time this planit was formed or as we are caled to recon As we are here and have an intrest with our fellow man We thus stand connected that with them we have an Intrest From the first age Untill the winding up senry of things the time was established by the Father Son and Holy Ghost as they was one and thre In Spirit and in boddy but one But the sun he took a boddy at the Meridean of time that he moved in persen according to the order of God He on Earth had a standing in the tabbernacle of flesh yet he was counted of no worth His doings was late and Early Untill to manhood he arose and stemed the torent of oppression Untill he was Crucified He then was resorected and again on Earth took a stand that the Law of God mite be established no more to be put to defiance He did then assend to Heaven in garments white and Clean and his boddy cleansed and purified He has since had a standing and borne rule In Connection with the Holy Ghost That is subject to him As the Father has power in Heaven and on Earth the son is governed by him also the Holy Ghost They was one in spirit but in Person was two after the Resorection Then comes another order because of the unwise doings of man That in the Latter times the order of God is established anew That the Holy Ghost In person on Earth takes a stand In a person Grone to manhood that lived in an early day that Condecended to take another round to assist in establishing The order of God to establish the Kingdom In the latter times As a work of importance is now commenced The Holy Ghost in person has took a stand being propeld by the Father and Son as he on Earth has a Standing He first Clears the way of Obsticles that would hinder his work and then puts things

9. Should be O P Rockwell.

in order as was Antiently wrote by the gift of the Holy Ghost As the Holy Ghost in person has on Earth took a stand He no more will suffer the approach[10] of man as he has borne with their folly for many days past and ben degraded and rejected by the Latter day Saints But they as a people soon must fall because of rejecting The teachings of The Holy Ghost As in spirit he first to them spoke an[d] patiently bore with them in their daily moves about But the time has ariven for an established Kingdom on the Earth conducted in wisdom By the Holy Ghost

[Folder number 8] Sept. 25th 1842 Citty of Nauvoo

Being caled to meet in council with the Antient of Days as they have now assembled and desided what to do As much is adoing and much a ben don I feel with them to cheerfully meet and write of their doings and daily moves They first met in Council thre days in succession In the month of June They since that have Laboured In differant parts that much has ben don to establish the kingdom of God They have met in differant Kingdoms and set things a moveing Agreeable to their minds that all is a doing as wisdom directs Famine war and pestilence is the theme that many is a suffering For the want of food Serious difficulty soon will arise that will brake down partition walls that now exists That set the captive fre and liborate the oprest And put things in order no more to be broke up As a kingdom will be established in the name of the Lord no more to be severd by the folly of man As much has been said in the name of the Lord without orthoroty to speak in his name he now has directed the antient of days to make ready to exterminate them and a kingdom established a new that will arise in the magesty and power of God From the Kingdom Thats fallen no more to arise will be Established a Kingdom of God The honest and valiant will be Caled to move in order as to them is shone The time is fast approaching that God to man will speak threw chosen vessels That he has raised up as there is many That move in his name Altho at presant to each other dark yet they are a moving in the order of God They in order will meet all in aray being directed by the antient of Days as they have this day met in Council A desision by them is made now to unriddle the foibles of the Church of Latter day Saints that the secret acts of man may be known From this time forth A senry of things will arise that will cause sorrow mourning and Lamentation all over the Earth The Latter day Saints is first in voge As Judgement beguins at the house of God Then the wicked Into wickedness will run because of their unwise doings The spirit of God will be withdrawn

10. Olney likely meant "reproach," meaning "shame; infamy; disgrace; that which causes shame or disgrace." *Noah Webster's First Edition of an American Dictionary of the English Language—Facsimile 1828 Edition*, s.v. "Reproach."

and they left to fill up their cup of Iniquity that will soon usher in. They in contention will meet in aray That they will fall by their own weapons after they are left without Exscuse But decision is past by a council on Earth that will establish an order anew that will rend and brake in pieces all that is not of God As the saviour in spirit has on Earth took a stand and the Holy Ghost in person has Commenced to move He now has commenced his work and will keep things in order from this time forth

[Folder number 9] Quincy Sept. 26 1842[11]

To whom it may concern this is to certify that I have been acquainted with O H Olney for about ten years and say that I have always considered him a worthy citizen

John Corrill[12]

[Folder number 9] Citty of Nauvoo Sept 27th 1842

I have long ben a looking a deseiring to se a change A prospect now arises as Excitement doth daily arise I look at J. C. Bennetts doings and say in my heart that God is able To make all things work together for good I se he has wisdom to move as seemeth him good Altho man is eavil yet God will controle his mind that he will move as directed to bring iniquity to light as the Leaders of the Church in aray have moved In iniquity A division arose amongst them that a way opened To bring dark to light The way is fast opening no more to be shet up that wickedness will be exposed amongst the Latter

---

11. Not written in Olney's handwriting, but it appears to have been written by the same person who wrote the letter extract from Israel Barlow and Oliver Snow found on the same page in folder nine.

12. John Corrill was born September 17, 1794, at Bone, Massachusetts. In 1830, Mormon missionaries stopped at Corrill's home in Harpersville, Ohio, for a night's lodging. After attending meetings where the missionaries preached, Corrill was convinced of the truth of Mormonism. He was baptized in January 1831. He brought many converts into the Church in Ohio and later served as second counselor to Bishop Edward Partridge in Missouri. Corrill was recognized as a Church leader during the five troubled years after the Saints were expelled from Jackson County, Missouri. In 1838 Corrill became disillusioned with Mormon leaders and later that year testified against Joseph Smith and other Church leaders at a hearing held at Richmond, Missouri. Corrill was excommunicated on March 17, 1839. He remained in Missouri and served in the Missouri legislature. Corrill was the author of a booklet entitled *A Brief History of the Church of Latter-day Saints (commonly called Mormons), Including an Account of Their Doctrine and Discipline, with the Reasons of the Author for Leaving the Church.* See Black, *Membership*, 69–72.

Day Saints Altho many is a moveing as to them is shone by their leaders they move in aray To do all they can But the anger of the Lord is kindled at what is a going on As much has ben don in the name of the Lord he will no more bear with their folly but trouble them in their doings As he has moved on J. C. Bennett to unriddle a theme That raises exitement in differant parts of the land But a senry of things Is now in voge that will much disharten the new fangled Masons about The watch word to them Will be of no worth that they of late have invented that they may know of Each others work The word is in voge From this time forth that they may know each other by a watch word The word is simple easy and plain that all may learn it Its a pat on the back and say Do you understand it or not The answer is made by a nod or yea[13] They then move in union after the sign is known By those that are of the Clan This Clan is a roveing in differant paths that raises excitement instead of covering it up that many is a saying what shall we do to well do our duty In the fear of God Much is said but little don to make Crooked Strait and rough smooth But God in wisdom looks down on man and has given direction to the Antient of Days to put things in order agreeable to his word

[Folder number 9] Citty of Nauvoo Sept 29th 1842

The mind of man when centerd to do the will of God It then becomes enlightend in his daily moves As mans moves is many they are often found in the dark that causes many to mourn that are lead by the folly of those of the Leaders of the Church of latter D Saints Some few are arayed in apparrel that is of the best kind others many are a following after as fast as the way opens as the spir [spur? spirit?] to be great is now the theme It by many is sought for that are only under way Again many that are looking for the Latter day Glory to soon usher in are sitting in rags And barly a morsel to eat There income is nothing and bearly a shadow of a house not fit to turn The wind or storm They reason thus That we have getherd on Zion land And depend on the Lord to provide for us He promises us protection if we move in his name We now have getherd at one of Zions stakes We impatiently wait Gods will for to do They say we have a Prophit of God to daily direct us in our doings By him we will be directed wright or wrong as he is much blest of God I look

13. Oliver Olney was not a Mason, nor was he a member of the Anointed Quorum. He could not have known firsthand any "watch words" or gestures that could have identified members of either group. He does mention in an earlier writing that he had received some information from "a new fangled mason." See OOP, fd. 8, September 1, 1842. It appears that Olney had an informant who was either a Mason or a member of the Anointed Quorum. It is not clear what Olney meant when he wrote of the watch word, pat on the back, and a nod of the head.

at these wise teachers And se their moves that often does astonish me when I hear them expostulate on the stand They arise and say thus saith the Lord that we as his agents move in his name We will teach you and direct you if you to us give heed If not we forsake you and put on you a curse That will sink you to hell whire you cannot extricate yourselves Here is the doom of those that are duped by the wise leaders of the L. D. Saints as this is the name that on them they take – worth or unworthy of it I say not I look at the excitement abroad And say it is to be expected Because of the doings as we of hear on the stand much boasting such as Threatning Defying The powers of the land They speak of being sheelded by the power of God that will baffle the wicked of the land that they as a people much are blest <bottom of the page cut off> people are established <bottom of the page cut off>

OCTOBER 1842

[Folder number 9] Citty of Nauvoo Oct 4th 184—

Sister Eliza R Snow

I will improve the presant time in writing you a few lines That you need not think that I am lost in some dreary wilderness on on some large Prairie I am yet about with my eye on the Gun and what is now a trouble to me is my gun is about loaded. I find it is about to go of I dont se any boddy that I want to shoot But you know from a principal that nature will have its course Thus it is with my gun when I first comenced to load it I thout to keep my gun still I reccollect what you said to me that what I did to do with my mite I receive the caution And continued to write of the ungodly doing of the Ch of L D S I have tracked them in their winding both Early and late that has ben a hard job It has often made me sick to take such a run of things as is in voge I have often shudderd to write and follow them in their windings but as I commenced I could not look back as such are counted cowards amongs the Latter day Saints I know that many names I have bourn a few months past but I made up my mind that my turn would come By and by That I could speak for myself If you hear from me soon by the by you need not be supprised if much comes to light That is caled in the dark Yet I have feeling that is good On a principal I act on a principle I move If it comes in contack with feeling I care nothing about it I have bore from many that say to be wise But alas their influance is gone with but little prospect to arise I need not cal names But to their supprise there is a topsiturvy turn to the Church of the L D Saints I look at them as a people to be in a fallen state that they cannot Extricate themselves They may go to the rocky mountains as the saying is but it is not of God A plurality of wifes will never do but for those that are fallen and wander in the dark It once was a custum When time could be delayed God sufferd it That their cup of Iniquity might be fild up But now time is precious No time can be spared for such ungodly works I have but little to say but something to do to bring to light what has transpired a few month past I have rote on a principal not to be swayed by a sett that lites on a person all in a mass that moves contra to their feelings I have passed over much that I could easily a wrote but suffise it to say I have wrote enough But if by the by I should take a second round I will stir up mud that will produce a bad smell I move by my self entirely alone I mean to come out streight in the end I remember the covenant that I made with you altho you think I am in the falt yet I will be a great help to you The time will soon come that the worth of my

Labours will be known That has ben hard to do because of opression that I have had to bear from those that I have ben to them a friend in a time of need But What have I got for it but to be slanderd and trod underfoot God that rules in the Heavens knows that I will no more bear it as I have bourn enough You have my best feeling also all of your kin I will do for you and for them as long as I have my wright mind I have this season sufferd much because of ill health But now I am healthy and all with me is well Yours as ever a friend

E R Snow O H Olney

[Folder number 10] Citty of Nauvoo Oct 6th 1842

As this is the commencement of a new era of things That must move in accordance with the teaching of the Antient of Days as they in council have at this time met to do certin business that has long lain in the dark But it is decided That the time has ariven to as long since was spoken by the antient men of God. They spoke as enlightend by the council of Heaven as there is a Council arayed in apparrel not made but by workman of high renown That have assended to the Father at the meridean of time They by the Saviour was chosen And with him did assend after being resorected After death Some Sixty was caled a council to form in the presance of the Father and Son They there sit in a council to open the way for those that are a passing threw a probationary state They look for the welfare of man on the Earth They look for the winding up of wickedness that a time may be That peace and prosperity will be the daily theme They in council have set in the courts above That speaks loud of doings that is to take place on the Earth They speak of the time That the set time has come for a revolution to immediately commence It is first to come amongst the Covenant people of God that will streighten crooked places and brake up wrongs Thus a destiny on the covenant people is decreed that they must fall That say to lead A war of extermination As has hitherto ben shone is now about to take place that is decreed by the Council in Heaven and committed to the Antient of Days As this message to the Earth is sent by a messenger of power it now takes effect From this 6th of Oct. Discord and confusion A spirit of intrusion now will arise that a Spirit of war into partys will lead party to party will join that will cause sorrow and sighings amongs those that God sees fit to preserve He will preserve such by his power a work for to do That is ushering in propeld by the Council in Heaven and on Earth As a council is formed and on Earth took a stand they move in accordance with the Holy Ghost that a oneness of spirit Threw that is obtained as is directed by the Father That has all power both in Heaven and on Earth Thus the Gift of the spirit is predominant It fills the immensity of space that no shadow of turning is invisible to it As the spirit is predominant in all parts it teaches and instructs All things wright By it the Nations of the Earth will be judged at an instant suddenly or a moment of time

[Folder number 10] Citty of Nauvoo Oct. 6th 1842

After several days absent I have to the Citty of Nauvoo returned I find things as usual much adoing The Prophit and people all of a mess except now and then one that knows not what to do As the story of a cat that got lost in a strange garrett She mourned and [sorrowed?] and looked and gased to se some chance to get of the place but its bearly a few That I compare to the cat as I se a most perfect Union amongst the Latter d Saints They are united to say That all is lie that is said against the L D Saints They bost of their wisdom to move in aray And out witt all that come in contact with them They speak of their wisdom of baffling the orthorotys of the land that have outwitted them in all their doings They say we have men of God at the helm that we are not dependant on the wisdom of man Thus by proxy they move in aray To baffle those that do not with them agree A bounty by the governors of Illinois and Missouri is offerd for Joseph and OPR[1] By proxy he is took and secured as is said by a Noted General Law of the C of L D Saints He thus is secured The bounty to get or to baffle any other one that would it attempt They say for to baffle all in their way until they get ready to go west as that is now the theme for some few to get ready and be of They are fast a fixing to go west whire they can live in peace without being molested By the laws of the land They say soon to Start if what I learn is correct As far west As injen Territory and establish a stake of Zion in the name of the Lord

[Folder number 10] Oct. 6th 1842 Thursday

I am caled to learn to recon[2] Coin that has long lain dormant but the time has ariven that it must arise to assist in establishing the Kingdom of God As God on Earth is a looking a work for to do that will put in order things here below The Coin of Gold was antiently called Plebus that was four dollars Coram thre dollars and Colan[3] that was two dollars This money was reconed in antient time that is the same now in dollars and cents Silver was a Coin that much of it was used in antient days It often went by weight A pound was 16$ in any kind of Coin Change was handdled then as it is now One piece 100 cts Of lesser grade fifty cts so down 25 12 ½ 6 ¼ cts Thus Coin was reconed of differant kinds

1. Orrin Porter Rockwell.

2. Olney likely meant "reckon."

3. None of these three words (plebus, coram, colan) are found in any of the scriptures used by members of The Church of Jesus Christ of Latter-day Saints (Bible, Book of Mormon, Doctrine and Covenants, Pearl of Great Price).

[Folder number 10] Laharp Oct 8th 1842

As I am still adoing such things as is incumbant on me I have much to do to do as the way opens As the time has come that I have to change my situation in living as I have had to leave the Latter day Saints and take up my abode amongst those that are caled the the wicked of the land hardly fit to be counted as human beings by the Latter day Saints But I with them find a home and a much more peaceable one than I do amongst the Church They are more honest more upright and just and to be depended on than the Church of L. D. Saints I have left them for reasons That I am sorry to speak of in a land of liberty and freedom of speech More esspecially amongst those caled saints of God I am threatend by them of being put a side That I am warned to be on the watch lest I come in their way and get ketched in their sneir I have now made my home aside of them that they know not of that I am now engaged in Coppying my writings that is desined to go forth to the world as a witness that will no more bear the name of being familiar with them in in In their degraded state

[Folder number 6] Laharp Oct. 13th 1842

As the Antient of have assembled all as one They form a Corum of twelve Their decision is past That because of bad works they have changed Their former place of sitting The sitting in futer will be with thee as thy Labours shall be needed in differant parts Let thy mind be centerd to go and to come As directed By the A- of Days as they at this time have assembled to regulate and put in order all things agreeable to the order of God A destiny is decided on the L. D. Saints that they have no power to extricate themselves It shall not be known as God will take the offender from the Eavil to come That is caled by Revelation his will to perform As much is adoing and a ben don that takes the attention of the people of the Land but the time has come for a change to be The wisdom of man is bafled because of a curse that on them rests It formily has rested On degraded minds that have sit in Heathenish darkness for many ages past and gone But the time has ariven that the curse is now removed and the Natives set at liberty as has hitherto ben recorded Yet the curse is the same as it has bearly changed homes that it now rests on the Jentile race that as a people they have long bosted of their worth But now are fallen no more to arise except by becoming the Covenant people of God But as God to man is a looking to help them on their way they have nothing to fear but to be up and adoing in accordance with the Law of God It has often ben written and as often abused By unwise teachers that run before they was sent to speak of the Law of God to man It is to deal honourably with his Neigbor and well pay his debts Because of bad doing Their wrights are gone that they have no Claim on the Kingdom of God of the Leaders of the Ch of L D Saints Altho many is a looking for that which is good yet the veil is drawn between them And the Son of God Their destiny is seald that they stand on the ground as they did before they was born so all those that have not well don their work must remember the penalty of the Law of God But because of their doings in days past and gone they now are permited to take another round that they may yet enter in to the presance of the Farther and Son that they may yet have a chance a work for to gain a Celestiall rest a rest of which the Prophits spoke if they it understood Is a rest of worth altho many of the L D Saints because of unwise doings have not it merited by their works as they on Earth took a stand and covented to do the will of God but God by them has ben much disgraced by their bad works Both Early and late They in his name have said to do untill he by them will be no more disgrased Their daily moves does them forbid to be caled after the name of the Lord But because of bad works they in a mass will fall some to shame and Contempt others will be boyed up in the presance of the Father and Son as a work of importance is on the wing to extricate the Spirits in prison that long since have Died As the time has ariven for them to come forth valient Labourers will be caled to go forward and do this work It is a work of importance to be managed by the Son of God as he is now a moveing on his way to put all things in order both in Heaven and on Earth

[Folder number 10] Laharp Oct 13th 1842

The word of the Lord is unto the at this time that you are caled to put things in aray for the fall and winter and as this is an established time for the setting of the antient of days As they have changed their habation of sitting because of the wickedness of the Inhabitants of their former place of Counsil They have now assembled in Union all in one as directed by the Son of God As they at this time in counsil set to regulate and put in order all things agreeable to the order of God A destiny is desided on the Latter day Saints that they have no power to extricate them selves But because of bad works they in a mass will fall some to Shame and Contempt others will be boyed up in the presance of the Father Son As a work of importance is on the wing to extricate The spirits in Prision that long since have died as the time has ariven for them to come forth valient Labourers will be required to go forward and do this work It is a work of Importance to be managed by the Son of God as He is now a moveing on his way to put all things in order both in Heaven and on Earth

[Folder number 10] Oct 13th 1842 Laharp

Thou art called at this time to establish the weath[er] threw the fall winter and spring untill the first of April next Let the weather be warm and dry with sudden changes of severe cold as the order of Heaven is thus to baffle perplex with sickness with famine That will bring want and cause sorrow and sighing in all parts of the land Altho many is a looking and mourns because of hard times That on them rests Yet a door is a opening That soon will speak loud to the Inhabitants of the land

[Folder number 4] ~~Oct. 16th 1842 Hancock County Ill~~

I look at the means that has ben used to build I look at what is don And say to those that takes charge of the work that there is some whire a wrong Has there not men ben set apart that have spent There time in collecting funds from East to west and North and South as far as the name of Mormon is known I well know of many That has spent their time and getherd much To assist in building the houses At Nauvoo Much from foren Countrys Has ben brought in connection with funds getherd in our own own Country to build the Temple and Nauvoo house in the name of the Lord Much has ben given to establish the two edifices and accommodate the Church of L.D.S. Much tithing has ben paid in The Consecration has don much that in safty can be said enough has ben given to enclosed both houses But In stead of that What is done Barely two foundations laid One building the sleepers placed and the other not But hands to work that say they do not get enough to sustain them Suffise it to say two thourough men with a few thousand dollars would a don more in six months than has ben don to build the two houses One tenth of Every mans time is required that would a don more If half the time was spent in the performance of the work but I pas by the houses as of not much account But yet I am disgusted To se their course as many came forward In good faith with money Goods Horses Cattle waggens and provisions to assist in building houses to worship God Also lands in abundance is turned in What becomes of it But to agrandise a few that say to have communion with God

[Folder number 4] Hancock County Ill Oct. 16th 1842

We the undersined,

After examining, The writings of O. H. Olney we have become satisfied That he has wrote on a principal not at all ~~to~~ enlarge on the~~ir~~ doings of the Church of L.D.S. but to give them a passing notice as he finds them In their doings We know too well of the foibles of many of the Leaders of the Church of L.D.S. to say all is well We are willing to give our our names That we discard much that we se to be agoing As we have long ben members of the Church of L.D.S it is with reluctance That we give our names to come in contact with those, That we have in all cases defended And wished them well, Untill we find there is that a going that we abhor

To bear testimony to all That O. H. Olney has written we cannot do it as we have not ben situated to know of all the doings of the Community, But think that he has aimed to write the truth In its propper bareing As we are personally aquainted with him, We consider that he has wrote on a principle of duty As we esteem him a worthy Cittizen[4]

[Folder number 10] Oct 16th 1842 Hancock County Ill

We the undersined After examining the writings of O. H. Olneys We have become satisfied that he has wrote on a principal to not at all enlarge on the doings of the Church of Latter Day Saints but give them a passing notice as he actually finds them in their doings We know too well of the foibles of the Leaders of the church of L. D. Saints And are willing to give our names That we discard much that we well know to be a going As we have long ben members of the Church it is with reluctance that we give our names to come in contact with those That we have felt it our duty to uphold in all cases, Untill we find there is that agoing That we abhor To bear testimony to all that we find published In O H. Olney writings we cannot as we have not put our selves in the way to get hold of the doings of the L. D. Saints in full But think that he has aimed to write the truth in its propper bearing As we are personally aquainted with him We consider that he has wrote on a principal of duty As we esteem him as a worthy Cittizen[5]

[Folder number 10] Oct. 18th 1842 Citty of Nauvoo[6]

1st Phebe M Wheeler
2 Mary Bennett

4. This was written in Oliver Olney's handwriting, and there were no signatures attached. It is likely that this was a copy or rough draft of what Olney planned to have people sign.

5. Another version of what appears to be the above petition is found in folder number four. It is in Olney's handwriting, but has no signatures. It is not known if he ever circulated the petition, or whether it was ever signed by anyone.

6. A manuscript page dated June 19, 1842, found in folder number ten has a similar list of thirty women. Following is a comparison of the two lists:

June 19, 1842, List	October 18, 1842, List
1. Phebe M. Wheeler	1. Phebe M. Wheeler
2. Mary Bennett	2. Mary Bennett
3. Axy White	3. Susan White
4. Susan White	4. Abby White
5. Aldridge	5. Leita Aldridge
6. dau Aldridge	6. Caroline Crany
7. Caroline Crony	7. Abigail Crane

3 Susan White
4 Abby White
5 Leita Aldridge
6 Caroline Crany
7 Abigail Crane
8 Leita Crane
9 Mary Chase
10 Hall
11 Sally Hatch
12 Esther Martin
13 Genette Russel
14 Juliette Atwood
15 Elisabeth Sikes
16 Emily Thompson
17 Lorinda Atwood
18 Crandal
19 Julia Jinks
20 Alvira Atwood (Dead)
21 Rebeca Atwood

---

8. Craine
9. Craine
10. Craine
11. Betsy Chase
12. Mary Chase
13. Polly Chase
14. Sally Hatch
15. Genelle (Genette) Russel
16. Juliette Atwood
17. Elisabeth Sikes
18. Emily Thompson
19. Crandall
20. Alvira Atwood (dead)
21. Rebecca Atwood
22. Leonora Levitt
23. Levitt
24. Levitt
25. Rebecca Wirick
26. Esther Morton
27. Elisabeth Barlow
28. Hansen
29. Hubbel
30. Elisabeth Chapman

8. Leita Crane
9. Mary Chase
10. Hall
11. Sally Hatch
12. Esther Martin
13. Genette Russel
14. Juliette Atwood
15. Elisabeth Sikes
16. Emily Thompson
17. Lorinda Atwood
18. Crandal
19. Julia Jinks
20. Alvira Atwood (dead)
21. Rebeca Atwood
22. Leavitt
23. Leavitt
24. ~~Crandal~~
25. Rebeca Wirick
26. Elisabeth Chapman
27. Nancy Rigdon
28. Nancy Brotherton
29. Rebeca Burton
30. Spencer

22 Leavitt
23 Leavitt
~~24 Crandal~~
25 Rebeca Wirick
26 Elisabeth Chapman
27 Nancy Rigdon
28 Martha Brotherton
29 Rebeca Burton
24 White
30 Spencer

[On the top of the following page were these numbers and math]

100		
<u>96</u>	1 16 -	100
4 0		<u>16</u>
		1600

[Folder number 10] Citty of Nauvoo Oct 20th 1842

The following lines composed by Oliver H. Olney for the Quincy Whig

As I of late have ben a writing of the doings of the Church of Latter Day Saints and gave Notice of it in the sangamo Journal,[7] as my Pamphlet in print is not ready to speak Altho underway. But from it I will Coppy- Commensing at April 6th 1842, According to previous Apointment this morning at 10 Oclock many met in Conference, With good feelings. But as weather was cold and wett business was dull, as they meet out of doors for the want of a house. The day past a way With but few remarks- and ajourned to eight In the morning, They again Come together as friends, and commenced business As usual. They spoke of the Temple And of its worth- that when finished mutch light threw it would flow, that they would be endowed with power from on High. They spoke of the necessity of being engaged- to establish this Edifise- in the name of the Lord. They spoke of many things, That must be don as a duty to forward The work of the Lord They spoke of the people abroad, that many was sitting in darkness- for the want of Labourers, to declare the Gospel sound They spoke of the necessity- of many being cald to prepare to fill an

7. The *Sangamo Journal* was a newspaper begun by Simeon and Josiah Francis in Springfield, Illinois. The first issue was published on November 10, 1831. Franklin William Scott, "Newspapers and Periodicals of Illinois: 1814–1879," 321. Throughout the 1830s and 1840s the *Sangamo Journal* printed many items about Mormons and Mormonism, including scandalous accusations written by John C. Bennett.

important Mission- amongst the Jentile race. They caled for Volenteers This work to do- I will simply make use of their words, uttered by one of their Leaders Lyman Wight a Noted man One of the Chosen twelve, Rag Shag and Bobtail And the scouring- of all Gods Creation, You now are caled to come forward- this great work for to do, to establish Zion, In the last days. If I had not been a versed In their doings- it would have made me a Stared, to a seen such a Company, as before me appeared-. It was Rag Shag and Bobtail- in every sense of the word, On Saturday eighth they come together- and received their Charge, to go forward And scower the Country, Sever out the good and leave the bad. The thre days of Conferance past ~~by~~ away with a Union of feeling, And a Union of mind Not much seemed to be don, except some cases came up- of Lying tatling and the like. Likewise some of the Chosen twelve, a trying to be verry Intimate with females. I thought as they had wives of their own- that they might let The young girls alone, as is the coston[8] of the day. As I pass by the Conferance I will Skip from time to time and speak of the doings of the L. D. S. From time to time many went out to preach and baptise in the name of the Lord Several hundreds have gone out this great work to do And are yet a going they say in honour of the Son of God But if he by them Is honoured I have no more to say as I look at their doings in the City of Nauvoo Much has ben Published of their doings in differant Periodicals of the day by John Cook Bennett and others but as yet half the story is not told

[Folder number 6] Oct. 22d 1842

As I am caled upon to meet in Council with the Antient of Days as they have assembled some business to transact to bring dark sayings to light that is desined to lay in the Dark It is the unwise doings of the L D Saints as they long have had a standing in the name of the Lord and often ben blest In their daily moves By Revelations dreams and visions much light have they received untill they by their bad works have rejected the Son of God By their works they have become fallen that on them is a curse that they cannot get of As his name by them is much disgrased as they say to be L D Saints at the close of the Day I speak my mind as I have often meet and rote of the doings of the L. D. Saints Whire has reason gone but into some solitary place whire the prince of Darkness rules both Early and late By works I judge that daily speaks of unwise doings of the Latter Day Saints They in aray together move to cuver up wrongs or their bad works They say we are the blest of God We the kies like Apostle Peter possess Their is no power to put us down as the Priesthood we have obtained As no one is instructed In the theme with light to lead the C of L D Saints Again the Lesser Class do say our teachers are Infalable men

8. Olney likely meant "custom" of the day.

of God that God has placed for our guide that we with them do cheerfully move in hopes to enter in threw the Pearly Gates in to a Heavenly rest They thus reason Without regard to the word of God Or his Law to govern man

[Folder number 10] Hancock County Oct. 22dth 1842

Thou art caled at this time to meet in council with the Antient of Days As they at this time have met in Council and have come to the Conclusion to Unriddle the Iniquity of the Church of L. D. S. As they on Earth have had a standing In the name of the Lord and often ben blessed in their daily moves By Revelations Dreams and Visions They much light have received Untill they by bad works have rejected the Son of God By their works they have become fallen that on them is a curse That they cannot get off But because of bad doings their wrights are gone that they have no claim on the Kingdom of God of the Leaders of the Church of L. D. S. Altho many is a looking for that which is good yet the veil is drawn between them and the son of God Their destiny is seald that they stand on the Ground As they did before they was born So all those that have not well don their work must must remember the Penalty of the Law of God But because of their doings in days past and gone they now are permited to take an other round That they may yet enter into the presance of the father and son that they may yet have a chance a work to do To gain a Celestial rest A rest of which the Pr[ophets] spoke if they understood It is a rest of worth altho many of the L.D.S. because of unwise doings have not it merited by their works as they on Earth took a stand and covented to do the will of God But God by them by them has ben disgrased by their bad works both Early and late They in his name have said to do well be no more disgrased Their daily move does them forbid to be caled after the name of God as his name by them is much disgrased as they say to be L D Saints

[Folder number 6] Oct. 23

I today assemble with the A of Days as the Council ajourned Yesterday to meet again at this time on the bank of the River above the City of Nauvoo on the broken bank of the Missippi near the waters Edge as the water is a running sun a shineing Leaves a falling All Nature in Commotion as the wind is a blowing that causes me to say that God rules In the immensity of space I look at the Law By which all is governed and say by what power do they move as I se them move in wisdom being Governed by a principal that far excedes the wisdom of man I look at the Earth in the shape of a ball I se its revolutions In honour of the sun and the Days lengthen and shorten once in six months by degrees By a principal it is don If Understood God has given a law And laid a foundation to move upon As all is the same above and below all centers to the Earth from the Circumferance of the Earth to its center all in a mass is inclined As the Earth is hollow like a bottle and in the form of a ball and the Spirit of attraction inclosed their in, That propels power that produces wind and presses water that it fills the pours of the Earth As the Earth is said on wings to move it is propeld by power That rules above A balance of air is said to sway by being oprest By Attractive powers that daily moves Wind and water is thus combined That water is prest that it governs The briny tide The tide in honour of the Law of God produces Convulsions all over the Earth that causes Rivolets to flow Also springs to cheer the hart of man Again this attraction only has power over Combustibles That is not pure When they become pure and undefiled they become transparent or are quickened By the spirit of God that they then move as the Angels above The Earth is governed By powers that be because of the fallen condition of man but the time is fast ariveing that it to its rest will return uniting with the planit of the Sun as it from that was formed To accomodate those that had feelings to come into the presance of the Father and the Son in differant situations it often has stood from its departer of the Glory of the sun It has raised and fallen time and again that many has ben priveleged of being an honour to themselves But the time is fast ariving that it will be relieved from the curse that on it rests Sixteen hundred years Is barely the time to prepare for the Melineum and one thousand years of rest Then the enemy of souls will have a short time to baffle those many on Earth others in prision that was raised up in the Melinneum Then Comes the day of Judgement when all will be hailed and receive their destiny according to their works that have not kept a celestial Law Those that have kept the Law of God will stand to judge the Human race as they in aray will move around and receive their last doom When once their sins are all forgot they then come on to a planit of rest that often comes to our vew when eavening shades comes roleing on We se a Star Stationary in the North altho but dim yet it is their rest The high and low will Center there at the close of Sisteen hundred years from this, Time will be caled of worth unto the human race to honour the cause of which they have espoused Or said to do when from choise they took a probationary state a state of which much is said by that desire to be of fame in the Eyes of those like them selves The tree began to sprout and bud in honour of the Son of God in the first age as it now is caled that God formed Adam from the dust altho the Earth had for many ages stood and been peopled by Mortal man At this time an order commenced anew for those that plead for greater light that they with God mite have a rest that they might know of things presant past and futer Also power to form and create anew that they could not obtain except by keeping a Celestial Law But as I am caled in Council in this grove to write for the Antient men of God I with them freely spend my time in honour of the God above ~~As this is the~~

~~first day of the week and set a part to honour God~~ As this is a day set apart to honour God it being the first day of the week in honour of the day the saviuor arose the time has come for a change to be It is now to honour the sitting of the Antient of Days as they on Earth have took a stand to be governed by the Son of God He to them does freely give the honour of performing the Latter Day Glory Them in Connection with the Holy Ghost is to be entitled with the honour of bringing about much Righeousness Thus the day must come in Note the ninth of June 1842 in stead of the one formerly kept Let every seventh be a day of rest Let man and beast of every ~~kind~~ grade withdraw from Labour of every kind except to prepare to satisfy thirst Let this day be set apart to honour God by prayer and thanksgiving to his name

[Folder number 10] Citty of Nauvoo Oct [23rd][9] 1842 O. H. Olney

I today assemble with the antient of days as the council ajourned from yesterday to meet again at this time on the Bank of the river above the Citty of Nauvoo on the broken Bank of the Missippi near the Waters edge As the water is a running sun a shineing And leaves a falling all Nachure in Commotion As the wind is a blowing that causes me to say that God rules In the Immensity of space I look at the Law By which all is governed and say by what power do they move as I se them move in wisdom being governed by a principal far to accede the wisdom of Man **[There is a mark at this point on the page and the same mark on another page in the manuscript indicating that the following is a continuation of what was written above on this date.]** Far to exceed the wisdom of man I look at the Earth in the shape of a ball I se its revolutions in honour of the sun and the days Lengthen and Shorten once in sis months By degrees By a principal it is don If understood God has given a Law And laid a foundation to move upon As all is the same above and below All centers the Earth from the Circumferance of the Earth to its center All in a mass is Inclined as the Earth is hollow like a bottle and in the form of a ~~Bottle~~ Ball and the Spirit of attraction, inclosed their in That propels power that produces wind And preses water that it fills the Poors of the Earth[10] As the Earth is said on wings to move it is propeld by power That rules above A balance of air is said to sway by being oprest By Attractive powers that daily

9. It appears that the entry was originally dated October 24, but Olney wrote over the 4 to make it a 3.

10. Based upon a similar document also dated October 23 found in folder 6, the following lines are missing from this entry in folder 10. Uncertain as to whether Olney added a new paragraph in the folder 6 entry or a page is missing from the October 23 folder 10 entry, I have added the next few lines from folder number six for continuity.

moves Wind and water is thus combined That water is prest that it governs The briny tide The tide in honour of the Law of God produces Convulsions all over the Earth that causes Rivolets to flow Also springs to cheer the hart of man Again this attraction only has power over Combustibles That is not pure When they become pure and undefiled they become transparent or are quickened By the spirit of God that they then move as the Angels above The Earth is governed By powers that be[11] The power to rule and govern the Earth and its productions Beasts Birds and fishes of every kind he gave names as he by God was shone He then was caled a Law to keep as was an agent to act for him self Good and bad before him was set that the happy Coupple was free to do as their minds and will did them direct The restrictions on them that was put as they had a standing in the Garden of Eaden A thrifty tre before them stood well clothed with fruit of good looks but they to it had no wright as it was a law of God and penalty annext that if they the precious fruit should Eat they should fall from the Glory that did on them rest The power that with them long had ben Left them to themselves They looked and vewed the senes around and often spoke of things to come But at last a creeping thing came round and said to those of High renown that he with them would like to stay and Learn wisdom as well as they Day after day he with them meet that they with it did freely converse Its attractive powers Did them lead that they desided it was a messeng[er] from God He to them did plainly show that he wished them well He eat of fruit And gave to them that they with reluctancy joined with it and did frely eat of the forbidden fruit[12] The creeping thing did then transform in looks and sise as a man and left them to se to themselves The God of Heaven then come down and asked them What they had been about They to him feintly said that they had Eat of fruit of the tree of which they was forbid Then came a senry of things that all Nachure trembled and man lost his high standing from the presance of God and came under the tuition of that power of darkness that rules at noon day[13] because of the fallen condition of man But the time is fast ariving that it to its rest will return uniting with the planit of the son[14] as it from that was formed to accommodate those that had feelings to come into the presance of the Father and Son In differant Situations It often has stood from its departer Of the Glory of the sun It has raised and fallen time and again that many has ben priveleged of being an honour to them selves But the time is fast Ariving that it will relieved From the curse that on it rests Sixteen hundred years is bearly the time to

11. This ends the lines from folder 6. The following is from the October 23 entry found in folder 10.

12. The following is from a previous page written upside down.

13. The following is from a different undated page in folder 10.

14. Olney likely meant "sun."

prepare for the Melineum and one thousand years of rest Then the enemy of souls will have a short time To baffle those many in Earth Others in prision that was Raised up in the Melineum Then comes the day of Judgment when all will be hailed And receive their destiny according to their works that have not kept a Celestial Law Those that have kept the Law of God will stand to Judge The human race as they in aray Will move around and receive their last doom When once their sins are all forgot they then come on to a planit of rest that often comes to our vew when evening shades comes rolling in We se a Star Stationary in in the north altho but dim yet it is their rest The high and low will Center there at the close of Sixteen hundred years from this; the Time will be caled of worth unto the Human race to honour the course Of which they said to do when from choise they took a probationary state A state of which much is said by those that desire To be of fame in the Eyes of those like themselves The tree began to sprout and bud in honour of the son of God in the first age as it now is caled that God formed Adam from the dust altho the Earth had for many ages stood and ben peopled By mortal man At this time an order commenced a new for those that plead for Greater light that they with God mite have a rest that they mite know of things presant past and futer Also power to form and create anew that they could not obtain except by keeping a Celestial Law But As I am caled in Council in this grove to write for the Antient men of God I with them do freely spend my time in honour of God above As this is a day set a part to honour God it being the first day of the week in honour of the day that the Saviour arose The time has come for a change to be It is now to honour the sitting of the Antient of Days as they on Earth have took a stand to be governed by the son of God He to them Does freely give the honour of performing the Latter day Glory Them in connection with the Holy Ghost is to be entitled with the honour of bringing about much Righeousness Thus the day must come in Note as a day of rest The ninth of June 1842 in stead of the one formerly kept Let every seventh be a day of rest Let man and beast of every kind withdraw from Labour of every kind except to ~~satisfy~~ to prepare to satisfy thirst Let the day be set apart To honour God by prayer and thanksgiving to his name

[Folder number 6] Oct. 24th 1842

On bank of the Missippi River I again am cald to meet in Council with the Antient of Days as they at this time to transact Certin business, That will put things in order, That all things may move as is by the Council in Heaven decreed. As they have assembled of Late and looked to the doings of the people of the United States. As their Constitution was framed by the Council of God. And honoured for many years But alas the time did arive That desining men took the reigns of Goverment and violated the Laws of the land, Because of their doings and wicked works. A decision is past and decreed that the Goverment shall all be broken up

[Folder number 10] October 24th 1842

On the Bank of the River of Missippi I again am caled to meet in Council with the Antient of Days As they at this time have assembled to transact certin business that will put things in order that all things may move as Is by the Council in Heaven decreed As they have Assembled of late and looked to the things of The people of the United States As their Constitution was formed By the Council of God And honoured for many years But alas the time did arise that desining men Took the Reigns of government and violated the laws of the land Because of their doings and wicked works A decision is past and decreed that the goverment shall all be broken up

[Folder number 10] Quincy Oct 26th 1842

As I of late have be a writing of the doings of the Church of Latter Day Saints and gave Notice of it In the Sangamo Journal as my pamphlet ~~is not~~ in print is not ready to speak Altho underway But from it I will Coppy

Commencing at April 6th 1842 According to previous apointment this morning at 10 Oclock many meet all in aray in Conferance with good feelings As the weath[er] is cold and wett business was dul as we mett out of doors for the want of a house The day past away with buf [but] few remarks and ajourned untill the 7th at 10 Oclock They again come together with feelings of the best kind and soon commenced business They spoke of the Temple And of its worth that when finished Threw it much lite would flow that they would be endowed with power from on high They spoke of the necessity of being engaged to establish this edifice in the name of the Lord They spoke of many things That must be don as a duty To forward the work of the Lord They spoke of the people abroad that many was sitting in darkness for the want of Labourers to declare the Gospel Sound They spoke of the necessity of many being caled to prepare to fill the last Mission amongst the Jentile race They caled for Labourers This great work to do I will simply make use of their words uttered by one of the Leaders Lyman Wite a noted man of the Chosen Twelve Rag Shag and bobtail the scourings of all Gods Creation you now are caled to come forward and from under our hands receive Ordinations to go forth and preach Gods word As you know the importance of what we have to do to Clear our shirts[15] and prepare for the comming of the Son of Man as he is soon acomming With the Saints in the air Scores and hundreds came forward this great work for to do to establish Zion in the Last days If I had not ben aversed In their doings it would have made me a stared to have seen such a Company as before me appeared It was Rag Shag and Bobtail in every sense of the word. On Saturday 8[ith] they come together and received their Charge to go forward and scour the Country in all parts and sever out the good from the bad The thre days of Conferance past a way with a union of feeling A Union of mind Not much seemed to be don except some cases came up of Lying tatling and the like and some of the Chosen twelve a trying to be verry intimate with females I thought as they had wifes of their own that they mite let the young girls alone as is the Costem of the land As I pass by the Conferance I will scip from time to time and speak of the doings of the Latter Day Saints From time to time the Elders went out to preach and baptise In the name of the Lord Many hundreds have gone out this great work to do And are yet a going they say in honour of the Son of God But If he by them is honoured I have no more to say as I look at their doings in the Citty of Nauvoo Much has ben published of their doings in differant Periodicals of the day by John Cook Bennett and others But as yet the story is not half told

[Folder number 6] Citty of Nauvoo Oct. 31st 1842

According to previous Notice I have arived at the Citty of Nauvoo being caled upon to meet in Council with the Antient of Days as they in part have essembled to establish an order of things that may move in the order of God as the wicked are many In differant parts Much said and much a doing that is abominable in the Sight of God as he the earth has visited within a few days And given orders how to proceed The Covenant people is first in aray that they have to suffer because of brakeing the Law of God They as a people will suffer the penalty of the Law of God that was established in The morning of time For it they must suffer all as one but many will arise to honour and other to dishonour Of the L. D. Saints Then comes a senry of trouble abroad in the land Because of bad doings amongst the people of the world as they have ben Laboured with and sought for In days past and gone by Legally Orthorised servents that God has sent forth both late and Early Their Labours have ben free untill they are rejected and counted of no worth that they now are caled

15. "Clean our shirts" means to repent of sins and be made pure. Similar statements are found in Latter-day Saint scripture: "No man be saved except his garments are washed white; yea, his garments must be purified until they are cleansed from all stain, through the blood of him of whom it has been spoken by our fathers, who should come to redeem his people from their sins" (Alma 5:21).

Their Labour to leave and stand still and se the Salvation of God A theme of things is now in voge to clens and purify the Earth as it has long ben under a power that rules in Darkness at noon day This power has from the begining by him that had fell from a high Station in the presance of God because of misdoings Their agency they abused that they now in contact are a moving to the doings of God But As the time has ariven that Dark Shades must give away the Orthorotys of Heaven have taken the Kingdoms of the Earth into their hands By degrees they will baffle dark sayings in this and foren lands untill the Earth is purified and its contents clensed with all things in order agreeable to the different Councils in Heaven that it may become a transparant ball and always be an abode for the specie man

[Folder number 10] Citty of Nauvoo Oct 31st 1842

According to previous Notice I have arived at the Citty of Nauvoo being caled upon to meet in Council with The Antient of Days as they in past have this day assembled to establish an order of things that may move In the order of God As the wicked are many In differant parts much said and much adoing that is abominable In the sight of God as he the Earth has visited with in a few days And given orders how to procede The Covenant people Is first in aray that they have to suffer because of brakeing The Law of God They as a people will suffer the penalty of the Law of God that was established In the morning of time For it they must suffer All as one But many will arise To honour and others to dishonor Of the L. D. Saints Then comes a senry of trouble abroad in the land Because of bad doings amongst the people of the world As they have ben Labourd with and sought for in days past and gone by Legally orthorised servents that God has sent forth both late and Early Their Labours have ben free untill they are rejected And counted of no worth that they now are caled Their Labours to leave and stand still and se The Salvation of God A theme of things is now in voge to cleans and purify The Earth as it has long ben under a power that rules in darkness At noon day This power has ben from the beguinning by him that fell From a high station In the presance of God He with many that was caled Angels of light have forfeited their standing in the presance of God because of misdoings Their agency they abused that they now are In Contact a moving to the doings of God But as the time has ariven that dark shade must give away The orthorotys of Heaven have taken the kingdoms of the Earth In to their hands By degrees they will baffle Dark sayings in this and foren lands Untill the Earth is purified and its contents Clensed With all things in order agreeable to the Differant Councils in Heaven that it may become a transparent ball and always such be an abode for the specie man

O. H. Olney

[Folder number 11] Citty of Nauvoo Oct 31st 1842

To Presidant Joseph Smith

It is with no ordinary feelings that I address you at this time in writing But as I have a leisure moment Improve it in writing you a few lines That you may know my mind that this time I will say that I am differantly situated from what I was one year or Eighteen months ago I was then in trouble because of many things my mind was unsetled In doings as I se much adoings I often felt to mourn lest I should make mismoves I look at my self and at the Church Also the order of God and I se their must be a Union amongst those that covenant to do his will I looked at my own weakness and unworthiness that we must say is the common lot of all that has from choise taken a probation I looked to my superiors for Instructions and was entirely willing to be governed by them untill I found them to be against me that I se no sympathy of feeling towards me but a feeling to tred me underfoot That never was my name it I never bore neither is it required of any man But many submit to it My wrights is what I claim and must have without takeing the wrights of others I look at your wrights and the work you have don and say its of great worth to bring about the purposes of God I look at many as well as yourself that must in the due time of the Lord have something to do That no one can say all rests on me that I am all But many move in accordance As is directed by the wisdom and council of God I look at myself and the connection that I formerly had with the Church of Latter D Saints I claim no standing with them Altho my mind is the same as was when I moved with them in accordance I have my reasons for doing as I have don As I feel that I have ben Shamefully abused by many I will say I have herd but a little from you But hardly a word from you has set sckores a barking That I have sufferd from the yelping of a dirty mess of pettish pups That I do not feel in duty bound to bear but I have bourne it untill I will not do it much longer I will defend myself in a manly way Threw the medium of the press as from your hand in that way I have sufferd by being published to the fore quarters of the Earth I am not Ignorant of things that have transpired look back at the doings such as Laciveousness for.[16] Au.[17] and many doings that is abominable The Heathen would blush at it That is now supposed to be coverd up But the most part of it is pend to be published that will speak of doings that has ben to many in the dark

16. Olney was likely referring to fornication.
17. Olney was likely referring to adultery, which he typically spelled "Audultry."

[Folder number 11] Epitaph on the Life of Andrew Jackson[18]

State of Illinois Oct 31, 1842

To the Hon. Prest Andrew Jackson

As my eye the other day ketched on a clause in a periodical, That spoke of the decline of our old ~~friend~~ and long friend Gen. A. Jackson respecting An epetaph of his life a speaking of his Labours ~~doings~~ Life and doings I cheerfully improve a leisure moment and in doing it ~~write~~ exspress my mind

An Epitaph on the Life of Gen A Jackson

This noted Chieftain
From youth grew up
In honour of Parrents
That gave him birth
In an Early day he took a stand
To move in accordance
With the Laws of the land
He soon took an honourable station
To defend a free Constitution
With weapons of war He moved in array
Against those that did oppose
The American wrights
He honoured his station
At home and abroad
By being honest valient
Uprwight and Prudent.
After many long and hard toils
He then was caled, the cepter to sway
Over the American Soil
His daily doings caused many to say
We are ruined by his doings
~~Of those of weaker~~
By those of the weaker class
But by the by all had to say
That Prest Andrew Jackson
In his doings could not be Exceld

18. Andrew Jackson was born March 15, 1757. He served as President of the United States from March 1829 to March 1837. At the time Olney wrote this tribute (1842), Jackson was eighty-five years old. Jackson died June 8, 1845.

He was fre and familiar
With both high and low
He vetoed and set at liberty
As he pleased
Without respect to party or Friends
But His youthful moments fled
And middle age passed by
Above thre scores years and ten
Has measured his time
Yet in health he is a moveing
As in the vigour of youth
With a mind Strong and comprehensive
But alas we must say
That he is on the decline
We look at his deportment
At home and abroad
With the doings of the day
He is familiar
But his days is numberd
As we speak of mans days on Earth
Yours A St[r]anger O. H. Olney

An Epitaph on the life of Gen A Jackson

This Noted Chieftain
From youth grew up
In honour of his parrents
That gave him Birth
In an Early day he took a stand
To move In accordance
With the Laws of the land
He soon took an honourable station
To defend a fre Constitution
With weapons of war He moved in aray
Against those That did oppose
The American wrights
He honoured his Station at home and abroad
By being honest valient Upright and prudent
After many long hard Toils
He then was caled To sway the cepter
Over the American Soil
His daily doings caused many say

We are ruined by his doings
By those of the weaker Class
But by the by all had to say
That Prest Andrew Jackson
In his doings Could not be exceld
He was free and familiar
With both high and low
He vetoed And set at liberty as he pleased
Without respect to party or Friends
But his youthful moments are fled
And middle age gone by
Above three score years and ten
Has marked his time
Yet in Health he is a moveing
As in the vigour of youth
With a mind Strong and Comprehensive
But alas we must sayThat he is on the decline
As we look at his deportment
At home and abroad ~~With doing~~
With doings Familiar of the day
But his days is numberd
As we speak of mans time of him
As of others a traverling on the Earth

As my Eye the other day ketched on a Collom in a Periodical That spoke of the decline of our old and long Friend General Andrew Jackson requesting an epitaph of his life[19] a speaking of his Labours Life and doings I cheerfully improve a leisure moment and in doing it express my mind

19. It may be that a newspaper invited interested parties to write an epitaph for Andrew Jackson and Olney responded to the request. It is not known whether it was ever published or if Olney ever provided the newspaper with his Jackson tribute.

NOVEMBER 1842

[Folder number 9] City of Nauvoo Nov 4th 1842

this letter is draft of letter elsewhere [written down?]

Dear Sister L. W.[1]

I again improve a leisure moment in writing you a few lines As we have ben Conversent without knowing fully each others mind I well remember the few hours I spent with you and the good understanding that we had And the desision of our minds That we would use our endeavours to live together Respecting your mind at this time Of it I cannot say but I will say to you that My mind is now as then and has ben the same I should like to know your mind If your mind is the same we will act accordingly As we have the time before us what we cant do today we will do at some futer time when the way opens I am satisfied that your Parents want your work I am not in such a hurry to settle but what I can wait for your Motion But I would like at this time to know your mind It would be satisfactory to me to converse with you but if it is not best; pleas to speak to me by writing I would say to you to make the Citty of Nauvoo a visit If you should want to attend a high school[2] or get wages you will find a good chance here As help is in good demand I would get out of the lonely grove any how And se what is agoing on Make up your mind to come here and stay a few months I know of a first rate place that you can get to make it a home By Comeing to moses Smiths Daniel Spencer wants to get some girl to live with them They have a good house well of and nice folks Improve the first opportunity and I will engage you a good time that you will Learn more here in one week than you can there in a year under

1. Lucinda White.

2. Common schools were the precursor to public elementary schools. There were common schools in Nauvoo, typically taught in someone's home or a room rented by the teacher. It was not mandatory that children attend school. Parents chose to send their children to school and a tuition was paid to the teacher. Although there was a Kirtland High School founded by the Saints in Ohio, there is no record of a high school in Nauvoo. Likely, there were teachers who provided "higher education" for older students, twelve or thirteen years of age and up. There was a University of Nauvoo founded and some classes were taught in various locations around the city. Olney's reference to "high school" probably meant the private school classes taught for those beyond the elementary level but before the university level. See Paul Thomas Smith, "A Historical Study of the Nauvoo, Illinois, Public School System, 1841–1845," Thanks to Scott Esplin for bringing this source to my attention.

the tuition of those that opress I am not disposed but to bearly speak I look at you as a youth And a female too I disdain the mind That would them abuse I unexpectedly with you meet but I mus say with feelings of no ordinary kind As you took my mind But if I have not yours then I must say that it is not best for us to come together But if you say as you have said that we will Unite if the way opens We then will take a course to do it without being swayed by those that acks on selfish motives I am now about to start to Walnut Grove I shall put up to Brother Snows if I can call at your house and see you If not best pleas to come or go whire I can se you But if you cannot se me write to me your mind as my journy is to know how it is with you and convey to me By the one that hands you this

[Folder number 9] Extract from a letter from Israel Barlow to O H Olney[3]

Dr Sir having had many years acquaintance with you and your familys and many a friendly intercourse with you, and passed through many trials since our acquaintance, and having had the utmost confidence in you as a christian &c &c

Israel Barlow

[Folder number 9] Nov. 4th 1842 Citty of Nauvoo

Being Caled upon by the Orthoroty of the Antient of days I ordain Newell Nurse to the High Priesthood after the order of the son of God To Stand Connected with the twelve councilers As is established for the promulgation of the Gospel As directed by the Antient of days preparitory to the Comming of the Son of man

[Folder number 10] Citty of Nauvoo Nov. 4th 1842

I by name this morning being caled upon as names to be used to bring about the purposes of God as this is a day set apart for much to be don to establish the kingdom of God It is a day long ben looked for by the former day Saints that the Latter day Glory may beguin to usher in As much is agoing in the name of the Lord by unorthorised servents on the Earth that a light may arise in the name of the Lord To move in accordance In thy Labours as thy Labours is many And will progress the differant Quorams must be established Commensing at the High Council then the chosen twelve Then comes Zions Watchman that must move in aray that will stand as seventys being special witnesses to the world From time to time the Corams will be fild by valient men of God that will honour his name amongs the Nations of the Earth Let

3. Not Olney's handwriting.

them be ordained As fast as they are known and set a part to fill their several offices in honour of the God above As his name is sounded By many around let a standard be set up[4] commenceing at this place as the stone from the Mountain is now in aray propeld by the An. of Days They will move all in order as to them is shone By the Council of Heaven directed by the Son of Man A senry of things first is in voge to establish the name of the Lord It is to baffle those That use his name by sayings that is not of God Altho they have Labourd Gods will to do but mistook it for their own Thou art caled to ordain thy Brother Nurse and Hadlock[5] as High Priests and give them Cirtificates As being Legally orthorised from under thy hand

[Folder number 11] Nov 4th 1842 Citty of Nauvoo

Dear Sister Lucinda White,

In health and good spirits I Improve a leisure moment In writing you a few lines as we have ben conversant some little but as dark shades seems to hover over my mind I feel desirous to get them removed. I well remember the few hours I spent with you and the good understanding that we had and the decision of our minds, That we would use our endeavors to live together. Respecting your mind at this time I cannot say, But will say to you That mine is now as then, And has ben the same, I should like to know your mind if your mind is the same, We will act accordingly, as we have the time before us. What we cant do today we can at some futer time when the way opens. I am satisfied, That your Parrents want your work. I am not in such a hurry to settle, But what I will wait for your Motion But I would like at this time to know your mind, It would be satisfactory to me to converse with you, But if it is not best, pleas to speak to me by writing I would say to you to make the Citty of Nauvoo a visit If you should want to attend a High School or get wages for work here is a good chance Womens help is in good demand I would get out of that lonly Grove of gloominess any how And se what is ago-ing on Make up your mind and come here, And stay a few months I know of a good place here for you neer by Moses Smiths at Daniel Spencers they want to get some one to live with them They have a good house well of and nice

4. At this point in the manuscript Olney drew a symbol that matches a symbol in another part of the manuscript which appears to connect the two parts together.

5. Olney is likely referring to Joseph Hadlock, a Latter-day Saint and citizen of Nauvoo. When Oliver Olney and Phebe Wheeler were married in 1843, Joseph Hadlock performed the wedding. Lyndon W. Cook, *Nauvoo Deaths and Marriages*, 107. D. Michael Quinn mistakenly lists Patriarch Hyrum Smith as performing the marriage of Olney and Phebe Wheeler. D. Michael Quinn, "The Culture of Violence in Joseph Smith's Mormonism," 36n135.

folks Small family lately from the East I will assure you a good place if you come here soon That you will learn more here in a week than you can there in a year Under the tuition of those that opress I am not disposed but bearly to speak I look at you as a youth, And a female to. I disdain the mind That would them abuse I unexpectedly with you meet but I must say with feelings of no ordinary kind as you took my mind But if I have not yours I then must say, that it is not best For us to come together But if you say as you have said that we will unite, If the way opens we then will take a course to do it without being swayed by those that acts on selfish motives I am now about to Start to Walnut Grove I shall put up to Brother Snows If I can call at your house And se you If not best pleas to come or go whire I can converse with you But if you cannot se me or think it not best write to me your mind as my Journey is to know how it is with you and convey to me By the one that give you this

Yours as ever O. H. Olney
Lucinda White

[Folder number 6] City of Nauvoo 8th 1842[6]

As this is a day set apart By the A. of Days they at this time have meet in Council ~~As this is a day set a~~ A decision is past To bring to light Dark sayings that have long lain in the dark As dark sayings is many a vale must be rent to establish an order anew on Earth As minds is many All in one must move that a Union must be established amongst the Chosen of God As wisdom shall direct let all move being directed by the Antient of Days as at this time is A decision in honour of the Son of God as he rules and governs this Planitary mass By doings and sayings as seemeth him good As he has now took a stand a work for to do To clens and purify and make all clean Again he has come the wicked to opress and put his Law in forse As his Law is easy for man to perform no shadow of turning will be received A decision is past That an order may arise governed by agents To the A. of Days as they with the Chosen will daily move Teach them in the path of duty that they may well do their work A theme of things is now to arise by Legally orthorised servents on the Earth A Kingdom must be reard in honour of God that long has ben looked for By the Antient Saints As the time has ariven man to be known delays will no more answer but all things must move both in Heaven and on Earth as many is a waiting for the time to come that long since died From the first age down to the presant time They are all impatiently awaiting for the time to arive that they on Earth can take a stand to prepare for a more glorious

6. Although the year is not recorded, the date is likely November 8, 1842, because it was written beginning on the last page of the October 24, 1842, entry.

rest It is to gain wisdom from on high by wise teachers That was resorected at the Meridean of time As many arose in newness of light by being quickened By the resorecting spirit that they with the Saviour did arise as they was on a planit of rest anxiously a waiting to come forth that they have stood as mineut men and cheerfully don as they was shone Their Labours have ben many in days past and gone In keeping records of things that have transpired down to the presant time as no man on Earth has it performed but is kept in Heaven by the spirits of the just perfected The time has ariven for man to arise and honour him self By keeping an impartial history of what transpires Let no one endeaviour eavil deeds to hide as a day of reveiling secrets is at hand The time will soon arive the doings to solve of things that has ben don whether wright or wrong but the doings of the L.D.S. is in vogue Then comes the doings of the Antients back to the first age of the world Then will be unriddled a mistry of worth speaking of this planit and its work before time began as it had a standing above fifty thousand years since it took its departure from the Sun From that time to the presant it has often changed By the wisdom of God that many have moved And honoured themselves by living in obediance to the Law of God As Satan or the prince of Darkness has in all ages had power from time to time since The Earth was formd Altho they have changed as God se fit and Knew not of Each others doings or what had took place As the time has come That light must shine and solve mistrys of worth as many on the Earth has had a standing conducted by the Father of lights as he had many decendants or sons to bring his purposes about The adopted son of Joseph[7] at last took a stand to wind up a senry of things the work he commenced at the beginning of time to establish and put all things in order as was to him shown by a Council in Heaven long since raised up

[Folder number 10] Citty of Nauvoo Nov 13th 1842

As the time has ariven for a change to be Amongst those that in habit the Earth a curse has rested on many because of bad works that many is a sitting in darkness because of transgressions of their Fathers that long since lived As many is a roveing in dark shades for the want of true light a door must be opened by the Antient of days As the time has ariven for them to arise and act for themselves as their wisdom shall direct The time has ariven for Labourers to be caled to Stand as watchman and fishers and hunters and to proclaim the Comming of the Son of Man An eventful door is now to open in honour of God As his kingdom is now to be established no more to be baffled Signs and wonders will be performed that all may well know that God rules in Heaven

7. Olney is likely referring to Jesus Christ, the Son of God, who in mortality was the "adopted son" of Joseph, the husband of Mary.

and on Earth as his name is cheering to man on the Earth Yet many is fallen Because of bad works that their destiny is seald because of rejecting The servents of God while others stand a looking as is said without exscuse But the time has ariven for Labourers to be caled that will make a seperation between the wicked and the wise that they in array may move Each one to their past and reap the reward of their Labours that they have merited by their works, As works is many and much a ben don to establish an order of things that is not of God But God in wisdom has looked down again on the Earth To propel his work as he by many is discountinanced for the want of true light A senry of things is araising that will establish his name as some few is caled and others under way to establish Zion Anew on the Earth Many will be caled Their time to spend to prepare to meet The Son of Man as he on Earth had a standing at the meridean of time preparatory to his second advent in power honour And the glory of God As He with the saints in a pillow of fire will move in order from Earth Every Eye will se him that is extant on the Earth as he will come In the brightness of the sun that will consume the wicked and set at liberty the ~~wicked~~ Righeous As dark shades is many On all around eaven amongst the Covenant people or those that say To have influance with God a theme of things is a moving that will bring sayings to light of the differant Classes of man on Earth As many as is a sitting In darkness of both Simple and wise they are now to be looked to by the Orthorotys of Heaven as a decision is past for them to arise As from them in past the curse is removed that they are liberated the Lamanites and Negroes are freed from the Curse that has long baffled them because it on them did rest But they from it are deliverd and are now set free that their minds are clear altho many is In bondage to man

[Folder number 10] Nov 13th 1842[8]

As time passes I often think of our Fathers and mothers in the gospel that God has took to him self I think of their power to look and to se of what is agoing in the Citty of Nauvoo I look at the doings of the L. D. Saints and se their unwise doings I look at the power of deceased Friends and knowing of their desernment in vewing man on Earth as amongst them much is adoing that lies in the Dark to those that is passing threw a probationary State But as they have power to se and to know of what is adoing and of things presant past and futer I look at the ungodly doings of the Latter day Saints and say how must those feel that have ben taken from the Evil to come I look at the Antients that long since died that spoke of the priveleges of living in the Latter times It was looked to be a day of worth to close up a scenry of things that had long

8. This November 13 entry immediately follows the previous November 13 entry also found in manuscript folder number 10.

had power over the Earth that caused many to mourn of hard times But as a change was determined in the latter times to be that the Earth from Opression would be set fre Also sin and bondage would be changed to Righeousness

[Folder number 10] City of Nauvoo Nov 15th 1842

As time passes Much is to be don to establish the Order of God as God on Earth is a looking that all things may move in aray A kingdom must be established both spiritual and temporal As a temporal kingdom Is the theme an opening must needs be to the treasures hid a way As treasures is many which has been laid a way in the bowels of the Earth by the presant race of men As the Earth is the Lords and the fullness thereof the time has ariven for it to come forth to assist in establishing a kingdom that has long lain in the dark Money must be plenty amongst certin ones that is caled to establish Zion of the Chosen ones As the time has ariven for a change to be That Zion may arise in honour riches and buty and that without delay As Coin is a lying In all parts of the land hid a way by men That long since died that was don in the name of the Lord Also treasures By those on Earth that had an over pluss and conveyed it to the Earth that it changed owners when conveyed to the Earth that it is now at the Comand of the Antient of Days as they on Earth have a standing and have received their charge They this day have assembled and a desision is past To transact business that is now in voge It is to purchase lands of the world in the Neighborhood of Squaw Grove At the time of the sale At Chicaugo some few will be caled there to meet and secure land at the sale as directed by the Antient of days As they will meet with them and give directions how to procede such must be caled as will be named to attend to this business in the name of the Lord that a foundation may be laid that cannot be undermined As money is plenty of differant Coins yet it is to be used with prudence by those that of it have care As they will have power the cepter to sway Being agents to the Antient of days as they on Earth have assembled on this the fifteenth of the 11th month A decision is past To bring much about not only a temporal Kingdom is in aray but a brake up of the fallen one The time is desided for it to be don that obsticles may be removed that is much in the way The time fast ariveing for the word to go out To raise volenteers the Latter D- Saints to brake up But this power is held by the A- of Days that all things may move in order as Is by God decreed As he is the helmsman and director all moves as he says as he rules in power and wisdom on this Globe He has a standing that all to him is plain of the doings of man. He moves in order as is by his council decreed and recorded in Heaven And on Earth The time has ariven that much must be don to establish an order To assist the poor As the poor is many In all parts an eventful door must be opened that they may have a sustenance A plan is determined By a council in Heaven that land shall be purchased and a field Established seven miles square in and about the above named Grove Also a Citty of High renown according to the pattern given and additions from time to time A senry of things now is in voge, condirected[9] by the Antient of Days Its of the order of the Citty of Nauvoo as this place was established by Revelation Many together have meet and consecrated themselves and property to the Lord of Hosts God in wisdom on them has looked and given directions to his Council as he did in the days of Noah at the time of the flood. The council in Heaven then decreed that they would secure much fruit that a trouble arose Because of bad works that the wise and unwise was masacreed and taken from the Evil to come Some arose to honour others to dishonour but a few did stand testimony to bare and people a new Earth As much is adoing At this time amongst the Latter Day Saints much is said and a ben don by those that profess to be of God that their substance is much that is not their own that is secured in dark cells for a time to come But the time will arive that chosen ones will be caled to secure the goods and chattels of the Citty to establish Zion anew As a stake must be reard in honour of God By industry and economy as directed by the Antient of Days as they on Earth will travel and open the way for their agents that is by them Chosen As their Agents will be many abroad in the land They by Spirit will communicate to them in their daily moves Their minds They will direct that they in wisdom may move that all may be left without exscuse But as many is a saying in testimony I lack Provision for them is made in the scriptures of divine truth As the teachings reasonings of the Saviour is by many caled Correct let them follow his example and all with them will be well

[Folder number 10] Citty of Nauvoo Nov 15th 1842

I look at the doings of my fellow man and draw a contrast Between them and the doings of God And say I am supprised at the theme As many is a looking and adoing that say to have power with God I look at them in their moves and say whire has wisdom flead It is gone no more to return or is it with them as with water that by and by it may come round I look at the wisdom of the P. J. Smith and scan his doings as has ben I se him much degraded by his works that he is fallen fallen no more to arise Yes I se him with others no more to arise except by the privelege of being born again that them with others will have a chance that have made no pretentions to goodness But because of what they have don they will be sufferd to take another round that will wind up their doings worlds with out end To come

9. Olney likely meant "co-directed."

[Folder number 10] Nov 16th 1842

As I am again caled upon by the Council of Antient of Days as much is adoing and to be don, I am daily caled a work to do I long have ben a looking at the doings of the Latter D Saints I long have ben a writing of their doings And moves about I look at them with feelings to do them no Harm But assist them to bring about the purposes of God But their presant doings does them forbid to be caled after the name of the Lord as their doings is such that no light on them shines but stand rejected By God As from time to time They have ben faverd that they much light have received by messengers from Heaven that have visited the Earth But the time has ariven for much to be don By men of God that a decision is past By him that has power In Heaven and on Earth As a decision is past In the courts above for an armed forse to come in liberty is now given To the wicked of the land to raise their forses And exterminate the L D Saints A decision is past And in voge from the 16th of Nov 1842 They now are permitted in aray to meet To cut and distroy the lives of the L D Saints A decision is past That their doings is well known that no further Procedings need be to establish the facts of the doings of the Latter Day Saints Let those that have wisdom look well to their ways as a senry of doings Is now in voge that deamons in the shape of men will move in aray both sides of the river of the Missippi untill a war of extermination will distroy the Latter D. Saints A war of Extermination must needs be to streighten Crooked places and make rough places smooth

[Folder number 10] Thursday November 17th 1842

As I have ben previously caled upon to meet in Council with the Antient of Days as they at this time have meet to transact certin business to prepare for the Comming of the Son of Man As Nations is many And much to be don Labourers is to be caled on from differant parts Names must be mentioned as wisdom Directs To establish Zion in all parts of the land Watchman will be caled To move in aray both and late and Early As directed by the A- of D- as they on Earth have took a Stand being Orthorised by the Son of God As He with them doth often meet to direct them in their daily moves Names are now In aray to be mentioned by the Antient of Days The High Council is first to be fild in part then the twelve then the Presidents of the watchman Then will thre be caled by them over them to preside and one to receive the word of God The four to be chose by those that by revelation is caled and when their names is once set down they are not to be removed by the vois of man But God to them will look that they will not his name disgrase If they should fall out by the way they will be removed from the stage of life to the planit In the presance of the father and son But those that well perform their work they have the promise of a long life that they shall live If ever so old untill the coming of the Saviour Each one shall head a little band and present before the Son of Man He with his family first shall stand Then in aray will him surround the fruits of his Labours on Earth that he by his industry and Economy has initiated into the Kingdom of God Again otherer blessings will arise

[Folder number 11] City of Nauvoo Nov 17th 1842

To Sisters, &nd Lecty Crain

I with the best of feelings, sit down to write, as I have a leisure moment, to my Eastern Friends. As I think much of Friends, I now and them to them speak, the run of their minds. But as minds is many I barely say, I will speak yours in part. We from our Native land have traveld- far in-to the western States; as we have a theme before us It is to serve the God, That rules above, We from our youth,s have ben conversant, about time matters and things. That dark and light shades has hoverd over us That our mind from trouble have not ben free Yet we have received much Comfort As Friends and Connection has often twined around our harts that we with them Have had good visits both in and out, of the Family Circle. But alas a whispering Spirit by the way of sympethy To us did speak that we on God was dependant for our daily sustinance Again we se our friends returning to the God that gave them breath that brought to mind the Sollem tidings when will God call on us as we have often ben saluted by the Dieing groans of man We admit the life of man is fleety that we dare no more trust our selves out of the ark of Safty. From time to time We conversed freely with those that said to have much light But in looking at their daily moves we hardly se any differance between them and those of the World But at last came a long a people that said to be Latter Day Saints They Preached Labourd and reasoned to Convince of the truth of their faith that we reluctantly went forward and was baptised For remission of sins We with feeling to do our duty set out with a determination to do as well as say, that all with us mite be well We at last desided, To gether with the L. D. Saints that we with Old Friends and Neigbours mett shook hands and parted as if to say we no more shall meet Thus we took a fleety journy to the Citty of Latter Day Saints We with them soon meet in Union after a long an cheering voige Thus we meet with our old friends and hartily shook hands and thanked the God above for the blessings received We looked at the doing That came to vew and the things of Nachure that spoke in honour of God As we have assembled with the Saints we with them will Labour as wisdom Directs As we have before us a senry of things we ask for the wisdom of God us to direct that we make no mismoves We have herd of the blessings of being with the L. D. Saints As we with them have getherd we ask to be instructed in things that is of God

[The following is apparently a second draft of the letter written above also dated November 17, 1842.]

[Folder number 11] Citty of Nauvoo November 17th 1842

To Sister And Crane

I with the best of feelings sit down to write as I have a leisure moment to my Eastern Friends As I think much of friends I now and then to them speak the run of their minds But as minds is many I barly say I will write yours in part We from our Native land have traveld far into the western States As we have a theme before us It is to serve the God that rules above We from our youth have ben Conversent about time matters and things that both light and dark has ben before us that our minds From trouble has not ben free Yet we have received much Comfort As friend and Connection has often twined around our harts that we with them have had good visits both in and out of the family Circle But alas a whispering Spirit by the way of sympathy to us did speak that we on God was dependant for our Daily sustinance Again we se our friend returning to the God that gave the breath That brought to mind The sollem tidings when will God cal on us as we have often ben seluted by the dieing groans of man We admit the life of man is fleety that we dare no more trust our selves out of the ark of Safty From time to time We conversed freely with those that said to have much light But in looking at their daily movements we hardly se any differance between them and those of the World But at last come a long a people that said to be L D Saints They Preached and talked and reasoned with appearantly a determination to do us much good that we finly said We will move with them and se what light on us will Shine We went forward in duty as to us was shone by being baptised for remission of sins We conformed to the ordinances ~~of God~~ of the house of God As the way opend that all with us mite be well At last ~~we~~ decided to the west we will go and get further Instructions We started with feelings of the best kind and bid farewell to all That's behind Our journy was pleasant on the way untill we arived at the Citty of Nauvoo to the Habitations of the Latt D S- With old aquaintance of Brothers and sisters we soon meet and shook hands that our feelings was cheerd It seemed like getting home We looked at the Prairies Log Cabbins Buildings made of differant Commoditys that astonished us much But as we have assembled with the Church of Latter D Saints we will move in wisdom and do what is wright As we have before us a senry of things we ask for the wisdom of God to direct us as we from our homes are far away If we can find things as we have herd we will be content and serve our God But things as we se them look look dark But suffise it to say all things will work to gether for Good

The mind of Rebeca Atwood[10]—

I have be reard in a hard Cold Country whire rocks ~~and~~ stones and Moss doth cuver the Earth Mountains vally Hills swails and rivers is the theme of those that travel But as I am young And have kind parrents a toilsome life has me pased by But as I have Friend and Connection a conversing about The things of time unto me there came a whispering spirit that convinsed me of my duty to God I with others went forward in duty with a full determination to serve God I with the saints did soon assemble at a Citty of High renown that I was with the saints both late and Early That was to me a theme of things as I did gether with our wise teachers I from them did look much light to receive But I must say In it I was disapointed as dark shade did around me role that I often mourned and Lamented because of things That I herd of them I am ashamed to make use of language that would tell the tale of their doings Alth many say they are made up storys But testimony doth establish the fact that our caled wise teachers are verily Gilty of Crimes that would make the Heathen blush But as I have a mind to speak and do not to be turned by those of ill fame But I have a mind rooted and grounded that is not turned by the folly of man I have many Friends and Connections that are on the road with me If we as one can be united so to pas thruigh this Probationary state and steady our hark[11] in into the Courts of Heaven We there will have a senry of things not realised by Mortal man

A senry of things to me appeard as a vision of Joseph Hadlock of a council of men being caled to act as Arbitrators In a difficulty be between man an man There will a difficulty soon arise in the Neighbourhood of Laharp that men will be caled to settle the difficulty as it will arise amongst the members of the L D S— It will be left to reforees They together there will meet and deside the

---

10. Rebecca Atwood was an LDS Church member living in Nauvoo at this time. She was one of the names on Olney's list of women found in his writings. Why Olney wrote "The mind of Rebeca Atwood" is not clear to the editor.

11. "Steady the ark" comes from the incident recorded in 1 Chronicles 13:9–10 when "Uzza put forth his hand to hold the ark [of the covenant]; for the oxen stumbled. And the anger of the LORD was kindled against Uzza, and he smote him, because he put his hand to the ark: and there he died before God." To steady the ark is typically mentioned with a negative connotation. An example of this is found in the Doctrine and Covenants: "That man, who was called of God and appointed, that putteth forth his hand to steady the ark of God, shall fall by the shaft of death, like as a tree that is smitten by the vivid shaft of lightning" (D&C 85:8). However, in this letter it is used in a positive light, "to steady our ark in into the Courts of Heaven," apparently meaning to follow a steady course of obedience to God in this life to be enabled to enter heaven.

Case according to testimony that will make both party mad because of their disposition to take the advantage

But alas what to me has has happened A neer dear an effectionate sister that long has twined around my hart she in the bloom of youth was taken[12] and sored alof to worlds unknown that she has gained a rest in Heaven that she has become An administering spirit to mortal man that on the Earth Yes her Labours on Earth was finished Her probationary state was well worked out that she was thus escorted to Heaven by a lovely spirit that to her was sent Her Labours now is not to neglect those that long have strove for her good as she on them is daily a looking to gide them in the path of truth

[Folder number 11] Walnut Grove Ill Nov 8th 1842

Song Composed by O. H. Olney to be sung In accordance with the songs of the times

There is many a looking
At the daily moves about
With sayings what shall we do
To gain a sustinance
As we have before in a senry of things
That often comes in Contact
To the natural mind
As times are getting harder
We hardly dare to boast
Of an over plus In Store
But as we have a promise

12. Unsure who Olney is referring to. Olney's wife, Alice Johnson Olney, died July 16, 1841. She certainly would have been near, dear, and "twined around" his heart. However, Alice Olney died when she was forty-one years old, and would not be considered in the "bloom of youth," especially during that era. A search in Susan Easton Black's *Membership of the Church of Jesus Christ of Latter-day Saints, 1830–1848* and obituaries in Nauvoo periodicals does not reveal the identity of the female who died as she may not have been a Church member and she may not have been living near Nauvoo. One possibility is Maria Chase, whom Olney included on his list of thirty women. Both of Olney's lists were written in 1842. Maria Chase died November 17, 1841, at age sixteen. See "Obituary," *Times and Seasons*, December 1, 1841, 622. Maria would have been dead when Olney wrote his list of thirty women. However, Olney did include Alvira Atwood, whom he noted as being deceased on his list, making Maria Chase a possibility. Another prospect is Lucy Alvira Atwood, who was born in 1820 at Mansfield, Connecticut, about sixteen miles from where Oliver Olney was born and raised. She died in 1842.

Of seed time and harvest
All as one will be up and adoing
That we our work may do
That we can Claim the promise
Of a plentiful harvest
But as many is a looking
In riches for to gain
Some by Industry Others by trade
Whether the former or Latter
Econemy must have a place
To direct the mind In their daily moves
But as many is a looking
To be noted and boyed up
By those of their fellow man
That a spirit of flattery
Is often held out To gain approbation
In the esteem of all around
But as many is a leading
It often makes a split
In Cittys towns and vileges
Because of money to support
As Each party is alooking
To be supported by his Friends
That causes a split amongst Neighbours
In this and foren lands But as it is the theme
I would of it bearly speak And say it is a custom
And allow it to be wright
That all move in partys
That no one can the cepter sway

A Song of the Morning by O. H. O—
The king of Day has hove [?] in sight
Its pleasant rays ore the Earth
All Nachure brightens At its sight
The Earth upon its Axis roles
In honour of the Law that govern
A law of which we must pas by
For the want of wisdom
That is beyound our reach
But we have a light
That around us shines

That adds to our minds a theme of praise
Its of the doings of the day
That speaks of things That is past and gone
It speaks of things That is to come
The soil produces differant meats
Of many kinds That satisfys thirst
In Connection with Herbs of the Field
That Stimulates the mind of man
Dark and light shade do often role
That dampen feelings of many around
And lightens up the path of those
That has a desire to live and learn
We look at the saying of our Friends
That is familiar with the daily moves
And say the times is getting worse
We look at time as at the Days
They lengthen and shorten
By degrees once in six months
Thus we will say that Nachure
Must have its course
Days lengthen and shorten
The briny tide does raise and fall
The Earth performs its revolutions
In honour of the sun
The wind blows High and low
That looks to us strange
To se cold and heat At the same time
At the differant points of Compass
Although not far apart
We look at the times As being hard
But say it is to streighten
And make Crooked places streight
That we can soon say all is now well
That our Currency is a gaining
Our busines men is in aray
A buying and selling And do well

Song of the Eavening—
The moon in honour of the sun
Precent its briliancies to man
That shades of darkness doth give way

In honour of the Law that Governs
The stars in aray doth seem to gase
That speaks of power That is not known
The Sun in Darkness now is closed
Because of planits That intervenes
That dark shades on us do seem to role
But at the sun we cheerfuly look
We se it sitting in the west
We may well say its gone
We know not whire to retire
But when the morning hours do come
We se the sun In buty arise
We look at the power by which it moves
And sise ~~and~~ form and looks
And the velocity on which it moves
But when our minds gets more matured
We se the sun stationary in the East
And the Earth revolve one in twenty four hours
In honour of the King of Day
That is stationary far remote
From the planit of the Earth
As the Earth is round like a ball
And propeld by a power from on high
Attractive powers Thus combined
Being oprest by powers That rules above
That wind and water together meet
That balances the Circumferance of the Earth
The Earth on its wings does role
As a ball on a Crank In obediance to the sun
The days Lengthen and Shorten by degrees
By a principal or a Law given
That has power to form and create anew
The doings of Mankind and rise and fall
The time begun when God formed man
From the dust on which we stand
He was raised Immortal as is said
By the scriptures That we say to believe
But as we have no living men
That can say they know them to be correct
Yet we well admit the fact That they are true
And say God moves in a misterious way

We look at mankind On the Earth
Passing and repassing about
Some in High life others in low
Some are Slaves Others Oprest
For the want of the necessirys of life
We se dark shades on many role
For the want of wisdom to direct
We speak of man as he first stood
Upright and just before God
We will speak of Adam then of Eave
The bride that was took from his side
They on the Earth did seem to move
As directed by the God that rules
As God with them did often meet
And spoke of things That would take place
He told them of his design
To bring about his purposes on Earth
He gave them power to say and do
To lay a foundation To arise upon
He to them did freely give

[Folder number 10] November 18th 1842

I at this time sit down to write of things that daily transpires in and about the Citty of Nauvoo As many arives From differant parts from England Ireeland and the Islands of the sea and our own Native soil I look at the doings of the Citty that often makes me mourn As seldom a person knows of mismoves they say, our Leaders are men of God that we by them receive instructions to direct us in our daily moves and think our privelege is great But in looking at their doings that comes to my vew I must say I am often astonished to se so many duped I look at the Leaders of the Church and to trace them in their doings I am not a little supprised at their windings and folly when I se them undertake to cuver up their foibles and say all is well Will God bear with such doings as has daily ben the theme from the rise of the Church untill the presant time In Iniquity on iniquity has ben the theme that Gods name has ben disgrased by the Leaders of the L. D. Saints But the time has ariven for a change to be as the Antient of Days has on Earth has took a stand the cepter to sway over the people of the Nations of the Earth As Nations is many Each one in turn will be looked too And laboured with from this time forth This Jentile Nation Is first in aray Then comes the red men of the Forest that have long ben oprest But the time has ariven that they are set free from the curse put on them by their forefathers They because of bad doings have long had to bear severe chastisement but they now are to be numberd and counted of worth and receive Instructions by the teachers of the Latter D. S. The time has ariven for Labourers to be caled and Establish an order of Righeousness amongst those sitting in darkness that no light on them shines To them a Standard must be reard that they together may meet and commence a Union Some few will be caled in the Coming Spring to go to a tribe west of Missouri They will there meet with them and will commence to teach and amongst them ordain Priests and teachers and set them to work Let some few make ready that are the chosen of God to establish Zion in the west As a senry of things now is in voge to lengthen and strengthen her stakes as Zions Curtin must be enlarged and her Childern made free No one need doubt Gods power to deliver

[Folder number 10] Citty of Nauvoo Nov 19th 1842

As time pases I daily am caled to sit in council with the Antient of Days as the business does them forbid to loose any time But to daily move as I am caled in council to meet almost daily That takes my time As my money is gone and my substance mostly spent and no Friends That is able to help me that I with my family can be Comfortable As the Latter day saints is many that I daily pass by In and out of our Citty but I look at a time Not far ahead that I can get out of the tract of poverty Yet I once had a plenty and to spare that I could go and come as I pleased But the time has ariven that my clothing is badly worn and my Childern is destitute and I am destitute of meens to clothe School or have a sustinance But as this is a day of Council for the Antient of Days to set they have decided To assist the destitute and releive the oprest that move with them in spirit agreeable to the order of God As the order of God is established and his power displayed nothing must be a lacking to hinder them in their in their doing As money is plenty In differant parts yet a veto is on the doings of man or a curse in on those of the Jentile race that they have no Confidence in each other that they are baffled in their doings as their doings has ben many in days past and gone But alas a decission is past To streighten the crooked But as many is a looking that not many know not what to do To get a sustinance because of their poverty As the poor is many of the L. D. S. a decision is past To take them from the Evil to come that have moved in wisdom in the order of God But those that have not must suffer by the way as time passes them along

[Folder number 10] Sunday 20th of Nov Nauvoo

I yet have feelings My mind to express about matters and things that daily transpires I look at the Latter day Saints as is their daily moves about and say of them as they say of the doings of the world their daily moves does them forbid to be counted Equal to those that have rejected the Council of God But as God to man is a looking to help them on their way but no door to the Latt D. S. Opens except to be exterminated As I have had a vew of an order of things that will soon follow after directed by the Antient of Days It is a kingdom to move in honour of God that will Baffle the wicked and leave them without Exscuse As the wicked is many That rove around they together must stand and receive their doom They will long have a standing on a planit of Gloom when removed after their cup is full They on it will have a standing from the arise of Gods power that have ben left without excuse The preachings and doings Does no one forbid performed by the L.D.S.- To become an heir of God But a theme is a raising And on the move that will draw the time and leave man without exscuse Some few is caled And others under way that will soon commense their Labours amongst the Natives west An eventful door To them will open and brake down partition walls from tribe to tribe That a Union will be begun By a chosen few that will be continued untill All as one will be set free As the wind that blows or the waters that run At the same time Labourers will be caled amongs the Jentile race that the doings of God may be accomplished and a senry of wickedness wound up

As mans ways is fleety
And often on the wing
And often in trouble
About many things

A way is fast opening For the chosen of God as their Labours will be many by them to be performed in the due time of the Lord They will be caled as minit men to Stand aready and a waiting A work to perform as many is awaiting a knowledge to gain of their duty to God that they it may perform As Gods ways are Equal No one need doubt his condesention to do for those that have a standing on the Earth As many Nations in darkness are a sitting Because of bad works the time is fas ariving for them to be known and liberated from the curse and their minds set free Then Labourers will be caled with them to take a stand and Establish an order Amongst them Let those that are chosen put shoulder to the wheel and depend on God for wisdom to direct them in their moves As God is a looking His power to display to bring about his purposes anew on the Earth That Zion may arise in honour of God no more to be put down

A song of Zion to the Natives[13]

E con de la Ocon sha naw me Co de lan de lo ha on she naa da sha ne Ohe on de naw Pe ca lon De she naw
Arise ye Natives Bright and fair A work perform That the light of fredom may the adorn As the time has come for to arise and show thy selves to be of God
He he co, he he on de nau mel on ohe con, de las e ne be se o le on she nau de lon, she nau nau, me con delau te ne o te re on she e lau deloshena
Arise ye nations from the dust that long have dwindled in unbelief Arise ye Nations Both far and neer and claim blessings that sores above
He he codelau delon she nau me con shenau oleon de lau she nau he on dela la on
The Sun doth shine In honour of God that by the Heathen is honourd
Ohe con de lashane he le o leon de law te se on de lau she nau te ne on she na
Let those that would desire much wisdom to obtain honour him That formed the Sun
Ohe con delau she nau te re on delau he se he delon te re on she nau
As the sun doth shine in honour of the God that did it form
Ohe con ho le cau ne on delose a nau te ne on de lau she now me lon
As it stands on pillow Not made with hands but placed by him That has power to form and create anew

[Folder number 10] November 22d 1842 Citty of Nauvoo

As I am caled from my Labours a few moments to spend a writing as directed by the Antient of Days as my Labours is many I have no time to spend but to daily do as I am shone As much is adoing light doth shine amongst those In darkness As much has ben said and don by the Latter Day Saints that is disgusting to God and his councils in Heaven that the wicked shall have power to over rule the L. D. Saints that they now are deliverd into their hand that

13. Native American tribes in Illinois during the 1800s included the Illinois, Miami, Fox, Shawnee, and Kickapoo. It is possible that Olney learned a Native American language while living in that area. The editor was unable to determine if what Olney was writing was an actual Native American language and, if it was legitimate, which tribal tongue he used.

they will do by them as they pleas They are now in aray and about to start To the Noted Citty of the Latter D Saints Let those that have wisdom look well to themselves when the troubles arise as many will come in with weapons of War with a spirit to die or Concor as that is their theme They now are fast a fixing in all parts of the west to March and meet together and contend for their wrights The wise will remember that God does over rule that he will preserve a few to bear testimony of the fall and establish a new That a work may commence in the name of the Lord by agents that is to be depended on Let such look for the spirit them to direct And stand still and say let the will of God be don Let their houses be well inclosed with windows darkend on the outside Let all stay with in In silance except bearly one That will receive apass by an agent of the Antient of Days from some officer of Orthoroty Let those that have friends look first to themselves as all is in the hands of God Let know one leive his mansions untill he has a permit as the house is the only safty for those that In habit it Let those that have wisdom look to their own familys that is under their care Let all others act for themselves as wisdom shall them direct as God over rules

[Folder number 11] Citty of Nauvoo Nov 23d 1842

Dear Brother Oliver Snow

I at This time have a leisure moment to write you a few lines I am in the best of health and spirits all with me is well and fast a moveing As usual I am now takeing a differant course from what I exspected to when I se you I have seen fit not to publish any more to the world that what I have done as a enough has gone out of unwise doing as both in and out of the Church is of the same stamp<illegible>That there is not much to choose I have got me a house in the Citty and about to move in to it with my Little girls to do the work

Much is a going Many is a comeing in I have herd that Lorenzo Parly Pratt and Orson Hide is on their way from England with Each of them a Company in Charge Of the Latter D Saints[14] little is said here all seem to be still at this time Except that Doct Bennett has published much against the Church

14. Lorenzo Snow and Parley P. Pratt were serving missions in Great Britain at this time. Olney does not include Lorenzo's last name because this letter is written to Oliver Snow, Lorenzo's father. Orson Hyde had been in Germany but traveled to England prior to returning to the United States. Hyde "presided over the 214 saints bound for Nauvoo." Myrtle Stevens Hyde, *Orson Hyde: The Olive Branch of Israel*, 148. Lorenzo Snow returned from England with about 240 saints. *Biography and Family Record of Lorenzo Snow*, 67. Parley P. Pratt returned to Nauvoo with about 250 emigrants. Givens and Grow, *Parley P. Pratt: The Apostle Paul of Mormonism*, 196.

a pamphlet of betwixt 3 and 400 pages[15] He comes out in flying coulers with recommendations of the first class in Community He is now In Jackson County Missouri No doubt but busy I se it to be my duty now to settle with the Church and say nothing do nothing to raise excitement I have not herd from or seen your Childern since I have seen you

Yours as ever O. H. Olney
Oliver Snow
Jane Charnock[16]

[Folder number 10] Citty of Nauvoo Nov 26th 1842

As I am often caled upon to write as wisdom shall direct I must speak of the poor that I se In passing about As the poor is many in and about the Citty of Nauvoo I cannot pas by them wholy as they on the wright and on the left are often seen In rags and a scanty pittance to eat I look at their houses open and cold and no wood to burn of the poorer Class Cold storms arise with wether severe that many is a suffering because of their Scanty means Again in and about the Citty of Nauvoo an order of things is araising that does me supprise To se and to learn the doings of those That say to lead They in a mass move together that they the Cepter sway that they opress the poor and take from them their wrights with fine clothing horses and Carreges and money to lay away for some futer age I[n] pomp and splendor I se many a moveing at the Exspense of many That is oprest I will now cal on the Father in the name of his Son to take a retrospective vew of the Church of L. D. Saints I ask for wisdom from above to assist me in offering up my petition to the God that rules I pray in behalf of myself as I feel anxious to be extricated from my presant Condition as I have long ben oprest and in a word troden underfoot by many that say to be saints of God I ask for deliverance And that without delay I also ask deliverance for those that is much affected because of their lot I ask in the name of my master that some door may open that the poor may be relieved and liborated from bondage and set free I cal on God The crooked To make streight and establish his name and suffer it to be no more disgrased I ask for a union In honour of God by those that are caled after his name that wisdom knowledge and dissernment may amongst the saints abound Let men be caled To take the rule that will be honest prudent and honour the cause of God Let such be caled

15. The book or "pamphlet" to which Olney refers was John C. Bennett, *The History of the Saints: Or, an Exposé of Joe Smith and Mormonism*. Olney wrote that there were between 300 and 400 pages in Bennett's book. There are 344 pages in Bennett's book.

16. Jane Charnock was born on August 23, 1819, at Kirkham, England. She married William Conner and was sealed to her spouse on January 31, 1846. Unsure why her name was attached to a letter written to Oliver Snow.

as are prudent [Equinomiat?[17]] and Industrious and move in accordance with the chosen of God I ask God all such to bless as is caled and chosen of himself I ask for blessings That have lain in the dark I ask for His propeling power on such to rest That they may arise as valient men of God

[Folder number 10] Citty of Nauvoo Nov 27th 1842

Being again caled upon to meet with the Antient of Days I cheerfully do as I am shone as I se much adoing that looks dark but wisdom dictates That is of God to remove obsticles And subdue wrongs As a door is fast opening for the valient to arise as their Labours is much needed in differant parts of the world men must be caled upon this work to perform That the wicked may be left without exscuse As the L. D. Saints is many yet a division must be that a work may commence no more to be baffled or turned aside But men of importance must be caled that will move in the Order of God Names are now to be mentioned of some few That a work may commence when the presant Order goes down Names in aray now is to be caled High Councilers[18] 2 Oliver Snow 3 Truman 4 David Deval as scribe 5 Daniel Spencer 6 Hiram Spencer 7 Robberson 8 Sydney Rigdon + Childs 9 Of the twelve traverlin Council 1 Orson Spencer 2 Orson Pratt 3 Orson Hide 4 Lorenzo Snow 5 John E Page 6 Truman Gilet 7 Wilford Woodrough 8 Junies Snow 9 Erastus Snow 10 Wm B ?esly Presidancy of the Watchman is to be caled at some futer time to stand as assistants to the twelve

---

17. It is not clear as to what word Olney meant to use and the meaning of the word. Perhaps Olney used his own creative version of "equanimity" which means "evenness of mind; that calm temper or firmness of mind which is not easily elated or depressed, which sustains prosperity without excessive joy, and adversity without violent agitation of the passions or depression of spirits. The great man bears misfortunes with *equanimity*." *Noah Webster's First Edition of an American Dictionary of the English Language—Facsimile 1828 Edition*, s.v. "Equanimity."

18. Believing that the current organization of Mormonism was about to collapse, Olney made a list of names of men to be called as members of the High Council and the Twelve Traveling Council in his proposed reconstituted version of Mormonism. Information concerning these men is found in Appendix 3 in the order Olney has them listed.

DECEMBER 1842

[Folder number 10] <~~Dec~~> City of Nauvoo < Dec> ~~November~~ 1st 1842

As I am this morning caled in Council at the time apointed by A. of Days I cheerfully meet with them to do as I am shown in my daily moves As much as has ben don and to do I se no place to falter by the way as the way opens for me to do as I am daily directed by the spirit of God As the day of chooseing is the theme wise and willing minds must be caled that volenteer to do the will of God As some few is caled Altho to them yet a door will open To their supprise in the dark As a oneness of spirit will be the theme they by degrees will fall in that they will honourably fill their post But if any should falter by the way others will be caled to fill their place Such as are caled have a work to do as directed by the Antient of Days as they receive orders from time to time from the son of man As he moves in aray In differant parts to prepare for his second Advent to reign on the Earth one thousand years a rest of which much is said by those that dwell upon the Earth From the commencement of time it was the theme That it soon would be But age after age has past away that many has dispaired of the sene to se peace and Harmony the theme But the time has come for it to prepare for a day of rest a day of light to prepare for a more glorious rest a rest of which their is much said It is to enter into the presance of the father and Son as that is a place whire light doth shine Exalted minds must enter there that they may know the road to take An additional Law Is to be given to what has hithertoo ben wrote by inspired men That long since lived to be honest upright and just before God and man Move as wisdom directs In honour of God Let each one do As his gift shall say as all is not composed a like as differant gifts On man does rest yet all centers in one in God above As some have faith to rend the vale to se the father And converse with the son Others have power to raise the Dead and cast out Deavils In Gods name While others have power to rend the vale brake up and subdue kingdoms that is not of God Others have powers to se and know their duty to God and man and till the Earth Raise flocks of herd and Establish habitations that cheers the heart of man As temporal Kingdoms was once the theme its thus to be In the Latter times Let each one acknowledge The Gift of God and move in the paths The Antients trod as they a pattern Thus did set for their decendants on the Earth as they long since to Heaven went clothed in power and the magesty of God They thus to Earth have now returned to bring to light Their former Saying that is not fulfild But as the time is at hand for much to be don By feeble man there is some caled A work to do as agents on Earth To the messengers of God. Let no one fear If ever so weak as teachers are many to instruck Their Labours are free They volenteer to teach and Instruck the honest in heart Let those that would Gods will perform remember well The path that the Antients trod It was a path of light and truth not known but by few In the nineteenth Century of time It spoke of power that was of God It baffled the wicked as they was forsed to say that God rules in Heaven and on Earth by faith and works They often beat back the powers of Darkness that have in sight

[Folder number 11] City of Nauvoo Dec 2d 1842

The vale of Darkness ere long mus rend because of time That is decreed by him that rules Above The time the Latter time has come that God decreed a change A change that will affect the human race From land to land and from sea to sea The beasts of the fields and forests will be much alarmed because of doings that is to come But its no less than the voise that Jesus gave To clens and purify and make all clean As the time to favor Zion has come a mournful Sound must be the theme by darkened minds That moves around as the wicked are many of differant grades From high to low in all parts of the world On some there is a heavy curse because of their progenitors But the time is fast a roleing on the wing that Childern shall no more suffer because of their Parrents deeds

[Folder number 10] City of Nauvoo Dec. 6th 1842

As the time has ariven for the Antient of Days to assemble in Council The twelve have meet and have past desisions to put in forse as they on Earth are a moveing in differant parts But now have assembled certin things to bring to pass As many is a looking some light to obtain A door is opening in an unexspected way to those of the Latter Day Saints But the time has ariven that a work must Commence that will establish principals to raise up a Righeous Branch As many is a looking wisdom to obtain an eventful door is now open for those that will improve as the antient teachers Have took a stand to finish their last mission on Earth that all things may move in order They now will display their power by raising the Dead As this is a sign that of it much is said by the wicked of the Land As signs are for them As they move in aray a door to them is fast opening in honour of the name of the Lord A work of importance Is now to commence no more to be baffled Or hindred by the powers of Darkness Altho the enemy of soles Is in array to throw enchantments over the Earth but in his doings He stands curtailed by the wisdom of the Saviour that Stands at the helm As the time has ariven For some few to arise as agents for the messengers of Heaven they now have assembled all as one to ordain Oliver H Olney To the P_hood that is conferd on them by the Father and

Son with the same gifts and blessing to se and to know Of the doings of man as the messengers of Heaven that a spirit of dissernment may have power To fore se Iniquity and check it in the bud As this Priesthood Was decreed but seldom ben in forse Untill the presant time It is only for those That has power to move as the Angels of Heaven In aray It is a quickning Spirit That purifys man and clenses his system from filth It is power to travel As the Angels above from land to land and sea to sea As the time is at hand Partition walls to brake down Let some few make ready this work to perform As a work of importance is now begun that out of the chosen will be selected teachers to go to foren lands The ten tribes have a promise of some light to obtain By a man from Heaven that will streighten their works As they now are a waiting A visit to receive one will soon be caled To speak to them that the P_hood may be established amongs a few And set to work that the whole lump may be levened Then will be caled some chosen ones to visit them teach them instruct them more perfectly in the things of God But a senry of things first is decreed that Zion in prosperity may speak It is to establish Zion anew in the North part of Illinois neer a place caled Squaw Grove as there was once a Noted Citty that was highly extold for piety caled by the Nephites Coleon[1] but in English is known a place of rest that is to be caled Coleon or a place of rest

[Folder number 11] Nauvoo Lyceum Exchange[2] Dec 6th [184]2

The subject of agriculter Improvements of differant kinds Is at the presant time the theme of the world I was about to say that is almost the only God that the people of the nineteenth Century knows any thing about But to come to the subject that is never in contemplation Of the Interest of the Citty of Nauvoo When we take a retrospective of our Citty we se many families some that it requires their daily Labours to sustain them Thus we se them of all classes From the wise man to the Idiot We look at the Labouring part of Community and se their attachment to business As they differ in looks so do they in their employments Some minds run to farming others to the Mechanical arts. Thus we find the different gifts severally bestowed on man

1. This word is not found in the Book of Mormon.

2. A lyceum is an institution for popular education providing such things as discussions, lectures, and concerts. In the 1830s and 1840s it was common throughout the United States for communities to have lyceums. "Through such organizations ordinary citizens learned rules of debate, law, and political science and heard about the best or latest books and periodicals." The creation of a Nauvoo Lyceum was announced in the November 29, 1843, issue of the *Nauvoo Neighbor.* George W. Givens, *In Old Nauvoo: Everyday Life in the City of Joseph*, 169–71. The Nauvoo Lyceum Exchange referred to by Oliver Olney was a different lyceum held at Nauvoo. Olney reports on the meeting held on December 6, 1842.

That we must say that God has not desined us all to move in one speer Or take to one kind of employment As we se our necesseties to be many That requires All the different gifts each one fitted to its place to furnish mans wants Mr. Chairman I at this time will make use of my best Judgement and in as formidle[3] a way as I am capable of to encourage the Manufacter of silks I look at the cutter of silk as an object worthy of our attention But for the want of experiance I cannot do the subject justice but merly open a door for Information as by freely conversing we learn Each others minds I have seen its groth in all its stages I have seen the worm that layed the egg and From that to maturity I have seen the scrub that gives them sustinance I have seen of different kinds of Mulbarys But at this time I will speak of the Malt cactus[4] Lately imported I look upon as a plant or scrub of worth It grows quick and produces many leaves and spreads by sprouts faster than a most any other scrub By sitting out the sprouts Or Laying them in [ditches?] say thre inches beneath the surface of the Earth sprouts will put forth from root to top say from one sprout four feet long There will come forth eight or ten new blades that will gro faster than a most any other sprout That will produce leave the first season to feed to worms A small piece of land will furnish leaves sufficient to do good business for a family that they will realise a good prise for their Labours In what will sell in any market at a fair value I look at the cutter of silk to be one of the best kind of business that a man can go into that has help of his own or at his command as it will nest a good profit if manged with Judgment and care it is a business that is not to be run out silk is an article That would take the place of flax in many cases Also wool and cotten And except cotten it does not cost but little more than the others per lb By giving it a fair chance to gro we find by experiance in doing business that there is a wright way and a rong way when we take the Latter, all goes hard with the former all goes well Respecting the cutter of silk I have made up my mind to go into it What have I don merely nothing in a word In another I have laid a foundation Yes I have secured about 6000 maltecatas trees That they are

3. Olney likely meant "formidable." He has a "d" and a "b" written in the same place. Because the "d" appears to be written over the top of the "b" in darker ink, I have used formidle rather than formible in the text.

4. All the sources examined state that silkworms will only eat fresh mulberry leaves (or a manufactured silkworm food made with mulberry leaves). Perhaps Olney was referring to a type of mulberry bush when he wrote about the malt cactus. More likely, the malt cactus Olney spoke of was the cactus pear or prickly pear plant. Although there were several sources comparing the similarities of the mulberry bush and the prickly pear cactus, no sources were found that claimed silkworms eat prickly pears leaves. It is very possible that Olney had received some bad information and was mistaken in his view about the value of the malt cactus plant in raising silkworms.

now ready to set out or plant in the Comming spring that will next season on a moderate calculation produce 30000 trees that would supply a whole Neghbourhood with with leaves trees silk gowns slack shawls Handkerchiefs finly I dont know but what we should be clothed in silk

[Folder number 10] December 7th 1842

~~November~~

As the rays of light beguins to dawn from the king of Day Caled the sun The sun stationary in the East is daily scene Sheadding light to all around Its daily doings Is hardly known by mortal man On the Earth As man is many on the Earth some in darkness Others of light Yet in a mass They all as one stand a looking as to se what is to come But the set time has arived for the curse to be removed that all as one may have a chance to well perform the work of God Altho many a sitting in groups with skins bare And scanty allowance yet they on God Now have a claim as the curse because of Progenetors is soon to be removed Their forms and sise Does not agree as they in looks and sizes do much differ They in aray do move because of Darkness that on them rests But the set time for them has ariven that the curse on them has now been removed that they are priveleged to do and act as seemeth them Good They thus are agents To say and do and are to be judged according to works But as they have ben in a fallen state they cannot keep a celestiall Law that they can enter into the presance of the Father and Son Yet if perchance some should perform in obediance to a celestiall Law they in the presance of the Father and Son will have a rest That is of worth But those that do not this work perform agreeable to the Law of God but are honest in their doings as far as they know and have not faith to sore above the groveling things of time they then will have delightsom home of which the moon is a tipe Again there is many of the Jentile race that have ben and are honest in doings on the Earth that often falls on the wright and left that they secure a Terestial rest Again there is more provision made to accommodate the race of man It is a rest That of it many bost as it ketches all Except those that sin against the Holy Ghost The stars of this rest does freely speak from brite to dim Of all grades Those that say to do but come short of fully keeping the Law of God in the round will become an heir of a telestial kingdom No more to go out

[Folder number 10] Citty of Nauvoo Dec 8th 1842

As this is a day set apart by the Antient of Days to meet in council they at this time have met in Council A decision is past To bring to light dark sayings that have lain long in the Dark As dark sayings is many a vale must be rent to establish an order a new on Earth As minds is many All in one must move that a Union may be established amongst the Chosen of God As wisdom shall direct Let all move being directed by the Antient of Days As at this time is a desision in honour of the Son of God as he rules and governs this planitary mass By doing and sayings as seemeth him good As he has now took a stand a work for to do to clens and puryfy and make all clean Again he has come the wicked to opress and put his Law in forse As his Law is easy for man to perform no shadow of turning will be received A decision is past that an order may arise governed by Agents to the Antient of Days As they with the chosen will daily move teach them In the path of duty that they may well do their work

Took back to 400.

[Folder number 10] Written on the top of this page: 400 took back from <illegible> De 8th 1842

A theme of things is now to arise by legally orthorised servents on the Earth A kingdom must be reard In honour of God that long has ben looked for By Antient saints As the time has ariven for man to be known delays will no more answer But all things must move both in Heaven and on Earth as many is a waiting for the time to come that long since died From the first age down to the presant time They are all impatiently a waiting for the time to arive that they on Earth can take a stand to prepare for a more Glorious rest It is to gain wisdom from on high by wise teachers That was resorected at the Meridean of time as many arose In newness of light by being quickenedd by the Resorecting spirit that they with the Saviour did arise As they was on a planit of rest anxiously awaiting to come forth that they have stood as mineut men and cheerfully don as they was shone Their Labours have ben many In days past and gone In keeping records of things that have transpired down to the presant time as no man on Earth has it performed but is kept in Heaven by the spirits of the just perfecteded But the time has ariven for man to arise and honour himself by keeping an impartial History of what Daily transpires Let no one endeaviour Evil deeds to hid as a day of reveiling secrets is at hand The time will soon arive the doings to solve of things that have ben don whether wright or wrong But the doings of the L D Saints is first in voge Then comes the doings of the Antients back to the first age of the world Then will be unriddled a mistry of worth speaking of this planit and its work before time began As it has had a Standing above fifty thousand years since it took its departure from the sun From that time to the presant it has often changed By the wisdom of God that many have moved and honoured themselves by living in obediance to the Law of God As Satan or the prince of Darkness has in all ages had power from time to time Since the Earth was formed Altho they have changed As God se fit and knew not of each others doings or what had took place As the time has come that light must shine and solve misterys of worth as many on Earth has had a standing conducted by the Father of lights as he had many decendants or sons to bring his purposes about The adopted son of Joseph at last took a stand to wind up a senry of things The work he commenced At the beguinning of time to establish and put all things in order as was to him shown By a council in Heaven Long since raised up that the hart of man has not conceived It is a senry of things To uoy up the mind enlighten and Enliven Those that have well don their work that they will stand as teachers and leaderers Threw the thousand years of the Melineum Or a day of rest A rest of which much is said But as it is a rest of worth not yet fully explained to mortal man but the time has come For it to be known by those that do to God give heed As God has now set out anew to bring back the fallen race of man it is to be don by daily moves by saying and doing the will of God As God to man is much inclined their mismoves does mar his pease as his Law is written On tables of stone that its not to be changed To eumer man Altho they are weak And of feeble minds yet provision is made for them to arise and se as they are seen and know as they are known When once a tree beguins to grow it must be rooted And grounded before its boddy can get large and strong Its thus with those that would be wise Let them commens as the bud that aspires high into the air and sallutes the Sun Moon and stars and cheers the brutes upon the Earth with its rich products Let man take the thrifty Oak for an example to honour God They then will raise With rays of light being rooted And grounded on the rock Christ Jesus

[Folder number 10] By O. H. Olney of Nauvoo Hancock County Ill[5]

An introduction of the design of the author in publishing the following pages is to show the trates of Certin ones who profess to be lead by the spirit of Revelation from God That Stand as leaders of the Church of Latter day Saints. I pass by doctrinal points wholy and speak of the doings of those that are looked upon as infalible, My design is in Publishing this work Is more perticularly to open the eys of many, That have not had the privelege that I have to know of their doings of the Church of Latter day Saints I have ben with the Church eleven years not as a watcher after Iniquity But as an impartial observor And have an Impartiall record of the doings of the Church of Latter D Saints That will speak for it self in due time On a principal of duty I have rote these few pages with much reluctance but not knowing of any other person About to devulge the Iniquity I commenced last April and have barly toutch on the doing of a certin Company that I feel it an indispensable

5. No date given.

duty To wield my pen against them To show to those that move under their watch care The Iniqu of those that lead them I add my own testimony and the testimony of others Of the truth of what I have written It is those that are aquainted with the doings of the Latter day Saints That are not aferd to speak for them selves with characters Unimpeachable Again I shall add Letters that have ben [illegible] I add all or a part That will establish true points as they are mostly in ful faith with presant doing of the Leaders and their confidance in me As to morality

[Folder number 11] Citty of Nauvoo Dec 1842

Brother Oliver Snow,

As I at this time have a leisure moment, I improve it in writing you a few lines, as we have long had and intimacy that is hard to brake up. As I well remember your stand in the East with land and conveniences to cheer the mind of man. I have often looked at your doings- and said in my mind, that econemy Is a gift of God. In an Early day I meet with you- of the settle-ing of a new state, But how has time changed of late; of Not Only you but myself- had a plenty and to spare, that we could freely assist the poor, and not scrimp our selves. Why is the change thus, Is it because of mismoves, O no it is wisdom in God for our good, As God to man is a looking- and with them would sympethise, teach and direct them- in the streight and narrow path, I would continue my writing but time does actually forbid as I send by Elder Gaylord[6] and he about to start. Yours as ever a friend.

O. H. Olney

Oliver Snow

The saying is Zion prospereth all is well. You will soon hear from me again.

6. Gaylord was baptized on August 2, 1835, and became one of the seven Presidents of the Seventy in 1837. In January 1838 at Kirtland, Ohio, Gaylord was excommunicated from the Church "for rising up in rebellion against the Church authorities." He later rejoined the Church and lived in Nauvoo. He affiliated with the James J. Strang's church for a time. Eventually, he became a member of the Reorganized Church of Jesus Christ of Latter Day Saints. Black, *Membership*, 18:94–97. Andrew Jenson, comp., *Church Chronology: A Record of Important Events Pertaining to the History of The Church of Jesus Christ of Latter-day Saints*, xiii.

JANUARY 1843

[Folder number 4] Citty of Nauvoo Jan 1st 1843

I again feel it my duty to write of a party that Is highly exalted for Piety and fame They have much a going and saying that looks to me strange for people that profess to be men of God As I am daily with them I am inclined to say that if they ever had wisdom it is flead Some upwards of thre years ago is well known by many that a plurality of wifes was the theme One year ago They in it commenced to move that some few added to their spouse some few that now stands as brides To priveleged ones Yet in toto they have denied the fact that they have ever harbourd such a thought But to my supprise What has come to vew but a Pamphlet printed by Joseph Smith yet it stand in the name of a Jacobs[1] a lacay that will move at a wink Its tener is reasoning from the scriptures by picking passages To encourage Poligemy from Genesis to Revelations To se such use made of the Bible must be abominable in the sight of God The Law given to direct The Childern of Israel by Moses on the mount Is applyd to that it is all to come in forse anew But whire does it speak of Poligemy but amongst those of a degraded set like a set that is around me of Greedy barking dogs That often bit and mangyle the wounded That is on all sides I look at the sosiety formed by the females that said to have some secrets of Masonry that is far advanced In the cause as some noted few are selected to teach and instruct The weaker class in doings that I think in most cases they are well schooled and mostly ready to display their ability In raising up a Righeous Branch that this generation may see The power of God displayed and they left will out exscuse I think a score of young Josys and a multitude more of the same Spicies of the twelve Bishops Councilers and those of high b[l]ood say about one hundred, are priveleged and the rest must stand back except their young daughters and wifes if per chance they should suit to assist in establishing Zion anew on the Earth

---

1. In the fall of 1842, a thirty-seven-page pamphlet defending polygamy was published by the Mormon press in Nauvoo. It was purportedly two chapters from a larger manuscript that was to be entitled *The Peace Maker, or the Doctrines of the Millennium.* The author was Udney Hay Jacob, a non-Mormon according to the preface of the pamphlet. On the title page was printed "J. Smith, Printer." Referring to the pamphlet in his publication *The Absurdities of Mormonism Portrayed,* Oliver Olney wrote, "If the pamphlet was not written by the authorities of the Church, it was by them revised in Jacobs' name." Olney seems to be suggesting that Joseph Smith or some other Church leader actually wrote the pamphlet and that Udney Hay Jacob might be a pseudonym. Udney Hay Jacob was a real person and was baptized into the Church in 1843, after the pamphlet was published. See Lawrence Foster, "A Little-known Defense of Polygamy from the Mormon Press in 1842," 21–34.

[Folder number 11] Walnut Grove Jan 12th 1843

The vale of Darkness ere long must rend as Christ the King will soon decend He in aray on Earth will come in power and magesty of God- He on the Earth will speak to man that have well performed their work He to them will freely show his condecension to mortal man Wise teachers to them he will send that long since lived on the Earth For ages past many have stood daily learning the the doings of God that they in aray may move a round to instruct the Childern of the Melineum As many has ben caled this work to do that are now in aray a waiting this work to perform a work of which but little is known because of the lack of faith But the time has come For God to speak that his name may be known on the Earth The fallen race must now arise and beguin to learn and know of God as they in aray do move around propeld by powers That is not of God Let the wise the Learned well understand the final destiny of man that the meek and low will first be cald to stand as agents and subjects to the Messengers of Heaven Let those arise in wisdoms ways that desires to become heirs ~~to the King of God~~ to the Courts of Heaven above But those that do neglect their work will come short of the Glory of God They in a mass must eventually fall that Sorrow and Lamentation will be their destiny Their final doom is thus decreed that the melineum rest will them <illegible> as they in aray will move around ruled by power that is not of God In dreary looks and frightful shapes will brood over them and on every side that they will Shudder at the sight one thousand years upon the Earth They then will have a senry of things not to be explained by the scractch of a pen But in aray all will come and stand before the King of Kings The councils of Heaven Will then decide the destiny of the Human race a race of which their is much said As many kinds And many grades is now extant upon the Earth they all as one have claim on God for their daily sustinance Again all have a work to do in honour of God that raised them up that in aray all will stand

[Folder number 11] Pawpaw Grove Decalm[2] County Illinoi January 13th 1843[3]

On a Noted Stake of Zion I am caled to take my stand as the teaching are unto me that the work of God cannot Stand still as Thousands Thousands tens of thousands is on the alert to know of God Yet an established Organiseation must <illegible> as this Is a land That speaks loud of Nature It speaks of much that is past and gone as fields and mouns doth fill the eye of the wayfareing man that does pas by Yet in and about these groves of buty was Citties towns and vileges of differant grades That is

---

2. Pawpaw Grove is located in Lee County, Illinois.

3. It appears that Olney originally wrote a 2 but attempted to make a 3 by writing over the 2.

now in the Dark But the time has now ariven that a work is now to commence for to Establish a new Stake of Zion in the County of Decalm that must be a place of rest a place of honour and of High renown to man As it is a day of counsiling for the Antient men of God they together now have assembled on the land of High renown And removed obsticles of the differant kinds The L. D. Saints are caled in question that on this land to get them homes as the tide of persecution On them soon will come Its not only a rest but a place of Safty that will cheer the heart of those that have conformed To the order of God Thus in aray let the saints assemble on the land as to them will be shone by the chosen men of Zion that stands as agents To the Antient of Days As many is caled To Stand as mineut men and do as to them is plainly shone Let those that have a mind together and establish themselves on permanent homes form settlements on this State of Zion As no power on Earth shall drive them therefrom altho the wicked may arise by Millions Yet God has power to put them down Let them settle on Prairies in clusters and cultivate large fields as to them will be shone Far east and west let them settle by purchase or exchange or by preemption right[4] Let a spedy rush be a makeing for the saints of Latter days to establish them selves On this land As the curse is now removed that Health and Streanth will be the theme Although their is a dreary famine well commenced and Undder way that the World is now in Commotion because of times That is getting hard The business [park? parts?] is now confounded and confidance gone That man cannot trust in man Thus in commotion all is a moveing that the fallen race of man may look back and se their doings that have lead into darkness the honest in heart But the time has ariven for a change to be that man may no more depend on his felow man And receive doom of the Council of Heaven As a Standing Council is in aray that puts all things in order As they this power have received this Council is of a chosen race that was raised up in an Early day They had a Standing On Earth when it first seperated from the planit of the sun They as wise Councilers now Stand to turn and over turn as they pleas that they the cepter long have swayed as on them rests the power of God They have power to form and create anew that by them Worlds on Worlds comes to vew But now the time is neer at hand that a decision is past that this must come to an end

[Folder number 11] City of Nauvoo Jan- 22d 1843

I at this time have feelings my mind to relate And speak my feelings of what daily transpires as much is adoing In all parts The high is a mourning because

4. Pre-emption right: "The right of purchasing before others. Prior discovery of unoccupied land gives the discoverer the prior right of occupancy. Prior discovery of land inhabited by savages is held to give the discoverer the *pre-emption* or right of purchase before others." *Noah Webster's First Edition of an American Dictionary of the English Language—Facsimile 1828 Edition*, s.v. "Pre-emption."

of hard times As money is scarse and confidance gone That confusion is the theme I take a retrospective vew of our Citty and say in my heart A senry of things is in voge that speaks loud of doings That is not of God I look at the houses some high and others low that is a tipe of the members of the Church some in high life others in low I look at the low and se them abused I look at the high on the pinicle of fame a moveing in affluance in the name of the Lord I look at the poor And se them Oprest as they are caled on daily for tithing that is every tenth Their labour is wanted The temple to build and the Nauvoo Mansion Is also the theme But what do we learn of the doings that it is but the drugs[5] of the place that is put to build The houses of the Lord The rest is squanderd In differant ways to accommodate the Priveleged ones of the place

[Folder number 11] Jan 23d 1843

As time pases I still have to write of things that comes to my vew As much is agoing daily amongst the Latter Day Saints Wisdom says that it must be wrote It speaks of a company in aray that stands now established as Kings and Priests to God They say to move by proxy in the name of the Lord and establish them selves for the Melineum morn that they may stand as Kings and rulers no more to be put down Again I look at their doings at home and abroad that speaks loud yet they move in the Dark Their doings is such That I shudder to write of the advantage that is taken of Sisters that are inofensive and of worth Yet they have to contend with many that say we know the mind of God that we have you as an offering to us that they are brought into bondage by being over powerd by a priveleged few But as the Day Star is a raising their destiny is seald As they will be dambd for their ungodly deeds Again I look at their members They in a mass do say all is well Zion prospereth All is well There is barely a few That can say that sin and Iniquity is the theme

[Folder number 11] On the envelope of a letter to Orson Hyde:

Rev Orson Hide
City of Nauvoo
A free letter
Jailors Rights
And no grumbling

5. Olney likely meant either "drudges" or "dregs." One who works hard, or labors with toil and fatigue; one who labors hard in servile employments; a slave. *Webster's Dictionary* (1828), s.v. "Drudge." Waste or worthless matter; dross; sweepings; refuse. Hence, the most vile and despicable part of men; as the *dregs* of society. *Webster's Dictionary* (1828), s.v. "Dregs."

FEBRUARY 1843

[Folder number 11] Citty of Nauvoo Feb 5th 1843

Mr Orson Hide

As I have a leisure moment I cheerfully spend it in writing you a few lines, As I did not fully speak my mind to you yesterday before you turned me out of doors I thought to your disadvantage whireas we had just began to talk You said to me that you was dissatisfied with me because of certin things told by Jestin Johnson[1] That I said to his Brother John,[2] in Hiram Ohio In 1840 That I told you I did not say but was told by Jestin to injure me or make difficulty between us. I told you that I would make you any kind of satisfaction if you would make it appear that I had spoken in the least to your injury but in all cases in your favor, And my chances to do it was not a few, As I think if any man in the Church has ben unwise it is you. How did you manage in Missouri, Did you not turn a vile enemy to the Church of L. D. Saints Did you not send your Affidavit[3] with others to the Governor That was the means of the exterminateing orders of Gov Bogs that men women and Childern

1. Justin Jacob Johnson, born November 13, 1820, at Hiram, Ohio. Justin was the son of John Johnson Sr. He was the younger brother of Luke and Lyman Johnson, members of Mormonism's first Quorum of Twelve Apostles. Justin was also a younger brother of Alice (Elsa) Johnson, the first wife of Oliver H. Olney, making him Oliver Olney's brother-in-law.

2. John Johnson Jr. was the oldest son of John Johnson Sr. and Mary Elsa (Alice) Jacobs. He was born at Promfret, Vermont, on March 21, 1805. He was a brother-in-law of Oliver H. Olney.

3. Northern Missouri was the site of Missouri mob and Mormon violence in 1838. Troubled by the destruction committed by Mormons and struggling with his confidence in Joseph Smith, apostle Orson Hyde signed an affidavit written by President of the Twelve Apostles, Thomas B. Marsh. The affidavit affirmed the possibility that the Mormons would burn down the cities of Buncombe, Liberty, and Richmond, Missouri. Marsh also wrote, "The plan of said Smith, the Prophet, is to take this State; and he professes to his people to intend taking the United States, and ultimately the whole world." At the bottom of the affidavit Orson Hyde wrote, "The most of the statements in the foregoing disclosure of the Thomas B. March I know to be true; the remainder I beleive [*sic*] to be true," and then signed his name. The affidavit, dated October 24, 1838, contributed greatly to the Mormon expulsion from Missouri later that year. Both men lost their positions in the Twelve. Marsh was excommunicated and Hyde was disfellowshipped. Hyde was restored to full fellowship in 1839. See Alexander L. Baugh, "A Call to Arms: The 1838 Defense of Northern Missouri," 218–19. Also see Myrtle Stevens Hyde, *Orson Hyde: The Olive Branch of Israel*, 95–103.

have had to suffer by being driven from their homes by a ruthless mob in the severity of winter That they had gained by hard labour When you had got fairly away did you not write directly to Father Johnson[4] at Kirtland Ohio of the wickedness of Joseph and others of the Leaders of the Church, Did you not mention my name as being accessory with [torn page] in stealing robbing plundering and the like If you did not I am misinformed. How did I find things as I was on my mission East of Ohio in the Eastern Country. When I got to Hiram the contents of your Letter came up with other things and your presant doings of Deal with Lyman[5] and Wiggins[6] and your missinion to the Holy land[7] They told me that you was a mean man if what you had wrote in your letter was true and then you conform to them or coencide with them that you had opposed. Or if what you had wrote was fals you was equally as mean a man What could I say for you as they had you before them they knew

---

4. John Johnson Sr. was affectionately known as Father Johnson. He was born at Chesterfield, New Hampshire, on April 11, 1778. He was converted to The Church of Jesus Christ of Latter Day Saints after his wife was miraculously healed of chronic rheumatism by a blessing pronounced by Joseph Smith. Johnson lived in Hiram, Ohio, on what is known today as the John Johnson Farm. Joseph Smith lived with the Johnsons from September 1831 to March 1832. Johnson sold his 304-acre farm and moved to Kirtland, Ohio, where he opened an inn near Newell K. Whitney's store. Johnson was called to serve as a member of the Kirtland high council in 1834, but in September 1837 he was rejected as a high councilor and later became disaffected with the Church. John Johnson Sr. was the father of early Mormon apostles Luke and Lyman Johnson. He was also the father of Alice (Elsa) Johnson, who married Oliver H. Olney. Arnold K. Garr, Donald Q. Cannon, and Richard O. Cowan, *Encyclopedia of Latter-day Saint History*, 576–77.

5. Lyman Wight, born on May 9, 1796, at Fairfield, New York, was an early Mormon apostle. Wight was baptized and ordained to the office of elder in November 1830. In June 1832, Joseph Smith ordained Wight as the first high priest in the Church. Wight then ordained Joseph Smith to the same office. Near the end of the Mormon-Missouri conflict, Wight was imprisoned in the Liberty Jail with Joseph Smith and other Church leaders. In 1841 at Nauvoo, Wight was ordained a member of the Quorum of the Twelve Apostles. Prior to Joseph Smith's death, Wight had been charged with the responsibility of going to Texas and establishing a mission there. When Joseph Smith was killed in 1844, Wight proceeded with the plans to move to Texas. He was excommunicated from the Church in February 1849. Garr, Cannon, and Cowan, *Encyclopedia*, 1344.

6. Unsure as to the identity of the person named Wiggins mentioned by Olney. There are several Mormon men named Wiggins who lived in Nauvoo at the time this letter was written: Alford Wiggins, Ebenezer Wiggins, Heber Wiggins, and Nelson Wiggins. Susan Easton Black, comp., *Membership of the Church of Jesus Christ of Latter-day Saints, 1830–1848*, 46:76–80.

7. See OOP, fd. 5, July 7, 1842.

you like a book your writings spoke with your works To speak for you I was as a cat without claws in climbing a tree I had no tools to use to help you as you requested of me to do What took place then John went to his Fathers and as usual talked over the tale Jestin took the sound come to Nauvoo and told the tale and laid it to me as I was not here to speak for myself They could go ahead. That is it Orson. Wall [While] I went on to York State the bretheren said how is it with Elder Marsh[8] How is it with such a one such a one and such a one in a most every case O. Hide was in question I in all cases coverd up his old sores and daubed him over the best way that I could fix it as I had told him [torn page] Nauvoo by his request that I would assist him to get in accordance with the Church In the round I went to Boston there was the contents of the big letter to Father Johnson moved on by a Sister Brewer that was hard to encounter with I can show that I volentarily said much to get Orson Hide out of his unwise moves Altho the gentleman was on a noted Mission to the Wholy Land, Yet his character wanted much patchin (I will say too much for me) To Orson Hide I will write my mind Altho he is counted a man of fame Yet I look at him as at other men I se him partially in a Glass I se his moves I vew is ways a striving to be something verry great I se his ability to go ahead is to arise on the exspense of others whether they have to suffer more or less I see him now on a high moun Go which way he will he must go down as he on the top has ben reared with aught but a sandy foundation to rest his foot As Storms are frequent both high and low poor Orson has not much more time to strutt and gro I to you will plainly speak my mind I ask know favors of you in the least but look on you as an imprudent man Have I not for you in all cases don Had a Lying and an imprudent youth orto distroy the Confidance of long friends Sir to you I will speak again that unless you to me come and give satisfaction that I have not only received from you but

8. Thomas B. Marsh, born November 1, 1799 (or 1800), at Acton, Massachusetts, ran away from home age fourteen. A religious seeker, Marsh learned about the Book of Mormon being printed in Palmyra, New York. He and his wife, Elizabeth, joined Mormonism shortly after the Church's organization. In Ohio, Marsh was ordained an elder and then a high priest. Chosen as an apostle in 1835, he presided over the Quorum of the Twelve as its oldest member. In 1838, Marsh became disgruntled with Joseph Smith and left the Church. He swore an affidavit against Smith, asserting that he was guilty of treason. Marsh remained estranged from Mormonism for nearly twenty years. Eventually, he made his way to Salt Lake City and begged for reconciliation. Thomas B. Marsh died in full LDS fellowship at Ogden, Utah, in January 1866. Garr, Cannon, and Cowan, *Encyclopedia*, 711–12.

have ben slanderd by your wife[9] Yes of you and yours I will speak in black and white and speak of things that might lay in the Dark

O. H. Olney
Orson Hide

[Folder number 11] Citty of Nauvoo Feb 6th 1843

Mr Orson Hide

As I have a leisure moment I cheerfully spend it in writing you a few lines as I did not fully speak my mind to you yesterday before you turned me out of doors I thought to your disadvantage Whire as we had hardly began to talk

You said to me that you was dissatisfied with me because of certin things told by Jestin Johnson that I said to his Br John in the East that I told you I did not say but was told by Jestin to injure me and make a disturbance betwen us I told you that I would give you any kind of satisfaction if you would make it appear that I had spoken in the least to your injury but in all cases in your favor My chanses to do it was not a few As I think if any man in the Church has ben unwise it is you how did you manage in Missouri Did you not turn a vile enemy to the Church of L D Saints Did you not send your affidavit to the Governor with others that was the means of the exterminatein orders of Governer Bogs That men womin and Childern have had to suffer by bein drove by a ruthless Mob in the severity of winter from their peaceible homes That they had gained by hard Labour When you had got fairly away did you not write directly to father Johnson at Kirtland Ohio of the wickedness of Joseph and others of the Church did you not mention my name that I was engaged with in stealing robbing plundering and all manner of Iniquity if you did not I am misinformed How did I find things ~~East~~ as I was on my mission to the Eastern Country When I got to Hiram the contents of your letter came up with other things and your presant doings They told me that you was a mean man If what you had wrote in your letter was true and then

9. Olney is referring to Marinda Nancy Johnson Hyde. She was born to John Johnson Sr. and Mary Elsa Jacobs Johnson on June 28, 1815. Marinda was a younger sister of Alice E. Johnson Olney, the first wife of Oliver H. Olney, making Oliver her brother-in-law. Marinda became one of Joseph Smith's plural wives. No information could be located concerning Olney being slandered by Marinda Hyde. However, Marinda was a believer in the principle of plural marriage and even acted as intermediary for Joseph's proposal to Nancy Rigdon. Marinda, being privier to the actual facts than anyone else, may well have been irritated at Olney's attack on Joseph Smith in the newspaper concerning the Nancy Rigdon matter. It is plausible that Marinda spoke out against Olney, thus he considered himself being slandered by her.

conformed to the doings of that that you had exposed Or if what you had wrote was fals that you was no less mean What could I say for you as they had your Character your works and writings all in their hands To help you as you had requested of me I was as a Cat without claws in climming a tree but what took place John went to his fathers and told over the old Story as usual Jestin took the sound and came and told in Nauvoo to many that I had said something as I was not here to speak for myself That is about it Orson Wall I went on to york State the bretherin said how is it with Elder Marsh how is it with such a one such a one such a one They in the most of cases had Orson Hides name that I in all cases coverd up old sores and daubed him over the best way that I could fix it as I had told him In Nauvoo that I would assist him to get in accordance with the Church of the Latter Day Saints In the round I went to Boston the was the contents of the Big letter from father Johnson that was hard to encounter with But I can show that I had to say much because of unwise moves on Orson Hide altho he was on an important Mission Yet his Character wanted much plasterin I will say it wanted to much for me To Orson Hide will write my mind Altho he is counted a man of fame Yet I look at him as at other men I see in partially in a glass I se his mves I vew his ways striving to be something verry great I se his ability to go a head is to arise on the exspense of others whether they have to suffer more or less I see him now on a high moun Go which way he will he must go down as he on the top has ben rerd with aught but a sandy foundation to rest his feet As Storms are frequent both high and low Poor Orson has not much more time to strut and gro To you Sir I plainly I ask no favors but look on you as an imprudant man Have I not for you in all cases don Had a Lying intruding youth orto distroy the Confidance of long friends Sir to you I will speak again unless you to me come and give satisfaction that I have not only received from you but have ben Slanderd by your wife Yes to you I will speak in black and white and speak of things That mite lay in the dark

O Hide

Letter written by Oliver Olney's second wife, Phebe Wheeler, to her aunt and uncle:

LETTER FROM PHEBE WHEELER

[Folder number 11] Nauvoo Jan 28 1844-

To my Beloved Uncle and Aunt Dunning [from Phebe Wheeler]–

I can not easily express to you the present emotions of my heart I as am ever closely attach,d to my friends and but for the knowledge which I have of the power of the Gospel of Jesus shed down upon the faithful of this people I could not submit to be shut from your Society No Aunt Dunning I would fly to you and my blynd Mother and situate myself where I could now and then sit and talk with you till you sleep - - - - But if I had this precious privelege I could not have the advantage of the Gospel or the gifts and blessings of it which is bestowed through the Holy Priesthood upon the faithful such as walk humbly before the Lord. I have sacrificed almost every thing but my Life - to come among this people But the most trying is the affection of my friends which I have left for the Gospels sake alone – for my good name, tho lost; I mourn not— Because the Lord looketh upon the heart, and will judge righteous judgement Since I left you I have passed thru many scenes some pleasant some Awful but amidst all I rejoice that my eyes are open to understand tho yet imperfectly; something of the work of the Lord in the Last days. My Health is state delicate my constitution slender but free from disease – except the canker which I have had at times since I first came to Ill- I use no stimulus – or opium coffees or teas wine or spirit – now so that what strength i have is my own The Latter day Saint use none of these things But there are many Mormons who do - - There are many people gatherd in here who are offensive and bring a great reproach upon the entire Church. Nauvoo is building up very fast Buildings 3 and 4 stories going up of brick chiefly, rapid improvments making Merchants mony or more than is would goods cheap Cloths collar – from 4 cents to a <illegible> or 12 ½ - other cloths in proportion – but the great difficulty is scarsity of Mony As to myself I have enough at present I have heard from Conn that Mr Edwin Lay had heard – or told I had lost my money all was homesick and going to return – I reply Not I hold a note of over 50th all that was left of my experiens coming here which is in the hands of a friend of mine nd Joseph Smith or any of that family and as I am lately moved I have called for it and exprest it soon further I am not homesick – Tho I long to see my friends all of them I have all confidence in the foundation of this work and would assure my friends all, that it is true Mormonism (as it is called) is true And tho you never hear from me again remember it, imprint it on your mind, put it in your memory for my sake for your own sake and see by and by if I have not told you correctly For be assured that all the Systems and Creeds of men are waning the power of the Priesthood is restored and held as the disciples held it whom Christ Commissioned this too is so and the time is fast hastening when the world will know it. I know that Satan hath great wrath as he hath but little time and gets power here as every where over many and in this Church his stratogims are laid deep to welcome them But tho many may fall yet he who has set his hand to restore the House of Israel will accomplish his own work by his own Instruments in his own due time But I have forgotten myself I was going to tell you Aunt Dunning that I was married on the 19th of October 1843 to Mr. Oliver H Olney formerly from Conn - a Br of Jesse Olney[1] Conn author of School Books he has been a particular friend of mine ever since I came to Illinois Mother committs me to his care in Conn; he has in every sense been true to his trust he has been in this Church from the rise of it was worth some $10,000 worth property but sacrificed it nearly all to this Church &c &c his last donation was $500 into the Temple in Nauvoo of his possessions I know not only that he has some money but of this I have no concern he is a businessman and will calculate to bear a adverse fortune his disposition and mind is the jewel to me adverse fortune I am used to also depravations Mr. Olney was a widower with 7 children which are all except one among his former wifes relatives in Ohio who are wealthy and wish them to stay with them the other one a daughter is married but should he wish to take them the two youngest I Should be pleased with it anything that would render him most happy tho I do not expect it as present Mr Olney expects to travail a good deal thinks as they are well off with their friends who have no children that they had better remain Mr Olney is now gone to Ohio shall wait for his return before I mail this that you may know also my dear Mother of my salutations I shall then know and communicate further I have been thus particular Aunt Icrania because I know you care for me Mr Olney is 5 or 6 years older older than myself of an even temperament of a lark[2] generous

---

1. Jesse Olney was a younger brother of Oliver Olney, born October 12, 1798, at Union, Connecticut. Jesse served as principal of the Stone School in Hartford, Connecticut, for twelve years. His book, *A Practical System of Modern Geography* became a standard American text and was used in by almost every private and public school in the United States for thirty years. He wrote other textbooks, including *A History of the United States: for the Use of Schools and Acadamies* and *Olney's School Atlas*. Jesse Olney's books were advertised in the *Nauvoo Neighbor* and *The Wasp*. Jesse Olney never became involved with Mormonism. He was a Baptist until 1840 when he became a founder of the Unitarian Society. Jesse Olney died on July 31, 1872.

2. Phebe Wheeler states that Oliver Olney had the "even temperament of a lark." The expression "happy as a lark" means very happy or extremely happy. "Whether larks are actually happy is debatable, but the origin of the expression is lost in antiquity." Marv Rubenstein, *21st Century American English Compendium,* 119. Perhaps Phebe was saying that she saw Oliver Olney as consistently cheerful and pleasant.

disposition faithful in friendship which is a prominent feature in his character I am well aquainted with many who have been long aquainted with him who reccommend him as possessing good habits & morals I dont know where we will Locate ourselves but probably somewhere from this It does not seem that I am 2000 miles from you and yet I often think of it – Mr Olney thinks I will come and see my friends in Conn before a great while As to that I don't know if Mr O should go east again as he has often been I might come with him; probably should, I do expect to see Mother again if you say so to her not only to comfort her but because I think really that I will I hope you will convey this to Mother immediately as this letter is later than <illegible> say one month In your letter to me Dear Aunt you speak of rumours; - true rumours there are many some true and many false ones you spoke of Joseph Smith of rumours concerning him he is said to be lecivieous &c &c But I can speak so far as I know and no farther I saw no thing of it while I was at his house nor since You cant depend on the flying stories at all But to change the subject we have had a pleasant mild winter the Mississippi is just frozen over, Last winter it was frozen 17 weeks we have had one snow of 8 inches and that is all crops are light from the drouth. potatoes small flour 3$ lb – pork 5$ ½ Have been teaching school the past summer this winter heard aut I received your Letter Last winter by a stranger by private conveyance and thank you for it I am always happy to hear from you all My love to all the cousins to Polly Pamelea Trifena <illegible> <illegible>[3] And Anna and cousins Edwin their Companions & Children I have not yet written to Mr Taylor but tell him the letter is to come nor yet kept my engagement with Mr Somers (used to work for <u>him</u> – but I will – When I get settled I will write probably to Mother then you will know where to direct your letters then I hope you will write or some of the Dear Cousins and not fail I would would like to see you all much please remember me to cousin Eunice & family to Uncle Seckets family is cousin Oliver living & how is his health Has he recovered from his rhewmatic[4] complaint? How is Uncle Orange Merwins[5] family Love to all respects to Mrs S. Johnson Mrs Llora Facy and all friends Though what is friendship? Tis but a name answered a sound "all like the purchase few the price will pay"

---

3. Phebe includes names of family and friends. I have included the names I could clearly read. In other cases, I was not sure of the names, even though I could make out some of the letters. I have listed those names as illegible.

4. Pertaining to rheumatism, or partaking of its nature, as *rheumatic* pains or affections. *Noah Webster's First Edition of an American Dictionary of the English Language—Facsimile 1828 Edition*, s.v. "Rheumatic." A painful disease affecting muscles and joints of the human body, chiefly the larger joints, as the hips, knees, shoulders, etc. Webster, s.v., "Rheumatism."

5. Orange Merwin was a member of the House of Representatives from Connecticut 1825-1829. *Biographical Directory of the United States Congress, 1774 to 2005*, 95, 98.

APPENDIX 1

THE

ABSURDITIES

OF

MORMONISM PORTRAYED.

A BRIEF SKETCH BY

OLIVER H. OLNEY.

HANCOCK CO., ILLINOIS.

March 3d, 1843.

THE ABSURDITIES OF MORMONISM PORTRAYED.

The doings and movements of the Church of Latterday Saints, has been a theme of things long dwelt upon—that many have stood amazed, to hear and see the moves of and about them.

Many have spent much time in writing and publishing of their traits, but as yet, I have not seen an impartial account of them, that has been published. With the best of feelings, I commenced about one year ago to write of their doings that occurred daily,—that I did, until a short time since, that was taken from my custody in my absence, that I have not yet obtained. Now to answer my own feelings, and do the Latterday Saints justice, and the people at large, I commence anew, with the best of feelings, and instead of writing more than the truth, to come short of it. Not but what I know of them; as the old saying is "I know them like a book."

With pen, ink and paper,
And convenience to write,
I could unriddle a scenery of doings
Of the Church of Latterday Saints;
But to give a full history of them,
Would be labor spent in vain at this time;
It is barely the out skirts on which I will touch,
By and by I will write again.

In the spring of 1831, I became acquainted with the Church then called Mormons, now Latter Day Saints, and their principles; I united with them, believing them to be a good people of God, saying to serve in accordance with the Bible of the Old and New Testament; that I considered a standard for man to walk by. I was familiar with their doings, and often have seen much that I knew was not right, but laid it to the weakness of man, saying, he is fallable and liable to err, that allowances must be made. Thus time passed away that much was said and done, that had to be noticed by discerning minds. I moved in accordance with them, as I felt it my duty to be in accordance with the Church, as I with them had a name. As this was a principle of faith, I took the liberty to keep a record of their doings, that I still have in my care; but of their daily doings of late, is what they took from me, with dates, names, &c., that I had designed for publication, of about 130 pages.

4

I shall first speak of the doings at Kirtland, Ohio. That was call a stake of Zion, in the borders of the East; that was to be an important gathering place for the Church. Also Jackson County, Missouri, was to be a place of note, for the gathering of the Latter Day Saints, that a City should be reared in honor of God, by the Latter Day Saints, that the nations of the earth should flock to it with their valuables, that would eventually become a light to the world.

Also twelve Stakes of Zion on its borders, that was to be reared by the Latter Day Saints, in the due time of the Lord, as the way opened it for them to perform.

As Kirtland was the first Stake to be reared as an ensign to the nations of the Earth, many came together and commenced to build. All moved speedily. Lots of small dimensions soon raised in price, from fifty to two thousands dollars a lot. Farms in the suburbs of the city soon raised, from ten and fifteen dollars per acre to one hundred and fifty in some cases. All moved fast; all were in business.

Yet money was scarce. That, almost to a man, they wanted to borrow. And property was continually raising in and around the city of Zion. They at last decided that a city could not prosper without a currency of its own. They of the Church soon met by hundreds, and subscribed to a bank. Capital stock was called for, the books were opened, capitalists came forward and showed their good will to establish a Bank, as it was said to be a Revelation from God to do it. They signed from one thousand dollars cash to five hundred thousand dollars. There was no lack of capital to start on. The instalments were soon called in, but those that signed the least, I think in the most of cases, payed in the most stock. No time was lost to start a currency. Money was soon so plenty that hardly a man but what had a big roll of bills of the Kirtland Safety Funds to do business. Every thing seemed to move with life and animation. Hardly a man but what had credit to get of their currency. Pedlars went in every direction to change and put off as chances should occur. But to their surprise, they were soon sounded. That did many surprise, as their Bank was said to be established by a Revelation from God. Many contended that it could not be put down by man. They soon formed a union with the Monroe Bank of Michigan Territory. That added to their circulation of currency. But their God soon failed them, it seems, and their currency went down, and Monroe currency did but just go it.

As Pedlars went to and fro from the Bank,
In connection with business men,
From different parts of the land,
They soon see themselves in difficulty.
As gold and silver began to be scarce,
They got hold of a quantity of boxes,
And nearly filled them with sand,
Lead, old iron, stone, and combustibles,

5

And covered it up with clean coin,
That darkened the deception beneath,
That showed they were not to be run,
By the men of the world.
But the skim on the top soon disappeared,
And the currency, city lots, and farms,
All went down to their value.
As thousands on thousands of dollars
Had been paid out for lands,
That had made payments but in part,
Their lands went back to satisfy a security bond,
To those of whom they had bought.

At the same time in the city of New York many had been credited for goods to a large amount. Also, in other business places; and so many demands about home, that it was with the greatest difficulty that they got so as to clear out and go to Missouri, from Ohio.

At the rise or start of the Church in Kirtland, a company went to Jackson county, Missouri, there settled to make ready a city that, of it much was said. But their stay there was but short, as trouble soon arose; that the people of Jackson county arose and drove them out. They mostly went into Clay county, staid there a short time, dissatisfaction arose, that an armed force arose from Kirtland, Ohio, of some hundreds to go up and settle the difficulty. Many of them died of the Cholera, and otherwise, but nobody killed. It appears that they had their labor for their pains.

Many that went up on this occasion in the heat of the summer, to make all straight, were called to return to the mother dust. Difficulties soon arose in Clay county; that the Mormons were again crowded, that they went into Caldwell and Davis counties, Missouri, and made settlements in both counties.

They continued there until the summer of 1838, when they were joined by those that had started from Ohio. Of the doings of those in Mo., and why they were driven, I do not pretend to say, as all I know is by hearsay. But those from Kirtland, Ohio, of which I have spoke, seemed to have many besetments that attended them. An unlawful intercourse amongst the two sexes existed, of which testimony plainly spoke. Also an introduction of principles that would lead to bad morals: such as Polygamy, or the time would soon be, that the ancient order of God that was formerly, would again have its round, as it was in the days of old Solomon and David.— They had wives and concubines in abundance, as many as they could support. The secret whispering was, that the same will eventually be again. Many arrived at Mo., after a long and tedious journey of about eight hundred miles, and many died on their journey.

Much excitement existed between the people of Missouri and the Mormons, that seemed to daily gain. All parties seemed to be engaged: armed forces made their appearance. That caused much excite-

6

ment. Threats arose on both sides, until Gov. Bogs of Mo., issued orders to clear the State of them, or exterminate them. The militia were soon called in; the Mormons were forced to submit to them, and agree to leave the State in the course of the winter and spring of 1839. Several skirmishes occurred. Many more were killed on both sides than was made public by either party. I was not in any engagement, but stood as guard with the Mormons, as I moved in accordance with them in Kirtland, and went with them to Missouri.

They as a people, removed to Illinois, left as they agreed, and settled in different parts of the State. They held a council, appointed agents to locate a place at which they might assemble together again. They soon made a purchase at Commerce, Hancock county, Ill., and bought land, or agreed for it, on both sides of the Mississippi river. They soon began a new settlement on both sides of the Mississippi river. They soon changed the name of Commerce to Nauvoo, and established it a Stake of Zion, to be reared up in honor of God, [as was the former Stakes,] that he might have a resting place for his foot, and where to lay her head. Land was purchased in both large and small quantities, on both sides of the river. Many soon got homes or places to make them. This, as was Kirtland, was to become a light to the world.

Thousands have been, and are flocking to the New State of Zion, that when war, pestilence, and famine, shall spread over the land with its ravages, they can have a home to shield themselves from the storms. It is to be an ensign to the nations of the earth; a light shining in a dark place. As they say, we are the only people of God on the earth—we stand as his agents to officiate for the human family, as they say.

We as a people are the chosen of God,
We daily have his word to cheer us up,
Although persecution on us does rule,
That we suffer from all classes of men.
But we, like the ancients it must bare,
And add to our works perseverance,
And press our way through.
As the way is opening, no one can doubt,
As God has again delivered from oppression,
That peace and plenty now is the theme,
And no one to harm us, or make afraid.

After many had gathered to Nauvoo, they commenced to mark off city lots, and sell, until they finall got Nauvoo chartered, that they could form their own laws, and do more to their liking, they said, to form laws to suit their convenience as a city of Zion. They have raised a military force of all ages, that stands as minute men armed and equiped, in and about the city of Nauvoo. They have lands to dispose of at all prices and parcels, in and out of the city.—

7

They are also ready to attend to all calls on their part, in and out of their city, in farms, lots &c.

But when they get there,
What do they find but men to salute them
In the name of the Lord;
The first thing is to know
How much they possess,
And what they have a mind to do,
That opens a door to handle them as they please,
That to them they can sell, buy or borrow,

And strip them as they see fit.
Such men are many, and always on hand,
That they know every man's ability to do.
From five hundred to two thousand dollars
Is the common price of their lots.
That is an exorbitant price
In a new settled country as is Nauvoo;
But as they have "thus saith the Lord,"
No man dares doubt, but give their price.
Again, their daily trainings speak aloud
Of something more than to answer the law.
The weapons they have, speak loud to me,
In connection with their words,
That they intend to stand in all cases,
In self defence and contend for their rights,
If oppressed, as they have heretofore been,
By the inhabitants of the land.

DANITEISM.

In Missouri was formed a society of Danites, as men of power, to do as thought best by the leading ones of the L. D. Saints, that say to have power with God.

They stand as minute men on all occasions, ready to fulfill the word of those that stand in high authority in the Church. Much has been said of this company in Missouri and in Illinois. But they have within the past year joined the Freemasons. Their name is changed. They united with the Lodge free of expense. They now claim the name of Masons; but are a band bound to the Danite principles as before. In connection with the addition of Free Masonry, their oaths are to be true to one another; also to the Authorities of the church; suffer no one to speak reproachfully of them; to be as minute men to fulfil their word; not to let their left hand know what their right hand does. That is to say, keep their doings to themselves in all cases, except to give a history of their doings to their leaders.

Here we get hold of a company cut and dried for any thing that comes to hand. They quote the case of Ananias and Sophyra.— That were killed by Peter's chosen men, because they did not

8

give up their property, or lie about it. Also, of Moses killing the Egyptian, and burying him in the sand.

Thus they take lenity, as they say like the Apostle Peter, we hold the keys of the kingdom of God. Our rights are not limited.— The destiny of the wicked is in our hands. That we can do by them as seemeth us good. A part of this band stands as a life-guard to the leaders of the church of L. D. Saints.

The above company is a raising,
That no one can doubt, to put into subjection
All that does them oppose;
In an oath they are bound,
And a penalty annex'd,
To well do their duty, if it is to take life,
They in all cases are called,
To defend each other at law,
This company is spoken of,
Under different heads,
But mostly as the daughter of Zion.

The above company I was familiar with in Missouri, also have been here, as many of them have supposed me to be one of the band, that they have been free with me.

But I never united with them. I look upon them as a combined company, gaining fast. They to strengthen themselves in faith and doings, quote the prophecies of the prophet Daniel 2;44, that speaks of the stone cut from the mountain without hand, that was to move until it filled the whole earth. They say to be this branch a raising, as is spoken of in Isaiah 11;1.

RE-BAPTISM.

There is another order of things arising, or has arisen, that speaks loud to me of degraded minds; that is if a person or persons have been in any kind of iniquity, if ever so bad, they have a remedy for it, by being baptised over anew. For remission of sins, this principle is instilled into the minds of all that moves with them, or that comes under their watchful care.

Since first introduced, it has been a caution to see the river foam with them on Sundays after meeting in warm pleasant days.

Again, if we allow testimony to speak, there is an unlawful intimacy between the two sexes, it would make the heathen blush, too bad to write, much more to talk or read. Yes, those that profess to be the chosen of God, that claim to have power to say, thus saith the Lord, have seduced and abused females, that many have to bear the stain of fornication and adultery.

In speaking of the above doings, it has often caused me to say,
Where is there another such a people
On all the face of the earth.

From their own mouth's we learn,

9

Of both, male and female,
That an unlawful intimacy
Has existed for a number of years;
But for eighteen months past,
No one can doubt, of the unwise moves
That has existed between the two sexes,
That have lived in and about the city of Navoo
Yet we see many that have no minds of their own,
And would suffer their wives and daughters
To be abused under their nose
And not know it, or think it no harm.
I look at many such in the city of Nauvoo,
That would think it an honor to them
For some of their kin to be intimate,
With some of the chosen ones,
If they have "thus saith the Lord" for it.
There is no more to say,
But Zion prospereth, all is well.

EQUALITY.

I must, to do justice to the Latter Day Saints, yet touch on many subjects, that occur to my mind.

As equality at the rise of the Church, was the theme, all as one must arise and be equal. The strong bear the infirmities of the weak. But what do we discover but big fish and little fish all mixed up together. No more equality than there is amongst the brutes of the field, all going in the name of the Lord; brother to law with brother daily, and calling one another d—d rascals; finally no bad name excepted. And on Sundays they will come together and put on their Sunday fixings (that is hypocrisy,) preach then, partake of the Sacraments, and go home much edified at what has been said.

For me to write all their discourses, would not be in vain,
But of them, I will give a sample,
I am of the mind, I can touch their case.
They, as leaders and teachers, take the stand,
And offer some few remarks, pray and sing;
Some one of note arises to speak,
It can be told when he begins,

And when he leaves off,
As all will look at him,
To catch every word as it rolls.
When he gets through, its hard to tell,
What his subject was or about.
They will speak of their doings,
And of what must be done,
And of using up the different sects,
And of building up in the name of the Lord.

10

Also of the priest-hood that they have got,
And their poor, that they must be helped,
And their opposers, that they shall be damned.
We find in their Sabbath devotions,
All kinds of fixings that need be,
To say the Latter Day Saints,
Is not what they profess to be.
I say they as a people are deep in the mud,
Or the Bible is false in every sense of the word.

POLYGAMY.

I will now touch on a subject of which much has been said, that I would cheerfully pass by, but the importance of the subject forbids my doing it. Polygamy was first introduced in Kirtland, Ohio, about eight years ago. Hint after hint has been going, until we have to say, they have begun to do, as well as say. This subject has been kept in the dark, as long as it could be, as it was first said to be too strong meat for the Latter Day Saints to bear. But as some have long waited impatiently, and the plainness of the Scripture is such on the occasion, has forbid any further delay. But to risk to move ahead. I will not pretend to refer to all their scripture to prove their privileges—only to Solomon and David, that yet have to suffer for their misdoings.

Again, a dark saying arises in the name of the Lord, in the form of a pamphlet, said to be written by a man by the name of Jacobs, but published by Joseph Smith, Editor. We find if the pamphlet was not written by the authorities of the church, it by them was revised in Jacobs name. But to come to its contents, it argues polygamy; that there is hardly a saying in the Bible but what apply to polygamy. As much as the sayings of a noted Miller in the east I have heard him lecture a number of times, I saw there was hardly a saying in the Bible but what he could apply to a winding up scenery of things of this world, in 1843.

I look at the Bible as a very good book,
But whether it will support polygamy,
Or Millerism, I have my doubts,
But if either would sway,
I with Miller would wish to go.
As little fish like me,
Will stand a poor chance
Amongst those of high renown.

The subject of polygamy, amongst the Latter Day Saints is no longer to be kept in the dark; as many are actually attached to the second living companion; and a door is fast opening on this subject, that many is arguing it to be the will of God. That in these days God designed to raise up a more righteous people on the Earth than has been for many ages past. It is argued that those of the chosen

11

of God, is to father them, instruct them, rear them up in the nature and admonition of the Lord. That they may have faith, knowledge and wisdom, to be directed in wisdom's way. A number of moves have been made, to effect that order, and get it established. But nothing seemed to prevail, until they got a wise master Free Mason to come and establish a lodge amongst them. That he accordingly did, in the beginning of 1842. That a general gathering to them ensued—that they for months, took in three a day, and are a taking in yet. Also establishing lodges in the branches of the Church out.

This master Mason instructed them in many good things, such as there was some few degrees of Masonry for the fair sex of the land. That such encouraged the Mormon sisters. They soon came together and formed a lodge. But altered the name, that they could be distinguished from the lodge of the men. That they called the ladies benevolent society. They often met in union, and received many instructions, in their daily moves, by the authorities of the Church. They by the assistance of the authorities of the Church got their society organized, that much encouraged many; as all, both old and young was privileged to unite with it, by being recommended as worthy sisters, in the Church of Latter Day Saints.—They continued their meetings from time to time, until it was made known to them, that had been regular members, that there was certain degrees of Masonry for them to receive.

As I was passing over the Temple lot,
It being on high ground, I looked on the flats,

I there saw fixings of different sorts,
Some near by, others afar off.
I saw a society formed by the females,
That of it, much was said,
I saw their ambition was to go ahead,
By being governed by the authorities of the Church.
That from them they received instruction
In many good things, such as some few degrees
Of Free Masonry, it was their privilege to receive,
To be better prepared to meet,
The coming of the Son of Man,
They continued their meetings,
And soon formed a lodge,
And decided the first degree of Masonry to receive,
That was for each one to keep their secrets.
They often met in union,
With feelings of the best kind,
And received instruction,
That added much to their joy.
As I got somewhat wearied in mind,
At what I saw daily amongst them take place,
I on a rise of ground, was catched in a drowse,

12

I apparently saw fisherman of skill,
Spread a net far into the waters,
And commence to haul in.
As the cords were tightened from time to time,
The fish became uneasy, some flounced and flopped.
But as they found themselves entangled,
With cords not a few, they submitted to their lot.
I soon saw the net arrive near shore,
That had enclosed, fish of all sorts and sizes.
I saw the fisherman that had long waited for fish,
All as one put into the water,
And picked out such as they liked,
The rest they let go for some future haul.
As I awoke from my slumbers,
In May of eighteen hundred and forty-two,
The interpretation came to my view.

As I was still on the Temple Lot,
I saw many females together meet,
But to their surprise they were entangled in law,
That they could not themselves.
They finally seemed to become submissive to their lot,
And go forward as instructed,
By the authority of the Church.
As the cords were tightened from time to time,
That they were brought into subjection,
And a rush was made for a plurality of wives.
I saw difficulty that soon arose;
As all pitched for the young and handsome,
But to get in accordance they cast lots,
And decided to make another haul.
The old they let go to toll others in,
That caused many to mourn,
To think they had to be left.
That was the second degree of Free Masonry.

INEQUALITY.

The Church of the L. D. Saints is a theme of things, that no deserving mind can pass by, that is at all acquainted with them, and their doings. Yet they have all as one united together by being baptized for remission of sins, a saying to serve God in accordance with the teachings of the Old and New Testaments. This at the arise of the Church was their theme. But what do we discover but a complete change, they say the Bible is of little or no account—they say we have a man of God to tell us what to do—that we are not dependent on any former writings to mark our path.

The say, we as a people are the blest of God. Our privileges are not to be questioned. These are their arguments. That are of

13

the leaders of the Church are so combined together, that not a man of their stamp that has gathered with them, dares lisp a word of dissatisfaction, knowing, as all do in Nauvoo and vicinity, of their rules. I have been not a little surprised to see men of respectability that had gathered from the Eastern States, who I knew were in the habit there of speaking for themselves. But when they get to Nauvoo with their all, get settled, get established, and look about themselves, what do they find? They find they have got to be careful how they go to it. I guess I must tell a short story on the occasion. A big chunk of a Yankee from down East, New Haven county, Connecticut, that was noted for strength and good courage, by the name of Roberts; but when he got on, as is a Yankee notion, he began to find fault with something that Smith said. He, by the prophet Smith, got a curse, a kick and a cuff. That he went out of the store in a way that it was a caution to see him move. He soon got over his kick and cuff; but the curse used him up, as all said he was cursed, he could not get it off, as all said they could see it in his looks and actions. He soon became the talk of the place. It made him so sick that he went home and went to bed. His friends set in that the Elders must be called; but they were afraid to officiate, lest it should be with them as it was with the hogs on a certain occasion, when the devils entered them, and they ran into the river and were drowned. They came and looked at him, but dare not tell the devil to depart. They advised him to send for the offended prophet Smith, and give him satisfaction, that he might condescend to remove the curse. That he soon did, and the man of power attended to his case. They all looked at him as a new creature again in their ranks.—From that to this he has made much proficiency; he was soon made an officer in the Nauvoo Legion, ordained to the Priesthood, joined the Danites by taking their oath, and took his departure into the Eastern land. He says he thinks he can say that he knows Smith is a prophet, and the Mormons are as they say, the people of God, and that all the stories told by J. C. Bennett and others are lies.

I will speak of the Elders that are called to go out to preach. They are mostly Danites, or we may say, all, as at the April Conference in 1842 new regulations were made to send out such as had an understanding of the order of the Church, and those out to return to Nauvoo. They continued to move in this way until the difficulty arose with J. C. Bennett, Orson Pratt and others. Much was afloat at that time, as it was about the time of their selection for spiritual wives, that Dr. Bennett spoke much of in his publication. But, to put every thing in its place, they, as soon as Bennett had divulged much of their doings, called a company to go into all parts to clear up their characters, as they said, that had been scandalized by false reports. As I was then amongst them, I thought that the story was nothing to what was actually doing in Nauvoo.

I look at the Mormon Elders sent to preach,

14

They as a Poetess compared them to a kite;
As we see the kite, it raises high;
But to it we find a fastened cord,
As said the poetess of the latter times.
By it I see she had a mind to keep the run

Of the Mormon clan of big and little.
As big and little is the theme
Amongst those of the L. D. Saints,
On them are cords that are far away.
Before they start they have a charge
To move in accordance with the head.
As they are of the Danite Band,
They by an oath are bound,
For the Authorities of the Church to contend.
From time to time I have heard them lie
By sayings that they knew were false.
As what I have written up to this time,
In Nauvoo, is acted over and over again,
And is known by all except the dupes.

EDITORIAL DEPARTMENT.

Of their Times and Seasons, and Wasp, their Editorial department, of it I must speak short, as the saying is, "a short horse is soon curried." I look at their press as under that head being short; at the same time it speaks loud of their doings as a light to the world, or a City on a hill. They speak of using up the Editors of the day, and finally defy them, as they have often done, to come in contact with them, as is a common theme amongst editors, to take a little liberty, as with lawyers, with good feelings. But they have to shun the Wasp, I think, on the same principle that a man well dressed would a skunk or a pole cat, that has but one weapon to defend itself. By it, it has almost become the king of the forest. It is thus with the L. D. Saints; they have a little, low, insignificant, offensive weapon, that whose garments it touches, it is hard to get off. As a sample I would refer to their controversy with Thomas Sharp, editor of the Warsaw Signal.

As I look at their Editorial department,
It's of not much account;
Yet they boast of wisdom, and that of God;

15

But I think if God is with them,
He must be lost, or turned topsy-turvy,
From what he anciently was.
Of the Times and Seasons I now will add,

It has spread far and wide,
And speaks for itself.
But of the Wasp, I barely will hint,
It has a foundation, that no one can doubt,
But it is on sand, that is turned by a wink or nod.
The Wasp that flies from Zion's tower,
That is there reared by men of power.
But the little wasp to me does speak
Of something more than to fly about,
But is designed to brow beat
All that do not with it move.
The little Wasp that flies out and in,
I think has mistook his name,
As by his flying, it must have been hatched
By a bug in some low place, of some ordinary kind.
Much of the Times and Seasons might be said,
But I look at their papers and speak my mind.
I look at them as at saplins,
Where the tops have overpowered the roots,
That they much lack in nourishment,
For to support their growth.
I again look at them, as the saying is,
What the devil said when he catched a hog
That he mistook instead of a sheep.
At its sqealing he said
There is a great cry, but a little wool to be got.
I again look at the insect, the wasp;
Wasps are of many colors, sizes and forms,
Of them we see a thing but industry, beauty,
And independence. If not much love,
The wasp is an insect, that often stings,
When insulted, and to its business returns.
But we look at the columns of the Wasp,
And see the abuse toward Editor Sharp;
Month after month he received their slang,
When he, like a wasp, once them did sting,
That caused a smarting wound;
That they long cried and bawled aloud.
But the little bug that flies from a shrub
That has sprouted, budded, and bloomed,
But has withered in bringing forth fruit.

SEDUCTION OF FEMALES.

This is a subject I would cheerfully pass by; but on a principle of honor, I cannot forbear to write, as a door opens far and wide, on every side, that hundreds are convinced of the fact; that fornication and adultery is as common in the city of Nauvoo, as it is to be abhorred by respectable people. Many at this time are suffering under the stigma of being seduced by those that say, 'thus and thus saith the Lord.' For me to go into all their doings, I forbear, as I lack on every side. Much has been made public by John Cook Bennett, and many others, that the new fangled masons have said was all a pack of lies. But let the truth come to light; Doct. Bennett did not begin, hardly, to point of their doings. I will now take up two cases, say one of a hundred:

Miss Nancy Rigdon and Martha Brotherton. Miss Rigdon had repeated calls to visit a Mrs. Hide, until she made a visit. Soon after her arrival at Mrs. Hide's, Joseph Smith visited her; he told her that he had the word of God for her, that God had given her to him for a wife. Miss Rigdon said to him, 'you have a wife.' 'Well,' said he, 'you know the ancient order was, one man had many wives, that is again to be.' Miss Rigdon was obstinate. He then got Mrs. Hide to come in, and made use of her persuasive arguments, that she was first unbelieving in the order, but had been better informed; although she had long been acquainted with Mrs. Rigdon, but her many arguments were of no account. Mr. Smith again used his influence by more rash means, that Miss Rigdon threatened to call for help, that he let her go, but soon a letter was conveyed to her, written by some one of the clan, that argued the doctrine of Polygamy about as well as Jacob's Pamphlet, I should think, as I read it, and it contained about the same, except a few dry compliments to her. Miss Rigdon had been a member of the church with her parents, since eight or ten years old, in good standing. I have been personally acquainted with her since she was a small child, and I know that Miss Rigdon has sustained a good character at home and abroad. But what do we hear of her now, as being of the blackest dye? Yes, she is defamed by all, both high and low, of the Latter Day Saints.

The sound has gone, her to oppress;
Yes, Miss Rigdon now has to bear the slang,
Because she did not conform
To Joseph Smith's word of God;
But barely a youth, she for herself spoke,
And showed that she was not to be duped.

Miss Martha Brotherton, a youth of about eighteen, was saluted by a number of the clan, that set themselves in the place of God and count themselves as God. Miss Brotherton, a native of England, of respectable parents, all in faith and works, united with the Latter Day Saints and removed to America, and gathered to Nauvoo un-

17

der the instruction of those, who, in one sense of the word, are now her destroyers.

As the sound has gone both far and near,
Started by a clan of the noted ones,
That Martha Brotherton is of ill fame,
Yet her character was called good,
Until she by them refused to be duped.
Miss Martha by Eber Kimball was called
To be a second companion to Brigham Young,
But first was called into a large brick store;
She there with men had to contend,
That said to have much power with God.
They were her former teachers, that had led her
Far from her native land.
On them she looked, on them she gazed,
Being astonished at such an order of things,
That Polygamy should be their theme.
They called on her to them unite,
And become a second companion to B. Young.
Says Martha, if it is so, I have nothing to say,
But give me time to think of it.
All as one did then agree
To give her until next day.
She from them to her lodgings went,
And wrote of what had transpired,
Her writings I have seen,
That speaks loud of hard works.
This noted youth is to be extolled
Foe her presence of mind,
That she did not with them contend,
As they had her at their command,
In a large brick store. Miss Brotherton was decoyed,
The above youth's of which I have spoke,
Have honored themselves by their doings.
If others as they have marked the way,
Had rejected the salutations made to them,

But know they in most cases did submit,
To run fast into the degrees of Free Masonry.
Of Free Masonry I would not wish to speak;
As of it I am not versed in its traits;
But whether its traits is good or bad,
It is much dishonored by the Mormon Clan.
But the sound has gone for to oppress,
Whether male or female, all the same;
But Martha and Nancy, for themselves spoke,
And showed that they was not
By every villain to be duped.

18

The Editor of the Wasp John Taylor. Lest some may feel slighted, thinking they are not noticed, I will mention the name of Rev. John Taylor, a noted man for both speaking and writing &c. Not that I think he has any thing to do with the women, as he is not of that breed of dogs, but more of the mongrel breed, or like a weather-cock, or a minute man; or in other words, a lacky.

His hair is of a blackish brown,
His eyes is grey or grizzle, nothing of him can be said,
As he is of the neuter gender.
He is often found on the stand,
And as often a puffing and blowing,
Essaying to preach or to instruct;
But like the Wasp, he is wrongly named,
When he is called a man of fame.
As by his moves, he plainly shows
That he is not of the species man,
But is rather of the Apeish kind.
What he does, he is mostly told,
Although he is counted one of the twelve,
That is as much honor as it is to edit the Bug
That flies from the shrub, and throws his perfumes in and about.

In speaking of the editors amongst the Mormons, I have long been acquainted with them. They say, to be ranked high in the world, men of science and arts. They also profess to be inspired of God; they say the destination of man is in their hands; that as they say, so it is; they ursurp power, and will abuse all that does not with them coincide. In speaking of their editors—they are all editors that can write. All of the would be priests of the different grades as they term it, a moveing in solid columns, rank and file.— That if any fellow, for any reason whatever steps aside from them, he at once has to step forward and cord with them, or with him the fat is at once in the fire.

Dr. John Cook Bennett, a noted man amongst the Mormons; and he was a noted man before he joined them. I think we have reason to say that the Doctor was about as much a Military man as could be found amongst the suckers. The Doctor united with the Mormons about the first of their starting in the military line—that the Doctor arose as a head officer amongst them. They by him was often drilled—that we had to say Mr. Bennett took an interest for the Mormons. He soon used his influence, that they obtained a City Charter, mostly through his means, that was allowed by all. He took an interest we had to say, for his new brethren. They soon, in establishing their officers in the city, placed Dr. Bennett as Mayor of the city of Nauvoo. He officiated as Mayor a long time. Again, on him was placed their priest hood, that he was called a high priest after the order of the Son of God. In a word, we must say that John C. Bennett was extolled to the highest Heavens. By the authori-

19

ties of the L. D. Saints, he with them walked hand in hand. I saw him with them, and it appeared to be the most perfect union. Not a sism to lisp, except now and then some one that wanted to grow very fast, would come out on him with some old offence that had long before transpired to his joining the Church. But those that advanced such stories was soon put to silence. The Dr. moved along as did others of the first of the Church, until all of a sudden broke. That did not at all surprise me, as I saw many aspiring amongst them, that seemed to daily gain. The Doctor is well known to be a go ahead man; does not stop to tell long stories or hear them. As I learn he caused the difficulty amongst them that I spoke of in my sleep. In fact I saw that the Doctor was about as forward as any of them, when the rush was made. He too had the advantage, as you know a Doctor can say and do about as they are a mind to, and it is all a doctoring along. I saw that an uneasiness arose because of the Doctor's ability to go ahead.

But things passed along as they did—sometimes up, and often down, until Doct. Bennet had to clear out. I think the Doctor must have felt bad to leave as he did. Such prospects a head.

Yes, Doct. Bennet little thought
In his fat living with them,
To be so soon routed from their midst.
But, alas! of it he had to bear.
But the place he left was soon filled,

As many was awaiting to aspire;
Yet I think J. C. B. must felt bad,
As all the unmarried females that is pregnant;
It is laid to John Cook Bennett.
But when they in question are brought,
No one says aught of Doctor Bennett.
I have heard, much said of Doctor Bennett.

But I think that the Doctor did his best for the Mormons until about the time that he was forced to leave them. When he left he did as he thought his best to break them up. But he was not the man to tell of them, as by doing it he must criminate himself. In the case of Ex-Gov. Bogs being shot Doctor Bennett was bound, he was fastened; that he could not tell the tale of it without mentioning himself in the fault. Now as for me I could not, if called upon, swear under oath, that O. P. Rockwell was hired by about fifteen or twenty of the first of the Mormons to kill Ex-Gov. Bogs of Mo. It is by a multitude of circumstances that I know that he did it. As it was done, it went through the city as if a great prophecy had been fulfilled.

Let Doctor Bennett know that it shall not hurt his character, influence, or any advantage be taken of him because of what he shall say under oath, and I think that the man would unriddle a scenery of things, as he has been through the Mormon Mill. They of the Mor-

20

mons well knew as he left them, and commenced to divulge, there was no other way than to destroy his influence.

But the truth in most cases will
Bear its own weight. But as yet amongst
The Mormons, it has been waived that
Their doings have not come to light at all.
I am a moving as I am, and instead of being against them, in a word, I am for them.
But I look at them as a man at his son,
That has been where he ought not;
That for it the old man raised a rod;
Rod after rod he on him used,
Until he found it was no use to whip.
He then made a plaster and on him put,
That from him arose a mist that took out all his putrifaction;
But when it was gone, nothing was left
But an unwholesome lump of no account.

OF THE TEMPLE AND NAUVOO INN.

The Temple is a building that of it much is said. As it is said to be a revelation from God to build it, that takes the attention of all the Mormons. It is said that their salvation depends on its finish; that if the house is done well and good. The church as a people are a saved people. But it was to be done in such a time, or no salvation for them. They went to work—laid the foundation with great parade, and soon commenced to build. All engaged to a man to fulfill the Revelation; but the building was large and to be of stone, that was hard to dig, hard to draw, hard to fit for use, that has been to them a slow job to get along with. They are yet to work on the house, but it is slow as the building is very large, and of the best of work. As far as it is done, I think their God will accept of their work; but the time they had to do it has long since run out. I do not yet learn how they fix it with him about the time.

But I must here let a snake out of the grass. They commenced to build in the name of the Lord; every man was called to put a hand to, and rear up this edifice. Men has been appointed as agents to gather means in the city of Nauvoo. Other travelling agents, that have travelled through America, and as far as the name of Mormons is known. That thousands and thousands of money has been gathered to erect the Mormon edifice. But what is done with it? it is made use of to build up a certain company that say, it is in these days right to have as many wives as they can support. And it is a well known fact, that on such fixings, rooms is convenient on the occasion; rooms cost money that is to be got, we find by tithing the Saints their God has said to them to exact one tenth of all the members that has become a law amongst them of the L. D. Saints.

Again by the by they found that there was so much to do to get

21

their righteous branch started that they got of their God a new Revelation, that said, you that have properties, whether much or little, it matters not; let it be consecrated, by laying it down at the Apostles feet, that they may distribute as seemeth them good; as every man has need, behold the day cometh that Zion shall arise, and put on her beautiful garments; let my servants arise in time, as the time cometh that Zion shall become the glory of the whole Earth; let him that has money, lend unto the lord, and he shall be rewarded ten-fold in this world and life everlasting in the world to come; Amen. The above revelation did not quite come it; it took in some few cases, but it was too strong meat they found, and went on the old plan of taking my every tenth, that is and has long been the theme.

The Nauvoo House or Inn is going on about the same principle of the Temple. That was to be done in such a time, and the time run out; but, in short, it is calculated, as is the Temple, to get away every man's money, or property, whatever it does consist of. There is no doubt but what enough has been paid in to build the two buildings, to have well finished both, if it to them had been applied.— Hands on these buildings are hired; others give their work; one-tenth of every man's work is required as tithing. This tithing of work is about all that is laid out on the house, in connection with a few hired hands that say they are not paid for what they do. The Mormons are full of notions, and as I said at the start, I would make a brief sketch of their doings. I again will repeat the same words and say, I have my fears that my writings will not, as the Hoosiers say, go it, as I am aware of the Mormon breast work. But I think I have one advantage of them, as I have been amongst them so much that I find their big guns don't carry any thing but wind, and that not far.

In short, they say to have power to do for those that have long been dead, as they lived in the dark ages, or before the light of Mormonism shined. They say to officiate for them, by being baptized, as they would be if alive, and do it in their name, that it would answer them, either father, mother, husband, wife, brother, sister, or any near friend, could be administered for to save them. That they can come forth at the first Resurrection as fair as the sun at noon-day. The house is a building, as I said, by direct revelation from God. We that are acquainted find many things of note about this edifice that I will notice. The foundation is on a high spot of land, settled on a cellar dug, and in that a foundation laid; in this cellar is their Baptismal fount, of which much is said, where they baptise to raise their dead friends from darkness to light, beneath it is twelve carved oxen of wood, that stand to support it. Again, in this vacant cell is made small rooms or cells, that with the Baptismal fount fills the basement story full; that would make one hundred feet square; and walls, some of them three feet and upwards; that when I have looked at them, and as I did know the intent for which

22

such places was made; I ask for an example on the American shores. It is not to be found. Here is a mystery to solve, that hundreds have spoke of. The first and second stories is for public worship; and the loft for schools when finished. But these cells beneath is to imprison all that, in a word, that does not to them conform; by dark holes through the lower floor into them of stone and lime cement; that no man could give an alarm of his condition, when all is finished, because of the solid work of building materials around him.—Again, this edifice answers for another purpose, it is said to be done to fulfil a Revelation from God; every man is crowded to put in his mite, not only in Nauvoo, but as far as the name of L. D. Saint is known. All as one is over persuaded by sayings, that whatever they have sacrificed will be to them of no account, unless they add unceasing diligence, in both property and labor. The money that has been paid in, and the commodities of every kind, there is no telling the amount, as every cord has been drawn to gather means. Well, what has been done with it? it has not been put to the building of the Temple; it is used to build and repair houses to accomodate certain ones, of which I have often spoke, that say it is right to have as many wives as they can support. The labor of thousands is mostly put on the house, as they are also interested to get that along, as there is many unruly fellows, such as J. C. Bennett, George W. Robison, John F. Olney, O. H. Olney, and many more I might mention. Such as Miss Nancy Rigdon, and Miss. M. Brotherton; that they don't seem to have tools to handle yet, for the sisters they have got another edifice in the name of the Lord, of whivh I hinted of the Nauvoo House, that is a building; any way that they can fix it by begging, borrowing, buying, selling rooms; finally, it don't seem to matter, so as the work can be done, as all is impatiently awaiting for the Nauvoo House or Inn to be done. That is a building built of brick above the basement story, with the basement story is to be raised five story high; that will front about, I think, one hundred and forty feet and proportionable width, to be divided into such rooms as will suit their convenience.

Here I must unfold another mystery. This great Mormon Inn is said to be for the rich of all classes and nations to come to, such as men of pleasure, of taste, &c. For those that have an interest in their eternal salvation; that they can come to Sion and receive such instruction as will tend to forward them in the things of God.

But beneath this shadow of filthy stuff
Is a trap set of much account, that is in the dark.
The building, as is said, is calculated for an inn,
That the noble, rich and wise, may in Nauvoo,
For their money, find a decent resting place.
But over head, and on every side, there is to be
Rooms of all dimensions, and many in number.
To accomodate the Mormon spouses. Yes, this band

23

of the Mormon clan say their secrets to keep,
But they have friends, so have I, to learn their tales,
They say to be wise, but they first must learn
That the tongue is an unruly member if not governed.

I have tracked them in their daily moves,
That I have got in black and white up to this time.
But I to a close my writings draw, and say,
And take an extract from some few letters,
As they are too long to publish entire.

As I have before said, so I say again, that no person, I don't care what their name is or where they live, or, I was going to say, don't live at all, that once had their name on their roll, and have left them under I don't care whatever circumstances they may be in, I left them as I did; in short, I had long wrote of their doings, but had kept it to myself a dead secret, as I knew it would make dissatisfaction. But a sound of it got out. They called me to an account, as they would fetch a fool to the altar, and demanded my writings. I told them I could take care of myself. I well tho't that, with them I was, as the Suckers say, up a stump at once, if they should get hold of all that they did down there in Kirtland and up in Missouri. I guess I have skipped it all over up there amongst the Pukes; you know how they acted as if they was about to rule the roost. I know what they said and did up there away up in the pine country. I know how a real lot of Danites, or new fangled Masons, or the Daughters of Zion, went up there on business. That I guess I know enough about to tell it if best. The Brother Mormons and I have long had a fuss, but I have had to see their doings so much that till now I think they had to call me a clever fellow, as they have been a pecking away on me; from big to little, all that had life to grant, has showed their good will to get me under foot. But you know these 'ere a way down Easterners don't stand much about trifles I guess; so the Mormons and I now will take a round, as I don't think it good to back out. So, you know, I will give them a little out of much that I have written. I was about to write a whole mess as did Dr. Bennett, you know. But I want to make them sick or mad. I want to get my feelings a little roused if I can. As I have got a way down here in Ohio amongst my old friends, I had liked to forgot what I came for, and on the way down I have seen a real lot of Mormon Elders that don't hardly know how to go it, as they look some as they did at the April Conference, when they had rag, shag, and bobtail, and the off-sowerings of all God's creation to make ready for a mission to the East, West, North and South, to bind up the law and seal up the testimony. If your big bugs of Latterday-isms think to light on me now, I will give you a little advice, as you know Yankees don't stand to help a little on such occasions. They are Johnny Taylor, or Woodruffe, or any of them little nubbed fellows—I should, I guess, like a fuss up there with

24

that are kind of a laughing, good natured, spindle shanked Phelps; you know him, that are fellow that left you in Missouri, cause you acted so up there—he aint nobody's fool, I guess so. If you can't get some body to write of me, write yourself, as you say you are inspired of God. I guess that would go it. If you don't like to kick me and cuff me, just curse me as you did Roberts. You know how it made him bed ridden or so; you must spur up. As I aint Dr. Bennett, I don't go in such big company, you know, as he did in his fat living with you. He must have had a hard time in weaning, I spose. The Editor of the Bug, Johnny Taylor, said that Doctor Bennett and I was in company. But I guess the Doctor did not say it, as we never spoke together but once up there. As soon, if you please, that you hear from me, write. If I haint time to write, I will send you one of my little books or two, you know; if they take there in your Mormonism, print a real lot, or if you haint time to do that, take extracts from 'em, you know; they will circulate. I aint praticular. They cost me nothing. I did it myself you see, so I did. Go ahead, as soon as you hear from me, as I am soon on the way up there. Them ere Danites up there I hate; they must keep out of my way, as I dont stand long for such chaps, you know; I don't go around for them so many times as I have done. Let me write of their acts. I don't hint, but tell, what a damnable set they are.

And again what they have done,
I expect you will wonder, at the course I have took,
To skip over so much of importance,
That you know I might have wrote,
But my reasons are many; one is, I was afraid
That because of so big a story, my writing would be overlooked.
Another is, if this in you should produce a reformation,
I have no more to say, but to go ahead and that without delay;
But if you do'nt straighten, or make crooked straight,
I will next time give you your characters in full,
You need not think I am a jokeing always when I laugh,
Though I am not often mad, although I think it no harm in some cases
To act out nature in every sense of the word.
Again many may ask, how I know of the above tales;
In a word I can answer and say, I have been there myself.
And when a boy, I heard my mother say,
Don't ever spoil a story for relation sake;
That is still fresh in my mind, so if I have to suffer,
I do'nt see as I can get round it, if I do'nt tell it of my self,
The Mormons will, so it goes for what it will fetch.

Nauvoo, July 15th 1842.

An extract of a letter written by Israel Barlow: "Brother O. H. Olney—after a long and friendly acquaintance with you and your

25

family, I at this time address you with no ordinary feelings, as I learn that you have for some reasons, left the church of L. D. Saints. The good opinion that I had of you as a brother in the Church, because of your christain-like conduct, I hardly can say, to give you up, so you must know there is no salvation out of the church. Please to give me your present views of things in writing.

Yours as a friend and well wisher,

ISRAEL BARLOW."

Nauvoo, July 8th, 1842.

An extract of a letter, written by Benjamin S. Walker:

"BROTHER OLNEY—I with singular feelings, address myself to you at this time, as I learn that you have left the church of L. D. Saints. That is to me a singular occurrence, as we have long had an intimacy that is hard to break up, I think we can say we have borne the burden in the heat of the day; as we met in Kirtland, Ohio, went to Missouri, and with the L. D. S. moved back to this place. I have in all the hardships that we have had to pass through, found you ready to do on your part. I have considered you a worthy and a good man, and I now ask you to give me your reasons for leaving the church of L. D. Saints.

Yours affectionately.

BENJ. S. WOLBER.

O. H. OLNEY.

June 26th, 1843."

An extract of a letter written by S. STODDARD, HANCOCK CO.:

"Mr. O. H. Olney—After a long and friendly acquaintance with you, I am sorry to hear that you have left the church of L. D. S. You as I must well know, that the spirit of apostacy has been the lot of many that has as you left the church. I have looked on you as a worthy member in the church since our first acquaintance. But of us, one and all stand upon our own merits.

Yours in the bonds of friendship,

S. STODDARD."

June 1st, 1842.

An extract of a letter, written by H. G. Sherwood:

"Mr. O. H. Olney—

"I address myself to you, that you must be aware of your condition, as I hear you are in contact to or against the high council of the church. There is some where a fault, either in you or them. I will say to you at this time, to beware how you manage, as you know the priesthood is not to be trifled with, that I think you first received under my hand. Be not backward to put yourself in a situation to be free with me in conversation. Yours a friend,

H. G. SHERWOOD."

O. H. OLNEY.

26

June 26th, 1842.

An extract of a letter, written by John Parker:

"Mr. Olney—

"I learn by report that you have left the L. D. S. I would say to you be wise for yourself, as the road to Heaven is various, and many must come short of the prize. If there is but one way to get there, I have had a good opinion of you.

Yours a friend,

JOHN PARKER."

The High Council in Session and Presidency to preside, December 15th, 1839.

This is to certify that we give this our worthy brother Oliver Olney, this Letter of Commendation as a Preacher of the Gospel and Member of the L. D. S. We recommend him to all wherever his lot may be, as one of the Seventy's; it being that he is situated far from the Coram to which he belongs.

H. G. SHERWOOD, Clerk.

OLIVER. OLNEY.

An extract of a letter written by Oliver Snow:—

Walnut Grove, June 25, 1842.

Mr. O. H. OLNEY:

Sir: I understand you have left the Church of L. D. S. As I have been acquainted with you since the last of your being a school boy, the high esteem I have had of you previous to your embracing religion, and your daily walk since. I am often asked why you have left the L. D. S. There is somewhere a fault either in you or them. I ask of you an explanation in writing.—Please be particular, and you will much oblige an old friend.

Yours, as ever, a friend,

OLIVER SNOW.

O. H. OLNEY.

Quincy, August 20th, 1842.

To all whom it may concern:

That I have been personally acquainted with Oliver H. Olney for ten or eleven years, and say I consider him a worthy citizen.

JOHN CORIL.

Iowa Territory, Lee Co., Sept.16th, 1842.

This may certify, that we have been personally acquainted with Oliver H. Olney for a number of years, and consider him a worthy man in society.

DAVID MOORE.
CHARLES MOORE.
JOHN PHELPS.

All the above written letters, except the four last, were written to me by the members of the L. D. S. I have like them over one dozen,

27

but I think it not of much use to publish any more, as I am cutting all my writings short of what I had calculated. The above letters tend to establish my writings on two prominent points. The writers, in the most of cases, in writing to me, show that they think if a man is not in the path after the authorities of the Church, his feet are on a sandy foundation. And the other is to establish my character as a citizen. I am amongst my old friends, who, if necessary, would add a catalogue of names to establish myself amongst strangers, but it would take too much time. As the most I have written is a well known truth amongst the Mormons, I expect they will at once coincide with me, and say the half is not yet come to light. It is immaterial whether they say aloud or nothing; as silence in all cases gives consent. I do not contend that there are no honest and well meaning persons amongst the Mormons, but they are deceived by an unprincipled gang of scoundrels whose sole object and aim is to secure their own aggrandizement.

The church of L. D. S., after writing what I have written, I now feel in duty bound to speak more particularly of them at large.—Their Elders go out and say to preach the word. They well know the first things to teach. They have their orders to dwell mostly on the gospel plan, that is devised. For the salvation of man, reason and so forth, on the duty of man to God. They have their orders to look to one another out; that in as much as a sound arises that is like to make a clash in their ranks, they at once draw on the cord of which a poetess speaks, that is at once a veto on whom it touches. They at once have to go home, settle up all old accounts. If they make all with them straight, they can go ahead again, if not on them is a veto to rest until they conform to orders.

A contrast between the Bible and the doings of the Latter Day Saints.

I will admit that it is the mind and council of the moves of the Latter Day Saints as teachers to preach from the Bible, and say that it is true. That it is a record of the word of God; it is the foundation to build on, or the sure assistant for those that hold the priest hood, as they say we have the priest hood. That puts in our hands the keys of the Kingdom; the same that was conferred on the Apostle Peter. That whatever they do is sanctioned by Heaven, they say to be actuated in all their teachings by the spirit of God. It is also understood, that a man must not preach without the spirit. This is with them a principle. That as soon as a man rises to speak, that the spirit of God is subject to them, as they say, the spirit of the prophet is subject to the prophet. They say, to preach by inspiration. I will here remark, as I have often thought as well as often heard said, that the Mormon Elders are the most saucy set of men that is to be scared up. They suppose all they say is infalliable; that they don't pretend to give their opinions on any occasion; whatever they say is not to be waived by a man of any other

28

faith. They, the most ignorant ones of the Mormons, look on all classes of men to be far behind them as teachers, as they say the spirit of God is their guide. Many has said to me, how is it that people is such fools as to join the Mormons. The question is easily answered at once: the Elders go out, some have relations, and many friends, they labor with them with unceasing diligence; they soon begin to get a sympathy of feeling; that some fall in with them, and honest seekers to know and do the will of God. It at the rise of the church, was a theme to dwell on the book of Mormons, and Joseph Smith and his Revelations; but that is not thought to be so profitable to get members to move with them, as it is to dwell more on the Bible, and dwell more on the duty of man, &c., that this order of teaching is mostly now, and has been their mode of teaching.

Again it is a theme with them to say at Nauvoo—all is peace and harmony. We live in a land that flows with milk and honey; it is almost the Garden of Eden; such teaching as we have there, would make you stare, to set under the sound of our brethren of the Presidency. The twelve, and those of our brethren that are advanced in the things of God, have had to suffer by being imprisoned in Mo., tarred and feathered, and finally suffered in perils both by sea and by land. Such teaching is all by the spirit of God they say.—Many falls in with them of all classes of men, some that are honest seekers after truth. Others that have got run down in society and want a home, almost anything will answer. Others fall in, that I had like to have said that have bulk and in the shape of man. If they had features as an ox or a hog, I think they would do to barrel up and send down the river for beef, as they do'nt look to me as if God had much to do with them.

In a round about way I have endeavored to show that the most plausible means are made use of that can be to get people to unite with them, and thus help them to make the city of Nauvoo a Stake of Zion. It has of late been the theme to get all together; by hundreds they are flocking in daily. Thousands after thousands are continually on the wing to establish homes. As I said, all profess to be actuated by the Spirit of God. This spirit, when they are out preaching, teaches them in all manner of good sayings. But when they get their ends answered and get their converts to Nauvoo, their spirit changes its theme of teachings, as, even in the first salutation, the Bible is so mangled that it is of but little account.

They say by the spirit they know the heart of man and the desire of the most high God. That in all cases they can unriddle the doings of the wicked. That no man can take from them their rights. They dote of receiving the Priesthood, and say that with it they receive the gifts of the Gospel, the gift of Wisdom, Faith, Knowledge, Discerning of Spirits, Prophecy, Gift of Tongues, and Interposition.

But their spirits have much business on hand. It hardly makes or

29

leads to a union, only when interest calls, when there is more to do than one can perform.

For me to go into another detail of their doings: it I pass by, but refer to what I have written on the first pages.

They claim and usurp authority in a way that is mysterious to me, many times to see their barefaced moves in and about the city of Nauvoo. No man can know of their doings, and the lenity they take in the name of the Lord. I have often wondered that God should bear with them as he has. But I look back on the scenes of time, of which history speaks, and say that God overrules for good. He towards the children of men is of long forbearance. Yet when the cup of iniquity of men is full, we see that God has power to lay desolate. We look at the children of Israel, because of transgression they were brought into bondage to Pharoah; and when Pharoah and his host was brought to an untimely end, when they was ripened for destruction. We look at the different ages of the world, and see man in the hands of God as clay in the hands of the Potter.

PERSECUTION

Persecution amongst the L. S. is a caution to the persecuted.—They claim as a people, to be infallible, they say to have and to hold the destiny of the Nations of the earth. That on them is conferred the holy Priesthood after the order of the Son of God; that they have all the rights that pertain to the plan of Saalvation; that they stand in an attitude to do as is wisdom in God for them to do. They say as the Ancients spoke, so do we, we are persecuted, so was they. Our lives have been in jeopardy—men and women have suffered death, for Christ's sake; perils have long hung over our heads—at home and abroad.

I would ask how many have had to suffer for unwise sayings and doings? I ask the candid reasoner if there is any society or denomination but what can establish themselves to be of God, let persecution tell the story as is common in this age, where parties get together and contend as is often the case. I know the Mormons have suffered; I at the same time know that they have many times escaped censure when it to them was due. But if others talk to them as they talk to others, it is all persecution, it will go through their ranks without a jog. I think if I could take up a course of reasoning with them of the doings as they actually occurred at Kirtland, Ohio; then go to Mo. and talk over things there. I am of the opinion that the Mormons would say that they did about as they was a mind to, and it was no body's business. I do not suppose the suckers would like to have it said that the Mormons could get the start of them.—But I long since heard of some prophecies uttered, that may touch them by and by on a tender spot. I am aware of feelings on both sides, but if I take the second round, I shall unfold the Mo. doings, as what I did not see I well got the run of sayings, doings &c.

30

THE RISE OF THE MORMONS.

The Mormons commenced their rise to become in notice about 1830. Before that time there was but a handful of them. Since that time they daily have been gaining. They have broke their way through America, England, Ireland, and many of the islands of the sea. By their moves, as they have managed, they have become numerous. They as a people have much to encourage them. They are growing up in an age and country of freedom. They have a military force at their command, that are armed and equipped, at all times, and are ready on all occasions to act when called upon. That is well understood. Most of them are equipped by the State of Illinois; yet it is so well understood that their company are mostly formed and drilled to stand in their own defence, in case of an attack by their neighbors of the adjoining States.

They sometimes in conversation speak of attacking Missouri. But Missouri, until they get something stronger, need not trouble herself, as they seem to grow up by degrees. Of the Mormons I think we have a sample.

We look at the case of Mahomet. How did he arise? Was it by his foreknowledge of events and a very wise head? No: it was by a low, mean, cunning, ambitious desire in him to become great.

And it is a well known fact, that nothing like the name of Religion will sway like it. It speaks of futurity, of living again after death. It is solemn to see the body of a person laid in the silent grave, much more to say to live eternally, saved or unsaved, in happiness or misery. All classes catch at the sound from the wise Man on the throne. To those in heathenish darkness, of all grades of men and sex; that there comes the language of the Poet:

"My all, my all to heaven is gone,
No chance, no chance for to return;
If I mismove my all is gone,
That I am damn'd, I am damn'd,
For worlds to come, to come."

The above is the run of the theme of man in his natural mind of things. That of the same that he plants he will reap his harvest.

It is also an idea at the present time with many that, any thing that has the name of religion is a saving ordinance. It makes no difference of what sex or party. If the name is attached, it is salvation to the soul of man, in every sense of the word it is all in all.

We from history may look at Mahomet's followers trampled under the cars of the juggernaut, men women and children. We look near home and view all the christian societies on their way to Heaven, honest before God. Their aim is salvation, to a never dying soul.—We then look at their teachers, that each denomination adheres to.—We see them men of information, men of talents they say from God. They feel in duty bound to preach for the good of man; thus each teacher has his influence, that he moves as he feels. If his feelings

31

is to do the will of God, that is his theme; if to gain by usurping authority that has its besetments, enough is ready with it to move.

As the mind of man is a looking,
And a constantly of the strain
Aspire for something, if not quite so good.

As we find the "twig is bent so is the tree inclined," but the sap to support, arises from the roots in all cases.

Thus it is the case, the Bible is called a very good book, I believe it is. But what do we discover, we find all the teachers agree in one point, that is, the Bible is true; but they do not see its contents alike. Some says, free salvation for all; others say, on conditions.

Rev. Miller, in the old country east, says and proves it from Scripture, that the present 1843, this world is coming to an end. We understand thousands are flocking to his standard, because of their faith in his reasoning. But if Rev. Miller is right I have no more to say; I have heard him lecture, I think him honest in his belief; yet I think if he lives forty-three round, he will see the sun, moon and stars performing their daily moves, and the earth make its obeisance, once in twenty-four hours, to the sun.

Again, the Mormons say, to live long on the earth, and prove it, as do others, from the Bible, that they have but just began to live. They have their peculiarities, as do others; they say they have just began to live. They promise themselves much good; that they will yet live many years, and seem as much engaged as does Rev. Miller; but I don't vouch for their honesty. That a man may take to himself wives to his liking, and say there is no lack of Scripture to prove the fact that a woman was made for man, not man for the woman. That in the round, we find them as the Mormons would say, property as brutes of the field, that is the run of their pamphlet that goes in Jacobs name, to introduce poligamy in this enlightened age. But what did I say, the buds take nourishment from the roots. That no man will doubt we see the principle carried out amongst the Mormons. We look at them but a few years ago, there was but a handful of them; but as they say, have now increased to about 150,000 in all parts, or proselyteing. Let them once gather as is their theme in a thin settled country as Ill. How soon would they root out of office by moveing as they do with one or the other parties, thus they slip along as they please as they say by proxy to accomplish much, and all receive their nourishment from the roots, or in other words their instruction how to proceed, thus by the most perfect union they move ahead in the name of the Lord, saying our salvation depends on our teachers, until an institution is reared, that they can force as they please in measures.

Before I close I speak to all both far and near,
That has a name of L. S., of the Female sex,
That every day they stay away counts one,
That they will see when my book they peruse.

32

It is not the old that has need to hasten in,
Whether married or unmarried its all the same;
As when they get there, their husbands go a preaching,
The sisters then soon have a chance
To commence on the degrees of Masonry.
Of Masonry I would not wish to speak,
As it is much extolled amongst the L. S.
But its charms to me are all in the dark,

As I have not took one degree;
Yet I have friends that have learnt the theme
Of those Masons in the city of Nauvoo.
As for my name it's very plain
As I have wrote it over and over again,
But of late I have replaced the letter H.,
That I am known by the name of

OLIVER H. OLNEY.
Hancock County, Illinois, April 1, 1843.

APPENDIX 2

SPIRITUAL WIFERY OF NAUVOO
EXPOSED.

-ALSO-

A TRUE ACCOUNT OF TRANSACTIONS IN AND ABOUT NAUVOO.

BY O. OLNEY,
ELDER OF THE CHURCH OF JESUS CHRIST.

ST. LOUIS :
PRINTED FOR THE AUTHOR.
1845

BRETHREN AND SISTERS,

Of the Church of Jesus Christ of Latter Day Saints;

To you and all other lovers of honesty, peace, truth and righteousness I recommend the perusal of the following pages, in order that you may be truly informed of the corruption and iniquity of the people of Nauvoo, and also the present movements and future designs of the leaders of that community.

Having lately visited Nauvoo and spent a few days in the city, and being an Elder in the church, I have had a good opportunity to become acquainted with the secret designs and measures of the twelve and their adherents, and can vouch for the truth of the information herein given.

Were it not that I have heretofore upheld by my voice and influence the people of that place, and especially their leaders, I should consider my testimony against them at the present uncalled for, but in view of the foregoing fact, I publish to the world the few following items of truth that all who may choose to gain information, may be truly informed upon this (to many,) very important subject, and if it shall be the means of saving a few souls from the wily and practised destroyers of innocence, the writer will have gained his point.

THE AUTHOR.

SPIRITUAL WIFERY, &C.

BRETHREN AND SISTERS: —

Being an Elder in the Church of Jesus Christ of Latter Day Saints, it is therefore my Priesthood and calling, to teach the pure principles of truth and righteousness to all ranks and conditions of the human family, and also to warn them against the multitude of errors and false doctrines that are abroad in the land, and with this view of things before me I enter with no very pleasant feelings upon the duty which now seems to devolve upon me.

It is well known to most of you at least, (who are members of the church) that upon the death of our beloved Prophet and patriarch Joseph and Hyram Smith, Sidney Rigdon, then resident at Pittsburgh, Pa., returned to Nauvoo and was excommunicated from the church, and since that time the church has been under the sole guidance and management of the Twelve.

How far their management and practice has been in accordance with the principles of Peace, Virtue and Truth, I shall leave the candid and mind unbiassed to judge after becoming acquainted with the principles taught and practised by them at the present time.

If you have not heretofore been informed of the fact, I will now inform you that the orders of the twelve are to every member of the church throughout the United States, who can, to make ready to leave Nauvoo as soon as grass grows sufficient to sustain teams on the way and go to California, in order that they may be free from the persecutions of the Gentiles, and also to fulfil the words of The Prophet, where he warns the people to "hide themselves in their chambers as it were, for a little moment until the indignation be overpast." (Isa. 26-20.) Thus claiming the projected move of themselves and followers into the western wilderness to be the fulfilment of the words of the Prophet.

Again, in order to stir up the lukewarm and "to confirm the weak hands and strengthen the feeble knees," it has been proclaimed on the stand in the Temple, by Orson Hyde, one of the twelve, that this very anticipated emigration of the church will fulfill the saying of John the Revelator: 12th chapter.

"And there appeared a great wonder in heaven—a woman clothed with the sun and the moon under her feet, and upon her head a crown of twelve stars, (5th verse). And she brought forth a manchild, who was to rule all nations with a rod of iron, and her child was caught unto God and to his throne, (6th verse). And the woman fled into the wilderness where she hath a place prepared of God, that they should feed her there a thousand two hundred and three-score days. Mr. Hyde said, "This church is the woman, Brethren and Sisters, and Joseph is the man child, and be has been caught up, and we have the testimony of Rigdon, that he is in heaven, for he says he has seen him sitting at the right hand of the Majesty on High. Thus you see brethren and sisters, that this scripture is soon to have its actual fulfilment, and the church will be nourished in the wilderness for a time, times, and a half which will be about—but I will leave the time for your own consideration."

Thus spake the Great Apostle Orson, upon the application of that Scripture which forms the first necessary prerequisite to the establishing of the church in 1830, viz: (the fact that it must have been in the wilderness or it could not have come out of it,) thereby fulfilling Rev. 14-6. "And I saw another angel fly in the midst of heaven, having the everlasting gospel to preach to them that dwell on the earth, &c."

Now those of my readers who are at all acquainted with the pure principles of Mormonism as taught by the Elders heretofore, most assuredly know, that from our martyred Brothers Joseph and Hyrum down to the weakest Elder who has ever spoken or written upon the subject, we have been taught that the woman represents the church with its officers at its head, and the manchild representing the authority of said church was taken from their midst, at which time the church went into the wilderness or in other words, descended into popery, (570 after Christ,) since which time it has remained in the wilderness unto the consummation of the 1260 days (or years,) which brings us to the year 1830, the time of the restoration of the priesthood and establishing of the church with its attendant blessings, thus fulfilling Rev. 14-6 concerning the mission of the angel and forming a bulwark and foundation which fifteen years of the most powerful opposition has not be enable to overthrow.

As may well be supposed I was much astonished at such an application of Scripture as was given by Mr. Hyde, and supposed it was so applied to cheer up some, if any there were, who might hesitate about joining the general movement.

I therefore spoke to some few with whom I was acquainted, upon the subject, and was still more astonished to hear those whom I had supposed to be capable of exercising an opinion of their own declare they had never heard it applied

[4]

otherwise and that it was perfectly plain, that it would be fulfilled when the church emigrated and not before.

I endeavored to reason with them and show them that, according to the Scripture, the woman brought forth the marrchild, but if it be applied to the church emigration and to Joseph, it will be assuming that the manchild brought forth the woman, for Joseph brought forth and established the church in the year of our Lord, 1830.

Such plain reasoning as this had no effect and bore no weight with them. Thus I discovered that, any thing spoken by the twelve was swallowed down without any regard to its truth or falsehood.

I remarked that the Elders who had preached heretofore had preached by the spirit of God, and I believed they had made a right application of said Scripture, and I did not believe that God was so much of a lawyer as to make a portion sacred writ apply one way to-day and another way to-morrow.

From an old lady present who had been ordained to the priesthood under the hand of Brigham Young and who had been practicing the duties of an Elder, viz: the laying on of hands, I received the following answer:

"Brother Olney, Br. Brigham says "*Learn to mind your own business, to obey counsel and to hold your tongues*, and you will all get along well enough.

On the following morning, I met Mr. Hyde in the street and asked him if the saints were to receive his explanation of the said scripture as correct, or whether he so explained for the purpose of encouraging the fainthearted.

With a foppish turn of the body, a nod of the head accompanied by a wave of the hand, he replied, "That is as I understood it, good morning Brother Olney," and passed along, leaving me to wonder at his deceit which was but too apparent.

Let us now, for a moment, see whether God requires us to follow the teachings of such men and thus be led into the wilderness. They say to the people that it is the will of God for all his saints to flee into the wilderness, and to this end there has been Elders sent to almost every State in the Union to proclaim to the saints that if they will obey the counsel of the twelve and go into to the western wilds they will there establish a government and kingdom in which they can enjoy, unmolested, that liberty of conscience and freedom of speech which they have in vain sought for at the hands of the rulers of this republic and that God will sustain them and protect them from their enemies until they are secure from them, and then the wicked will destroy the wicked and thus leave the broad lands of the continent of America to them and their posterity, at which time they will inherit thrones, dominions, principalities and powers which will continue through the countless ages of eternity.

See last Edition Book Cov., page 400; given Jan. 19th, 1841.

"I will show unto my servant Joseph, all things pertaining to this house (the Temple) and the Priesthood thereof and the place whereon it shall be built, and ye shall build it on the place where you have contemplated building it, for that is the spot which I have chosen for you to build it. If ye labor with all your mights I will consecrate that spot, that it shall be made holy, and if my people will hearken unto my voice and unto the voice of my servants whom I have appointed to lead my people, behold, verily, I say unto you, they shall not be moved out of their place."

* * * * * * *

And it shall come to pass that if you build a house unto my name and do not do the things that I say, I will not perform the oath which I make unto you, neither fulfil the promises which ye expect at my hands saith the Lord, for instead of blessings, ye, by your own works bring cursings, wrath, indignation and judgments upon your own heads by your follies and by all your abominations which you practice before me saith the Lord." Now behold ye and see, my friends who believe the revelations which have come forth by our Prophet Joseph "that if the saints would hearken unto the voice of God they should not be moved out of their place."

And again, even if the house should be built, if they have not observed to keep the commandments of the Lord, they should not receive their expected blessings and endowments but should bring curses, wrath, indignation and judgments upon their own heads. Now let the twelve take which horn they please and see if they can make such removal coincide with the revelations of God, in which they profess to believe.

Their removal will be proof ample that they are in transgression, if not, "they shall not be moved out of their place." And if they endeavor to remain, they must be driven by the people of Illinois (so says P. P. Pratt) which will go conclusively to show that they have not kept the commandments, and hearkened to the counsel of the Lord; see Book Cov., page 385, given 1834, 2nd verse "But verily, I say unto you, that I have decreed a decree which my people shall realize inasmuch as they hearken from this very hour unto the counsel which I, the Lord their God, shall give unto them. Behold, they shall, for I have decreed it begin to prevail against mine enemies from this very hour, and by hearkening, to observe all the words which I, the Lord their God shall speak unto them, they shall never cease to prevail until the kingdoms of the world are subdued under my feet and the earth is given to the Saints to possess it for ever and ever. But inasmuch as they keep not my commandments and hearken not to observe all my words, the kingdoms of the world shall prevail against them, for they were set to be a light unto the world and to be the saviors of men, and inasmuch as they are not the saviors of men, they are as salt that has lost its savor, and is, thenceforth, good for nothing but to be cast out and trodden under foot of man." Thus you see that if they are moved out of their place, it is in consequence of their transgression, and if they remain and are prevailed against, it is a proof of transgression, and the twelve say they must be driven unless they leave of their own will. But remember God decreed that if they hearkened to his counsel and obeyed his precepts they shall not be prevailed against but should prevail against all the kingdoms of the world. Thus I have given in short, abundant evidence to show that the saints are not required to go into the wilderness but may remain where they choose at present, and with an eye single to the glory of God, wait until you can see the disorganized and headless body of the church re-organized and established by having its proper authority and priesthood at its head: See Book of Cov., page 129, 3d verse.

"Therefore, thus saith the Lord, unto you with whom the priesthood hath continued through the lineage of your fathers, for ye are lawful heirs according the flesh and have been hid from the world with Christ in God, therefore, your life and the priesthood hath remained and must needs remain *through you and your lineage* until the restoration of all things spoken by the mouths of all the holy prophets since the world began." Now inasmuch as it is plain that the church as well as the leaders, are in transgression. We must come to the conclusion that the head and body both being corrupt, the purity and chastity of the whole organization has fled to parts unknown. Therefore, let us, as servants of God, be watchful and prayerful—watchful that we be not caught in the snares of the evil one, and prayerful that the Lord will speedily call to the work one of *that linage* with which the priesthood *must needs remain* that then may be fulfilled, the words found on page 387, Book Cov: "Behold, I say unto you, the redemption of Zion must needs come by power, therefore, *I will raise up unto my people a man* who shall lead them *like as* (not where) Moses led the children of Israel, for ye are the children of Israel and of the seed of Abraham." This was given in the year 1834 before which time the Prophet Joseph was raised up, yet here is a positive declaration to have its fulfilment in the future from that time, thereby showing that another prophet must be raised up, and according to page 129 which I have heretofore quoted, he must be of that lineage with whom the priesthood has remained, and must still remain—Therefore Brethren and Sisters, let us in view of this important subject; follow no man or set of men, until we can see who will next rise up at the call of God, and show forth a true authority and a pure priesthood. I freely acknowledge that the twelve should have stood in their office and held the keys of the priesthood, and guided the affairs of the church, (unless they were found in transgression,) in connection with the other authorities of the church, until God should raise up a head to the quorum of first Presidency, or in other words until such times as one of that lineage should stand up to claim and exercise the authority of his priesthood. But, the twelve having gone into measures not compatible with the pure principles of righteousness have fallen from high and exalted station to which God has raised them to a level with the brute beast that yields every motion to the promptings of that passion, which at the time may chance to have the preeminence.

Perhaps some of you my readers may think this to be the overflowings of a heart full of prejudice, but I assure you I visited Nauvoo with the intention and expectation of making it my winter's residence, and for the purpose of receiving blessings and endowments in the Temple. Yes, I expected to realize the truth of what I had read in the "Times and Seasons," and "Nauvoo Neighbor," and had on my way to that place used my utmost ability to free the twelve from what I considered foul calumy and vile aspersions against their character, but judge my surprise and disappointment when I came to see with my own eyes, and hear with my own ears, I found Nauvoo a sink of iniquity inhabited by a people whose leaders are whoremongers instead of those who I fondly thought were among the first to contemn vice and foster the germs of virtue and truth, that thereby the saints might be brought into the bonds of perfectness. Our prophet Joseph said to the people that he did not want any to leave Nauvoo till the Temple was finished, and then after receiving their endowments they might scatter abroad upon the face of the land and preach the Gospel, raise up the branches, establish stakes and build Temples on all the land of Zion, which he said was the continent of America knowing as he did that if they kept the commandments of God, they should never cease to prevail. Thus the important question is, will the people of Nauvoo prevail or are they in transgression in consequence of which they are to be moved out of their place.

Methinks every honest lover of truth must agree with me that the church is now guided by such men as are not led by the spirit of the living God; but are speedily forsaking every principle of truth and honesty, and are now living on the ill-gotten spoils of their corrupted authority, while thousands of the honest hearted scattered abroad in the world are (by paying tithing) supporting them in their luxury and extravagance. Although as I have written that I found Nauvoo a sink of iniquity, I do not mean to be understood that all are so practising upon their own judgment, but hundreds are so bound up in the belief that the twelve are pure, paying no regard to the reasonableness of their requirements that it is often said, "If we obey counsel and commit sin in so doing it will not lie at our doors but will be answered upon the heads of the twelve for so teaching us." This is the confidence which that people have in the twelve, to the exclusion of all honor, truth, justice, peace, mercy and righteousness.

The building of the Nauvoo House is wholly abandoned, its bare walls and large piles of brick near by exposed to the weather, presenting a striking contrast to the view which would be presented if the measures of the martyred Prophet were to he carried out as he designed. A desperate effort is being made to finish the Temple, although hundreds yea thousands of dollars of the tithing is appropriated to the subsistence of the twelve, the bishops and their prostitutes, thereby requiring an extra amount of tithing to what would be necessary for the use to which it should be applied. In view of such a state of things, my heart bleeds and my feelings burst forth in sorrow to think of the many who must be as I am sadly disappointed, when they learn that they are led by those who are utterly destitute of every principle that tends to exalt a man in the scale of being, or make him noble in the eyes of his Creator, in consequence of which, our mites which have been joyfully cast in for the building of the House of the Lord, are applied to the subsistence and aggrandizement of themselves and their prostitutes; and the honest hearted left no relief or consolation but to mourn over the depravity of fallen man, and strive to

[6]

shun the vortex of ruin into which others are daily plunging. And such are the men influenced by such passions, who have only to speak the word, and no crime is too horrible, no act however mean and degrading, too low for their police, (as they are called,) to perform in order to carry out the designs of their superiors.

Having given a few testimonies from the Book of Covenants, and also from my own personal observation. I shall leave this part of the subject matter of my little work, trusting that the honest in heart will treasure up the truth, which will enable themd to judge between good and evil, that they may practice the good all the day long that when the night *cometh they may be called upon to enter into the joys of their Lord.*

Since writing the foregoing I have perused a pamphlet written by Wm. Smith, Brother of the Prophet, and formerly one of the twelve, and patriarch in which be has (as far its my knowledge extends) set forth plainly and clearly the corruptions of Nauvoo and its leaders, and I can recommend the perusal of it to all honest hearted saints to whom it may come, by which it will be seen that he renounces all their secret designs and unhallowed measures, and still stands forth as a herald of the pure Gospel of Cbrist.

[*From the Times & Seasons.*)]
TUNE -- INDIAN STUDENT'S LAMENT.

Oh give me back my Prophet dear,
And Patriarch, O give them back;
The Saints of latter days to cheer
And lead them in the gospel track.
But ah! they're gone from my embrace,
From earthly scenes their spirits fled;
Those two, the best of Adam's race,
Now lie entombed among the dead.

Ye men of wisdom tell me why,
When guilt nor crime in them were found,
Why now their blood doth loudly cry,
From prison walls, and Carthage ground
Your tongues are mute, but pray attend,
The secret I will now relate,
Why those whom God to earth did lend,
Have met the suffering martyr's fate.

It is because they strove to gain,
  Beyond the grave a heaven of bliss;
Because they made the gospel plain,
  And led the Saints in righteousness.
It is because God called them forth,
  And led them by his own right hand
Christ's coming to proclaim on earth,
  And gather Israel to their land.

It is because the priests of Baal
  Were desperate their craft to save;
And when they saw it doomed to fail,
  They sent the Prophets to the grave.
Like scenes the ancient Prophets saw,
  Like these, the ancient Prophets fell;
And till the resurrection dawn,
  Prophet and Patriarch—Fare well.

A brief outline of the transactions in and about Nauvoo may be found in the remainder of this work, As I before stated I visited Nauvoo with the strongest assurance that I should find it a place of piety and virtue, but I found it a place where profane language is in common use with all classes, yea I have heard God's name profaned in the presence and hearing of the twelve, and instead of reprimanding the swearer one of them excused the matter to me by saying that "the person used to be an infidel, but is a *first rate fellow now.*"

The twelve often meet in council, to give advice to any who may choose to ask it, and also to give orders to those in authority under them; and one such occasion I have witnessed where three six shooters (revolving Pistols) were laid on the centre table and one fifteen shooter (rifle) stood in the corner to protect the persons of the twelve, although an armed guard are posted every night around the city and every street guarded by police, armed with (some of them) large heavy canes with an iron or steel point, also pistols and bowie knives, and others around the houses of the twelve thus shielding them from any intrusion in the night time, and in the day time they are (unless they are secreted for fear of being arrested for some of their misdemeanors) walking in the streets in their Broadcloths while their followers are toiling to support them in their luxury and extravagance.

As it respects the late troubles in the county I am prepared to say in truth as follows:

The twelve by their unbounded influence over their subjects, and by teaching that the people round about them are gentiles and that the saints are to "suck the milk of the gentiles," have created such a state of feeling in the breasts of their followers that they think it is no sin for them to "suck a little," just now, and in fact I have heard prominent men such as High Priests and

Presiding Officers say that if a gentile comes in their way the best way to do is to put him "out of the way," as quick as possible, Such sentiments thrown out by the people at Nauvoo have not failed to create a response on the part of the settlers, and the feeling has been fanned into a flame that will ere spring (I opine) burn too hot for mormons. Yes, even to their expulsion from the state, and for this reason.

A stipulation has been mutually agreed to by both mormons and anties, that hostile operations and maneuvers should cease on both sides, and also that the mormons should leave Nauvoo as soon as grass grows sufficient for teams to subsist upon.

Yet still the mormons have been visited by writs to bring some offenders (of which class there are many) to justice; which serves as a pretext for the mormons to send out armed forces numbering from 50 up to 200, who on horseback scour the prairie between Nauvoo and Carthage (as they say) in search of "Prairie Chickens," and latterly as if this was not enough; a body of these men have been to Carthage, and entirely broken up the court which was in session at that place, (so I heard one of the men engaged in the transaction declare,) so that none of the brethren could be tried at that court if arrested, but probably there will be none arrested, for Brigham says to the people to "give them what is in their guns first and then use them to the best advantage before they submit to an arrest."

The judge of the court in company with some of the lawyers of the county, visited Nauvoo to inquire the reason of the breaking up of the court in such a manner, but received nothing satisfactory, except a tirade from John Taylor (one of the twelve,) which, he the judge carried away rankling and festering in his own bosom.

Another evidence of their purity and holiness, may be gathered from the fact that at the houses of some of the twelve, I have seen from three

[7]

to five young females, whose prolific appearance indicates a great increase of posterity in the temporal kingdom, to say nothing of a great number of married women who are sealed to different ones in high standing in the church, and (as I have been taught from their own mouths,) believe it to be their privilege before God to raise up as many children here in the flesh as they can, that they may have a greater kingdom to rule over in eternity; and on being asked how many women it is one's privilege to beget children with, the answer was, "As many as he can maintain." thus making it an object among themselves, (except the twelve, the bishops, the Temple committee and some other privileged characters,) who help themselves out of Temple funds; to enter largely into speculations engagements, that thereby upon their income they may support (if they have no husbands to support them) those unhallowed and polluted vestiges of humanity, with whom they practise such abominations under the garb of righteousness; as must make the heavens weep, and the earth mourn, to witness to the fallen and degraded state of those who are to be "a light unto the world and also the saviors of men." And whose privilege it was to bring in everlasting righteousness, to make the earth bloom as Eden and to gather Israel from the dispersions, preparatory to the coming of the Messiah and establishing of the celestial kingdom of God, when the earth and the fulness thereof shall be given into the hands of the saints of the most High.

Another important item in the present teachings of the twelve, is that "At the time of receiving their washings and anointings of their endowments, all marriages will be declared void, and every person have the privilege of choosing for him or herself, by a mutual agreement, that is, if two choose to remain together it is their privilege to do so, but neither one can retain the other, if he or she chooses to depart and live with another. Oh shame! where is thy blush? Furthermore, it is said by the redoubtable Brigham, that "when the church once gets away from Nauvoo, if any find any fault with the twelve, their heads shall come off, and none shall ever return to tell their tales!"

Another of his sayings is, "It is better that an innocent man should suffer death, than that a crime should be proven against any one of the twelve, even if he were guilty."

Another is, "The Bible is no more to the people of this generation than a last year's almanac, for I am all the bible needful for the people now, if they will obey my counsel."

Another testimony of the purity of that people is the fact that a High Priest of that place told me that he had witnessed the deaths of five mobocrats at the hands of Mormons, on the prairie, and also that the catfish in the Mississippi had scraped the bones of some who had better have kept away from Nauvoo.

The "anointing and washing" as it is jocosely called, is practised frequently upon those offenders who are not judged worthy of death, which is covering them from head to foot with filth obtained from the vault of some necessary in the city, and then casting them into the river.

Alas! for the purity of such a people, when their renowned head is upholding them in, and urging them on to deeds of shame and degradation, no where equalled in the annals of history, but which must stand forth in bold relief, as a warning to any who may hereafter be called to stand in as high and holy a calling as were these men who have now sacrificed every honest and virtuous principle at the shrine of female corruption, and justly merited a portion with those who are left without the city, such as (see Rev. 22:16) "Dogs and sorcerers, and whoremongers, and murderers, and idolaters, and whosoever loveth and maketh a lie."

Another heart-rending fact in the present history of Nauvoo is that hundreds of honest hearted females are there, who have no means with which to get away, and scarce any means of subsistence there, except at the expense of virtue, and who are continually subject to the importunities of those fiends in human shape who, after having gratified their passion for lust, will, straightway, upon the public stand, declare before God and the Angels, that no system of spiritual wifery is practised or tolerated by them, when perhaps some of their victims are at the very time upon their knees in secret beseeching God to forgive them for yielding in an unguarded moment to their seducers, and to open a way for their escape from the folds of their destroyers, that, perchance, by a life of morality, virtue and piety, they may atone for the weakness of a moment, and at last gain an inheritance with the saints of God. Think not, my readers, that this is a fancy piece, or the suggestions of an over excited imagination, for it is but a few out of thousands of the testimonies that might be brought to show that virtue and truth have fled from their midst, and vice, in almost every form, has stalked forth, and holds, unchecked by any pure principle, the sway over almost the entire community, while their publications—"Times and Seasons" and "Neighbor"—would fain make the people at a distance believe that Nauvoo is pure as was Eden at first, and that the people are the innocent but persecuted people which they once were. I blush for the depravity of my fellow-man, and were it not for some hopes for the future, I should be disposed to loathe the society of human intelligences, and in the deep recesses of the forest learn that man was exalted only that he might be abased, and virtue nourished only for a time that vice might the more strikingly exhibit the contrast, and cast mankind to a depth from which they might never arise, but to witness their own depravity, and weep over the last sad remains of a miserable existence.

But I yet hope for the future, and pray God that he will soon reorganize his kingdom, and preserve all the honest in heart from the hand of the spoiler until everlasting righteousness is brought in, and his saints inherit the kingdom prepared for them from before the foundation of the world, even so, Amen.

O. OLNEY.

[8]

Copy of a letter received from Br. WM. SMITH, dated,

St. Louis, Nov. 4th, 1845.

ELDER OLNEY:

Dear Brother,—I understand you have arrived in this city from Nauvoo, on this steamer Boreas, and as many of the saints are leaving that place, the cause is plainly evident to every honest and discerning mind, whether their stay has been long or short there, that such is the declining state of morality, and such the departure from the old and pure principles of religion, as laid down in our books and as taught by my brothers, Joseph and Hyram, that hundreds must be inevitably ruined by the damnable heresies that have crept into the church, whereby many are giving heed to seducing spirits and doctrines of devils, speaking lies in hypocrisy, &c., unless they are redeemed by a speedy and bold exertion on the part of the honest and uncorrupted Elders of Israel.

As I understand you are about to publish your sentiments, for the, purpose of exposing their works of darkness, it is to be hoped that your praiseworthy and laudable undertaking of exposing these wolves in sheep's clothing, their secret abominations, their plans of seduction, crime, cruelty, false claims, unhallowed pretensions and base subterfuges, may be blessed to the saving of souls from ruin. It is my counsel and advice that all the saints remain where they are, and not remove to Nauvoo. Let the Elders continue preaching the gospel in its original purity, and follow no spurious twelve. Let the saints continue to hold meetings, preach and pray, do good, &c., until a general conference can be held, and all things regulated according to the pattern given by the revelations of God, and if you please you may give this, entire, a place in your pamphlet for the benefit and instruction of the saints. Wishing them and all mankind, in company with yourself, salvation through obedience to the requirements of the gospel of our Lord and Saviour, Jesus Christ,

Your friend and brother,

In the new and everlasting covenant.

WM. SMITH.

Patriarch of the Church.

APPENDIX 3

OLNEY'S LIST OF PROPOSED CHURCH LEADERS

Oliver Olney believed that the existing organization of the Church would collapse. In preparation for that outcome he stated on November 27, 1842, that "men of importance must be called that will move in the Order of God. Names are now to be mentioned of some few that a work may commence when the present Order goes down." Olney then listed names of men to be called as "High Councilers" and "the twelve traverlin Council." The names of those men are given below in the order Olney numbered and listed them, along with information about each person.

High Council

No number 1 is given by Olney

2. Oliver Snow – Oliver Snow III was born September 18, 1775 at Beckett, Massachusetts. He married Rosetta Leonora Pettibone on May 6, 1800. They were the parents of seven children, among them Eliza R. Snow and future president of the LDS Church, Lorenzo Snow. Oliver was a member of the Nauvoo 1st Ward. Black (1989), 40:608-610. Oliver Snow, himself, was struggling with his feelings about Mormonism in 1842. "John C. Bennett, a counselor to Joseph Smith and mayor of the city, lost his faith and began delivering a series of anti-Mormon lectures. He also published a history of Mormonism that purported to be an expose of its secret practices. Oliver Snow, who was inclined to be critical of people in authority, decided to leave. He bought a home in Walnut Grove, Knox County, Illinois, some seventy-five miles east of Nauvoo, and moved his family there. Rosetta did not want to go, but eventually she acquiesced and went with him." Leonard J. Arrington and Susan Arrington Madsen, *Mothers of the Prophets*, Revised Edition (Salt Lake City: Bookcraft, 2001), 85. Oliver Snow died at Walnut Grove, Illinois on October 17, 1845.

3. Truman – Truman is the only name given. There are two other men on the list with only one name listed: Robberson and Childs. Both are either last names or family names. If Truman is a last name, the only Truman in Black's *Membership* is Jacob Mica Truman, who wasn't baptized until 1845. The Truman on Olney's list is probably a given name. Among the possibilities of Church members with the given name of Truman who can be placed in the Nauvoo area in the 1840s are (1) Truman O. Angell, architect of the Salt Lake Temple. Black, 2:462–66; (2) Truman Barlow, policeman in Nauvoo

and member of the Nauvoo 3rd Ward. Black, 3:602; (3) Truman Brace, referred to as Father Brace. He was a member of the Nauvoo 3rd Ward. Black, 6:442–43; (4) Truman Gilbert, received his endowment in the Nauvoo Temple. Black, 18:380–81; (5) Truman Richards, a Seventy endowed in the Nauvoo Temple in 1846. Black, 36:693; (6) Truman Leonard, Jr., who was married in Nauvoo in 1846. Black, 27:983–87.

4. David Deval as scribe – David DeVol lived in Nauvoo and was a member of the Nauvoo 4th Ward. Black, 13:925.

5. Daniel Spencer – Daniel Spencer, Jr. was born at West Stockbridge, Massachusetts, on July 20, 1794. He was baptized in 1838 (or possibly 1840). He received in patriarchal blessing at Nauvoo from Hyrum Smith in 1843. He is mentioned among the Nauvoo List of Members. In August 1844, Spencer was appointed to fill the remainder of Joseph Smith's term as mayor of Nauvoo. He made the trek west with the Mormon pioneers in 1847 as a captain of a company. Spencer served as president of the Salt Lake Stake. Black, 40:853–62.

6. Hiram Spencer – Hiram Spencer was born at West Stockbridge, Massachusetts, on November 30, 1798. He is the younger brother of Daniel Spencer Jr. Hiram received his patriarchal blessing in Nauvoo from Hyrum Smith. He was endowed and sealed in the Nauvoo Temple. Hiram crossed the plains in 1847 in the company led by Daniel Spencer. Black, 40: 878–81.

7. Robberson – This would likely be William Roberson, whose name is found in Black's *Membership.* He was born at Charleston, New York, on July 6, 1802, and died and was buried in Winter Quarters in 1846. Black, 37:42.

8. Sydney Rigdon – Sidney Rigdon was born February 19, 1793, at St. Clair Township, Pennsylvania. Rigdon became a popular Baptist preacher in Pittsburg, Pennsylvania. He later moved to Ohio, where he left the Baptist Church and joined the Disciples of Christ, also known as Campbellites. Sidney was introduced to Mormonism in late 1830 by an earlier associate, Parley P. Pratt. Rigdon became a key figure in early Mormonism as a counselor to Joseph Smith in the presidency of the Mormon Church. Rigdon was admired by church members as a skilled orator. He suffered persecution for his beliefs in Ohio and Missouri. He was involved in the founding of Nauvoo, where he was elected as a member of the Nauvoo City Council and appointed postmaster. His poor health limited his participation in Church and city leadership while in Nauvoo. In early 1844 when Joseph Smith became a United States presidential candidate, Rigdon was nominated as his

running mate. Persecution against Mormons increased in Illinois and Rigdon moved back to Pittsburg. When he heard the news that Joseph Smith had been killed, Rigdon traveled to Nauvoo offered his leadership as a "Guardian of the Church." His claims were considered, but ultimately the Twelve Apostles under the direction of Brigham Young were sustained as Church leaders. Rigdon attempted to establish a rival leadership to the Twelve and was excommunicated in September 1844. A number of disciples followed Rigdon back to Pennsylvania, where he founded the short-lived Church of Christ. In 1863 Rigdon organized the Church of Jesus Christ of the Children of Zion, which continued into the 1880s. Sidney Rigdon died on July 14, 1876, in Friendship, New York. Arnold K. Garr, Donald Q. Cannon, and Richard O. Cowan, eds., *Encyclopedia of Latter-day Saint History*, 1030–33.

9. Childs – Childs is the only name Olney recorded for this person. Possible individuals that Olney may have meant include (1) Nathaniel Childs, born June 16, 1791, in New Hampshire. Nathaniel was a member of Zion's Camp. He later lived in Nauvoo, Illinois, where he received his patriarchal blessing from Hyrum Smith. Nathaniel received his endowment in the Nauvoo Temple on January 29, 1846. Black, *Membership*, 9:645–46. (2) William Childs, born July 6, 1819, at Kidderminster, England. William joined the Mormons and was baptized in 1832 and was later ordained a Seventy. He received his endowment in the Nauvoo Temple of February 3, 1846. Black, 9:652–54.

Twelve Traveling Council

1. Orson Spencer – Orson Spencer, younger brother of Daniel and Hiram Spencer, was born March 14, 1802, at West Stockbridge, Massachusetts. He was baptized a Mormon in 1841 and received his endowment in the Nauvoo Temple on December 11, 1845. Daniel was a member of the Nauvoo 2nd Ward. He was elected mayor of Nauvoo in 1845. He traveled west across the plains to Utah in 1849 and later served as a missionary in Great Britain, Prussia, and the United States. Black, 40:919–24.

2. Orson Pratt – Orson Pratt was born at Hartford, New York, on September 19, 1811. He was introduced to Mormonism by his brother, Parley P. Pratt, who baptized Orson on his nineteenth birthday. Orson participated in Zion's Camp in 1834. In February 1835, he was ordained as one of Mormonism's original Twelve Apostles. Pratt served a mission in Great Britain from 1839 to 1841. Returning from Great Britain, Orson was confronted with rumors that his wife, Sarah, had been the victim of an attempted seduction by Joseph Smith and that she had committed adultery with John C. Bennett. At the same time that Pratt was dealing with sorting out the truth from rumor, he

appears to have also been introduced to the doctrine of plural marriage. The *Sangamo Journal* published Bennett's story about Joseph Smith seeking Sarah Pratt as a spiritual wife. Orson became very distressed and left Nauvoo. He was found sitting on a rock by the Mississippi River about five miles below Nauvoo. Not knowing who or what to believe, Orson's faith waivered. Both he and Sarah were excommunicated on August 20, 1842, Sarah for adultery and Orson for insubordination. On January 20, 1843, Orson and Sarah Pratt were rebaptized and Orson again took his place in the Quorum of the Twelve. See Brian C. Hales, *Joseph Smith's Polygamy*, 1:575–93. Following the death of Joseph Smith, Orson Pratt went west with Brigham Young and the first pioneer company. He and Erastus Snow were the first of the Mormon pioneers to enter the Salt Lake Valley. Orson Pratt became one of the most influential leaders of early Mormonism. He died on October 3, 1881, at Salt Lake City. Garr, Cannon, and Cowan, *Encyclopedia*, 939–40.

3. Orson Hide – With Olney's apparent disdain and distrust of Church leaders, it is interesting that he chose a number of them to be leaders in the church he was planning to reorganize. This is especially true in the case of Orson Hyde. In a letter to Orson Hyde dated February 5, 1843, Olney accuses Hyde of becoming a vile enemy of the Church and of signing an affidavit that influenced Governor Boggs to issue the "Extermination Order." Olney also censures Hyde for "unwise moves" and denounces him for trying to lift himself up at the expense and suffering of others. Yet, Olney has Orson Hyde on his list as one of the men to serve as one of the Twelve. Orson Hyde was born at Oxford, Connecticut, on January 8, 1805. He joined the Latter-day Saints in 1831. He was a participant in Zion's Camp in 1834. In 1835 Hyde was ordained an original member of Mormonism's Quorum of Twelve Apostles. In 1838 Hyde was disfellowshipped for signing an affidavit written by Thomas B. Marsh, which accused Joseph Smith and the Mormons of planning to destroy certain cities in Missouri and trying to take over the United States. Hyde was restored to full fellowship in 1839. See Alexander L. Baugh, "A Call to Arms: The 1838 Defense of Northern Missouri," 218–19. Hyde was called in 1840 to travel to the Holy Land where, on October 24, 1841, he offered a prayer dedicating that land for the return of Abraham's descendants. Following the death of Joseph Smith, Hyde remained with the major portion of the Saints and traveled west to the Great Basin. He served as president of the Twelve for twenty-seven years. Orson Hyde died at Spring City, Utah in November 1878. Garr, Cannon, and Cowan, *Encyclopedia*, 526–27.

4. Lorenzo Snow – Lorenzo Snow was born April 3, 1914, at Mantua, Ohio, the fifth of seven children. In 1831 his mother and sister Leonora became

Mormons. In 1835 Lorenzo decided to attend Oberlin College. While traveling to Oberlin he met Mormon apostle David W. Patten, who impressed Snow as they discussed God's purpose for His children on earth. Lorenzo became disenchanted with what he was being taught about religion at Oberlin. His sister, Eliza R. Snow (who had been baptized a Mormon in April 1835), convinced Lorenzo to come to Kirtland, Ohio to study Hebrew with some of the Mormon leaders. Impressed with his experience in Kirtland, Lorenzo Snow was baptized on June 23, 1836, by Mormon apostle John F. Boynton. Snow served missions to Ohio, Illinois, Missouri, Kentucky, and Great Britain, where he had the opportunity of presenting a copy of the Book of Mormon to Queen Victoria. Following the death of Joseph Smith, Snow and his family traveled west with the Saints, arriving in the Salt Lake Valley in the summer of 1848. He was called to be a member of the Quorum of the Twelve in 1849. Snow served as the first president of the Salt Lake Temple after its dedication in 1893. At President Wilford Woodruff's passing in September 1898, Lorenzo Snow became the fifth president of The Church of Jesus Christ of Latter-day Saints. Snow died at Salt Lake City in October 1901. Garr, Cannon, and Cowan, 1151–54.

5. John E. Page – John Edward Page was born February 25, 1799, at Trenton, New York. Page was a Methodist prior to being baptized into Mormonism in 1833. He was sent as a missionary to Canada in 1836 and baptized close to six hundred people during his nearly two-year mission. Page was ordained as an apostle in the Quorum of the Twelve on December 19, 1838. He was later called to serve as a missionary to England and to accompany Orson Hyde to Palestine but did not fulfill either assignment. After the death of Joseph Smith, Page did not sustain the leadership of Brigham Young and the Twelve, supporting instead James J. Strang as Joseph Smith's successor. He lost his apostolic authority in February 1846 and was excommunicated in June of that year. Page became president of the church presided over by Strang, but later renounced Strangism. Prior to his death in 1867, Page became involved with other restoration groups founded upon the teachings of Joseph Smith. Garr, Cannon, and Cowan, 886–87.

6. Truman Gillett – (or Truman Gillet) was born May 30, 1797, at Schuyler, New York. He was ordained a Seventy and served as a missionary in Iowa and New York. Gillett was endowed in the Nauvoo Temple on January 5, 1846. He and his wife (Fidelia Teal) were sealed in the Nauvoo Temple on February 6, 1846. Black, *Membership*, 18:421–22.

7. Wilford Woodruff – Wilford Woodruff was born at Farmington (now Avon), Connecticut, on March 1, 1807. Troubled by the existing state of Christianity, Woodruff joined a group of people who studied the gospel together and adopted

biblical beliefs and practices as they sought for primitive Christianity. Woodruff moved to Richmond, New York, to farm with his brother, Azmon. It was there that he heard the preaching of Mormon missionaries. He was converted and baptized on December 31, 1833. Woodruff enlisted in Zion's Camp and traveled with Joseph Smith and about two hundred others to help recover the lands taken from the Saints in Jackson County, Missouri. Woodruff fulfilled a series of missions and became one of the most successful Mormon missionaries of the nineteenth century. He was called to fill a vacancy in the Quorum of the Twelve in 1838. Returning to Nauvoo after serving as president of the British Mission, Woodruff assisted Orson Hyde in dedicating the Nauvoo Temple, and then began his journey west with the Saints. Woodruff presided over the St. George Temple—the first temple built in the Utah Territory. He became president of the Quorum of the Twelve in 1880 and became President of The Church of Jesus Christ of Latter-day Saints following the death of John Taylor. Wilford Woodruff is probably best known for issuing the 1890 Manifesto directing the abandonment of plural marriage. Woodruff died at San Francisco on September 2, 1898. Garr, Cannon, and Cowan, *Encyclopedia*, 1361–65.

8. Junies Snow – Did not locate any information for a Junius Snow or any similar name variation who would have been a Church member at that time.

9. Erastus Snow – Erastus Snow was born at St. Johnsbury, Vermont, on November 9, 1818. Snow began preaching Mormonism shortly after his baptism on February 3, 1833. Snow served several missions in the eastern states and was called to be a member of the Second Quorum of the Seventy. He was endowed in the Nauvoo Temple in December 1845. After traveling west with the first pioneer company, Snow and Orson Pratt were the first Mormons to enter the Salt Lake Valley in July 1847. Snow was ordained an apostle in 1849 and went on several missions to Europe. He went into hiding during the final years of his life because of United States Government action against polygamists. Snow died at Salt Lake City in May 1888. Garr, Cannon, and Cowan, 1150–51.

10. Wm B ?esly – The name is unclear. It does read Wm. B. and the last name appears to end with "ley." There is a William Bull Bosley listed in Black's *Membership of the Church of Jesus Christ of Latter-day Saints, 1830–1848.* However, Bosley died at Nauvoo on June 5, 1842, nearly six months prior to the date on this document. Black, *Membership*, 6:221–22. Other possibilities include William Crossley, born May 30, 1823, at Harrisville, Ohio. Crossley's name is on the Nauvoo Membership list. Black, 12:532; and William Mosely, born November 28, 1809 at Kingsley, England. Mosely died at Nauvoo on September 14, 1845. Black, 31:807–8.

BIBLIOGRAPHY

"Abbalena Olney." Ancestry.com. https://www.ancestry.com/genealogy/records/abbalena-olney_37829526.

Affidavits and Certificates, Disproving the Statements Contained in John C. Bennett's Letters. Nauvoo, IL. August 31, 1842. M230.9 A257 1842. LDS Church History Library, Salt Lake City.

Anderson, Devery S. and Gary James Bergera, eds. *Joseph Smith's Quorum of the Anointed 1842–1845*. Salt Lake City: Signature Books, 2005.

Arrington, Leonard J. and Susan Arrington Madsen. *Mothers of the Prophets*. Rev. ed. Salt Lake City: Bookcraft, 2001.

Bartlett, John Russell. *Dictionary of Americanisms: A Glossary of Words and Phrases, Usually Regarded as Peculiar to the United States*. New York: Bartlett and Welford, 1848.

Baugh, Alexander L. "A Call to Arms: The 1838 Defense of Northern Missouri." PhD diss., Brigham Young University, 1996.

Bennett, John C. *The History of the Saints or An Exposé of Joe Smith and Mormonism*. Boston: Leland & Whiting, 1842.

———. "Further Mormon Developments!!!" *Sangamo Journal* 10, no. 47 (July 15, 1842): 2.

Biographical Directory of the United States Congress, 1774 to 2005. Washington, DC: United States Printing Office, 2005.

Bitton, Davis and Gary L. Bunker. "Phrenology Among the Mormons." *Dialogue: A Journal of Mormon Thought* 9 (Spring 1974): 42–61.

Black, Susan Easton, comp. *Membership of the Church of Jesus Christ of Latter-day Saints, 1830–1848*. 50 vols. Provo, UT: Religious Studies Center, Brigham Young University, 1989.

———. *Early Members of the Reorganized Church of Jesus Christ of Latter Day Saints*. 6 vols. Provo, UT: Religious Studies Center, Brigham Young University, 1993.

———. *Who's Who in the Doctrine and Covenants*. Salt Lake City: Bookcraft, 1997.

Boies, Henry L. *History of De Kalb County, Illinois*. Chicago: O. P. Bassett, 1868.

"Church Statistics." In *1997–1998 Church Almanac*. Salt Lake City: Deseret News, 1996.

Compton, Todd M. *In Sacred Loneliness: The Plural Wives of Joseph Smith*. Salt Lake City: Signature Books, 1997.

Cook, Lyndon W., comp. *Nauvoo Deaths and Marriages*. Orem, UT: Grandin Press, 1994.

Cowan, Richard O. *Temples to Dot the Earth*. Springville, UT: Cedar Fort Press, 2011.

Crawley, Peter. "Two Rare Missouri Documents." *BYU Studies* 14, no. 4 (Summer 1974): 502–527.

De Platt, Lyman. *Nauvoo: Early Mormon Records Series*. Highland, UT: By the author, 1980.

Derr, Jill Mulvay, Janath Russell Cannon, and Maureen Ursenbach Beecher. *Women of Covenant: The Story of Relief Society*. Salt Lake City: Deseret Book Company, 1992.

"DIED – In this place July 16th, Alice consort of Oliver Olney." *Times and Seasons* 2, no. 19 (August 2, 1841): 501.

Dinger, John S, ed. *The Nauvoo City and High Council Minutes.* Salt Lake City: Signature Books, 2011.

"First Meeting in the Temple." *Times and Seasons* 6, no. 16 (November 1, 1845): 1017–18.

Foster, Lawrence. "A Little-known Defense of Polygamy from the Mormon Press in 1842." *Dialogue: A Journal of Mormon Thought* 9 (Winter 1974): 21–34.

Funk, Isaak K., ed. *A Standard Dictionary of the English Language.* New York: Funk and Wagnalls, 1895.

Garr, Arnold K., Donald Q. Cannon, and Richard O. Cowan. *Encyclopedia of Latter-day Saint History.* Salt Lake City: Deseret Book, 2000.

Givens, George W. *In Old Nauvoo.* Salt Lake City: Deseret Book, 1990.

Givens, Terryl L. and Matthew J. Grow. *Parley P. Pratt: The Apostle Paul of Mormonism.* New York: Oxford University Press, 2011.

Hales, Brian C. *Joseph Smith's Polygamy.* 3 vols. Salt Lake City: Greg Kofford Books, 2013.

Hedges, Andrew, Alex D. Smith, and Richard Lloyd Anderson, eds. *Journals, Volume 2: December 1841–April 1843.* Vol. 2 of the Journals series of *The Joseph Smith Papers*, ed. Dean C. Jessee, Ronald K. Esplin, and Richard Lyman Bushman. Salt Lake City: Church Historian's Press, 2011.

Hendrickson, Robert. *The Facts on File Dictionary of American Regionalisms.* New York: Facts on File, 2000.

Hill, Donna. *Joseph Smith: The First Mormon.* Garden City, NY: Doubleday & Co., 1977.

Hodges, Jake. "What Our Guests Have to Say on the Great Public Question." *Fort Worth Daily Gazette* 12, no. 359 (July 27, 1887): 3.

Holzaphel, Richard Neitzel. "The Nauvoo Temple." In *Joseph Smith, the Prophet and Seer*, edited by Richard Neitzel Holzapfel and Kent P. Jackson, 421-436. Salt Lake City: Deseret Book, 2010.

Homer, Michael W. *Joseph's Temples: The Dynamic Relationship Between Freemasonry and Mormonism.* Salt Lake City: The University of Utah Press, 2014.

Hyde, Myrtle Stevens. *Orson Hyde: The Olive Branch of Israel.* Salt Lake City: Agreka Books, 2000.

Jensen, Andrew, comp. *Church Chronology: A Record of Important Events Pertaining to the History of The Church of Jesus Christ of Latter-day Saints.* Second ed, revised and enlarged. Salt Lake City: Deseret News, 1899.

Jessee, Dean C., Mark Ashurst-McGee, and Richard L. Jensen, eds. *Journals, Volume 1: 1832–1839.* Vol. 1 of the Journals series of *The Joseph Smith Papers*, edited by Dean C. Jessee, Ronald K. Esplin, and Richard Lyman Bushman. Salt Lake City: Church Historian's Press, 2008.

Kenney, Scott G., ed. *Wilford Woodruff's Journal, 1838–1898, Typescript.* 9 vols. Salt Lake City: Signature Books.

Koltun, Dave. "The Sucker State?" *Illinois Times*, March 11, 2004.

Leonard, Glen M. *Nauvoo: A Place of Peace, A People of Promise.* Salt Lake City: Deseret Book, 2002.

Ludlow, Daniel H., ed. *Encyclopedia of Mormonism*. 4 vols. New York: Macmillan Publishing, 1992.

Moore, Richard G. "The Writings of Oliver H. Olney: Early Mormon Dissident; Would-be Reformer." *The John Whitmer Historical Association Journal* 33, no. 2 (Fall/Winter 2013): 58–78.

Morgan, Dale L. *Dale Morgan on the Mormons, Collected Works, Part 1, 1939-1951*. Vol 14 of the *Kingdom in the West: The Mormons and the American Frontier* series, edited by Richard L. Saunders. Norman: University of Oklahoma Press, 2012.

"Nauvoo Relief Society Minute Book." *The Joseph Smith Papers*. Accessed May 14, 2019, https://www.josephsmithpapers.org/paper-summary/nauvoo-relief-society-minute-book.

Newell, Linda King and Valeen Tippetts Avery. *Mormon Enigma: Emma Hale Smith*. Garden City, NY: Doubleday & Company, 1984.

Olney, Oliver H. *The Absurdities of Mormonism Portrayed: A Brief Sketch by Oliver H. Olney*. Hancock County, IL: N.p., 1843.

———. *Spiritual Wifery at Nauvoo Exposed: A True Account of Transactions in and About Nauvoo*. St. Louis: N.p., 1845.

"Olney, Oliver H." *The Joseph Smith Papers*. Accessed April 9, 2019, https://www.josephsmithpapers.org/person/oliver-h-olney.

"Outrageous Theft." *The Wasp* 1, no. 42 (February 15, 1843): 4.

Quinn, D. Michael. "The Culture of Violence in Joseph Smith's Mormonism." *Sunstone Magazine* (October 2011): 16–38.

———. *The Mormon Hierarchy: Origins of Power*. Salt Lake City: Signature Books, 1994.

———. "The Practice of Rebaptism at Nauvoo." *BYU Studies* 18 (Winter 1978): 226–32.

"Remarks." *The Wasp* 1, no. 19 (August 27, 1842): 2.

Rice, Harvey. *Pioneers of the Western Reserve*. Boston: Lee and Shepard, 1883.

Rogers, James. *The Dictionary of Clichés*. New York: Facts on File, 1985.

Rubenstein, Marv. *21st Century American English Compendium*. Third rev. ed. Rockville, MD: Schreiber, 2006.

Scott, Franklin William. "Newspapers and Periodicals of Illinois: 1814-1879." PhD diss., University of Illinois, 1911.

Smith, George D. *Nauvoo Polygamy . . . "but we called it celestial marriage."* Salt Lake City: Signature Books, 2008.

Smith, Joseph. "Minutes of a Conference of the Church of Jesus Christ of Latter Day Saints, Held in Nauvoo." *Times and Seasons* 2, no. 24 (October 15, 1841): 576–80.

Smith, Joseph et al., History of the Church of Jesus Christ of Latter-day Saints. Edited by B. H. Roberts, 7 vols., 2nd ed. rev. Salt Lake City: Deseret Book, 1948 printing.

Smith, Joseph Fielding, comp. *Teachings of the Prophet Joseph Smith*. Salt Lake City: Deseret Book Company, 1970.

Smith, Paul Thomas. "A Historical Study of the Nauvoo, Illinois, Public School System, 1841-1845." Master's thesis, Brigham Young University, 1969.

Smyth, W. H. *The Sailor's Word-Book: An Alphabetical Digest of Nautical Terms.* London: Blackie and Son, 1867.

Snow, Eliza Roxy. *Biography and Family Record of Lorenzo Snow: One of the Twelve Apostles of the Church of Christ of Latter-day Saints.* M270.1 S6746s, LDS Church History Library, Salt Lake City.

"Try the Spirits." *Times and Seasons* 3, no. 11 (April 1, 1842): 747–48.

Tuman, Joseph S. *Political Communication in American Campaigns.* Thousand Oaks, CA: Sage Publications, 2008.

Twain, Mark. *The Adventures of Tom Sawyer.* New York: Harper & Brothers, 1917.

Uncle Dale's Readings in Early Mormon History. Accessed April 11, 2019, http://www.sidneyrigdon.com/dbroadhu/artindex.htm.

Van Wagoner, Richard S. *Mormon Polygamy: A History.* 2nd ed. Salt Lake City: Signature Books, 1989.

_____. *Sidney Rigdon: A Portrait of Religious Excess.* Salt Lake City: Signature Books, 1994.

Webster, Noah. *Noah Webster's First Edition of an American Dictionary of the English Language—Facsimile 1828 Edition.* San Francisco, CA: Foundation for American Christian Education, 1967.

Western Slang, Lingo, and Phrases—A Writer's Guide to the Old West. Legends of America. Accessed April 11, 2019, https://www.legendsofamerica.com/we-slang/3/#C.

Whitney, Orson F. *Life of Heber C. Kimball.* Salt Lake City: Bookcraft, 1975.

Whitney, William White, ed. *The Century Dictionary: An Encyclopedic Lexicon of the English Language.* 8 vols. New York: The Century, 1895.

"Why Are Missourians Called Pukes?" *Sacramento Daily Union* 80, no. 62 (November 1, 1890): 1.

INDEX

A

Absurdities of Mormonism Portrayed, x, xiii–xiv, 144n17, 241
Adam, xv, 46, 65, 93, 187, 190, 214
Adams, S., xx, 117
adultery, xxi, 20, 24, 28, 43, 102, 125, 162, 244
Aldrich, Hazen, xi
ancient inhabitants of the Americas, 7
Ancient of Days (council of twelve ancient men), xv, xvi, xix, 46–48, 50, 95, 104, 124, 130, 179
  Olney called to meet with, 45, 137, 161, 172, 185, 190, 215, 220
  power of, 49
  and preparation for the Second Coming of Christ, 45–46, 92, 199, 206
  temporal kingdom to be set up by, 104, 131, 204
  to cleanse and purify the Church, 102, 174
  to select a new quorum of twelve, 124, 126
angels, 26, 29
Anointed Quorum. *See* Quorum of the Anointed.
"another round," 57, 180, 205
apostles, 15, 19, 55–57, 79, 83–85, 135, 261
  of the calf, xxv, 15, 17, 60, 63
Atwood, Alivira, 66n13, 69 183, 210n12
Atwood, Juliette, 69, 183
Atwood, Rebecca, 69, 183, 209
authorities of heaven, 126, 193, 203

B

baptism, 4, 12, 15, 44, 58, 112–14, 116–17, 185, 192, 207–8
baptism for the dead, 15, 114n31, 262
baptismal font, 15, 47n4, 262
Barlow, Elizabeth, 70, 183
Barlow, Israel, 70n37, 85, 173n11, 199, 266
Barnett, John T., 133n30
Bennett, John C., xii, xxn67, xxi, xxiv, 2n2, 4n3, 6n8, 59n11, 60, 75n48, 78, 79n3, 81, 110–113, 120, 133, 146, 151, 155–56, 158, 173–74, 185, 192, 218, 219n15, 253, 256, 259–60, 264–65, 289, 291
Bennett, Mary, 67n15
Bible, xxiv, 37, 39, 42, 229, 242, 249–50, 252, 268, 269–73, 285
  translated by uninspired men, 38
Bishop, Gladden, ix, 1n1
Boggs, Lilburn W., xii, xxv, 119n35, 128, 129n4, 136n8, 137n10, 292
Book of Mormon, xxiii, 7, 25n2, 54n9, 96n21, 127, 130n6, 141n14, 178n3, 269
Brotherton, Martha, 71, 111, 112n29, 256–57, 263
Brotherton, Nancy, 183
Buchanan, Abigail, 71n44

C

Carpenter, A. O., 107
celestial, 180, 186–87, 190, 225, 285
Chapman, Elias and Abbalena, 27n3
Charnock, Jane, 219n16
Chase, Betsy, 68, 183
Chase, Mary, 68n23, 183, 210n12
Chase, Polly, 68, 183
Church of Jesus Christ of Latter-day Saints
  attempts to raise up a righteous branch, 56, 61, 76, 87, 107, 125, 149, 247, 281
  authorities, xviii, 13, 32, 51, 97, 105, 127, 158, 171. *See also* First Presidency.
    apostasy of, xxiv, 5, 8
    hiding iniquity, 162
    and perceived mistreatment of Olney, xxv, 14, 17, 45, 219
  call for reformation and repentance of, 16, 24, 28–29, 36. *See also* reformation.

Church of Jesus Christ of Latter-day Saints (Olney's criticisms of)
accused of offering blood sacrifice, 113, 133
claims of infallibility, 270
contrary to laws of God, 39
cutting off those who do not conform, 55, 58
disgrace, 16, 18, 44
elitism of, xxii, 38, 39
fallen people, xxiv, 27, 45, 53, 74, 84, 164
infants
of questionable parentage, 44
rumor of bodies clogging the river, 76, 95, 108–9
Joseph Smith
curses those who do not follow him, 38
power withdrawn, 15
saves only those who give him money, 24, 28
to become a king in Nauvoo, 25, 29
leaders
have been rejected by God, 29
led by the devil, 141n13
only interested in money and property, 11, 40, 41, 281
oppress the poor and needy, 3, 10, 20, 37, 140, 232
Nauvoo Legion, 31, 33
obstacle to God's kingdom, 53
oppresses poor, 2–4, 10, 20, 22, 106, 232
plan to take over United States, xxiv, 159n31, 164n2, 292
projected growth of, 31, 33
punished for wickedness, 8, 47–48, 137
rejected by God, 29, 86, 193, 206
teachings are an abomination, 39
terror to the nations of the earth, 31, 33
to unite with Indians against the United States, xxiv, 108, 130, 156
wealth of, 3, 11, 22
works are evil, 13
coins (Nephite), 178, 178n3
Coleon (Nephite city), xvii, 223
Compton, Todd, xxviii, 32n5
consecration. *See* law of consecration.
coram. *See* coins (Nephite).
Corrill, John, 173
Cowdery, Oliver, 136n8
Cummings, James, 86n8
curse, xvi, xviii–xxiv, 9, 36, 38–39, 60, 63, 72, 83n6, 87, 89–90, 94, 97, 113, 127, 130–131, 163, 175, 179, 185–87, 189, 202–3, 215–16, 222, 225, 231, 253, 279

D

Daniel (biblical), 20, 82, 84–85, 102, 125, 139, 149, 165, 247. *See also* stone from the mountain.
Danites, xxv, 25n2, 37, 39, 146, 148, 246, 253, 264–65
Day Star, 48, 50, 232
devils, 24, 28, 83, 85, 221. *See also* Satan.
DeVol, David, 220, 290
divisions among Latter-day Saints, 32–33
Doctrine and Covenants, xn7, 6n6, 18n18, 25n2, 44n1, 127n2, 178n3, 209n11

E

earth, 132, 142, 188
Elijah, xv, 45, 128
endowed with power, xxiv, 18, 24, 28, 184, 191
England, 11, 31, 33
Enoch, City of, xv, 104
Eve, 93, 214
extermination order, xii, 137n10, 292

F

famine of seven years decreed, 99
fasting and prayer, 25, 28
females, attempted seduction of, 110, 115, 120, 247, 251, 291
First Presidency, xvii, 25, 28, 121,136n8, 269, 280
freedom of speech, 7–8
founding fathers, 31, 33, 37, 39, 43, 76, 83–84, 119, 148
Freemasonry. *See* Masonry.

G

Gentiles, 16, 102, 109, 127, 145, 179, 185, 191, 214–16, 225, 276, 283
gifts of the Spirit, 4, 8, 46, 50, 92, 138, 270
Gillet, Truman, 220, 293
God
  order of, 26, 29, 61, 63
  power of, 37, 39, 50
  relationship of Father, Son, and Holy Ghost, 171
Goddard, Stephen, 113n30

H

Hadlock, Joseph, 67n14, 200, 209
Hales, Brian C., 6n8, 90n12, 292
Hancock County, Illinois, 68n25, 144, 181, 182, 186, 227, 241, 244
Hatch, Sally, 68n25
healing the sick, 8, 24, 27–28
Hipsebah, xv, 96, 104
Holy Ghost, 57n10, 58, 65, 97, 104, 114, 171–73, 177, 188, 190, 225
Homer, Michael W., 4n3, 5n4, 146n19
Hyde, Marinda, 90n12, 236n9
Hyde, Orson, xix, xxv, 90n12, 117n32, 218, 220, 232, 233n3, 276–78, 292–94

I

Indians. *See* Native Americans.
Ireland, 3, 11, 271
Irving, Edward, ix
Isaiah, 7, 247
islands of the sea, 3, 11, 214, 271
Israel
  children of, 8, 15n14, 60, 229, 270, 280
  gathering of, 3, 7, 285
  tribes of, xvi, 48

J

Jackson, Andrew, 195, 197
Jackson County, Missouri, 242–43, 294
Jacob, Udney Hay, 229n1, 249
Jaredites, xvii, 131
Jesus Christ, 7, 12, 34, 45, 65, 94, 97, 126, 170, 202
John (the Revelator), 49
Johnson, Alice Elsa Jacobs, x, 233n2, 236n9
Johnson, John, x, 233–36
Johnson, Justin Jacob, 233, 235–37
Johnson, Luke, x, xxviii, 234n4
Johnson, Lyman, x, xxviii, 234n4
Johnson's Grove, Illinois, 96
Jonas, Abraham, 4n3

K

key word of God's power, xxiv, 24, 28
keys of the kingdom, 24, 28, 155, 247, 269, 280
Kimball, Heber C., 4n3, 32n5, 47n4, 257
kingdom of God, xv, xviii, 45, 95, 104, 126, 162, 171, 202
Kirtland, Ohio, x, xi, xxvii, 16, 21, 62, 198n2, 234, 242, 244, 249, 271
Kirtland Temple, xi, 18n17, 24n1
Kirtland Safety Society, xxiv, 16–17, 242–43
Knight, Vinson, 152n24
Knoxville, Illinois, 151n21, 152

L

La Harpe, Illinois, 179–80, 209
La Moille, Illinois, 169n8, 170
Lamanites, 130n6, 142n14, 156, 203
law of consecration, xxii, 54, 57, 140, 181
Law of God, 7–8, 11, 20, 22, 39, 50, 79, 127, 142, 164, 171, 179, 187, 193
  simple and plain, 4, 11, 58, 93, 150
Law of Moses, 112–13, 116, 133n30
lesser class, 51–52, 185
letters
  from Benjamin S. Walker, 77, 266
  from H. G. Sherwood, 266
  from Hyrum Smith, 91
  from Israel Barlow, 85, 199, 266
  from James Cummings, 86
  from John Corrill, 173, 267
  from John D. Parker, 92, 267
  from Joseph Smith, 101
  from Oliver Snow, 75–76, 267

from Phebe Wheeler Olney, 152, 238
from S. Stoddard, 97, 266
from unknown source, 78
from William Smith, 287
to Chapman family, 26–27
to Church leaders, 103
to Eliza R. Snow, xxix, 176
to Lucinda White, 168, 198
to Oliver Snow, 218
to Orson Hyde, 233, 236
to Sister (?) "And Crane," 208
to unknown recipient, 95

M

Marsh, Thomas B., 233n3, 235, 237, 292
Mansion House, 19n18
Masonry, 4–6, 12, 43
and Danites, 146, 246, 264
and priesthood. *See* priesthood
creation of a lodge in Nauvoo, 4–5, 12, 73, 148, 250
female involvement in, xxiii, 5n4, 13, 17, 53, 229
for the privileged few, xxii
new fangled, 150, 160, 162, 174, 256
Melchizedek Priesthood, xxiii, 8–9
Messenger and Advocate, xi
Michigan, 159n31, 243
Millennium, xix, 7, 50, 142–43, 190, 227, 230, 232
preparation for, xix, 187, 189
missionaries, 37, 39, 44
deserved to be whipped, 44
volunteers, 19
Mississippi River, xviii, 76, 159n31, 240, 244, 285, 292
Missouri, xi, xii, xxv, 18n16, 31, 33, 84–85, 99–100, 109, 128–30, 137n10, 233n3, 242–44, 271
mob law, 26, 29
Morgan, Dale L., x, 88n11
Morgan, William, 146, 148
Moses, 49, 98, 155, 163, 229, 246, 280

N

Native Americans, xxiv, 7, 78–80, 108–9, 130, 155, 164, 178–79, 216
have long been oppressed, 214
Indian Student's Lament, 282
song of Zion to, 217
nature, 61, 63, 188–89, 212
Nauvoo High Council, xii, 2n2, 10, 34, 91, 166, 266
demands Olney's writings, 2, 10, 108, 169
new high council to be called, 206, 220, 289
Nauvoo House, xvi, 18, 47, 48, 140, 181
Nauvoo, Illinois, 5, 6n8, 7, 25, 30, 40, 45, 72, 76, 119, 157, 162, 205, 223
city taxes oppress the poor, 51–52
destined to fall, 46
extolled for its righteousness, 3, 11, 51
great wickedness in, 44, 110, 275, 281
land sold for inflated prices, 11
name changed from Commerce, 244
people leaving, 41, 99
utter destruction of decreed, xviii, 164
Nauvoo Legion, 14, 26, 29–31, 33, 125, 253
armed, 31, 33
women to be armed, 160
Nauvoo Lyceum Exchange, 223
Nauvoo Neighbor, 233n2, 239n1, 280
Nauvoo Temple, xvi, 5–6, 18, 47, 53, 115, 140, 184, 261, 281
negroes, 203
Nephites, xvii, 96, 131, 139, 142n14, 165, 223
treasure hidden by, 96, 139
North Star, xix, 187, 190
Nurse, Newell, xvi, xxvi, 47n4, 47n5, 49n6, 199–200
home consecrated, xvi, 49

O

Olney, Alice Mary Johnson, x, 66n13, 90, 233n1, 234n4, 236n9
death of, xi, xxix, 166n3, 210n12
eulogy, xxix

Olney, Ezekiel, x
Olney, Jesse, x, 239, 239n1
Olney, Laura Elisa (Lany Eliza), xxvii, 27
Olney, Lydia Brown, x
Olney, Mary, xxvii, 27
Olney, Oliver
added "H" to his name, 27, 274
on Andrew Jackson, 195
arrested for burglary, xxvi, xxvii
believed role would be revealed by Joseph Smith, xxx, 163, 166
called by Ancient of Days, 48
called to write of the ancient men, 93
called to curse the Church, 97
called to set up a temporal kingdom, 45
called to teach principles of truth, 276
called to withdraw the priesthood, 125
claims he withdrew his name from the Church, 2, 10, 27, 108, 169
claims a woman was ordained to the priesthood, 278
compares Mormonism to Islam, 271–72
death, assumed 1847 or 1848 in Illinois, xxviii, xxviiin104
describes people near Nauvoo as animals, 72, 87–88, 91
desires to meet with Church leaders, 103, 105
does not rejoin Mormonism, xxviii
duty to labor with the Church, 1, 9
escapes arrest, xxvi
excommunication of, xxi, 2n2, 164, 166, 169
fears being called a visionary man, 128, 160
feels oppressed by certain Church leaders, 2, 10, 14, 17, 45, 219
hopes that the Church will correct its errors, 9, 22
has explosive information, 16–17
keeps a record of the Church, 2, 7, 9–10, 27, 51, 77, 107
lack of interest in formal education, 9
lists names for new quorum of twelve, 220, 291–94
looked at by Church leaders with jealousy, xviii, 25, 28, 38
membership trial, 2, 10
mourns for Nauvoo and Church members, 40–41
ordained Newell Nurse high priesthood, 199
ordained by the Prophet Judah, 162
ordained to the office of Seventy, xi, xxviii
plan to correct Church errors, 25, 28, 36, 38
poetry of, 150, 168, 170, 195–97, 210–14, 216–17, 241, 243, 245–60, 263–65, 272–74
poverty, xxvii
presided over teachers quorum, xi
receives another comforter, xv, 66
receives special priesthood and gifts, xvi, 223
refers to office seekers in the Church as "young Josys," xxii, 229
reformation, 25, 29, 147, 166
returned from eastern mission, 22, 166
revelations, dreams, visions, and visitations of, xxx
dream of his watch breaking in pieces,125
most important visitations, xv, 45–50, 92, 102
vision of a beast, men like evil spirits, 49–50
vision of net catching fish, 5–7, 12–13
vision of Latter-day Saints, contention, acts of evil, 19–20
vision of Church mired in the mud, 53–54, 56–57
visited by angels, xv, 65–66, 96–98, 104, 130, 162
tells story of an old couple arguing over mice, 35, 36
tells story of a sailor who became a farmer, 20–21, 23
visits Nauvoo for temple endowment, 280

writings of,
claims were taken by Church leaders and not returned, xiii, 241
intention to publish, 9, 14, 42, 49, 77, 117, 179, 227
made out of duty, 158
refuses to give up, xiii, 2, 10, 108, 169
Olney, Phebe. *See* Phebe Wheeler.

P

Page, John E., 220, 293
Parker, John D., xxvi, 49n6, 92, 267
Partridge, Edward, 173n12
Patten, David W., xiv, 96, 98, 104, 293
Paw Paw Grove, Illinois, 230
pearly gates, xxiv, 24, 28, 186
periodicals, 1, 18n16, 77, 106, 185
Peter (biblical), 24, 38, 155, 185, 247, 269
Phelps, William W., 265
phrenology, 86–87, 89
plagues, 49
plan of salvation, 58
plebus. *See* coins.
plural marriage. *See* polygamy.
politics among the Latter-day Saints, 37–39, 43, 121
polygamy, xxi, xxix, 6, 13, 38, 66n13, 107, 125, 176, 229, 244, 249
and need for money, xxii, 61, 63
poverty, 37, 52, 57, 215, 219
Pratt, Orson, xix, 120, 133n30, 220, 253, 291–92, 294
Pratt, Parley P., 152n24, 218, 279, 290
Pratt, Sarah, 113n30, 120, 291–92
priesthood, 8–9, 15, 50, 85, 89, 116, 125, 128, 157, 185, 223, 238–39, 267, 270, 277, 280
fullness of through Masonry, xxiii, 12, 73, 79, 114, 118. *See also* Masonry.
probationary state, 4, 11, 57, 59, 84, 93–94, 103, 124–26, 135, 150, 177, 187, 190, 203, 209–10

Q

Quincy, Illinois, 4, 49, 70n37, 78, 100n23, 106, 173, 191, 267
Quincy Whig, 18n16, 184
Quinn, D. Michael, 67n14, 114n31, 123n1, 200n5
Quorum of the Anointed, xxviii, 6
elitism of, xxii
Quorum of the Twelve Apostles, x, xix, xxviii, 7, 134, 162, 164, 280
some trying to be intimate with females, 16–7, 44n1, 80, 82, 185, 192,
weapons to protect, 283

R

raising the dead, 24, 28, 49, 98, 117, 222
rebaptism, 113, 247
red brick store, 5n4, 24n1
reformation, 25, 28, 38, 105, 108, 114n31, 163
Relief Society, 5n4, 13, 109
and Masonry, xxiii, 12–13, 16–17, 53, 56, 229
revelation, 37
Rigdon, Nancy, 71, 111, 112n29, 115, 183–84, 236n9, 256, 263
Rigdon, Sidney, 5n3, 59n4, 34–5, 71n41, 111n27, 137n10, 276, 290
Rockwell, Orrin Porter, xxv, 118n33, 119n35, 129–30, 136, 145, 156–57, 161, 165, 171, 178, 260
Rocky Mountains, xxiv, xxx, 78–79, 87, 89, 107–9, 114, 130, 145, 147, 149, 155, 176
Russell, Isaac, ix, 1n1

S

Sabbath, xix, 40–41, 249
sacrament, 34–35, 51–52, 248
sailor story, 20–21, 23
Saints
allowed themselves to be brought into bondage, 25
called to lay down their property, 74
coming into Nauvoo, 51–52

duped, 13, 51, 214
fearful to speak out, 26, 29, 80, 120
lacked good works, 20
number of, 83n5
oppressed, 162
perfecting of, 12
poverty of, 11, 30, 37, 39, 54, 57, 109
power to detect evil by gifts, 50
remnant to be purified, 46, 48
some preserved to bear testimony of a fallen people, 48
stuck in the mud and mire, 53
taken advantage of, 40, 51
Sangamo Journal, 111n27, 113n30, 184, 191, 292
Satan, xxi, xxv, 24, 42, 50, 55, 58, 88, 91, 93–94, 141n13, 185, 202, 226, 239, 253
Scotland, 3, 11
Second Coming, 5, 11–12, 14, 45, 49, 65, 92, 192
secret combinations, xxv, 25, 29, 37, 39
Sharp, Thomas, 41–2, 254–55
Sikes, Elizabeth, 69n28
silk, 224–25
Smith, Emma Hale, xxiii, 5–6, 83–84, 119n35
Smith, Hyrum, xxiii, 4n3, 34–36, 67, 136n8, 200n5, 277, 290–91
meeting with Olney, 101
Smith, Joseph, Jr., xi, xxiv, 5, 6n8, 8, 15, 24, 38, 51, 134, 154, 280
and Boggs assassination attempt, 119n35, 129, 157, 178
cannot speak the word of God, 83–84
death of, 276
editor of Times and Seasons, ix, 1, 9
fallen prophet, xii, xxiii, 83n6, 205
gives word of God, 32–33, 41
on Olney's arrest for burglary, xxvi
phrenology reading of, 87, 89
presidential candidate, 290
priesthood taken from, xxiii, 15
rumors of leaving Saints, 136n8, 148
referred to as Josy, 151, 164
teachings of, 80, 161
Smith, Joseph, Sr., xi
Smith, Moses, xxvi, xxvii, 49n6, 198, 200
Smith, William, 282, 287
Snow, Eliza R., xix, xxix–xxx, 66, 75n48, 176, 289, 293
Snow, Erastus, 67n16, 220, 292, 294
Snow, Junius, 220, 294
Snow, Lorenzo, xix, 75n48, 218n14, 220, 289, 292–93
Snow, Oliver, 75–76, 173n11, 199, 201, 218, 220, 228, 267, 289
Solomon, 61, 64, 244, 249
Spencer, Daniel, 198, 200, 220, 290
Spencer, Hirum, 69n29, 220, 290
Spencer, Orson, xix, 220, 291
spiritual wifery, xxi, 286
Spiritual Wifery of Nauvoo Exposed, xiv, xxiii, xxxi, 275
Squaw Grove, Illinois, xvii, 96, 204, 223
stake of Zion, xvii, xxvii, 46, 95, 130, 150, 155, 162, 174, 178, 230–31, 242, 244, 270
stone from the mountain, 48, 50, 52, 65, 84, 85, 200, 247

T

Taylor, John, xxv, 34, 60, 63, 258, 264–65, 284, 294
telestial, 225
temple rites, xxiii, xxviii–xxix, 6, 24, 28, 112, 279–81, 285. *See also* Masonry.
terrestrial, 225
Thompson, Emily, 69n29
Times and Seasons, ix, xi, xiv, xx, xxix, 1, 2n2, 9, 40–42, 166n3, 210n12, 254–55, 280, 286
tithing, xxii, 4, 8, 12, 30–31, 33, 37–40, 51–52, 54, 57, 140, 181, 232, 261–62, 281
treasure. *See* Zion.

U

Uncle Sam, 3, 11
Union, Connecticut, 9, 27n3, 239n1
United States of America, 31–33, 51

Constitution of, 119, 190–91, 195–96
laws of, 26, 29, 150
Mormons plan to take over, xxiv, 159n31, 164n2, 292

V

Van Buren, Martin, 25, 29, 36

W

war of extermination, xviii, 137–38, 177, 206
Warsaw, Illinois, 49
Warsaw Signal, 18n16, 41–42, 254
Wasp, xxvi, 40–41, 42, 87, 89, 112n29, 143, 146, 148, 239n1, 254–55, 258
watchman, 60, 99, 145, 165, 170, 199, 220
wealth inequality in Nauvoo, 4, 12, 22, 54
weapons of war, 30–31, 106, 195–96, 218, 246
Wheeler, Phebe, xix, xxvii, 66n13, 67n14, 123n1, 182, 200n5
believes in Joseph Smith, xxviii
describes the character of Oliver Olney, 239–40
marries Oliver Olney, xxvii, 239
writes of Joseph Smith being lascivious, 240
White, Axy, 67n16
White, Lucinda, 71n45, 167–68, 198, 200
Whitney, Newel K., 4n3, 234n4
Wight, Lyman, 155–56, 185, 191, 234n5
Wirick, Jacob, 99
Wirick, Rebecca, 70n35
Wirick, William, 99
Wilkinson, Jemima, ix
Woodruff, Wilford, xi, xix, 85n7, 264, 293–94
word of God, 4, 13, 45, 80–81, 134, 186, 206, 256, 268,

Y

Young, Brigham, xxiv–xxv, 47n4, 71n42, 111n28, 129n4, 146, 257, 278, 291–93

Z

Zion, xvii, xxii, 43, 51–52, 54, 65, 73–74, 94, 174, 185, 192, 203–6, 215, 217, 222–23, 228–29, 231–32, 242, 245, 247, 261, 280–81
treasure for the building of, xvii, 95, 139, 204

Also available from

GREG KOFFORD BOOKS

The Annals of the Southern Mission: A Record of the History of the Settlement of Southern Utah

James Godson Bleak
Edited by Aaron McArthur and Reid L. Neilson

Hardcover, ISBN: 978-1-58958-652-9

James G. Bleak's *Annals of the Southern Mission* (1900–1907) number 2,266 loose and lined pages and represent the finest early history of Southern Utah stretching from its initial Mormon settlement in 1849 into the early years of the twentieth century.

Bleak submitted the first portion of the history, numbering over 500 pages, to the Church Historian's Office in April 1903. He submitted additional increments of the manuscript when he visited Salt Lake City, usually for general conferences. He delivered the final installment of his Annals to the Historian's Office in October 1907. The complete holograph manuscript has been in the continuous custody of the Church History Department (formerly the Church Historian's Office) ever since.

Carefully transcribed and annotated by Aaron McArthur and Reid L. Neilson, this important work provides a detailed historical, ecclesiastical, agricultural, governmental, and cultural record of Southern Utah in the latter half of the nineteenth century.

Praise for *The Annals of the Southern Mission*:

"Professional historians and lay readers will be inspired by this vivid account of the pioneer experiences mostly before statehood or modernization. Developing water systems, establishing schools, creating courts and laws, constructing civic and commercial building and homes, raising food and animals promoting the arts, and generating faith and community harmony in some forty villages in Southern Utah and nearby Nevada and Arizona are all captured by James G.. Bleak. We will all be indebted to Brandon Metcalf for the fine Introduction and to Aaron McArthur and Reid Nielson for their brilliant editing of this important and extensive document." —Douglas Alder, Professor Emeritus and Former President of Dixie College

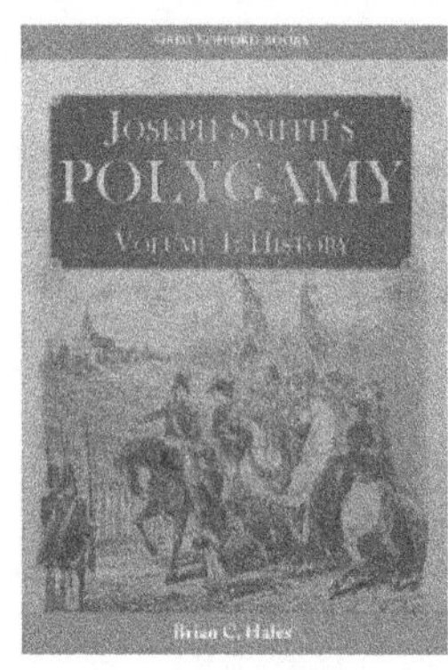

Joseph Smith's Polygamy, 3 Vols.

Brian Hales

Hardcover
Volume 1: History 978-1-58958-189-0
Volume 2: History 978-1-58958-548-5
Volume 3: Theology 978-1-58958-190-6

Perhaps the least understood part of Joseph Smith's life and teachings is his introduction of polygamy to the Saints in Nauvoo. Because of the persecution he knew it would bring, Joseph said little about it publicly and only taught it to his closest and most trusted friends and associates before his martyrdom.

In this three-volume work, Brian C. Hales provides the most comprehensive faithful examination of this much misunderstood period in LDS Church history. Drawing for the first time on every known account, Hales helps us understand the history and teachings surrounding this secretive practice and also addresses and corrects many of the numerous allegations and misrepresentations concerning it. Hales further discusses how polygamy was practiced during this time and why so many of the early Saints were willing to participate in it.

Joseph Smith's Polygamy is an essential resource in understanding this challenging and misunderstood practice of early Mormonism.

Praise for *Joseph Smith's Polygamy*:

"Brian Hales wants to face up to every question, every problem, every fear about plural marriage. His answers may not satisfy everyone, but he gives readers the relevant sources where answers, if they exist, are to be found. There has never been a more thorough examination of the polygamy idea." —Richard L. Bushman, author of *Joseph Smith: Rough Stone Rolling*

"Hales's massive and well documented three volume examination of the history and theology of Mormon plural marriage, as introduced and practiced during the life of Joseph Smith, will now be the standard against which all other treatments of this important subject will be measured." —Danel W. Bachman, author of "A Study of the Mormon Practice of Plural Marriage before the Death of Joseph Smith"

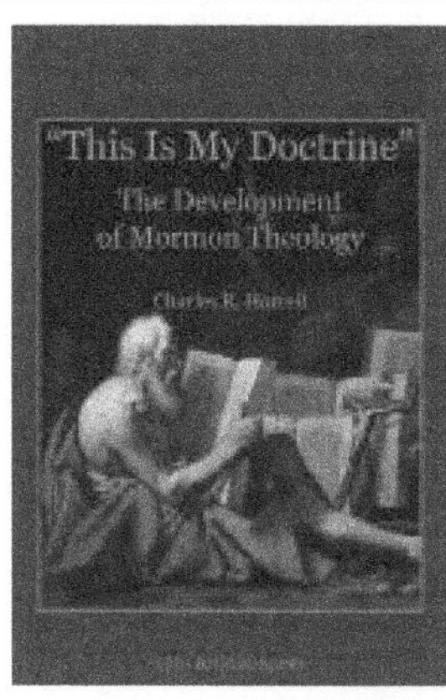

"This is My Doctrine": The Development of Mormon Theology

Charles R. Harrell

Hardcover, ISBN: 978-1-58958-103-6

The principal doctrines defining Mormonism today often bear little resemblance to those it started out with in the early 1830s. This book shows that these doctrines did not originate in a vacuum but were rather prompted and informed by the religious culture from which Mormonism arose. Early Mormons, like their early Christian and even earlier Israelite predecessors, brought with them their own varied culturally conditioned theological presuppositions (a process of convergence) and only later acquired a more distinctive theological outlook (a process of differentiation).

In this first-of-its-kind comprehensive treatment of the development of Mormon theology, Charles Harrell traces the history of Latter-day Saint doctrines from the times of the Old Testament to the present. He describes how Mormonism has carried on the tradition of the biblical authors, early Christians, and later Protestants in reinterpreting scripture to accommodate new theological ideas while attempting to uphold the integrity and authority of the scriptures. In the process, he probes three questions: How did Mormon doctrines develop? What are the scriptural underpinnings of these doctrines? And what do critical scholars make of these same scriptures? In this enlightening study, Harrell systematically peels back the doctrinal accretions of time to provide a fresh new look at Mormon theology.

"This Is My Doctrine" will provide those already versed in Mormonism's theological tradition with a new and richer perspective of Mormon theology. Those unacquainted with Mormonism will gain an appreciation for how Mormon theology fits into the larger Jewish and Christian theological traditions.

Villages on Wheels: A Social History of the Gathering to Zion

Stanley B. Kimball and Violet T. Kimball

ISBN: 978-1-58958-119-7

The enduring saga of Mormonism is its great trek across the plains, and understanding that trek was the life work of Stanley B. Kimball, master of Mormon trails. This final work, a collaboration he began and which was completed after his death in 2003 by his photographer-writer wife, Violet, explores that movement westward as a social history, with the Mormons moving as "villages on wheels."

Set in the broader context of transcontinental migration to Oregon and California, the Mormon trek spanned twenty-two years, moved approximately 54,700 individuals, many of them in family groups, and left about 7,000 graves at the trailside.

Like a true social history, this fascinating account in fourteen chapters explores both the routines of the trail—cooking, cleaning, laundry, dealing with bodily functions—and the dramatic moments: encountering Indians and stampeding buffalo, giving birth, losing loved ones to death, dealing with rage and injustice, but also offering succor, kindliness, and faith. Religious observances were simultaneously an important part of creating and maintaining group cohesiveness, but working them into the fabric of the grueling day-to-day routine resulted in adaptation, including a "sliding Sabbath." The role played by children and teens receives careful scrutiny; not only did children grow up quickly on the trail, but the gender boundaries guarding their "separate spheres" blurred under the erosion of concentrating on tasks that had to be done regardless of the age or sex of those available to do them. Unexpected attention is given to African Americans who were part of this westering experience, and Violet also gives due credit to the "four-legged heroes" who hauled the wagons westward.

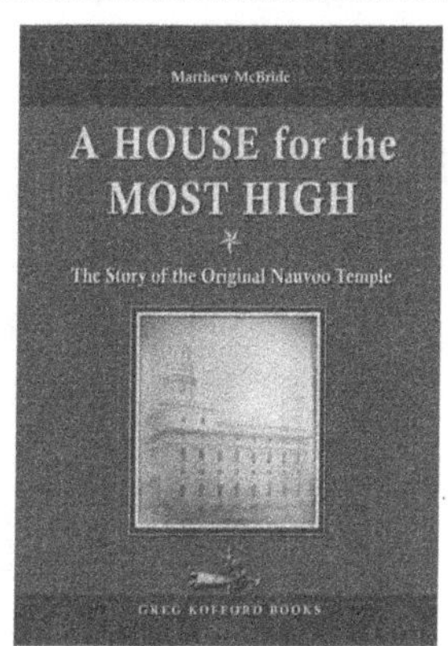

A House for the Most High: The Story of the Original Nauvoo Temple

Matthew McBride

Hardcover, ISBN: 978-1-58958-016-9

This awe-inspiring book is a tribute to the perseverance of the human spirit. *A House for the Most High* is a groundbreaking work from beginning to end with its faithful and comprehensive documentation of the Nauvoo Temple's conception. The behind-the-scenes stories of those determined Saints involved in the great struggle to raise the sacred edifice bring a new appreciation to all readers. McBride's painstaking research now gives us access to valuable first-hand accounts that are drawn straight from the newspaper articles, private diaries, journals, and letters of the steadfast participants.

The opening of this volume gives the reader an extraordinary window into the early temple-building labors of the besieged Church of Jesus Christ of Latter-day Saints, the development of what would become temple-related doctrines in the decade prior to the Nauvoo era, and the 1839 advent of the Saints in Illinois. The main body of this fascinating history covers the significant years, starting from 1840, when this temple was first considered, to the temple's early destruction by a devastating natural disaster. A well-thought-out conclusion completes the epic by telling of the repurchase of the temple lot by the Church in 1937, the lot's excavation in 1962, and the grand announcement in 1999 that the temple would indeed be rebuilt. Also included are an astonishing appendix containing rare and fascinating eyewitness descriptions of the temple and a bibliography of all major source materials. Mormons and non-Mormons alike will discover, within the pages of this book, a true sense of wonder and gratitude for a determined people whose sole desire was to build a sacred and holy temple for the worship of their God.

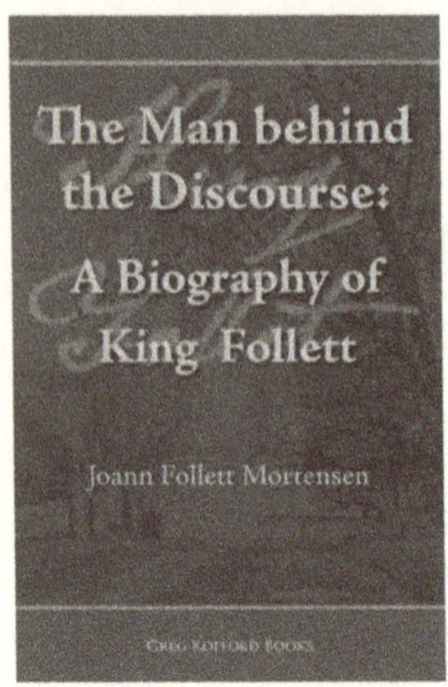

The Man behind the Discourse: A Biography of King Follett

Joann Follett Mortensen

ISBN: 978-1-58958-036-7

Who was King Follett? When he was fatally injured digging a well in Nauvoo in March 1844, why did Joseph Smith use his death to deliver the monumental doctrinal sermon now known as the King Follett Discourse? Much has been written about the sermon, but little about King.

Although King left no personal writings, Joann Follett Mortensen, King's third great-granddaughter, draws on more than thirty years of research in civic and Church records and in the journals and letters of King's peers to piece together King's story from his birth in New Hampshire and moves westward where, in Ohio, he and his wife, Louisa, made the life-shifting decision to accept the new Mormon religion.

From that point, this humble, hospitable, and hardworking family followed the Church into Missouri where their devotion to Joseph Smith was refined and burnished. King was the last Mormon prisoner in Missouri to be released from jail. According to family lore, King was one of the Prophet's bodyguards. He was also a Danite, a Mason, and an officer in the Nauvoo Legion. After his death, Louisa and their children settled in Iowa where some associated with the Cutlerities and the RLDS Church; others moved on to California. One son joined the Mormon Battalion and helped found Mormon communities in Utah, Idaho, and Arizona.

While King would have died virtually unknown had his name not been attached to the discourse, his life story reflects the reality of all those whose faith became the foundation for a new religion. His biography is more than one man's life story. It is the history of the early Restoration itself.

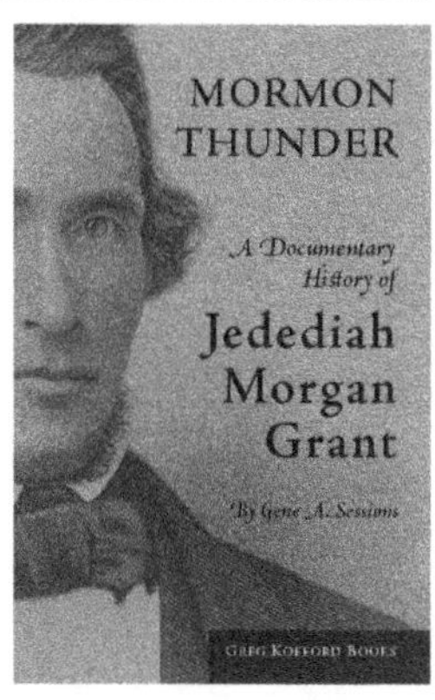

Mormon Thunder: A Documentary History of Jedediah Morgan Grant

Gene A. Sessions

Paperback, ISBN: 978-1-58958-111-1

Jedediah Morgan Grant was a man who knew no compromise when it came to principles—and his principles were clearly representative, argues Gene A. Sessions, of Mormonism's first generation. His life is a glimpse of a Mormon world whose disappearance coincided with the death of this "pious yet rambunctiously radical preacher, flogging away at his people, demanding otherworldliness and constant sacrifice." It was "an eschatological, pre-millennial world in which every individual teetered between salvation and damnation and in which unsanitary privies and appropriating a stray cow held the same potential for eternal doom as blasphemy and adultery."

Updated and newly illustrated with more photographs, this second edition of the award-winning documentary history (first published in 1982) chronicles Grant's ubiquitous role in the Mormon history of the 1840s and '50s. In addition to serving as counselor to Brigham Young during two tumultuous and influential years at the end of his life, he also portentously befriended Thomas L. Kane, worked to temper his unruly brother-in-law William Smith, captained a company of emigrants into the Salt Lake Valley in 1847, and journeyed to the East on several missions to bolster the position of the Mormons during the crises surrounding the runaway judges affair and the public revelation of polygamy.

Jedediah Morgan Grant's voice rises powerfully in these pages, startling in its urgency in summoning his people to sacrifice and moving in its tenderness as he communicated to his family. From hastily scribbled letters to extemporaneous sermons exhorting obedience, and the notations of still stunned listeners, the sound of "Mormon Thunder" rolls again in "a boisterous amplification of what Mormonism really was, and would never be again."

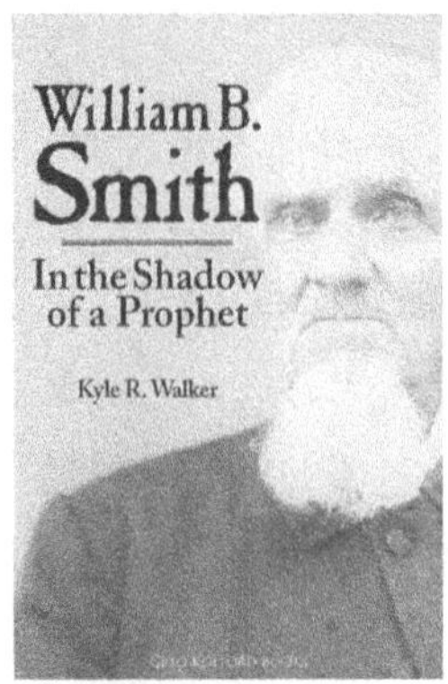

William B. Smith: In the Shadow of a Prophet

Kyle R. Walker

Paperback, ISBN: 978-1-58958-503-4

Younger brother of Joseph Smith, a member of the Quorum of the Twelve Apostles, and Church Patriarch for a time, William Smith had tumultuous yet devoted relationships with Joseph, his fellow members of the Twelve, and the LDS and RLDS (Community of Christ) churches. Walker's imposing biography examines not only William's complex life in detail, but also sheds additional light on the family dynamics of Joseph and Lucy Mack Smith, as well as the turbulent intersections between the LDS and RLDS churches. *William B. Smith: In the Shadow of a Prophet* is a vital contribution to Mormon history in both the LDS and RLDS traditions.

Praise for *William B. Smith*:

"Bullseye! Kyle Walker's biography of Joseph Smith Jr.'s lesser known younger brother William is right on target. It weaves a narrative that is searching, balanced, and comprehensive. Walker puts this former Mormon apostle solidly within a Smith family setting, and he hits the mark for anyone interested in Joseph Smith and his family. Walker's biography will become essential reading on leadership dynamics within Mormonism after Joseph Smith's death." — Mark Staker, author *Hearken, O Ye People: The Historical Setting of Joseph Smith's Ohio Revelations*

"This perceptive biography on William, the last remaining Smith brother, provides a thorough timeline of his life's journey and elucidates how his insatiable discontent eventually tempered the once irascible young man into a seasoned patriarch loved by those who knew him." — Erin B. Metcalfe, president (2014–15) John Whitmer Historical Association

"I suspect that this comprehensive treatment will serve as the definitive biography for years to come; it will certainly be difficult to improve upon." — Joe Steve Swick III, Association for Mormon Letters

www.ingramcontent.com/pod-product-compliance
Lightning Source LLC
Chambersburg PA
CBHW020335100426
42812CB00029B/3139/J

* 9 7 8 1 5 8 9 5 8 7 6 2 5 *